Irish literature since 1990

MANCHESTER
1824

Manchester University Press

Irish literature since 1990

Diverse voices

edited by Scott Brewster and Michael Parker

Manchester University Press

Manchester and New York

distributed in the United States exclusively
by Palgrave Macmillan

Published by Manchester University Press
Oxford Road, Manchester M13 9NR, UK
and Room 400, 175 Fifth Avenue, New York, NY 10010, USA
www.manchesteruniversitypress.co.uk

Distributed in the United States exclusively by
Palgrave Macmillan, 175 Fifth Avenue, New York,
NY 10010, USA

Distributed in Canada exclusively by
UBC Press, University of British Columbia, 2029 West Mall,
Vancouver, BC, Canada V6T 1Z2

British Library Cataloguing-in-Publication Data
A catalogue record for this book is available from the British Library

Library of Congress Cataloging-in-Publication Data applied for

ISBN   978 07190 7563 6   *hardback*

First published 2009

18 17 16 15 14 13 12 11 10 09   10 9 8 7 6 5 4 3 2 1

Typeset
by Graphicraft Limited, Hong Kong
Printed in Great Britain
by MPG Books Group

Contents

Acknowledgements

We would like to thank our contributors, and Matthew Frost at Manchester University Press, for their patience, good humour and wise counsel as this volume was being assembled.

We would also like to acknowledge formally the following publishers for granting permission to use quotations:

from *The Irish for No* and *Belfast Confetti* by Ciaran Carson, by kind permission of the author and The Gallery Press, Loughcrew, Oldcastle, County Meath, Ireland, and Wake Forest University Press.

from *Other People's Houses*, *Flight* and *Juniper Street* by Vona Groarke, by kind permission of the author and The Gallery Press, Loughcrew, Oldcastle, County Meath, Ireland, and Wake Forest University Press.

from *To a Fault* by Nick Laird by permission of the author and Faber and Faber Ltd. US permission: copyright © 2006 by Nick Laird. Used by permission of W.W. Norton & Company, Inc.

from *Selected Poems* by Michael Longley, published by Jonathan Cape, reprinted by permission of The Random House Group Ltd and Wake Forest University Press.

from *There Was Fire in Vancouver*, *Between Here and There* and *The State of the Prisons* by kind permission of the author and Carcanet Press.

from *Site of Ambush*, *The Second Voyage*, *The Rose Geranium*, *The Magdalene Sermon*, *The Brazen Serpent*, *The Girl who Married a Reindeer* by Eiléan Ní Chuilleanáin, by kind permission of the author and The Gallery Press, Loughcrew, Oldcastle, County Meath, Ireland, and Wake Forest University Press.

Notes on Contributors

Neal Alexander is a Lecturer in English at Trinity College Carmarthen, University of Wales. He co-edited (with Shane Murphy and Anne Oakman) *The Other Shore: Cross-currents in Irish and Scottish Studies* (2004) and has published essays on literary representations of Belfast, Northern Irish fiction and poetry, and the autobiographies of W.B. Yeats and R.S. Thomas. He is currently working on a book-length critical study of Ciaran Carson.

Scott Brewster is Director of English at the University of Salford. He co-edited *Ireland in Proximity: History, Gender, Space* (1999), and has published widely on Northern Irish poetry, the Gothic, deconstruction and psychoanalysis. *Lyric* will appear in the Routledge Critical Idiom series in 2009. He is currently President of EFACIS (European Federation of Associations and Centres for Irish Studies).

Lucy Collins is a Lecturer at the University of Cumbria and was a research associate at Boston College Ireland in 2007–8. She has published widely on modern Irish poets including Austin Clarke, Thomas Kinsella and Eilean Ní Chuilleanáin, as well as on American poetry from the 1950s onwards. She is currently completing a monograph on contemporary women's poetry from Ireland.

Joanna Cowper studied English Literature at the University of Durham, where she developed an interest in twentieth-century Irish and American poetry. Following her graduation, she embarked upon a career in marketing in the publishing industry, completing the CIM Professional Diploma in Marketing before returning to academic study at Oxford University. She is currently working as Marketing Manager for two Oxford-based companies, and frequently contributes material to a range of historical publications.

Heidi Hansson is Professor of English Literature at Umeå University, Sweden. Her main research interest is women's literature, and she has previously published in the fields of postmodern romance, nineteenth-century women's cross-gendered writing, and Irish women's literature. She has recently completed a full-length examination of the nineteenth-century writer Emily Lawless, *Emily Lawless 1845–1913: Writing the Interspace* (Cork University Press, 2007) and the edited collection *New Contexts and Readings: Re-Framing Irish Nineteenth-Century Women's Prose:* (Cork University Press, 2008). She is also the leader of an interdisciplinary project about foreign travellers to northern Scandinavia in the nineteenth century, and is working on a study of gendered writing about the region.

Liam Harte lectures in Irish and Modern Literature at the University of Manchester. His books include *The Literature of the Irish in Britain: Autobiography and Memoir, 1725–2001* (2009), *Modern Irish Autobiography: Self, Nation and Society* (2007), *Ireland Beyond Boundaries: Mapping Irish Studies in the Twenty-First Century* (co-edited with Yvonne Whelan, 2007) and *Contemporary Irish Fiction: Themes, Theories, Theories* (co-edited with Michael Parker, 2000).

Jennifer Jeffers is Professor and Director of Graduate Studies in English at Cleveland State University. In addition to numerous articles, she is the author of *Britain Colonized: Hollywood's Appropriation of British Literature* (Palgrave Macmillan, 2006), *The Irish Novel at the End of the Twentieth Century: Gender, Bodies, and Power* (Palgrave Macmillan, 2002) and *Uncharted Space: The End of Narrative* (Peter Lang, 2001), the editor of *Samuel Beckett* (Garland, 1998), and co-editor of *Contextualizing Aesthetics: From Plato to Lyotard* (Wadsworth, 1998). Her new book, *Beckett's Masculinity*, is forthcoming.

Jerzy Jarniewicz is a Polish poet, translator and literary critic, who lectures in English at the universities of Łódź and Warsaw. He has published nine volumes of poetry, six critical books on contemporary British, Irish and American literature (most recently studies of Seamus Heaney and Philip Larkin), and has written extensively for various journals, including *Poetry Review, Irish Review, Cambridge Review*. His poetry has been translated into many languages and presented in international magazines and anthologies. He is editor of the literary monthly *Literatura na Świecie* (Warsaw) and has translated the work of many novelists and poets, including James Joyce, John Banville, Philip

Roth, Edmund White, Seamus Heaney and Craig Raine. In 1999 he attended International Writers Program in Iowa, and in 2006 was writer-in-residence at Farmleigh, Dublin.

Mária Kurdi is a Professor in the Department of English Literatures and Cultures at the University of Pécs, Hungary. Her principal fields of research are modern Irish literature and English-speaking drama. Her books include *Codes and Masks: Aspects of Identity in Contemporary Irish Plays in an Intercultural Context* (Peter Lang, 2000), and a collection of interviews made with Irish playwrights (2004). In 1999 she guest-edited the Brian Friel special issue of the *Hungarian Journal of English and American Studies*, several essays from which form the core of the book *Brian Friel's Dramatic Artistry: "The Work Has Value"* (Carysfort Press, 2006), which she co-edited with Donald E. Morse and Csilla Bertha. In 2005 she guest-edited another special issue of *HJEAS*, in memory of the work of Arthur Miller. She is also the author of scholarly articles and editor of an anthology of critical material on Irish literature.

Vivian Valvano Lynch is Professor of English at St. John's University, New York. She holds a doctorate from State University of New York at Stony Brook (SUNY Stony Brook). She has published essays on James Joyce and on contemporary Irish and Irish-American authors, including Rona Munro, Sebastian Barry, Seamus Deane, Jennifer C. Cornell, and William Kennedy, and is the author of *Portraits of Artists: Warriors in the Novels of William Kennedy* (Rowman and Littlefield, 1999). She regularly reviews for *The Irish Literary Supplement*, of which she is a co-editor, and for *The James Joyce Literary Supplement*.

John McDonagh is a Senior Lecturer in the Department of English Language and Literature at Mary Immaculate College, University of Limerick. He is the author of *Brendan Kennelly – A Host of Ghosts* (Liffey Press, 2004) and editor, with Stephen Newman, of *Michael Hartnett Remembered* (Four Courts Press, 2006). He is also an Associate Editor of the *Irish Review of Books*. His latest book, *A Fine Statement – An Irish Poets' Anthology*, was published by Poolbeg Press in November, 2008.

Shane Alcobia-Murphy is a lecturer at the School of Language & Literature, University of Aberdeen. He has written two monographs on Northern Irish culture: *Governing the Tongue in Northern Ireland*

(Cambridge scholars Press, 2005) and *Sympathetic Ink: Intertextual Relations in Northern Irish Poetry* (Liverpool University Press, 2006). He has edited a number of books on Irish and Scottish culture, including *To the Other Shore: Crosscurrents in Irish and Scottish Studies* (2004) and *Beyond the Anchoring Grounds: More Crosscurrents in Irish and Scottish Studies* (2005). He is currently writing a monograph on Medbh McGuckian, co-editing a collection of essays on her work with Richard Kirkland, and co-editing the fourth volume of essays in the *Crosscurrents* series.

Michael Parker is Professor of English at the University of Central Lancashire. His publications include *Seamus Heaney: The Making of the Poet* (Macmillan, 1993), *The Hurt World: Short Stories of the Troubles* (Blackstaff, 1995), *Contemporary Irish Fiction: Themes, Tropes, Theories* co-ed. with Liam Harte (Macmillan, 2000). His latest book, *Northern Irish Literature: The Imprint of History 1956–2006* (Palgrave Macmillan, 2007), is an interdisciplinary study exploring literary texts and the political, historical and cultural contexts that shaped them. He is currently working on *Seamus Heaney: Legacies, Afterlives* (Palgrave Macmillan, 2011), a major new study of the poet's writing to date.

Martine Pelletier lectures in English and Irish studies at the University of Tours, France. She has published widely on Brian Friel, Field Day and on contemporary Irish and Northern Irish theatre. Among her recent contributions are articles for *The Book in Ireland*, edited by Fabienne Garcier, Jacqueline Genêt & Sylvie Mikowski, published by Cambridge Scholars Press in 2006 and in *The Cambridge Companion to Brian Friel*, edited by Anthony Roche (2007).

Ondrej Pilný is Director of the Centre for Irish Studies at Charles University, Prague. He is the author of *Irony and Identity in Modern Irish Drama* (2006) and editor of *Global Ireland: Irish Literatures in the New Millennium* (with Clare Wallace, 2005), *Time Refigured: Myths, Foundation Texts and Imagined Communities* (with Martin Procházka, 2005), and an annotated volume of J.M. Synge's works in Czech translation (2006). Most recently, he has co-edited a special journal issue on *Samuel Beckett: Textual Genesis and Reception* (with Louis Armand, *Litteraria Pragensia* 17.33, 2007). His translations include plays by Brian Friel, Martin McDonagh and J.M. Synge, and Flann O'Brien's *The Third Policeman*.

Stephen Regan is Professor of English at the University of Durham. His publications include *Irish Writing 1789–1939: An Anthology of Irish Literature in English* (Oxford University Press, 2004), *The Nineteenth-Century Novel: A Critical Reader* (Routledge, 2001), *The Eagleton Reader* (Blackwell, 1998), *Philip Larkin: The New Casebook* (Macmillan, 1997), and *The Politics of Pleasure: Aesthetics and Cultural Theory* (Open University Press, 1992). He has also written numerous articles on the work of modern Irish writers, including W.B. Yeats and Seamus Heaney. He is the founding editor of *The Year's Work in Critical and Cultural Theory*, published by Oxford University Press. His most recent book (co-edited with Richard Allen) is *Irelands of the Mind: Memory and Identity in Modern Irish Culture* (Cambridge Scholars Press, 2008).

Anthony Roche is Associate Professor in the School of English, Drama and Film at University College Dublin. He has written widely on twentieth and twenty-first century Irish theatre. Recent publications include the chapter on 'Contemporary Irish Drama: 1940–1960' in *The Cambridge History Of Irish Literature* (2006) and *The Cambridge Companion to Brian Friel* (2006), which he edited. A revised and expanded second edition of his book *Contemporary Irish Drama* will be published by Macmillan Palgrave in 2008.

Clare Wallace is a lecturer in the Department of English and American Studies at Charles University in Prague. She is author of *Suspect Cultures: Narrative, Identity and Citation in 1990s New Drama* (2006) and is editor of *Monologues: Theatre, Performance, Subjectivity* (2006) and *Stewart Parker Television Plays* (2008). Co-edited books include *Giacomo Joyce: Envoys of the Other* with Louis Armand (2002), *Global Ireland: Irish Literatures for the New Millenium* with Ondrej Pilný (2006) and *Stewart Parker: Dramatis Personae and Other Writings* (2008) with Gerald Dawe and Maria Johnston. She has contributed essays to *The Theatre of Marina Carr: "Before Rules was Made"* (2003), *Engaging Modernity* (2003), *Extending the Code: New Forms of Dramatic and Theatrical Expression* (2003) and *Beyond Borders: IASIL Essays on Modern Irish Writing* (2004).

Part I
Contexts

1

Changing history: the Republic and Northern Ireland since 1990

Michael Parker

Someone asks me for directions, and I think again. I turn into
A side street to try to throw off my shadow, and history is changed.
(Ciaran Carson, 'Turn Again', *Belfast Confetti*, Gallery, 1989)

Given the variety and energy of Irish creative and critical writing and
its contribution to re-thinking relationships, histories and futures
within and beyond Ireland, the first decade of the twenty-first century
seems an opportune moment to examine and evaluate the literary
voices that continue to enhance and enrich contemporary Irish culture.
The book that follows consists of seventeen chapters focusing on the
drama, poetry and autobiography fiction published since 1990, but also
reflecting upon related forms of creative work in this period, including
film and the visual and performing arts. The 'diverse voices' in the title
refers not only to the variety of creative talents currently at work in
Irish letters, but also to the range of perspectives brought to book here,
from scholars scrutinising Irish writing in very distinct parts of Europe.
As well as from Ireland, contributors have been drawn from the Czech
Republic, France, Hungary, Poland, Sweden, the UK and USA, which
in itself reflects the strong and sustained international interest in and
popularity of Irish literature.

The period covered by the book, 1990–2007, has witnessed
significant developments within Irish culture and society, which have
shaped and transformed the writing and reading of identity, sexuality,
history and gender. In order to set this remarkable, transformational
time into some perspective, it is appropriate to look back at Ireland's
sorry political and economic state during the first half of the 1980s. A
sharp, general downturn in western economies, generated partly by the
1979 oil crisis, had left Ireland particularly vulnerable. Unemployment
reached alarming levels between 1979 and 1984, when an estimated
16.4 per cent of the workforce were jobless.[1] As a result of the recession,
at least a million people in the Republic were reliant on social benefits,

a European report established in 1983. Crime levels began to soar particularly in the major cities, like Dublin and Cork, and drug abuse became an increasingly pressing issue.[2] 'Despondency seems to be on the increase', noted one commentator working for the Institute of Public Administration, adding that 'the intractability of our problems' appeared to have 'sapped our will to solve them'.[3]

Not least among the seemingly intractable problems faced by the Irish and the British Governments in the 1980s was the continuing violence in Northern Ireland. There the 1980–81 Hunger Strikes 'seared deep into the psyches of large numbers of people . . . Community divisions had always been deep, but now they had a new rawness'.[4] One unanticipated outcome of the strikes, however, was a profound and enduring change in the republican movement's long-term strategy. Sinn Féin's success in mobilising votes for the hunger-striker, Bobby Sands, and then subsequently his agent, Owen Carron, in the Fermanagh/South Tyrone by-elections of 1981 had convinced republicans of the merits of contesting elections. As a consequence, between 1982 and 1985 the party contested four polls in Northern Ireland and began to campaign with greater conviction in the Republic. It was alarm at their results in Westminster and the Dáil that provided much of the impetus for the Anglo-Irish Agreement of November 1985, which would transform British–Irish relations and the whole course of the Troubles. This arose directly from the fears of Margaret Thatcher, the British Prime Minister, that in rejecting the New Ireland Forum and its findings she had placed in jeopardy the possibility of 'a new relationship' and 'joint action'[5] by Britain and Ireland to resolve the northern crisis. However, unionists in the North were outraged by the Agreement, in particular by the creation of an Intergovernmental Conference, in which for the first time ministers and officials from the Republic would be given the opportunity to discuss not only security issues, but also political and legal matters. They also strongly objected to Article 4 in the Agreement, which made it clear that if devolved self-government were to be restored this would have to be on the basis of power-sharing. In an attempt to destroy this pact between the British Government and a foreign state which 'coveted their land',[6] the Ulster Unionist and Democratic Unionist Parties combined forces to mount a massive demonstration at Belfast City Hall on 23 November, attracting a crowd estimated variously at between 100,000 and 200,000 people. Following the overwhelming endorsement of the Anglo-Irish Agreement in the House of Commons, all fifteen unionist MPs resigned their seats in order to force by-elections which they believed would demonstrate the strength of hostility in the Protestant community. In the event the strategy proved at best a partial success; they did secure 418,230 votes for their anti-Agreement stance, but lost a seat to their main nationalist opponents.[7] In the wake of what was supposed to be a peaceful 'day of action' in March 1986, there were major clashes between protestors and the RUC, which resulted in forty-seven policemen requiring medical treatment and over 230 complaints about intimidation. Over the next three months over 500 police homes were attacked by loyalist gangs, forcing 150 families to flee for their safety. Almost immediately after the DUP leader, Ian Paisley, condemned these attacks, they ceased.[8] One lesson that took another twenty years to be absorbed by both British and Irish Governments was that a political settlement in Northern Ireland could not be made to work if a major grouping there withheld its consent.

The collapse of the Soviet empire in eastern and central Europe in the late 1980s was not without its repercussions for the crisis in Northern Ireland. Unlike constitutional nationalists like John Hume and Seamus Mallon, with whom they were engaged in secret talks, Sinn Féin believed that the British still harboured colonialist and imperialist designs on Ireland, and that they were hanging on there because of a need to protect Atlantic air and sea routes from the Soviet threat. In November 1990 a key speech by the Northern Ireland Secretary, Peter Brooke, sought to disabuse them of this view and reiterated the British government's willingness to engage in dialogue with them.[9] Instigated by Hume, and forwarded to the Provisional IRA in advance, Brooke's speech declared that the British Government had 'no selfish strategic or economic interest in Northern Ireland: our role is to help, enable and encourage. Britain's purpose ... is not to occupy, oppress or exploit, but to ensure democratic debate and free democratic choice'.[10]

Quickened partly by the ongoing northern crisis, cultural debate in the Republic reached a higher level of intensity and sophistication in the 1980s as a result of interventions by a diverse range of writers, artists and intellectuals from both sides of the border. Journals like the *Crane Bag* and *Irish Review*, organisations like the Derry-based Field Day, poems like those of Seamus Heaney and Eavan Boland, plays like those of Brian Friel and Frank McGuinness, all enabled re-readings and re-imaginings to occur, and so paved the way for the new perspectives associated with the 1990s. The preceding decade witnessed increasing strains in the intricate relationship between the Catholic Church and the State, particularly over the ethics of family policy. These were very much a sign of what was to come in the following decade when many of the traditionalists' victories were overturned. Conservative groups in Ireland in the early 1980s who backed the Catholic Church's opposition to abortion sought to prevent the Irish Constitution ever legalising the procedure. They proposed an amendment to the Constitution guaranteeing the foetus 'the right to life'. Their proposals were put to a referendum in September 1983, and won the day; of the 50 per cent of the electorate who voted, just over 42,500 more people supported the amendment than opposed it. The same year witnessed Senator David Norris's attempt to decriminalise homosexual acts between adults. Although Norris's bid to liberalise Irish law was rejected in the Irish Supreme Court, five years later the European Court of Human Rights declared that such law breached his and other gay men's 'human rights and fundamental freedoms'. In what turned out to be one further setback for those seeking change in Ireland, a plan by Garret Fitzgerald's Fine Gael administration to reverse the 1937 Constitution's ban on divorce suffered a heavy defeat in June 1986, again as a result of the ability of traditionalist forces to mobilise opposition to change.

By general consensus, one of the most conspicuous signs of the seismic cultural shift that was beginning to take place in Irish society was the election of Mary Robinson to the Presidency of the Irish Republic in November 1990. A 46-year-old lawyer, she had an impressive record of successful advocacy behind her, and had been preoccupied with women's rights since the early 1970s and gay rights in the 1980s. In the mid-1980s she had resigned from the Labour Party out of principled opposition to the Anglo-Irish Agreement, on the grounds that it had sidelined and ignored unionist opinion. When her candidacy as an independent was first mooted, few would have credited her with much chance of securing the post, particularly in a competition which included such experienced and gifted politicians as Fianna Fáil's Brian Lenihan or Fine Gael's Austin Currie. Yet following an inspired and energetic campaign – and in spite of mean-spirited, chauvinist, personalised attacks on her – she triumphed in the second count. Tellingly, in a victory speech she thanked the women of Ireland 'who instead of rocking the cradle rocked the system', but commended all those who 'with great moral courage' had 'stepped out from the faded flags of the Civil War and voted for a new Ireland'.[11] As Alvin Jackson notes, Robinson's election serves an example of 'the extent to which Irish women have been responsible for their own empowerment'.[12] One of her first acts as President was to light a candle and set it in the window of Aras an Uachtaráin, her official residence, in a symbolic attempt to re-connect the new Ireland with the lost millions of the Irish diaspora, whom she was effectively calling back home.

The years of Robinson's and subsequently Mary McAleese's Presidencies have coincided with a period of unparalleled expansion in the Irish economy, which one investment banker at Morgan Stanley likened to the roaring economic advances in the Asian Pacific by coining the phrase 'Celtic Tiger'.[13] Amongst the most important contributory factors behind the boom was the development of the European Single Market and surge in the US economy. Multinational corporations and investors from Europe and the USA found the Republic highly attractive because of its exceptionally low corporation tax, its stability in industrial relations, and its highly skilled, well-educated, English-speaking workforce. Successive Irish governments proved adept at fiscal management, and the restructuring of the economy and taxation initiated by Haughey and his Finance Minister, Ray MacSharry, in the late 1980s continued under Bertie Ahern and Charlie McCreevy. Between 1995 and 2001 growth in the industrial sector averaged 15 per cent, far outstripping increases in the rest of Europe. In a reversal of the situation that had existed for much of the twentieth century and the whole of the 1800s, emigration ceased to be a major factor in the Irish economy and immigration, necessary to supplement the workforce, became an increasingly important issue.[14] While unemployment fell to 4 per cent, half the EU average, domestic property prices and sales of what hitherto might have been deemed 'luxury' goods soared.[15] As critics of the Celtic Tiger phenomenon point out, however, this sudden wealth has not been distributed equably.[16] Most of its beneficiaries are located in the major cities and their suburbs, in which roads are now often gridlocked, public transport unable to cope, schools oversubscribed and houses unaffordable for young first-time buyers.[17] Alarmingly, 20 per cent of the Irish population still exist below the poverty line.[18] Opposition parties made much of this social and economic imbalance during the May 2007 election, yet still lost.

What came to be seen as the Robinson era witnessed also major changes in social legislation, particularly in relation to the politics of sexual relations and reproductive practices. An early sign that several issues seemingly 'addressed' in the 1980s required revisiting was the X case of February 1992. This involved the fate of a fourteen-year-old rape victim, who, as a result of the 1983 amendment act, was initially denied legal permission to travel to Britain for an abortion.[19] Subsequently the Supreme Court overturned this ruling, on the basis that 'a threat to the life of an expectant mother (including the possibility that she might commit suicide) was grounds for an abortion'.[20] Around this same period of time, controversy was reignited over the sale of contraceptives. This had been legalised in 1979, but contraceptives were only available on prescription to married couples. Partly because of threat posed by AIDS, in the mid-1980s and early 1990s

these restrictions were relaxed and there was an increase in the avail-
ability of condoms to young unmarried people. Following the passing
of a government bill of 1993 homosexual acts between consenting
adults were made legal, and two years later after another acrimonious,
hard-contested referendum the Irish people agreed to modify the
Constitution permitting divorce when couples had been living apart for
more than four years.[21]

These liberalising measures made it onto the statute books in part
because of a series of crises that destabilised the Catholic Church in
Ireland during the 1990s, which caused considerable diminution in
its authority. Even before the Bishop of Galway, Eamonn Casey, was
exposed as the father of a child in May 1992, unease at the Church's
near-hegemonic position within the state had been growing.[22] A succession of exposés in the press and on television soon established the
fact that he was far from being the only cleric to have abused his power.
In another high-profile case, Father Brendan Smyth spent three years
resisting extradition to Northern Ireland, where he faced charges of child
sexual abuse going back to the 1960s. It was not until January 1994
that he agreed to stand trial at Belfast Crown Court, where he admitted
his guilt in respect to seventeen charges. Catholics and non-Catholics
north and south of the border were particularly shocked by revelations
in an Ulster Television documentary that Church authorities were
aware that he was a paedophile, yet had simply shifted him from one
parish to another in the vain hope that this might curtail his activities.[23]
Further equally disturbing evidence of cruelty, abuse and clerical
hypocrisy was placed before the public once more in *States of Fear*, a
three-part film broadcast on RTE broadcast in the spring of 1999.[24]
This detailed the physical, sexual and psychological violence meted
out in a variety of institutions managed by religious orders until quite
recent times. Responding to these revelations in her book, *Goodbye to
Catholic Ireland* (2000), the journalist Mary Kenny denounced not only
the Church, but also the Irish state, the middle classes and the media
for utterly failing in their duty of care.[25]

In the course of the 1990s and since, several prominent politicians
and leading business-figures in the Republic found themselves under
investigation, facing charges of criminality, corruption and hypocrisy.
One of the earliest tribunals set up by Charles Haughey's government,
the Hamilton enquiry, uncovered crooked business practices and tax
evasion in the beef trade. In January 1992, while Justice Hamilton's
investigations were in their early stages, Charles Haughey felt compelled
to resign as Taoiseach over renewed allegations that in the early 1980s
he had been aware that two 'unfriendly' political journalists had had

their phones tapped by officials working in the Justice Ministry. It was not, however, until the McCracken, Moriarty and Flood Tribunals delivered their verdicts that the extent and scale of corruption in the Republic became widely known. From the McCracken hearings in July 1997 it emerged that Haughey had received payments from Ben Dunne of Dunne's Stores totalling £1.3 million, most of which was deposited in a Cayman Islands account so as to avoid detection and tax; when called to account about these matters Haughey claimed at first to be ignorant of the details of his affairs, which were handled entirely by his old friend and financial adviser, Des Traynor.[26] From the Moriarty Tribunal (1999–2000) the Irish public learnt that since the 1960s Haughey had consistently lived far beyond his means, and had frequently relied on 'donations' from unidentified businessmen and property developers to help him manage his debts.[27]

Haughey's good name was not the only casualty of the tribunals. What they exposed was that 'a culture of tax evasion had been tolerated among Ireland's elite for many years',[28] and how, in the words of Fintan O'Toole, 'organized crime' was not the sole 'preserve of shifty working-class men', but also 'carried out by respectable, beautifully tailored members of the upper middle class'.[29] That the Irish people were able to cope with so many shameful disclosures about their political, business and religious leaders is, as Terence Brown suggests, indicative of the new confidence and national self-belief generated by the economic, social and cultural advances of the 1990s, presided over by Mary Robinson and Mary McAleese. Questions about their probity continue to be asked of politicians. In response to a newspaper article, in late September 2006 the Taoiseach, Bertie Ahern, admitted that in the early 1990s, when he was serving as Finance Minister, he had been given loans of £33,000 to enable him to pay legal fees arising from separation proceedings.[30] Taking the stand at the Mahon Tribunal a year later, Ahern stressed that to date 'no evidence had ever been unearthed that he took bribes',[31] and that his heavy ministerial responsibilities in the 1990s meant that he had not been in the habit of retaining receipts for funds received. In spite of continuing allegations and intense media scrutiny of his financial dealings, Irish voters returned Ahern for a record third consecutive term in office following the May 2007 elections.

Not least among the factors which fostered a new, positive mood on the island was the considerable progress made during the 1990s in resolving the crisis in Northern Ireland. Another key turning-point in what came to be termed 'the peace process' came in 1993. The year began with nineteen civilians murdered by paramilitaries and, in March, the bombing by the Provisional IRA of a shopping precinct in Warrington, which killed two children, Johnathan Ball (aged 3) and Tim Parry (aged 12). The degree of revulsion generated by these murders in Britain and Ireland matched that which followed the 1987 Enniskillen bombing. At this very juncture, separate, secret talks between leading members of Sinn Féin and Albert Reynolds's Dublin Government, British Government representatives, and John Hume of the SDLP were gathering in momentum. In mid-December 1993, another important development occurred when the British and Irish Prime Ministers, John Major and Albert Reynolds, signed a joint statement declaring their commitment to removing 'the causes of conflict', enabling all parties 'to overcome the legacy of history', fostering the 'healing' of 'divisions'.[32] The Downing Street Declaration incorporated *both* the Irish people's right to self-determination *and* the principle of consent, without which there would be no prospect of Irish unification. The British offered no timetable for withdrawal from the province, though it did commit itself 'to encourage, facilitate and enable' dialogue on the 'new political framework'.[33] While keen to encourage republicans to abandon armed struggle in favour of constitutional politics, Major could not afford to alienate unionist opinion. Five times the issue of consent features in the Declaration; in which the British Government promised 'to uphold the democratic wish of a greater number of the people of Northern Ireland', whether to remain within the Union or become part of 'a sovereign united Ireland'.[34]

Throughout spring and summer 1994, the Sinn Féin leadership engaged its core supporters in dialogue over their proposed strategy in the radically altered, post-Declaration political climate. Despite the fact that a Provisional IRA ceasefire had been mooted as a possibility at several points in the preceding years, their announcement on Wednesday, 31 August, that 'a complete cessation of military operations' would take effect 'as of midnight' was greeted with amazement and euphoria by large numbers of people in Ireland and Britain. A headline in the northern nationalist *Irish News* hailed the Provisionals' statement as marking the start of 'A New Era', while *The Guardian* spoke of 'The Promise of Peace', and 'an historic resolution of Northern Ireland's bloody Troubles'.[35] Nationalist Belfast and Derry witnessed instant scenes of jubilation, yet these only served to fuel suspicions within the unionist community that the Westminster Government must have struck a deal with republicans.[36] However, six weeks later, on 13 October 1994, there was further cause for optimism when loyalist paramilitaries declared their own ceasefire. Quickly, however, the issue of arms decommissioning proved a stumbling-block to progress, and the IRA's unwillingness to destroy their weapons resulted in Sinn Féin's exclusion from all-party talks.

Over the next two and a half years unionist scepticism and republican frustration intensified. In early 1996 the Provisional IRA ended its ceasefire. It was only restored after Labour's victory in the Westminster General Election of May 1997. Evidence that Tony Blair, the new Prime Minister, viewed Northern Ireland as a priority can be seen from meetings with David Trimble of the UUP and John Bruton, the Taoiseach, which he hosted on successive days soon after his arrival in Downing Street. His Northern Ireland secretary, Mo Mowlam, repeatedly stressed the need for a new ceasefire and the government's keenness to include Sinn Féin in talks. Tony Blair's announcement on 25 June that all-party discussions in Northern Ireland would be resumed in September was designed to lure the republican movement back into dialogue. The restoration of the ceasefire in mid-July facilitated Sinn Féin's admission into political negotiations, initiating the process which eventually resulted in what came to known as the Good Friday/Belfast Agreement of 1998. The Agreement reiterated that a united Ireland could only come about 'with the consent of a majority of the people of Northern Ireland'.[37] The Irish Government undertook to introduce momentous changes to their constitution, modifying articles 2 and 3 which laid claim to the territory of Northern Ireland. A section on 'Policing and Justice' announced the setting-up of an independent Commission 'to make recommendations for future policing arrangements in Northern Ireland',[38] arrangements which would require widespread support in both communities.

In the immediate aftermath of the signing of the Agreement, the omens looked positive. In the referendum held on 22 May 1998, 71.1 per cent of Northern Ireland's voters supported its attempt at creating a historic compromise. However, an exit poll carried out on behalf of the *Sunday Times* suggested that while 96 per cent of nationalists approved of the deal, 45 per cent of unionists did not. Over half of unionist 'No' voters cited plans for early prisoner release as the principal reason for their opposition, though 18 per cent spoke of their fear that the Agreement signalled a drift towards a united Ireland.[39] A few months later, dissident republicans were responsible for the worst single atrocity in the Troubles' history, when on Saturday 15 August they exploded in Omagh's town centre a 500lb bomb which claimed the lives of twenty-nine people and two unborn children, and injured 360.

The Omagh bombing highlighted the need for progress on decommissioning. Throughout the following year the republicans' unwillingness to destroy their weapons remained a major cause of contention, delaying the formation of the Executive. It was not until midnight on 1 December 1999 that devolved government was finally restored in Northern Ireland. Following a report in January 2000 from the

International Commission on Decommissioning that they had received 'no information from the IRA as to when decommissioning will start',[40] the power-sharing Executive was immediately faced with a huge crisis. After only seventy-two days of self-government, the province's new institutions were suspended by the Northern Ireland Secretary, Peter Mandelson. On this occasion devolution was restored after a relatively brief period, following an undertaking from the Provisionals that they would 'initiate a process' to put their arms 'completely and verifiably . . . beyond use'[41] and consent to allow regular inspections of their sealed arms dumps by two leading international statesman, the former Finnish President Martti Ahtisaari and the ANC's Cyril Ramaphosa.

By the time the Executive and Assembly resumed work on 29 May 2000, unionist community support for the Agreement was increasingly ebbing away. A by-election in the autumn saw the second safest UUP seat in the province fall into DUP hands. Many unionist voters clearly preferred the uncompromising line on power-sharing with republicans taken by Ian Paisley's Democratic Unionist Party. In the years following the Good Friday Agreement, political support for the parties that figured so prominently in the negotiations – the Ulster Unionist Party and the SDLP – continued to decline.

While paramilitaries from both communities considerably curbed the scale of their violence from the mid-1990s onwards, they continued to be involved in racketeering, robberies, drug-dealing and punishment beatings. Incidents such as the robbery of the Northern Bank in December 2004 and the fatal stabbing by republicans of Robert McCartney, a 33-year-old Catholic, in January 2005, fuelled distrust in the province. As a consequence, the announcement by the Independent Monitoring Commission in September 2005 that the Provisional IRA had completed the process of decommissioning did not lead to the Executive resuming office. Although the Irish and British Prime Ministers regarded this as a 'landmark development',[42] they regretted that it had not 'happened a long time ago'.[43]

When on 4 October 2006 the Independent Monitoring Commission issued a report concluding that the Provisional IRA was no longer a threat to peace and stability in Northern Ireland, the stage was set for a further attempt by Tony Blair and Bertie Ahern to resolve outstanding differences between the main parties, the DUP and Sinn Féin. The St Andrews Agreement, unveiled by Tony Blair and Bertie Ahern on 13 October, called on them to embark on a consultation process to encourage their supporters to accept power-sharing (DUP) and to endorse the authority and police in Northern Ireland (SF). Days later, a senior British Government official commented that: 'This time everybody will be inside the tent, including Ian Paisley. If he is in government with Martin McGuinness, then it is well and truly over'.[44] His optimism proved well-founded, as in early May 2007 devolved government returned to Northern Ireland when the DUP's Ian Paisley and Sinn Féin's Martin McGuinness were sworn in as leader and deputy of the Northern Ireland Executive. A vital task yet to be undertaken is how *officially* to commemorate the 3,600 dead of the Troubles. Writing within three months of the restoration of power-sharing, Fintan O'Toole argues that

> it demands an approach to the past that is not exclusive; and it requires a belief that truth is a value in itself, rather than a form of tribal vindication. A process that could meet those needs would not merely honour the dead, but disarm the habits of thought that helped to kill them.[45]

It is fitting to see in Northern writing since 1990 just such an attempt to remember the dead.

Certainly since the 1990s, much has changed utterly on the island of Ireland. As will be seen from the chapters that follow, writing in the Irish Republic and in the North has begun to accommodate an increasing diversity of voices which address themselves not only to issues preoccupying their local audiences, but also to wider geopolitical concerns, particularly since 11 September 2001 and the outbreak of the war in Iraq in 2003. One of many manifestations of this growing global consciousness was an anthology entitled *Irish Writers Against War*, published by Conor Kostick and Katherine Moore, which brought together writers from both sides of the border to deprecate the proposed invasion as 'not-thought-through' and 'wildly disproportionate'.[46] The anthology included a Preface written by Brian Friel, poems by Seamus Heaney, Brendan Kennelly, Medbh McGuckian, Sinéad Morrissey and Theo Dorgan, and prose extracts by Roddy Doyle, Jennifer Johnston, Eugene McCabe and Bernard Mac Laverty.

The work debated and celebrated in *Irish Literature Since 1990: Diverse Voices* reflects the greater and growing cultural self-belief which has developed under both political jurisdictions. This new confidence in encompassing worldwide issues in their writing is perhaps not unconnected to the example offered by Ireland's former President, Mary Robinson, who took up the post of UN High Commissioner on Human Rights on leaving office in September 1997. In both positions she has worked imaginatively, bridging differences by sensing parallels between the history of her home country and that of vulnerable states today.

Notes

1 Terence Brown, *Ireland: A Social and Cultural History 1922–2002* (London: HarperCollins, 2004), p. 316.

2 Ibid., pp. 317–18. Whereas in 1970 a total of 70 people in the Republic were convicted of drug offences, by 1983 the figure was 1,822.

3 Quoted in Brown, p. 319.

4 David McKittrick and John McVea, *Making Sense of the Troubles* (Harmondsworth: Penguin, 2001), p. 146.

5 Kevin Boyle and Tom Hadden, *Ireland: A Positive Proposal* (Harmondsworth: Penguin, 1985), p. 101.

6 Words from a speech made by Ulster Unionist MP Harold McCusker in the House of Commons on 18 November 1985.

7 Seamus Mallon, the SDLP's deputy leader, won Newry and Armagh. His party only chose to contest four marginal seats.

8 Ed Moloney and Andy Pollak, *Paisley* (Dublin: Poolbeg, 1986), p. 397.

9 In a speech of November 1989, quoted in McKittrick and McVea, p. 99, Brooke stated that 'at some stage a debate might start within the terrorist community' about the efficacy of armed struggle. He continued, 'Now, if that were to occur, if in fact the terrorists were to decide the moment had come when they wished to withdraw from their activities, then I think the government would need to be imaginative in those circumstances'.

10 Thomas Hennessey, *The Northern Ireland Peace Process* (Basingstoke: Palgrave, 2001), p. 69.

11 Quoted in Brown, p. 360.

12 Alvin Jackson, *Ireland 1798–1998* (Oxford: Blackwell, 1999), p. 387.

13 Alex Davis, John Goodby, Andrew Hadfield and Eve Patten (eds), *Irish Studies: The Essential Glossary* (London: Arnold, 2003), pp. 44–5.

14 This is picked up in the essays that follow, particularly in the drama section. See also Brown, p. 386.

15 Brown, pp. 383–4.

16 See, for example, John Gormley's attack in 'The Celtic Tiger', *Resurgence*, issue 200 (May/June 2000), www.resurgence.org/resurgence/issues/gormley200.htm (accessed on 20 October 2007).

17 See Owen Bowcott's 'A Boom Too Far', *The Guardian*, 21 May 2007, p. 17.

18 Davis et al., p. 45.

19 Elements of the X case were fictionalised by Edna O'Brien in her 1996 novel, *Down by the River*.

20 Brown, p. 365.

21 Davis et al., p. 72.

22 See Brown, pp. 366–7.

23 Following exposure of the shortcomings in the Irish government's handling of Smyth's extradition, the Taoiseach, Albert Reynolds, felt compelled to resign his post.

24 Liam Harte points out that throughout the 1980s and 1990s evidence of institutional abuse had emerged, particularly following the publication

of a number of harrowing memoirs from abuse survivors. One book in particular, Paddy Doyle's *The God Squad*, caused a sensation in 1988.

25 See Brown, pp. 370–1.
26 Colm Keena, 'When Fact replaced Rumour', *Irish Times*, 14 July 2006, p. 8.
27 Colm Keena, 'Living Beyond his Means', *Irish Times*, 14 July 2006, p. 9.
28 Brown, p. 378.
29 Qtd in Brown, p. 378.
30 'Irish PM admits receiving loans', BBC News, 26 September 2006, http://news.bbc.co.uk/1/hi/world/europe/5383352.stm (accessed on 20 October 2007).
31 Henry McDonald, 'Ahern Comes out Fighting at Anti-corruption Tribunal', *The Guardian*, 14 September 2007, p. 26.
32 'The Downing Street Declaration', in Marianne Elliott, *The Long Road to Peace in Northern Ireland* (Liverpool: Liverpool University Press, 2002), p. 207.
33 Ibid.
34 Ibid. Paul Bew and Gordon Gillespie (eds), *Northern Ireland: A Chronology of the Troubles* (Dublin: Gill & Macmillan, 1999) p. 285, state that the UUP leader, James Molyneaux, had a hand in drafting the final text.
35 Quoted in Richard English, *The Armed Struggle: A History of the IRA* (London: Macmillan, 2003), p. 286.
36 A poll in the *Belfast Telegraph* in early September found that 56 per cent of respondents believed the ceasefire formed part of a secret deal.
37 *The Good Friday (Belfast) Agreement*, 'Constitutional Issues', I ii, in Elliott, p. 224.
38 Ibid., 'Policing and Justice', p. 3.
39 See Hennessey, *Peace Process*, p. 192. Here he draws attention to the massive slippage in unionist support for the Good Friday Agreement in the period leading up to the referendum. In mid-April, 70 per cent of UUP voters endorsed the Agreement, but by mid-May this had fallen to 52 per cent; the drop in approval from DUP voters was even more dramatic, slipping from 30 per cent to 3 per cent over the same period.
40 Quoted on cain.ulst.ac.uk/othelem/chron/ch00.htm.
41 Quoted in English, p. 329.
42 Bertie Ahern, quoted 26 September 2005, http://news.bbc.co.uk/1/hi/uk/4283720.stm (accessed on 20 October 2007).
43 Ibid.
44 Quoted in Henry McDonald, 'Blair's last-ditch deal saved Irish talks', 15 October 2006, http://politics.guardian.co.uk/northernirelandassembly/story/0,,1922980,00.html (accessed on 20 October 2007).
45 Fintan O'Toole, 'Truth and Tribalism', *The Guardian*, 21 July 2007, p. 36.
46 Brian Friel, in *Irish Writers Against War*, eds Conor Kostick and Katherine Moore (Dublin: O'Brien Press, 2003), p. 7.

2

Flying high? Culture, criticism, theory since 1990

Scott Brewster

Lucy McDiarmid begins her review of *The Cambridge History of Irish Literature* by reflecting on the upholstery of Aer Lingus seats, which features quotations from James Connolly, Yeats, Shaw, and lines from the sixteenth-century anonymous Gaelic lament for Kilcash. The quotations on the seats knit together the recurrent dynamics of Irish culture and society that have been interwoven since the twelfth century: tradition and modernity, arrival and departure, native and foreign, art and politics, Irish and Anglo-Irish, the Gaelic and English tongues. The soft furnishings also showcase Irish writing in its broad sense: literary and political writing, and both official languages in Ireland (we could also braid in Ulster-Scots, Hiberno-English and so on). This intricately layered fabric, with its subtle range of shades, might give material articulation to Declan Kiberd's vision of Irish cultural studies as a multi-coloured quilt.[1] Yet the celebration of Irish writing is not only an expression of national confidence; it also serves an external audience. The seats display an Irishness that can be readily commodified, and which the former national carrier (it was privatised in 2006) can transport and market abroad. The upholstery asks the travelling eye to recognise the integrity of its vision, and share its self-definition, of an Ireland realised through its writing. Irish culture thus confidently declares itself, and has clearance to go anywhere. Writ large in the interior décor of the passenger cabin is the reality that Ireland is now a global brand, as McDiarmid observes:

> Gradually, since the 1960s, and more intensely since the 1990s and the early days of the Celtic Tiger, Ireland has been presenting itself to the world for international recognition: the Aer Lingus upholstery and the first three volumes of the Field Day Anthology of Irish Writing are low and high versions of the same impulse, phenomena from the same wonder decade as the election of Ireland's first women President, the awarding of the Nobel Prize for Literature to Seamus Heaney, and the signing of the Good Friday Agreement.[2]

To the hall of fame on the airline seats we might add John Banville (2005) and Anne Enright (2007) as recent Booker Prize winners, and Paul Muldoon as the winner of the Pulitzer Prize for Poetry and the Griffin International Prize for Excellence in Poetry in 2003. Heaney and Muldoon have also been successive Oxford Professors of Poetry. This is part of the wider, continual branding of Irish culture, from the worldwide appeal of its folk traditions to its 'postmodern' reiterations.[3] As Diane Negra and others have recently demonstrated, Irishness constitutes an elastic reference point that is at once everywhere and nowhere.[4]

The aircraft metaphor is also invoked by Claire Connolly to scrutinise contemporary Ireland:

> What does Ireland look like? Is it Ireland itself or its image that confronts the viewer? Where do you need to be in order to get a clear view? And, finally, is the cost of critical comprehension a rejection of the rich texture of the terrain, or can these layered images (land, home, mountain, veins, skin, paper) themselves enhance our interpretations?[5]

For all its mobility and panoramic perspective, the aerial view is not enough: the lofty, carefree perspective unencumbered by the soil and by geographical boundaries still needs to be grounded in the multi-layered terrain it overlooks. This is to stress that Irish cultural history has never been organised around false dichotomies of exile and rootedness, insularity and cosmopolitanism: air and earth, flight and fixity are trajectories in constant, and often productive, tension. As Connolly points out, the eighteenth and nineteenth centuries provide ample evidence that 'the experience of those who lived on the island had both an Irish and an international dimension'.[6] The conventional oppositions of east–west and north–south that have shaped modern Irish culture must also now be re-thought in global terms. The new routes of exchange are not just between Ireland and Britain, Northern Ireland and the Republic, Ireland and America, but also between Ireland and an eastward-leaning Europe, and between Ireland and the developing world. As we shall see, it is the case that contemporary Ireland has more people – returning natives, tourists, migrant workers, asylum seekers – flying in than flying out.

To tease out this aerial metaphor yet further, we might also reflect on the death of Tony Ryan, founder of Ryanair, in early October 2007. The Ryan family issued a statement that expressed pride in 'his spirit of enterpreneurship which created enterprise and opportunity for many people in this country and abroad'. Dan Loughrey, chair of Ireland's Air Transport Users Council, remarked that Ryan would be remembered as someone who 'revolutionised the aviation industry in Ireland and abroad'.[7] Ryan's success, reflected in the company he launched, epitomises a distinctive brand for modern Ireland. Ryanair emerged from humble origins in the 1980s, carrying small numbers of passengers between Ireland and the UK, to become one of the most successful European carriers. Under the leadership of Michael O'Leary, it has earned a reputation as a bullish advocate of fare-slashing, cost-cutting air travel, and has been involved in a protracted takeover battle with Aer Lingus since 2006. Aggressively expansionist, and willing to use airports situated away from the main European hubs, Ryanair's no-frills approach seems to offer greater social mobility, very much in keeping with the model of an expanding Europe of small, ambitious nation-states that enthusiastically embrace the potential (and the risks) of globalisation.

Whereas, at the beginning of the twentieth century, the Irish Revival had fiercely rejected many aspects of the 'filthy modern tide', the situation appeared to have been reversed by the end of the century (and into a new millennium) with the enthusiastic embrace of modernity. Yet this antithesis does not bear rigorous scrutiny. Both periods, which harnessed various forms of cultural production to (re)define Irishness amid rapid social and economic change, were at once animated by, and ambivalent towards, modernisation. The Ryanair story might suggest that innovative, competitive Ireland is finally surfing the wave, yet much of Ireland's economic development has been underpinned by foreign capital investment, and its skilled but relatively low-cost workforce is subject to decisions made in boardrooms thousands of miles away. An offshore subsidiary of multinational capital, Ireland is at once at the cutting edge of globalism and vulnerable to its instabilities. It can thus identify with China and India, as well as with the great centres of corporate power, and its experience of going global involves continuing inequalities as well as buccaneering expansion.

Just as Ireland's position within the global economy must be questioned, so its status in relation to 'global' culture also requires careful scrutiny. Since the early 1990s, the tourist industry has yoked together commerce and culture in ways that have variously reaffirmed and challenged its established brand identity. Even as Ireland fashions an image as a high-tech knowledge economy and a dynamic hub for global commerce, the tourist industry markets heritage, a rich literary culture, celebrated folk traditions and unspoilt (but 'interpreted') landscape at the Atlantic fringe of Europe. Michael Cronin and Barbara O'Connor have charted the distance travelled between the publication in 1924 of Daniel Corkery's *The Hidden Ireland*, which chronicled the culture that had existed outside the Anglo-Irish Big House, and *The*

Hidden Ireland: Accommodation in Private Heritage Homes, a tourist brochure that appeared in 1998. The latter, which airbrushes out a history of poverty and land conflict from its picture of elegant gardens and tree-lined parks, 'articulates the values of a new Ireland whose self-image is crucially mediated by tourism'.[8] Tourism has been central to modernisation in Ireland, but it is now two-way traffic. The old antithesis between native and visitor has begun to break down, as a prosperous Irish population holidays at home and abroad, indulging in retail tourism, visiting heritage and craft centres and enjoying golf and fishing breaks, their lifestyle choices mirroring those of foreign tourists. In their mutual reliance on 'symbol-processing', the tourism and culture industries have a symbiotic relationship.[9] Yet this symbol-processing conceals anomalies. As Cronin and O'Connor emphasise, there is still a Hidden Ireland, one characterised not by cosmopolitan patterns of consumption but by deprivation and 'vastly restricted social mobility'.[10]

Hugh Linehan observes that '[f]or the last 40 years the Irish government has had a schizophrenic attitude to promoting its image internationally, torn between presenting itself as a modern, dynamic society ideal for investment by multinational conglomerates, and an idyllic, prelapsarian culture unsullied by the twentieth century'.[11] We might recall here the evocative advert for Caffrey's Ale in the mid-1990s, with its potent blend of flame-haired maiden, horse clattering down a village street, and plangent traditional music juxtaposed with the pulsing beat of a crowded bar in urban USA. This symbol-processing also harks back to the Industrial Development Authority's 'Young Europeans' posters in the 1980s, which proclaimed the Republic as both a romantic rural paradise and a perfect site for multinational investment. Thus the advertising campaign could situate sharply suited executives against the backdrop of unspoilt landscapes, Newgrange and neo-Gothic castles. Luke Gibbons argues that this 'neo-traditionalism' with its 'fabricated relationship to the past' could happily co-exist with the new information technologies, since it manipulates the past 'in order to establish new hierarchies in the present'.[12]

Thus the apparent congruence of cultural and economic success may conceal a fearful symmetry between socio-economic and cultural dependency. One recent essay, for example, has suggested that Ireland's prominent position in world literature may be more questionable than at first appears.[13] The universalising model of development would situate Ireland as a marginal culture in the context of wider European and Atlantic modernity. In this account, the traffic is inevitably one-way, with the margin a pale imitation of the centre. In the current moment, Ireland is in thrall to the dominant values, and the consumer

technology, fashion, music and cinema that emanate from the metropolitan centre (even if inward investment means that many of these products are produced in and distributed from Ireland itself). Any Irish
cultural production that registers on the world stage can be relatively
easily assimilated, homogenised, branded. As such, there would be no
sense that Ireland could invent, initiate or challenge this hegemonic
dominance. Far from being a belated participant in the modern world,
however, the Irish experience from the nineteenth century onwards
has often been of exposure to modernisation in its rawest forms. In the
contemporary period, this capacity for rapid change has led to the
significant liberalisation of laws on homosexuality, and the Republic
has also led the way on social and environmental legislation, such as
the ban on smoking in public, and a law on the disposal of plastic bags.
Equally, Irish culture has not just been malignly affected by modernisation: it has often helped to drive it. Cities across the globe have vivid
Irish heritages and histories, the product of waves of emigration that
obliged Irish people to adopt new languages, customs and practices with
startling speed. Culture has played a crucial role in projecting Ireland
outwards onto a worldwide stage, a process that has intensified in recent
years. As Paddy Logue has claimed: 'Our cultural influence extends
through the whole world in many different forms. This process has been
called the hibernicisation of Europe but it is fair now to talk about the
hibernicisation of the world. Our music, dance, films, pubs, literature,
theatre, athletes are everywhere'.[14] While there is a degree of hyperbole
about this statement, it testifies to a creative confidence in Irish artists
that can be traced in this volume.

Thus Ireland's historical experience refutes simplistic margin/centre,
tradition/modernity polarities. This ability to navigate but not be
engulfed by an expanding world, to harness modernisation but to remain
equivocal about its benefits, is perhaps epitomised in recent years by
the political campaigning of Bono and Bob Geldof. The government
reception held for U2 by Charles Haughey after their North American
tour in 1987, when they had graced the cover of *Time* magazine, marked
'the extent to which acceptance of popular music has been seen as a
necessary part of modernization'.[15] An Irish band had truly gone
global, yet it was U2's international success that gave Bono a platform
from which to question the impact of globalisation. Equally, Bob
Geldof's credentials as an activist who has mounted a passionate and
provocative challenge to the First World since the 1980s have been
arguably enhanced rather than vitiated by his comfortable negotiation
of the elite political sphere and royalty. The energy and anger driving
much Irish popular music in the late 1970s and early 1980s, reflected

in the campaigning of Bono and Geldof, can be set against the inter-
nationalism of acts such as the Corrs, Boyzone and Westlife in recent
years. Whereas the former period was characterised by the questioning
of pieties, this export brand wore its connection to Ireland relatively
lightly.[16] In contrast, Geldof and Bono operate as critical insiders who
exploit a consumer appetite for Irish culture both to challenge and
mobilise metropolitan audiences to redress the inequalities of globalisation. Both figures may emblematise the 'new-Irish intersection of money,
art and politics',[17] but they also represent dissenting voices. A comparison
can be drawn between their central involvement in the 'Make Poverty
History' campaign and the Robinson Presidency. Her election as the
first female President of the Republic was regarded as an unambiguous triumph of the modern over tradition, and she was constructed by
some as the face of liberalising, corporate Ireland. Robinson, however,
strongly questioned the impact of globalisation during her Presidency
and in her subsequent role as UN Commissioner for Human Rights.
These examples attest to a 'sophisticated critical awareness of the
nature of today's international order [that] is in marked contrast to the
parochialism which characterises dominant views of Irish society'.[18]

The 'Celtic Tiger' may have already receded into myth, but the ongoing debates over the impact of this creature do not centre on economic
or fiscal reform; more fundamentally, they engage in a struggle for
the past and for the future. Roy Foster characterises the competing
views of the Tiger phenomenon as a contest between 'Boosters' and
'Begrudgers'.[19] The Booster camp can certainly marshal an array of
impressive statistics to demonstrate the Republic's remarkable transformation. A National Economic and Social Council (NESC) strategy
document declared in 1999 that 'Ireland reinvented itself during the
1990s', and by some measures this 'reinvention' has continued apace.
In 2004 the *Economist* ranked the Republic second in its league table
measuring 'quality of life', and it has also been placed at the top of
list of 'most globalised' countries. Yet others have argued that the
predicate of this 'new' Ireland has been 'subservient integration into
a radical free-market or Anglo-American informational capitalism',
and a pattern of growth that produces extreme disparities in wealth.[20]
The Celtic Tiger phenomenon was subjected to astringent criticism from
many quarters. John Waters acerbically termed it 'Ireland's first secular
miracle . . . if a miracle is defined as a happening for which nobody can
provide a rational explanation'.[21] The 'virtual reality' of its boom was
founded upon 'the successful exploitation of subsidies, tax concessions
and other loopholes by multinational industry'.[22]

The divergent responses to the Tiger opened up another front in
the conflict between revisionists and anti-revisionists. While the main
debates over revisionism have been well rehearsed and cannot be dealt
with here[23] – indeed many of the contentious exchanges had taken place
before the 1990s – we can survey the battles for the past and the future
since 1990 on two fronts: the attitude in cultural texts to the perceived
stagnation and repression of the De Valera era, and the attitude to
commemoration. In both cases, previous historical moments are read
through the prism of competing versions of the 'new' Ireland.

Revisionist historiography had set itself to demystify the national story,
freeing the study of Irish history from partisanship and popular senti-
ment. The impulse to question entrenched assumptions and cherished
pieties can be traced in a wide range of cultural production. In his introduction to *Soho Square*, an anthology of contemporary Irish writing,
Colm Tóibín declared that the forty writers featured

> have nothing in common except a beginning under the same sky, the
> same uncertain weather. And there is no collective consciousness, no
> conscience of our race, no responsibilities, no nation singing in unison.
> Instead diversity, the single mind and the imagination making themselves
> heard.[24]

Here, the Republic has finally broken the shackles of the past and can
enter an enlightened, pluralist future. Numerous literary and cinematic texts in the 1990s – for example, Patrick McCabe's *The Butcher
Boy*, Brian Friel's *Dancing at Lughnasa*, John McGahern's *Amongst
Women*, Jim Sheridan's cinematic retelling of John B. Keane's *The Field*,
Neil Jordan's *Michael Collins* and Martin McDonagh's *The Leenane
Trilogy* – rehearse this narrative. Frank McCourt's *Angela's Ashes*, quickly
translated onto the cinema screen, was a way of laying to rest a past
of poverty and parochialism, of saying both to the Irish diaspora, and
to the native Irish, that 'we have arrived'. As Joe Cleary has observed,
what marks this tendency is its obsessive return to the grim period of
'autarkic development' associated with De Valera.[25] The implication is
that the apparent triumph of modernisation has brought about economic,
cultural and psychological transformation, illuminating the 'dark age'
of insularity, conservatism and underdevelopment that marked the
early years of the Republic.

The worlds evoked by these narratives now appear temporally far
distant to a contemporary audience, and the rapid translation of
McCabe, Friel and others from page or stage to screen may itself be
a marker of modernisation, but this 'fixation' with the rural Ireland
of the past suggested an inability or unwillingness to 'respond in

interesting or challenging ways to the demands of the present'.[26] It leads Cleary to conclude that

> the fact that contemporary Irish society continues to rely so heavily on invocations of the darkness of the past to validate its sense of its own enlightenment is not very reassuring. Such a society equips itself neither with the imaginative resources nor the strategies required to meet the challenges of the future.[27]

Anti-revisionists have argued that such narratives strip contemporary Irish identity of its subversive potential, leaving it 'sanitised and . . . remarkably accommodating to the dominant elitist project of sub-servient assimilation into multinational capitalism'.[28] In this account, culture is a mere 'handmaiden' to the Republic's economic transforma-tion. Debbie Ging has argued that, with the move in Irish cinema towards easy, 'globally-digestible' narratives such as *Into the West* and *Waking Ned*, 'Irish identity has become more a global commodity than a means of critical self-questioning', and there is little evidence from the film of Celtic Tiger that 'postmodernism heralds a plurality of marginalised voices'.[29]

Yet this is far from the whole story. Many artists have charted Ireland's modernisation with considerable ambivalence in the last two decades. Nicholas Daly has contrasted the 'whimsical globality' of films such as Peter Ormrod's *Eat the Peach* (1986), with its celebration of syncretism and 'local' appropriation of international influences, to Neil Jordan's cinematic version of *The Butcher Boy* (1998), which 'captures some of the shock of Ireland's abrupt baptism into the new global order' by showing the cataclysmic impact of modernisation on 1960s Ireland.[30] In Alan Parker's *The Commitments*, the confident familiarity with global popular culture provides an escape route, as Dublin's Northside identifies with the black underclass in United States, and embraces 'a new transatlantic freedom'.[31] The absence of the Catholic Church and indifference to the Northern Troubles increase the film's universalism. In their ability to forge connections with the outside world, the young Irish can go anywhere. Yet the recourse to soul music does not simply represent the carefree abandonment of the past: Jimmy Rabbitte's claim that the Irish are 'the niggers of Europe' recalls a real and recent colonial past when Ireland was 'at the back door of Europe'.[32] While Alan Parker's celebratory film reflects the increasing optimism of the early 1990s, Roddy Doyle's original novel was set amidst the chronic unemployment and economic crisis of the previous decade, a period that continues to cast its shadow over the heady Celtic Tiger years. Similarly Jordan's *Michael Collins* engages equivocally with new possibilities. Jordan acknowledged that the production was possible only after the IRA ceasefire of 1994, yet its contemporary currency was problematically filtered through its deployment of the Hollywood gangster genre. The film was criticised for its anachronistic allusions to the Northern conflict (such as the car-bomb used to kill the RIC detective brought to Dublin Castle) but the forces and attitudes it examined had been deemed anachronistic and alien in modern Ireland, even if in reality they hadn't 'gone away' in the North. Responses to the film may have been shaped as much by frustrations over the course of the peace process prior to the Good Friday Agreement as by its aesthetic failings. The film leaves both the state-building past and the peace-making present as open questions.[33]

Michael Collins begins with a scene of personal recollection that hovers between mourning and mythologisation, and this moment dramatises the prominence of commemoration throughout the 1990s. This was a period of many anniversaries that could be remembered, and whose significance could be claimed, in very different ways across the island. The decade included the 75th anniversaries of both the Easter Rising and the Battle of the Somme, the 150th anniversary of the Great Famine, and the bicentenary of the United Irishmen's rebellion in 1798 and of the founding of the Orange Order. The impetus was towards inclusive, rather than partisan, forms of commemoration that highlighted both contradictions and affinities between different traditions. This self-consciousness about memory shaped debates not only amongst professional historians and politicians, but also in the mass media, the museum and heritage industries, and in school classrooms. The child-abuse scandals in the period epitomised the importance of acknowledging and reclaiming lost narratives that 'spoke' to the present. The therapeutic dimension to historiography, which stressed the emotional and the psychological, while giving rise to some questionable interpretations, may have been in part a reaction to the 'shallow amnesia'[34] of the modernising project. The role of soldiers from southern Ireland in World War I was recognised, and Tony Blair's acknowledgement that the British government could have done much more to alleviate suffering during the Famine was accepted by some as a quasi-apology, and a significant contribution to the Northern peace process, but, for some, bore little relation to the historical facts of the 1840s.

While such competing interpretations at least suggested a healthy dialogue about the importance of history, the past was at the same time being ruthlessly commodified. Traumatic events were packaged for consumption and history came with a business plan. A Famine Theme Park stretching over 200 acres was opened in Limerick, and a group of bronze figures representing famished victims adorned Customs House

Quay. Yet these enduring markers of a calamitous historical moment had to end promptly by 1998 to make way for commemorations of the 1798 rebellion and the next set of heritage 'opportunities'.[35] Revisionist and anti-revisionist camps alike could argue that history was being manipulated to airbrush conflict from the past for the benefit of the heritage and tourist industries, whether by recycling hoary myths and nationalist verities, or by neutralising the North as a site of political conflict and marginalising those who question the merits of economic liberalism and labour flexibility.

Despite the strategic silences and evasions in relation to the past since 1990, however, it is hard to reject Carla Power's assertion that 'thanks to the boom, Ireland has awoken from its nightmare, and instead of escaping it, the Irish are increasingly willing to explore it'.[36] Yet there are significant challenges to this optimism. As the conclusion to *Reinventing Ireland* pithily comments, '[th]e affluent Irish city-dweller can choose between 20 different kinds of cheese but has no idea whether his/her job will be there next week'.[37] This comment at once celebrates and pulls up short the pace of change in contemporary Ireland. The *Riverdance* phenomenon exemplifies the breakneck transformation of the Tiger era. As Fintan O'Toole has commented, after its initial appearance as part of the intermission in the Eurovision song contest, *Riverdance* 'became, quite self-consciously, a parable of the modernisation of Irish culture'.[38] Michael Cronin shows how this parable is a 'hymn to speed', from the emphasis on fast footwork and the roadshow that flows 'unimpeded through global space' to the 'giddy pursuit of global profit' that impels the Riverdance organisation.[39] *Riverdance* is symptomatic of the wider 'chrono-politicisation' of Ireland, whereby continuity gives way to frantic acceleration, and the past is obliterated by a headlong dash for the future.

This flow was rather more impeded in spring 2007, when Galway, one of Europe's fastest-growing, and wettest, cities spent a number of weeks without a water supply due to contamination, resulting from underinvestment in treatment plants and unrestrained property development in this tourist hotspot. For around 90,000 homes, there was not an unbottled drop to drink, and the Archbishop of Tuam had to find unpolluted water to bless, lest his parishioners were poisoned. It is all too tempting to discern a metaphor for modern Ireland in the Church's sanctification of commercial spring water, but it was a striking demonstration of the potential social and environmental chaos unleashed by uninhibited economic growth. In response to the crisis, an EU Commission spokesperson confirmed that Ireland has 'one of the worst water qualities in Europe'.[40]

This imbrication of features – Ireland as a fantasy space, characterised by discontinuity and virtuality, contested pasts and futures, and uneven development – finds apt expression in Seán Hillen's *Irelantis*, a series of paper collages produced in the mid-1990s.[41] The arresting juxtaposition of postcards and photographs, depicting contemporary cityscapes, topographical features and monuments from antiquity, presents Ireland, like the 'original' Atlantis, as a mythical lost island. Hillen rewrites the iconographic legacy of John Hinde's tourist postcards from the 1950s and 1960s, but his series might also be seen as an ironic and defamiliarising counterpart of the IDA's 'Young Europeans' posters. Fintan O'Toole sees Hillen's collages as an attempt to negotiate between stability and breakneck transition:

> Irelantis is, of course, contemporary, globalised Ireland, a society that became postmodern before it ever quite managed to be modern, a cultural space that has gone, in the blink of an eye, from being defiantly closed to being completely porous to whatever dream is floating out there in the media ether. But this Ireland is also everywhere and nowhere. Hillen is dealing with displacement in a world where all borders – political, cultural and psychological – are permeable.[42]

Hillen's modes of composition and dissemination blend 'traditional' craft and virtual reality: the collages are fashioned with scalpel and glue, but they can be freely downloaded from the web. In its reference points – the 'ether' of the popular media, tourist imagery available through 'real' low-cost travel and virtually at the click of a mouse in and beyond IT-savvy Ireland – the *Irelantis* series is at once celebratory and oppositional, ludic and critically engaged. As Connolly argues, Hillen's self-conscious art occupies 'a space between scepticism and reverence',[43] since he does not merely deride and dismiss Hinde's nostalgic images, or the government-sponsored tourist kitsch, of an Ireland that may never have been. Rather, *Irelantis* acknowledges that Ireland inhabits not only the realm of the Baudrillardian hyperreal, but also a conflictual space between the apparently ubiquitous simulation and commodification of Ireland and the fleeting evocation of 'a cultural space that has gone'.

This sense of a vanished space where dreams continue to dwell amid displacement and permeability can be discerned in 'The Oracle at O'Connell St Bridge, Dublin' (1995). Skyscrapers that symbolise the miraculous rise of Corporate Ireland tower above the heart of the state-building enterprise in Ireland, including the GPO, the statue of O'Connell, and the classical ruins that evoke Delphi. The gleaming, unreflective oracle of the future overshadows these loci of wisdom, worship and illumination. The Delphic site in Hillen's collage, at once ancient and future-oriented, recalls an episode in Shaw's *Back to Methuselah* (1921), which is set in Galway in the year 3000. Visitors from the 'Eastern Island' come to consult an oracle in Galway, a region where dwells a colony of long-lived and sagacious people. These ancients have long ago outgrown any sense of Irishness; their prede-cessors had first exported nationalism to the world so successfully that all national problems were solved, and then returned to Galway having lost their unique selling point, only to find that place no longer satisfied their aspirations. Now bound only to realism, this utopia abjures romantic notions of place and nation. The idealism of the much more fallibly mortal visitors withers away under the discouraging scrutiny of Galway, and to touch the oracle brings death. Roy Foster observes that late twentieth-century Ireland belies Shaw's satirical vision of the Irish future: it is no longer a case of having the world and losing Ireland.[44] In contrast to the Galway oracle, the site of Hillen's oracle offers both abiding connections to nation and place and utopian possibilities. It is uncertain whether the flaming red skies that overhang the office build-ings and O'Connell Street in Hillen's collage presage divine revelation or impending judgement and disaster (uncannily evocative both of the arrival of the alien fleet in *Independence Day* and the destruction of the Twin Towers in September 2001). According to Colin Graham, this apocalyptic strain in Hillen's collages does not pit the comforts of nation, authenticity and origin against postmodern fantasy, 'a sincere nostalgia blinkering itself to ironic pastiche'. Rather, it shows how Ireland not only casts itself 'into the future in order to be realised' but 'also turns inside-out the underlying need for the future, disarming the crisis of what the future might be by forcing it to exist in a "plethora" of cul-tural images'.[45]

The rise of Irish Studies since the 1980s can be seen in the context of this simultaneous exposure to, and critical examination of, the process of globalisation. Literary criticism has remained a central disciplinary component of Irish Studies, and Irish criticism could not remain immune to the theory wars that convulsed literature departments on both sides of the Atlantic in the 1980s. These debates demonstrated how literary and cultural production could be conceptualised in terms of discourse, hegemony and subject formation, and how various cul-tural forms were enmeshed within a wider, complex cultural politics.[46] By the start of the 1990s Irish literature, and Irish Studies more widely, was encountering theory in a sustained fashion. Yet, as Terry Eagleton has acknowledged, just as cultural theory could illuminate aspects of Irish culture, so Ireland could cast light on the 'repressions and evasions' of theory, since categories central to the Irish experience – such as class, revolution and ideology – had often been dispensed with in the 'postmodern age'.[47]

At a time when facets of Ireland's literary history were being recovered or critically reappraised – with women writers accorded new prominence, and both the early modern period, and 'indigenous' Irish modernism, being more fully appreciated – what constituted 'Irish literature' came under rigorous scrutiny. The publication of the first three volumes of the *Field Day Anthology of Irish Writing* in 1991 represents a critical and historical landmark. The Field Day Theatre Company's regular theatre production had halted in the same year (it suspended operations in 1993), and from this point its 'counter-hegemonic'[48] project turned towards academic publishing. Outlining the rationale of the *Anthology*, Seamus Deane asserted that

> [t]here is a story here, a meta-narrative, which is, we believe, hospitable to all the micro-narratives that, from time to time, have achieved prominence as the official version of the true history, political and literary, of the island's past and present.[49]

The nature and validity of this meta-narrative, and the process of canon-formation, in the *Anthology* provoked a vigorous and often hostile response. Damian Smyth described the project as 'the most arrogant and challenging example of such a neo-Romantic, totalising vision to be produced in Europe', in which 'there seems to be something primordially continuous about "Ireland" and "being Irish" over a 1500-year period'.[50] Smyth's review betrays a clear hostility both to Field Day's interpretation of Irish history and to its deployment of theory. Yet Deane's very invocation of *grands* and *petits récits* invited a questioning of the relationship between the micro- and meta-narrative. In 1990 Eamonn Hughes pointed out how the identification of Field Day with critical theory enabled a recognition that its enterprise was not doctrinaire but one 'which is alert to the world beyond the constrictions of Irish cultural debate'.[51]

Field Day's reaction to the controversy over the marginalisation of women's contribution to the history of Irish letters in the first three volumes exemplified this reflexiveness.[52] The omission was all the more glaring given that one crucible of the nation-building, the Abbey Theatre, had appointed its first female artistic director, Garry Hynes, in 1990. Her three-year tenure saw provocative productions of John McGahern's *The Power of Darkness* and Sean O'Casey's *The Plough and the Stars*, and included European and American plays in the repertoire. Deane quickly acknowledged the 'unconscious' prejudice that had led to the exclusion of women from the first three volumes.[53] The limitations of the *Anthology* were exposed, and subsequently addressed, precisely because Irish Studies had opened up to the critical interrogation for which Field Day's founders had originally appealed in the 1980s. Two further volumes were commissioned, and their diversity of critical perspectives on Irish women writers represented not only a necessary revision but also a continuation of the project. The new volumes stressed a plurality of traditions and sounded out different voices obscured by dominant discourses of nation and identity in modern Irish history, and also maintained the presiding spirit of the previous books by letting the 'minor' and the 'great' mingle, and by articulating a broad understanding of the connections between literature and other forms of cultural production.[54] Roisin Higgins has claimed that, since feminism does not posit statehood as its ultimate goal, gender as the organising principle for the volumes 'opens up debate rather than conscribing it and admits the stories of the dispossessed'.[55]

This rethinking of the relation between gender, sexuality and the nation was paralleled in the field of social policy. Membership of European Union not only brought improvements to the infrastructure of Northern Ireland and the Republic, it also had a major impact on the social agenda, including divorce reform in the Republic in 1995. In Northern Ireland in June 2006, five gay couples were the first in the UK and Ireland to have their civil partnerships legally recognised. The DUP's opposition to the granting of equal rights to gay people – graphically expressed by Ian Paisley Jr's hostile comments on homosexuality – was attacked by the other main parties, including the late David Ervine of the Progressive Unionists. This picture is uneven, however. Northern Ireland is still permitted to opt out of the abortion legislation that pertains in the rest of the UK, and the main political parties continue to oppose changes to abortion law. Constitutional questions have persistently taken precedence over social issues.

The gay activist Kieran Rose has situated the final decriminalisation of male homosexuality in the Republic of Ireland in 1993 within a *telos* of national liberation:

> While there are obvious contradictions in Irish attitudes, GLEN [Gay and Lesbian Equality Network] knew that there was a tradition of tolerance, which was benign, and based on a belief in fairness and justice. GLEN knew that there were real and positive traditional Irish values, arising from the struggle against colonialism and for civil, religious and economic rights, which could be activated, and the demand for equality was attuned to this heritage.[56]

Tradition is invoked here as the driving force of radical social change, and there is a perceived commonality between nationalism and other forms of activism in the long historical struggle against discrimination and oppression. In a speech to the Seanad in June 1993, Senator David Norris, a prominent figure in the campaign to reform the laws on homosexuality, praised the Lower House of the Dáil for 'effectively wiping the lingering shame of British imperial statute from the record of Irish law'. In celebrating this 'Irish solution to an Irish problem', however, Norris nonetheless implicitly recognised (while attempting to deflect with humour) that homosexuality remained a 'problem' for many in the Republic: 'May I reassure the House that should two young men or two young women hold hands at a bus stop in Dublin the island will not be overwhelmed with earthquakes and turbulence, nor will the world come to an unexpected end'.[57]

Nor was this 'Irish problem' confined to its island boundaries. The controversy in the early 1990s over the involvement of the Irish Lesbian and Gay Organisation (ILGO) in the New York St Patrick's Day parade mingled sexual politics with definitions of Irishness. The Ancient Order of Hibernians, made official custodians of the parade in 1994, vigorously opposed the ILGO's participation, and video footage of the 1996 event shows male spectators shouting 'queers go home' at members of the organisation. The resistance to the ILGO suggested that homosexuality was not part of the Irish diaspora in the USA, but the abuse provoked a more profound question: where should 'queers' go home? Should they go back to now-progressive Ireland? It is a queer reversal of the nostalgic return to the old country, and a queer echo too of the fate of Oscar Wilde, a figure 'at home' in English society until becoming outcast after his conviction under the 'imperial statute' referred to by Norris. As Kathryn Conrad argues, the AOH attitude to the Irish American lesbian and gay community was an attempt to legitimise a conservative version of identity, one that excluded certain groups in order to ensure 'an airtight narrative of descent'.[58] As these examples demonstrate, the entanglements of ethnicity, sexuality and gender since the 1990s have become 'internationalised', but not in ways that confirmed a margin-centre or backward-progressive division. Siobhán Kilfeather has emphasised that Mary Robinson's Presidency not only changed the tone of public life and political exchange, it also enabled Irish feminists to focus more fully on global debates, such as those surrounding immigration, development and multiculturalism.[59]

Another contentious feature of Ireland's going global has been the vigorous debates regarding the validity and cogency of postcolonial studies for a reading of Irish history and culture. The proponents of 'travelling theory', some argued, were exporting fashionable critiques that often had little purchase on the particularities of the Irish climate, and there was a whiff of intellectual neocolonialism concealed in the 'post'. A number of central, definitional questions have been posed for Irish postcolonial studies: is Ireland a modern nation-state or ex-colony; does it have a 'First' or 'Third' World consciousness; to what extent has colonialism shaped Ireland's historical development; has the conflict in Northern Ireland been a continuation of colonialism? These questions have generated a great deal of debate since 1990 but they should not be put in 'either–or terms'.[60] This may testify to the reality that 'the question of where Ireland belongs has yet to settle into a single answer or set of answers'.[61]

Again, Field Day constitutes an instructive case study. The introduction of postcolonial theory, alongside the controversy involving the inclusiveness of the *Anthology*, has proved a particularly vexed issue in analyses of the Field Day enterprise. Deane's introduction to *Nationalism, Colonialism and Literature* declared that Ireland's current condition was 'above all, a colonial crisis'.[62] The book included essays by Edward Said, Frederic Jameson and Terry Eagleton that had originally appeared in the fifth pamphlet series. These star turns did not prove uniformly successful, as evidenced by Said's construction of Yeats as 'a homogenous decolonizing subject'.[63] Edna Longley criticised the dominant colonial/ postcolonial framework of Field Day that inappropriately annexed Ireland North and South: 'Strange collusions are taking place: holiday romances in a postcolonial never-never land'.[64] Liam Kennedy saw 'the Field Day tendency'[65] as in danger of propping up ultra-nationalism, whose 'threadbare' rhetoric 'can be seemingly modernised and given a patina of legitimacy through identification with genuine liberation struggles in the Third World'.[66] Indeed, Deane's statement about the necessity of new modes of critical thought seemed at once to question and reaffirm essentialism: 'Everything, including our politics and our literature, has to be rewritten – i.e. re-read. That will enable new writing, new politics, unblemished by Irishness but securely Irish'.[67] Yet, as Colin Graham has argued, Field Day aligned itself with a developing postcolonial critique of the nation that sought to look beyond notions of 'origin, identity and affiliation' offered by the 'nation-narrative'.[68] Graham and Richard Kirkland emphasise that the diasporic nature of Irish historical experience, and its relationship with Britain, have 'enabled the study of Ireland to be opened out to alignment with most definitions of globalization', and the suspicion that Irish postcolonial criticism 'underwrites the triumph of the independent post-colonial nation' is misplaced.[69] Thus, while the 'external' has already been here a long time, it has not disabled 'local' autonomy or specificity.

Under the Field Day imprint, Irish postcolonial theory has gone global. Field Day now has its base in the Keough Institute for Irish Studies at the University of Notre Dame, USA, with an outpost in St Stephen's Green, Dublin. Aidan Arrowsmith notes that its benefactor Donald Keough, formerly CEO of Coca-Cola, 'may know something about the empires and globalisation which recur as Field Day preoccupations', and while this situation might threaten to induce compromise, complicity and political quietude, it can also generate 'intriguing tensions'.[70] Given its enviable market position, Field Day has become 'Irish Studies' leading brand',[71] but it may stand as a weather vane of Irish cultural criticism more generally. An export-driven, transnational enterprise, it is in part subject to the process of modernisation that it critiques, but it also remains constantly alert to the assumptions and demands of the circuits of exchange it navigates.

Since the 1990s, the category of ethnicity in the European context has been at once comforting and disconcerting in a continent emerging from the Cold War, and this ambivalence towards ethnic difference informs the current tensions surrounding immigration and asylum. The rhetoric of liberal tolerance and pluralism can cloak suspicion and intolerance within many First World countries. Again, Ireland offers a distinctive perspective on the contemporary experience of migration and relocation. Current estimates calculate the Irish diaspora as seventy million people worldwide, compared with a population of five million in Ireland. These diasporic communities have often been the repository of nostalgic and essentialist attitudes that tourism has exploited and, as the Keough–Field Day association suggests, inward investment has sometimes followed suit. Yet reverse migration, and the increased self-confidence that accompanied economic expansion, has meant a reappraisal of these historic affiliations, as Mary Robinson's 1995 address to both houses of the Irish parliament suggested: 'if we expect that the mirror held up to us by Irish communities abroad will show a single familiar identity, or a pure strain of Irishness, we will be disappointed. We will overlook the fascinating diversity of culture and choice which looks back at us'.[72] Robinson's celebration of heterogenous diasporic identities also had implications north of the border. The peace process would of necessity ask all the people on the island to acknowledge the 'diversity of culture and choice which looks back at us'. Whether the current settlement in the North has promoted plurality or consolidated division is a moot point, of course. While Brian Walker has recently suggested that changes in Irish identity, by admitting both unionists and nationalists to a 'global network' of millions, 'may well have important consequences for changes in Northern Ireland',[73] it is possible to argue that the Agreement institutionalised the normative and essentialist categories that had sustained sectarian division before and during the Troubles.[74]

As Breda Gray has shown, Irish identity is increasingly promoted as diasporic, but in a period 'characterised by an intensification of transnational processes', the concept of the nation can also become a site of struggle.[75] Thus the question of Irishness is not only about Irish migrant identities that are fashioned elsewhere, but how other migrant identities might reconceive Irishness, given that the Republic is now defined by imported rather than exported labour. The popular assertion that Ireland has no racism has been placed under severe interrogation since the late 1990s. Michael Breen and Eoin Devereux have shown how the Irish media presents those at the social margins – travellers, immigrants and asylum seekers – as problems 'rather than offering any analysis of the sociological realities that underpin the experiences of those groups'.[76] The negative, inflammatory or hostile headlines simplify or efface the complex socio-economic forces that drive migration, and suggest that attitudes are little different in Ireland from those in many other European countries.

The issue of race was airbrushed out of discussions surrounding the referendum on citizenship rights in 2004, in favour of 'managerial' questions of how to deal with immigration across the Republic. In response to this climate, the monthly *Metro Eireann* was established in 2000 by the Nigerian immigrants Abel Ugba and Chinedu Onyejelem as 'Ireland's Only Multicultural Newspaper'. Yet its first issue worked hard to minimise the impact of cultural difference on contemporary Ireland, stressing that immigrants and those from ethnic minorities were united in wanting to 'contribute to the development of Ireland' and required only a 'free hand' to do so. The language of the market, and the evasiveness of the term 'development', suggest that these new arrivals will readily accommodate themselves to the economic liberalism and labour flexibility demanded by 'multicultural' contemporary Ireland. Yet there remains a racial hierarchy in place.[77] Emigration is no longer the defining pattern, but immigration in the present moment can exacerbate existing social inequalities as much as it encourages inclusiveness. The accelerating shifts in labour markets, and their impact on a rapidly changing society, seem set to ensure that multiculturalism will remain an open question for the Republic and Northern Ireland.

It will have become apparent that in a variety of ways the Irish experience of modernity can cast revealing light on the dislocations of global development. In the present moment, both parts of Ireland can find meaningful affinities, for example, not just with its fellow EU member states, but also with accession countries in Eastern Europe and emergent economies elsewhere in ways that do not collapse their different situations into some uniform 'postcolonial' condition. No doubt questions of connection still need to be asked closer to home, too. Back in 1991, George Watson commented that '[w]e cannot begin to study and relate properly to Europe until we have made ourselves aware of the differences of real complexity within these islands'.[78] Since the late 1990s, following the power-sharing agreement in the North, and devolution in Scotland and Wales, the complexity of political and cultural alignments across the two islands has increased significantly. Yet Joe Cleary has argued that Irish Studies also must situate Ireland's development within comparative frameworks that stretch beyond the horizon of Western Europe. For example, the appellation 'Celtic Tiger' connected the Republic with the 'tiger' economies of East Asia. The point, Cleary stresses, is not to find perfect symmetry between Ireland and other former colonies; it is rather 'to think the ways in which specific national configurations are always the product of dislocating intersections between local and global processes that are not simply random but part of the internally contradictory structure of the modern capitalist world system'.[79]

This discussion has surveyed the responses within cultural production and cultural criticism to Ireland's rapid economic transformation and its equivocal benefits. In 1985 John Wilson Foster claimed that the 'critical condition' of Ireland was inseparable from 'the condition of criticism in Ireland'.[80] One cannot equate the Republic's economic transformation and the Northern peace process with the 'success' of Irish cultural criticism since 1990, but the creative and critical work surveyed in this volume has responded to the sense of crisis invoked by Foster and by Field Day with boldness and energy. It is our hope that this collection avoids an airy and superficial embrace of diversity, and instead acknowledges the possibilities and problems for Irish culture in an age when people, resources and information move at dizzying speed across national boundaries. Gerry Smyth has recently reflected on how Irish Studies has changed through the computer-based production and dissemination of research, and he proposes that the theory and IT 'revolutions' are fundamentally linked. He identifies three terms in Irish cultural history – Theory⇔Tiger⇔Technology – that are locked together in a paradoxical relationship that is both mutually supportive and mutually interrogative. Each term connotes particular practices that have undergone massive change in a relatively short period of time; together they provide the discursive matrix from which modern Irish Studies has emerged.[81]

Whilst theory and technology can be harnessed together to meet the challenges of the future, modern Irish cultural criticism faces a Tiger in thrall to a notion of community 'based on the acquisition of property, portable and otherwise, irrespective of the health (physical, mental or emotional) of the environment in which it exists'. If this criticism is to retain 'a role in relation to the identity which it ostensibly serves as its pretext, it must be to mitigate the manipulative logic of the prevailing socio-economic climate, and to promote an acknowledgement of the principles of empathy, interdependence and love'.[82] Smyth rightly acknowledges that this remains a 'utopian' vision, but it is no more or less virtual than the vision projected from a computer screen, a tourist brochure, a business prospectus – or an aircraft window.

Notes

1   Declan Kiberd, *Inventing Ireland* (London: Jonathan Cape, 1995), p. 653.
2   Lucy McDiarmid, review of Margaret Kelleher and Philip O'Leary (eds), *The Cambridge History of Irish Literature* (Cambridge: Cambridge University Press, 2006), *Times Literary Supplement*, 6 October 2006, p. 3.
3   See Wanda Balzano, Anne Mulhall and Moynagh Sullivan (eds), *Irish Postmodernisms and Popular Culture* (London: Palgrave, 2007).
4   Diane Negra (ed.), *The Irish in Us: Irishness, Performativity, and Popular Culture* (Durham, NC and London: Duke University Press, 2006).
5   Claire Connolly, 'Introduction: Ireland in Theory', in Claire Connolly (ed.), *Theorizing Ireland* (London: Palgrave, 2002), p. 2.
6   Ibid., p. 3.
7   BBC News, http://news.bbc.co.uk/1/hi/business/7026921.stm, accessed 8 October 2007.
8   Michael Cronin and Barbara O'Connor, 'From Gombeen to Gubeen: Tourism, Identity and Class in Ireland, 1949–99', in Ray Ryan (ed.), *Writing in the Irish Republic: Literature, Culture, Politics 1949–1999* (Houndmills: Macmillan, 2000), pp. 166–7.
9   Ibid., p. 177.
10 Ibid., p. 182.
11 Hugh Linehan, 'Myth, Mammon and Mediocrity: The Trouble with Recent Irish Cinema', *Cineaste*, Contemporary Irish Cinema Supplement Vol. XXIV: 2–3 (1999), p. 46.

12 Luke Gibbons, *Transformations in Irish Culture* (Cork: Cork University Press/Field Day, 1996), pp. 89, 91.

13 See Joe Cleary, 'The World Literary System: Atlas and Epitaph', *Field Day Review* 2 (2006): pp. 197–219.

14 Paddy Logue, Introduction to Logue (ed.), *Being Irish* (Dublin: Oak Tree, 2000), p. xvii.

15 Brian Trench, 'Popular Music', *The Blackwell Companion to Modern Irish Culture*, ed. W. J. McCormack (Oxford: Blackwell, 2001), p. 482.

16 Although Gerry Smyth has argued that the Irish boyband phenomenon bears an affinity to the showband tradition. See his *Noisy Island: A Short History of Irish Popular Music* (Cork: Cork University Press, 2005).

17 R. F. Foster, *Luck and the Irish: A Brief History of Change 1970–2000* (London: Allen Lane, 2007), p. 148.

18 Peadar Kirby, 'Contested Pedigrees of the Celtic Tiger', in Peadar Kirby, Luke Gibbons and Michael Cronin (eds), *Reinventing Ireland: Culture, Society and the Global Economy* (London: Pluto, 2002), p. 26.

19 Foster, *Luck and the Irish*, p. 8.

20 Peadar Kirby, Luke Gibbons and Michael Cronin, 'Introduction. The Reinvention of Ireland: A Critical Perspective', in Kirby, Gibbons and Cronin (eds) *Reinventing Ireland*, p. 3.

21 John Waters, *An Intelligent Person's Guide to Modern Ireland* (London: Duckworth, 1997), p. 9.

22 Ibid., p. 133.

23 See, for example, Ciaran Brady (ed.), *Interpreting Irish History: The Debate on Historical Revisionism, 1938–1994* (Dublin: Irish Academic Press, 1994), and Willy Maley, 'Nationalism and Revisionism: Ambiviolences and Dissensus', in Scott Brewster, Virginia Crossman, Fiona Becket and David Alderson (eds), *Ireland in Proximity: History, Gender, Space* (London: Routledge, 1999), pp. 12–27.

24 Colm Tóibín, 'Introduction', in Tóibín (ed.), *Soho Square: New Writing from Ireland* (London: Bloomsbury, 1993), p. 9.

25 Joe Cleary, 'Modernization and Aesthetic Ideology in Contemporary Irish Culture', in Ray Ryan (ed.), *Writing in the Irish Republic: Literature, Culture and Politics 1949–1999* (Basingstoke: Macmillan, 2000), p. 108.

26 Ibid., p. 115.

27 Ibid., pp. 126–7.

28 Kirby, p. 27.

29 Debbie Ging, 'Screening the Green: Cinema under the Celtic Tiger', in Kirby, Gibbons and Cronin (eds), *Reinventing Ireland*, pp. 177, 193.

30 Nicholas Daly, 'From Elvis to the Fugitive: Globalisation and Recent Irish Cinema', *European Journal of English Studies*, 'Postcolonial Ireland?', 3: 3 (December 1999): 273.

31 Luke Gibbons, 'The Global Cure? History, Therapy and the Celtic Tiger', in Kirby, Gibbons and Cronin (ed.), *Reinventing Ireland*, p. 92.

32 Ibid., p. 94.

33 Luke Gibbons, 'Narratives of the Nation: Fact, Fiction and Irish Cinema', in Connolly (ed.), *Theorising Ireland*, p. 74.

34 Connolly (ed.), *Theorising Ireland*, p. 13.

35 On collective remembering and celebration in the period, see Roy Foster, *The Irish Story: Telling Tales and Making It Up in Ireland* (Harmondsworth: Penguin, 2002), pp. 23–36.

36 Carla Power, 'What Happened to Irish Art?', *Newsweek*, 20 August 2001, p. 45.

37 Peadar Kirby, Luke Gibbons and Michael Cronin, 'Conclusions and Transformations', in Kirby, Gibbons and Cronin (eds), *Reinventing Ireland*, p. 204.

38 Fintan O' Toole, *The Ex-Isle of Erin: Images of Global Ireland* (Dublin: New Island Press, 1997), p. 153.

39 Michael Cronin, 'Speed Limits: Ireland, Globalisation, and the War against Time', in Kirby, Gibbons and Cronin (eds), *Reinventing Ireland*, pp. 63–4.

40 *The Guardian*, 17 April 2007, p. 19.

41 The series can be viewed at www.irelantis.com.

42 Fintan O'Toole, 'Introducing Irelantis', in Seán Hillen, *Irelantis* (Dublin: Irelantis, 1999) p. 5.

43 Connolly (ed.), *Theorising Ireland*, p. 10.

44 Foster, *Luck and the Irish*, p. 185.

45 Colin Graham, *Deconstructing Ireland: Identity, Theory, Culture* (Edinburgh: Edinburgh University Press, 1999), p. 27.

46 We might cite here landmark works such as David Cairns's and Shaun Richards's *Writing Ireland: Colonialism, Nationalism and Culture* (Manchester: Manchester University Press, 1988).

47 Terry Eagleton, *Heathcliff and the Great Hunger: Studies in Irish Culture* (London: Verso, 1995), p. x.

48 See Richard Kirkland on the Field Day enterprise in *Literature and Culture in Northern Ireland Since 1965: Moments of Danger* (London: Longman, 1996), pp. 121–48.

49 Seamus Deane (ed.), 'Introduction', *Field Day Anthology of Irish Writing* Vol. 1 (Derry: Field Day, 1991), p. xix.

50 Damian Smyth, 'Totalising Imperative', *Fortnight* 309 (September 1992) 26.

51 Eamonn Hughes, 'To Define Your Dissent: The Plays and Polemics of the Field Day Theatre Company', *Theatre Research International* 15: 1 (spring 1990), p. 69.

52 For reactions to the exclusion of women from the Anthology see, for example, Edna Longley in *The Living Stream: Literature and Revisionism in Ireland* (Newcastle upon Tyne: Bloodaxe, 1994), pp. 34–6.

53 Cited in Francis Mulhern, 'A Nation, Yet Again: The Field Day Anthology', *Radical Philosophy* 65 (autumn 1993), p. 25.

54 Angela Bourke, Siobhán Kilfeather, Maria Luddy, Margaret MacCurtain, Gerardine Meaney, Máirin Ní Dhonnchadha, Mary O'Dowd and Clair

Wills (eds), *The Field Day Anthology of Irish Writing, Vols 4 and 5: Irish Women's Writings and Traditions* (Cork: Cork University Press, 2002).

55 Roisin Higgins, ' "A Drift of Chosen Females": *The Field Day Anthology of Irish Writing*, Vols 4 and 5', *Irish University Review* 33: 2 (autumn/ winter 2003), p. 405.

56 Kieran Rose, *Diverse Communities: The Evolution of Lesbian and Gay Politics in Ireland, Undercurrents*, Pamphlet Series (Cork: Cork University Press, 1994), p. 4.

57 Cited in Kathryn A. Conrad, *Locked in the Family Cell: Gender, Sexuality and Political Agency in Irish National Discourse* (Madison: University of Wisconsin Press, 2004), pp. 52, 53.

58 Ibid., p. 66.

59 Siobhán Kilfeather, 'Irish Feminism', in Joe Cleary and Claire Connolly (eds) *The Cambridge Companion to Modern Irish Culture* (Cambridge: Cambridge University Press, 2005), pp. 96–116, p. 114.

60 Joep Leersen, '1798: The Recurrence of Violence and Two Conceptual-isations of History', *Irish Review* 22 (1998), p. 45.

61 Claire Connolly, 'Postcolonial Ireland: Introducing the Question', *European Journal of English Studies* 3: 3 (December 1999), p. 260.

62 Seamus Deane, 'Introduction', in Deane (ed.), *Nationalism, Colonialism and Literature* (Minneapolis: University of Minnesota Press, 1990), p. 6.

63 Aaron Kelly, 'Reproblematizing the Irish Text', in Aaron Kelly and Alan A. Gillis (eds), *Critical Ireland: New Essays in Literature and Culture* (Dublin: Four Courts, 2001), p. 126.

64 Longley, p. 28.

65 Liam Kennedy, *Colonialism, Religion and Nationalism in Ireland* (Belfast: Institute of Irish Studies, 1996), p. 179.

66 Kennedy, 'Modern Ireland: Post-colonial Society or Post-colonial Pretensions?' *The Irish Review* 13 (1992–93), pp. 107–21, p. 118.

67 Seamus Deane, *Celtic Revivals: Essays in Modern Irish Literature 1880–1980* (London: Faber, 1985), p. 58.

68 Colin Graham, ' "Liminal Spaces": Post-Colonial Theories and Irish Culture', *The Irish Review* 16 (1994), p. 31.

69 Colin Graham and Richard Kirkland, 'Introduction', in Graham and Kirkland (eds), *Ireland and Cultural Theory: The Mechanics of Authenticity* (Houndmills: Macmillan, 1998), pp. 3–4.

70 Aidan Arrowsmith, 'New Field Day Dawning', *Irish Studies Review* 15: 1 (February 2007), p. 84.

71 Ibid., p. 86.

72 Mary Robinson, 'Cherishing the Irish Diaspora'. Address to the Houses of the Oireachtas, 2 February 1995 (Northern Ireland Political Collection: Linen Hall Library, Belfast).

73 Brian Walker, ' "The Lost Tribes of Ireland": Diversity, Identity and Loss Among the Irish Diaspora', *Irish Studies Review* 15: 3 (August 2007), p. 278.

74 As outlined by Andrew Finlay, 'Irish Studies, Cultural Pluralism and the Peace Process', *Irish Studies Review* 15: 2 (August 2007), pp. 333–46.
75 Breda Gray, 'Transnational Negotiations of Migrancy', *Irish Studies Review* 14: 2 (May 2006), pp. 207–23.
76 Michael Breen and Eoin Devereux, 'Setting up Margins: Public Attitudes and Media Construction of Poverty and Exclusion in Ireland', *Nordic Irish Studies* 2: 1 (2003), p. 90.
77 See Maureen T. Reddy, 'Reading and Writing Race in Ireland: Roddy Doyle and *Metro Eireann*', *Irish University Review* 35: 2 (autumn/winter 2005), pp. 377–9.
78 George Watson, 'All Europeans Now?', Proceedings of the Cultural Traditions Group conference, 'All Europeans Now?' (Belfast: Institute of Irish Studies, 1991), p. 55.
79 Joe Cleary, 'Misplaced Ideas? Colonialism, Location and Dislocation in Irish Studies', in Connolly (ed.), *Theorising Ireland*, p. 104.
80 John Wilson Foster, 'The Critical Condition of Ulster', in Michael Allen and Angela Wilcox (eds), *Critical Approaches to Anglo-Irish Literature* (Gerrards Cross: Colin Smythe, 1989), p. 86.
81 Gerry Smyth, 'Tiger, Theory, Technology: A Meditation on the Development of Modern Irish Cultural Criticism', *Irish Studies Review* 15: 2 (May 2007), p. 133.
82 Ibid., p. 134.

Part II

Drama

3

Home places: Irish drama since 1990

Clare Wallace and Ondřej Pilný

To appraise Irish theatre of the recent past is an ominous task; to attempt to predict what might be remembered in the future a treacherous one. From 1990 to mid-2006 the Irish Playography database lists 842 plays, devised pieces and adaptations produced in Ireland by Irish theatre companies and other commercial bodies. Since 1990 critical interest in Irish theatre has grown rapidly, spurred on in part by the Abbey Theatre centenary in 2004 and reassessments of its history, in part by the emergence of a vibrant new generation of playwrights and the international success of a handful of Irish directors and dramatists.

In his introduction to *Druids, Dudes and Beauty Queens* Dermot Bolger relates an anecdote about four women in the audience at the end of one of his plays: 'Two stood up to give the actors a standing ovation . . . while their two companions resolutely sat with their arms folded, disliking what they'd seen so much that they steadfastly refused to clap'.[1] Such contrary reactions, likely to end in 'a blazing row',[2] appealed to Bolger as an ideal response to a theatre production. Responses to the changes in Irish society, economy and culture in this period seem similarly split between outright rejection and standing ovation, and provide a challenging terrain for contemporary theatre and its criticism. The following survey will consider three aspects of Irish theatre since 1990 in an effort to establish a context for the chapters in this section. It will focus initially on writing for theatre from both established writers and the generation that emerged in the early 1990s, then will turn to the theatre scene (directors, theatre companies and performance); and finally consider the critical energies around theatre up to the mid-2000s.

Plays and playwrights

Irish theatre is renowned for its literary character; drama which is verbal rather than the physical is to the fore. Depending on one's predilection this may be its greatest quality or its long-term limitation; either way, traditionally it has been a theatre of the playwright, the text and the power of the word. Attempts to sum up what Irish drama is about tend to revolve around the questions of identity in relation to the nation. Thus, in *Twentieth-Century Irish Drama*, Christopher Murray observes succinctly that

> Irish drama is a long, energetic dispute with a changing audience over the same basic issues: where we come from, where we are now, and where we are headed. Alternatively, these questions comprise history, identity, home or a sense of place, and visionary imagination.[3]

The transformation of Ireland in the 1990s has meant that such questions remain at the top of the agenda, not merely for playwrights, but for Irish society and culture as a whole. At a time of much-publicised and selective prosperity, of returned, deracinated emigrants, combined with the influx of racially 'other' immigrants and the more general commodification of ethnicity, Irish identity has, unsurprisingly, been in the throes of some considerable redefinition. The status of Ireland's Celtic Tiger economy, the effects of consumerism and globalisation are the subjects of considerable debate. As Michael Böss and Eamon Maher have noted in their introduction to *Engaging Modernity*, positions taken in this debate tend to indicate the chief and quite divergent 'attitudes to modernity'.[4] A prominent, generally positive, approach is to be found in the work of National Economic and Social Council economist Rory O'Donnell, and has also been widely disseminated in popular form through the journalism of Fintan O'Toole. Accordingly the changes experienced since the mid-1990s are seen to be as progressive and necessarily moving away from the traditional nationalist model of economy and social organisation, towards further European integration and a process of 're-invention'.[5] In direct opposition to this view, Peadar Kirby argues that in contrast to the 'invention' of Ireland in the 1890s, the 're-invention' of Ireland in the 1990s has occurred 'through the actions of market-accommodating business and political elites rather than through popular social and cultural contestation of the dominant order'.[6] Compared then to the nationalist Ireland that preceded it, neo-liberal Ireland is of false provenance and can perhaps lead only to the abyss of post-national disempowerment.

Ultimately attitudes in this debate reveal how globalisation has involved more than an accelerated process of commodification in the cultural sphere. As a result of the development of mass media, telecommunications, computer technology and the upsurge in migration, traditional senses of national identity based on race and place have been rendered problematic.[7] What then does this mean for Irish drama? In an article in an *Irish Theatre Magazine* series assessing the state of Irish theatre in 2003, Scottish theatre critic Joyce McMillan notes that Irish theatre's strongholds have traditionally maintained an 'accomplished tradition of public storytelling through performance', eloquence and 'engagement with the life of the nation'.[8] Though globalisation may be notoriously difficult to define, having acquired in the last decade the qualities of a shibboleth,[9] in its contemporary incarnation it involves the transformation of how the world is perceived spatially and temporally. As such, its impact may test these strongholds, for as

> nations become less significant as political units, and we move into a world in which new media and faster communications create different networks of kinship and organisation across much larger distances, Irish theatre inevitably faces a huge crisis of identity, a deep question about who the audience now is, and how it should be addressed.[10]

The fallout of the triumphalist materialism of the 1990s, coupled with loosening bonds between nation and identity, continue to present a challenge for the new playwrights of the 1990s and those who follow.

Yet while the 1990s did herald a break with various aspects of twentieth-century Ireland and Irishness, a reconfiguration of Irish identity was evident in Irish drama well before the rhetoric of globalisation. When in 1992 Tom Kilroy surveyed his own 'generation of playwrights' which grew up in a country characterised by poverty and isolation, he noted how this group – whose early work dates from the 1960s – witnessed and wrote of the transformation of a traditional culture and the accompanying pangs of a changing identity. In Kilroy's view this work struggled to connect the past with the present, to the extent that the drama produced between the 1960s and the 1980s was notable for its self-consciousness, written by 'agnostic believers and uneasy patriots, reluctant farmers and local cosmopolitans, incredulous parents and recalcitrant, elderly children, citizens of a country not always identical to the one of their imaginations'.[11] Kilroy's generation of playwrights – Brian Friel, Tom Murphy, Hugh Leonard and Tom MacIntyre – emerged at the beginning of a long second wave of engaged and engaging Irish drama (following the first wave at the beginning of the twentieth century). In the 1980s they were joined by a younger set of talented theatre writers including, among others, Stewart Parker, Dermot Bolger, Frank McGuinness, Sebastian Barry, Christina Reid, Marie Jones and Declan Hughes.

Although the destinies of these writers are inevitably varied, most have continued to be of importance to Irish drama to the present day.

Murray lists Brian Friel, Tom Murphy, John B. Keane, Tom Kilroy and Hugh Leonard among the 1960s dramatists of canonical status.[12] Of these, Friel and Murphy now occupy absolutely central positions in the modern Irish dramatic canon. Friel has continued in the manner sketched by Kilroy, as a 'highly formal artist',[13] working with themes mapped out in his earlier work of history, memory, forms of identity and exile, and verbal and nonverbal communication. Indeed, for Friel the period is bounded by two major plays, *Dancing at Lughnasa* (1990) and *The Home Place* (2005), which frame a number of new pieces – *Wonderful Tennessee* (1993), *Molly Sweeney* (1994), *Give Me Your Answer, Do!* (1997), *Afterplay* (2002), *Performances* (2003) – and adaptations – *A Month in the Country* (1992), *The London Vertigo* (1992), *The Yalta Game* (2001) and *The Bear* (2002). Although appreciation of Tom Murphy has been slower to gather momentum, the Abbey Theatre's Tom Murphy season in October 2001 marked a breakthrough celebration of his work. The reputation of plays like *The Gigli Concert* (1983) and *Bailegangaire* (1986) has continued to grow, and Murphy's new work – *The Wake* (1998), *The House* (2000), *The Alice Trilogy* (2005) – adds to what is now a substantial oeuvre.

Simultaneous with the development of the group of established writers listed above, the 1990s saw a dynamic new generation of playwrights come to the fore. A number of these have achieved considerable success both internationally and in Ireland; the best known at this time include Marina Carr, Martin McDonagh, Conor McPherson, Enda Walsh and Mark O'Rowe. Along with their immediate predecessors the work of these playwrights might be examined in terms of various stylistic and thematic tendencies. These tendencies do not map out a fixed or comprehensive typology of contemporary Irish drama, rather they are best regarded as currents that at times intermingle, at times diverge, and at other times cut across each other with turbulent effect.

One of the most powerful and provocative of these currents is the tragic–mythic to be found in both new writing and adaptation. In *Theatre Stuff* (2000) Marianne McDonald noted over thirty adaptations of Greek tragedy that had been produced since 1984,[14] and the number has even swelled further since then. Among the most recent are Seamus Heaney's version of Sophocles' *Antigone* entitled *The Burial at Thebes* (2004) and Conall Morrison's *Antigone* (2003); however, perhaps more interesting are new plays that draw upon a combination of the mythic and tragic as does the work of Marina Carr. *The Mai*, *Portia Coughlan*, *By the Bog of Cats . . .* and *Ariel* grapple with the possibility of grafting the tragic onto the contemporary through powerful, often self-mythologising protagonists, and the cadences and idioms of Irish

Midland speech. Yet despite the local references Carr's work eschews narrow naturalism, addressing violent and destructive ontological conflicts and primal forces in human nature. The result is that sometimes the graft threatens to overpower the organism, raising once more the question of the role of tragedy in today's drama and in a present-day context.

A further noteworthy recent example of the tragic–mythic is to be found in Vincent Woods' *A Cry From Heaven* (2005) based on the medieval tale of Deirdre and the Sons of Uisnach. As Harvey O'Brien has pointed out in his review of the production, Woods' version 'takes the form of classical drama, a tale of the tragic folly of those who oppose the Fates, built around larger-than-life human archetypes, who share weighty exchanges in sombre tones'.[15] This may sound like a recipe for disaster in modern theatre, but under the direction of Olivier Py the production was given an expressionistic treatment that shocked some sectors of the Abbey Theatre's summer audience,[16] and testified to a renewed energy in unorthodox performance on Irish stages.

Currents of experimentalism run but intermittently through Irish dramatic writing, and are perhaps more fruitfully discussed in combination with performance. Nevertheless, experimental, non-naturalistic approaches are to be found in the work of Tom MacIntyre – particularly in *Good Evening, Mr Collins* (1995) – and in plays such as Dermot Bolger's *The Lament for Arthur Cleary* (1989) and *One Last White Horse* (1991), and in Woods' impressive mummers' play, *At the Black Pig's Dyke* (1992).

A more acclaimed feature of Irish drama and one of its most marketable features is the lyric–narrative. In this period Friel's *Dancing at Lughnasa*, Billy Roche's *Wexford Trilogy: A Handful of Stars, Poor Beast in the Rain, Belfry* (1992),[17] Sebastian Barry's *The Steward of Christendom* (1995) or Conor McPherson's *The Weir* (1997) are fine models of this stylistic strand. The plays maintain a naturalistic frame in which a story unfolds via careful character development and rich contextual reference. These are classic examples of a type of Irish play praised by Joyce McMillan above that wins audiences with a delicate, if formally conservative, blend of linguistic skill, human interest and carefully crafted narrative structures, while being marked by an engagement with individual and/or collective history.

Running parallel to the lyric–narrative is another very popular and traditional form, the melodramatic–comic play. A playwright who has had much success with this particular formula is Marie Jones. *A Night in November* (1995), *Women on the Verge of HRT* (1999) and *Stones in his Pockets* (2000), each of which is unashamedly populist in its humorous and clever narrative trajectory, provides neat, audience-pleasing resolutions. Melodrama, like tragedy, relies upon catharsis and in this sense may prove an interesting indicator of latent social unease. As Peter Brooks argues in *The Melodramatic Imagination*, the form 'starts from and expresses the anxiety brought by a frightening new world in which the traditional patterns of moral order no longer provide the necessary social glue. It plays out the force of that anxiety with the apparent triumph of villainy, and it dissipates it with the eventual victory of virtue'.[18]

Of the playwrights who emerged in the 1990s Martin McDonagh has most successfully provoked a great deal of dissent that belies considerable anxiety and insecurity around perceptions of Irishness. McDonagh preserves most of the elements of melodrama – suspense, sensational episodes and romance – though unambiguously happy endings are in short supply. In *The Beauty Queen of Leenane* (1996), *The Cripple of Inishmaan* (1996), *A Skull in Connemara* (1997), *The Lonesome West* (1997) and *The Lieutenant of Inishmore* (2001) these elements are liberally seasoned with satirical stereotypes of Irishness and stage Irishry. McDonagh's work, despite being embedded in the traditional formulae of Irish drama, also bears a close affinity with British 'in-yer-face drama' of the 1990s, serving the audience a cocktail of blood, gore and offensive language hitherto unseen on an Irish stage.[19]

The confluence of melodrama and satire in recent Irish drama is perhaps best illustrated in the adventurously quirky musical comedy *Improbable Frequency* (2004–05) by Arthur Riordan and Bell Helicopter. The play follows the fortunes of crossword enthusiast and British spy Tristram Faraday in wartime Dublin, where he discovers the laws of probability are being distorted and Ireland's neutrality preserved by PAT (a Probability Adjustment Tank), a secret weapon created by Austrian scientist Erwin Schrödinger. Playfully renovating performance conventions, *Improbable Frequency* also humorously unravels the conventions of the history play, so beloved of Irish playwrights.

The history–memory play maintains an important role, however. It was pioneered by Friel and developed in Sebastian Barry's work throughout the 1990s, and new playwrights have also explored this thematic stand. Elizabeth Kuti's *The Sugar Wife* (2005) depicts Samuel Tewkley, a tea and coffee merchant, and his wife, Hannah, and their encounter with an English anti-abolitionist and a former American slave and campaigner. Though set in nineteenth-century Dublin, the play explores themes of business and social responsibility, philanthropy and exploitation that all have significant resonance in the present day.[20]

One of the greatest challenges in Irish drama from 1990 to 2006 has been how to produce theatre that can deal with or respond to contemporary conditions. Attempts to address this issue are the final current flowing through recent Irish drama to be discussed here. Playwright Declan Hughes has vociferously rejected what he sees as the nostalgic preoccupations of traditional Irish drama, calling for a 'second way of reacting to the collapse of cultural identity in the world: to reflect it, to embrace it, to see it as liberating . . . what we need more than ever are clear-eyed writers who will take the trouble to view the world as it is, in all its complexity, and will then speak the truth'.[21] Yet how playwrights have approached the business of 'speaking the truth' inevitably reveals a spectrum of interests and methodologies ranging from naturalistic plays by Hughes like *Digging for Fire* (1991) or *Shiver* (2003), or Jimmy Murphy's *The Muesli Belt* (2000); the non-naturalistic, issues-based performance pieces by Donal O'Kelly such as *Farawayan* (1998) or *The Cambria* (2005); plays that take Irish politics as a theme or that reflect upon Northern Ireland, like Gary Mitchell's *In a Little World of Our Own* (1997) and *Loyal Women* (2003), or the docudrama *Bloody Sunday* (2005) scripted by British journalist Richard Norton-Taylor; to plays that fit within the experiential aesthetic of 'in-yer-face' drama like Mark O'Rowe's *Howie the Rookie* (1999) and *Made in China* (2001), and Enda Walsh's *Disco Pigs* (1996) and *Sucking Dublin* (1997). Such a list can only begin to suggest the range of possible inflections of contemporary experience, anxieties and conditions to be found in Irish drama today.

Practitioners and performance

A focus on the state of playwriting alone can give a somewhat distorted picture of Irish theatre as a whole. Theatre cannot belong solely to writers no matter how brilliant their work may be; it necessarily encompasses all the other agents and agencies that physically realise a performance on stage and invest it with meaning. The strength of the role of the writer in Irish theatre has often led to the diminution of the roles of director and performance practices in the ways in which theatre has been traditionally perceived and studied. Since 1990, however, some critics and scholars have drawn attention to this deficit and have begun to propagate a discourse around these aspects of Irish theatre. In a collection of essays on *The State of Play: Irish Theatre in the Nineties*, Anna McMullan reviews the contemporary Irish independent theatre sector. She cites the Arts Council report *Views of Theatre in Ireland 1995* in which attention is drawn to how the dominant role of the writer has resulted in 'artists and audiences [being] under-exposed to theatre conceived and made in other ways'.[22] McMullan's point is that performance is 'making a comeback'. This may be in terms of 'a wider range of performance conventions' being deployed by new playwrights like Marina Carr, Sebastian Barry and Dermot Bolger, as well as independent theatre groups who are devoted to performance and physical theatre such as the Galway group Macnas.[23] Irish theatre's preoccupation with language and text as a means of plumbing the depths of post-colonial identity may also be understood vis-à-vis the complex issues of transmission and posterity. If texts have pasts and futures, arguably performance (in the sense of physical/non-verbal theatre or dance) is frequently a matter of the present and presence. The former may invite reflection; the latter seems primarily engaged with the experiential. Yet, as McMullan rightly points out, '[r]efocusing on performance may [also] offer a new way of looking at the texts of the Irish theatre tradition, and at how this tradition may be opened up, regenerated, and made more inclusive'.[24]

From the perspective of 2006, what can be said of the state of performance, the role of theatre companies, performers and directors? Certainly the diversification observed and predicted by McMullan has been gaining momentum. The following paragraphs will pick out a few highlights. Garry Hynes, the co-founder of the Druid Theatre Company in 1975, is probably Ireland's most important living theatre director. As artistic director of the Abbey Theatre from 1990 to 1993 she provocatively challenged the very notion of a national theatre representing the nation. The nation she asserts was and continues to be 'a collection of fictions',[25] and as Ireland changes, the National Theatre must circumvent the risk of becoming 'hostage to one or other version of being Irish'.[26] Since her term at the Abbey, Hynes has been involved in numerous seminal projects. Her commitment to challenging new writing is evidenced in her discovery of the playwright Martin McDonagh, which led to the now (in)famous Druid productions of the Leenane Trilogy, and her direction of Marina Carr's *Portia Coughlan* (1996), *By the Bog of Cats . . .* (1998) and *On Raftery's Hill* (2000). Most recently in 2004 Hynes and the Druid Theatre company have revisited all of J.M. Synge's work in their cycle of productions entitled *DruidSynge*, thus marking 'Druid's commitment to affirming Synge's place in not simply the Irish, but the international theatre canon'.[27]

Lynne Parker, like Hynes, is co-founder of one of Ireland's major independent theatre companies, Rough Magic, and has worked extensively as a director with other companies and theatres across Ireland and the UK. Rough Magic was formed back in 1984 by Parker and Declan

Hughes and initially produced work by non-Irish playwrights including Howard Brenton, David Mamet, Caryl Churchill and Michael Frayn. From this starting point Rough Magic began to develop a base of original work, often written by performers and directors involved with the company such as Hughes, Gina Moxley, Donal O'Kelly and Pom Boyd. In 2001 the company inaugurated the Seeds Initiative in association with the Dublin Fringe Festival to develop and stage new writing in Ireland. A second round of the initiative was launched in 2004, and was followed up by Seeds III in 2006, in each case strengthening further the international dimension of the training provided to the young artists selected to participate in the project. The fruits of Rough Magic's propagation of new writing can been seen in impressive new plays like Morna Regan's *Midden* (2001) and Kuti's *The Sugar Wife*. Among Parker's recent directing projects has been the irreverent and surreal musical comedy *Improbable Frequency* discussed above.

The 1990s and early 2000s also saw the rise of a number of talented performers who also write and/or direct. This type of alternative theatre practice has complicated the traditional perception of authorship, described by Brian Singleton and Anna McMullan as 'the male playwright producing narratives of postcolonial cultural stasis or male impotence'.[28] Influenced by Stanislavski, Meyerhold, Grotowski and Eugenio Barba, Jason Byrne as artistic director and co-founder of Loose Canon Theatre Company (1996) leads a full-time ensemble of performers in an ongoing actor training programme. The company's philosophy foregrounds the role of the actor in the theatre experience. Since 1996 they have produced principally works of Elizabethan and Jacobean drama (*Julius Caesar*, *Coriolanus*, *Hamlet*, *Macbeth*, *The Revenger's Tragedy*, *The White Devil*, *The Duchess of Malfi*) as well as modern European classics such as Ibsen's *Hedda Gabler*. In overtly claiming a genealogy of performance/directing, Byrne is remarkable for his attempts to consciously connect with performance traditions that have conventionally not had much foothold in the Irish theatre scene.

Another challenger of the formulae of text-based theatre is the performer/practitioner Olwen Fouéré. As one of Ireland's more formally adventurous artists, Fouéré has become an important feature of the contemporary Irish theatre, acting across the range from the classics of modern drama to avant-garde performance. With composer Roger Doyle, she is artistic director of Operating Theatre (founded in 1980), which has been responsible for various experimental pieces such as *Here Lies (Antonin Artaud)* (2005), *Passades* (2004) or *Angel/Babel* (1999). Fouéré's commitment to powerful physical performance provocatively marks out a new territory on the contemporary Irish scene.

Finally, although it has oft been the target of criticism for its conservatism, Ireland's National Theatre has been home to much dynamic
new theatre since 1990. While fostering new writers like Marina Carr
and Mark O'Rowe, the Abbey has also continued to celebrate canonical
authors like Brian Friel, Tom Murphy and John B. Keane. The Abbey's
centenary in 2004 attracted critical and popular (re)consideration of its
role as a national theatre. However, the centenary celebrations also were
the focus of much controversy when it was revealed that the theatre
was in serious financial straits. Since 2005 reform has been ongoing,
with the theatre's new director Fiach Mac Conghail working to change
its organisational structures and, in conjunction with the government,
to secure a new location for it at Dublin's George's dock. Relocation
of the theatre will open another chapter in the life of Ireland's best-
known dramatic institution, providing it with renewed creative impetus
for the next century.

Criticism and commentary

As mentioned at the outset, critical interest in Irish drama since 1990
has mushroomed. First, a number of detailed studies have emerged which
re-assess the multifarious interconnections of canonical Irish drama with
politics. Among these, Nicholas Grene's *The Politics of Irish Drama*
(1999) and Lionel Pilkington's *Theatre and the State in Twentieth-Century
Ireland* (2001) deserve special mention, the former for its perceptive
textual criticism, and the latter for offering a challenging new perspective
on Ireland's national theatres.[29]

Detailed overviews of recent drama have been provided both
by Anthony Roche's *Contemporary Irish Drama: From Beckett to
McGuinness* (1994) and Christopher Murray's *Twentieth-Century Irish
Drama: Mirror up to Nation* (1997). These have been complemented
lately by the new *Cambridge Companion to Twentieth-Century Irish
Drama*, edited by Shaun Richards (2004), which sketches a map of
the territory for the general reader. Apart from that, a kaleidoscope of
opinions on the state of the art is offered by volumes of critical essays
such as *The State of Play: Irish Theatre in the 'Nineties*, ed. Eberhard
Bort (1996), *Theatre Stuff*, ed. Eamonn Jordan (2000), *Codes and Masks:
Aspects of Identity in Contemporary Irish Plays in an Intercultural
Context* by Mária Kurdi (2000), and *Druids, Dudes and Beauty
Queens*, ed. Dermot Bolger (2001), together with full-length studies
such as Margaret Llewellyn Jones's *Contemporary Irish Drama and
Cultural Identity* (2002).

Carysfort Press (Dublin) has become an important venue for publications on theatre (not only Irish), including *Theatre Talk: Voices of Irish Theatre Practitioners*, eds Lilian Chambers, Ger Fitzgibbon and Eamonn Jordan (2001). Carysfort have also embarked on a series of volumes dedicated to the most important recent playwrights, starting with *'Stages of Mutability': The Theatre of Frank McGuinness*, ed. Helen Lojek (2002) and *'Before Rules Was Made': The Theatre of Marina Carr*, eds Cathy Leeney and Anna McMullan (2003), followed up by *Out of History: Essays on the Writings of Sebastian Barry* (2006) and *The Theatre of Martin McDonagh*, eds Lilian Chambers and Eamonn Jordan (2006). The series represents a priceless resource for future scholarship, especially as it often – apart from offering new work – also makes available the best of the earlier articles on these playwrights, complemented with programme notes for individual productions, interviews and other supplementary material.

In addition, *Irish Theatre Magazine*, launched in 1998, filled the gap left by *Theatre Ireland*. The *ITM* dedicates significant space to the voices of young theatre critics and is a true hub for the most topical debates; in fact, its pages provide a fairly accurate picture of the current strengths and shortcomings of Irish theatre practice, and also fresh critical perspectives and desires. The preoccupation with Irish theatre as the theatre of a nation – as noted above – is still in evidence; however, it is accompanied by a struggle for a more international theatre, instigated by close contact with cutting-edge European theatrical practices and experiments. Significant coverage is given to alternative forms of theatre (particularly physical and dance theatre and performance) – often in fledgling state in Ireland as yet – and to fringe productions; this in turn demonstrates a wish for a more diverse scene in terms of genre.

The turn of the century has also witnessed a growing importance of online resources. Among these, the Irish Playography stands out in a remarkable manner. Launched by Theatre Shop in 2003, it aims to list all Irish plays produced since the formation of the National Theatre. The project is now nearing completion, and makes Ireland one of the very few countries worldwide to have such a comprehensive database available to practitioners and researchers in an electronic format. Moreover, Theatre Shop has just transformed itself into an Irish Theatre Institute, a body which has been sorely lacking in Ireland. Its Strategic Statement for 2006–12 makes for a fascinating read and raises high expectations indeed: apart from continuing extensive research, the Institute plans to focus primarily on the promotion of Irish

theatre and drama internationally, enabling access to unpublished or
out-of-print playscripts and materials, developing a national theatre
policy, and offering advice and consultation services to the theatre
sector. If the Playography is anything to judge by, Irish theatre is bound
to benefit immensely from the enterprise.

The three chapters that follow discuss some of the most topical issues
which have emerged in Irish drama and theatre since 1990. Starting
from the premise that drama is primarily 'a genre concerned with contradictory forces and unresolved problems' (p. 60), Mária Kurdi looks
at innovative ways in which it has addressed the fact of gender inequality in contemporary Ireland. She focuses particularly on the staging
of the female body, seen both as 'a sign of social positionality and
cultural experience associated with the symbolic' and a reflection of the
'individual desire to remain undefined by communal discourses' (p. 61).
The subversive and/or transformative potential of performing female
corporeality is documented in a detailed analysis of three plays by women:
Gina Moxley's *Danti Dan*, Emma Donoghue's *Ladies and Gentlemen*,
and *By the Bog of Cats* . . . by Marina Carr. Kurdi's interpretation of
Danti Dan stresses above all the deployment of mimicry as a strategy
which in the hands of a rebellious teenager dismantles established gender
roles and approaches to sexuality. Despite the fact that this brings about
'disorder and destruction', it also aptly exposes latent oppressive tendencies within the social system (p. 67). *Ladies and Gentlemen*, on the
other hand, is a play which 'introduces the practice of female cross-
dressing as a performative strategy to re-negotiate the ontological status
of gender' (p. 68). The delightful mixture of vaudeville, memory play
and metatheatre offered by Donoghue indeed shows that gender can
be experienced as a 'subversive performance' (p. 69). Moreover, Kurdi
argues that the complex emotions involved in the scenes from 'the
protagonist's memoryscape' may be communicated only through the
language of the body (p. 70). Finally, miming is observed again in *By
the Bog of Cats* . . . , but this time as a target of mockery. Characters
are revealed hypocritically imitating respectability in sharp contrast to
the desire 'to transgress institutionalised fixities and the binaries of
gender and class' (p. 73). In this context, the staging of corporeality
serves according to Kurdi as an instrument of demarcation, outlining
the boundaries between the world of 'the settled community' and the
'liminal realm of otherness' (p. 72). And although Carr's drama does
not explicitly address issues of gender politics in the manner of the
two former plays, Kurdi maintains that the pathos of *By the Bog of
Cats* . . . is bound to stir the audience into thinking about such issues

nonetheless. What comes out very clearly of Kurdi's discussion is that identity should be understood as a set of performative acts rather than static characteristics. Moreover, the stage might – in Kurdi's view – serve as a laboratory (Jill Dolan's term) in which experimentation is used to negotiate 'socio-cultural inscriptions' (p. 76) such as gender roles and attitudes concerning sexuality, and thus bring about requisite social change.

Carr's work is also explored by Anthony Roche, though from quite a different perspective. Roche's chapter focuses on an exceptional moment in Irish theatre history: in the period 2002–03, there were no fewer than three instances of Irish playwrights putting a contemporary politician on stage, while previous representations of this kind had been extremely rare in Ireland. The three plays in question – Marina Carr's *Ariel*, Sebastian Barry's *Hinterland* and John Breen's *Charlie* – all based their central character on the former Taoiseach, the late Charles J. Haughey (1925–2006), and all in the context of tragedy. The term 'controversial' cannot perhaps fully describe Haughey; on the one hand, he was the undeniable author of many essential steps leading to the economic boom of the 1990s, but at the same time clearly one of the most corrupt leaders Ireland has ever had. Roche – prompted by the Shakespearean allusions in the three plays, together with Haughey's apparent propensity for quoting the Bard – looks at how the Haughey character compares with Shakespeare's tragic heroes and famous manipulators. He finds an interesting parallel in Julius Caesar, riven by 'ongoing internal struggles' very relevant to Haughey's career (p. 94), and also notes Eileen Battersby's linking of the politician with Richard III. The latter he finds to be a very apt analogy, and only regrets that no other of the histories have been considered: although these may not be so deeply lodged in people's memories, they could provide metaphoric images of Irish political life 'which would prove more immediate and less flattering' than any allusions to the tragedies (p. 96). At the same time, though, Roche points out the extent to which artists have been among the chief beneficiaries of financial policies introduced by Haughey: due to legislation unique in Europe, writers may live in Ireland without paying tax on their earnings. This brings Roche to a rather unsettling question, namely to what extent are, for instance, playwrights 'mired and implicated in the same financial double standards which the former Taoiseach promoted?' (p. 87).

Finally, Martine Pelletier extends the consideration of politics and ethics in Irish drama of the period. Her contribution addresses the phenomenon of immigration and some of the attempts by Irish playwrights and practitioners to stage it. She looks at five plays – Brian Friel's *Dancing at Lughnasa* and *The Home Place*, Donal O'Kelly's *Asylum, Asylum*, Elizabeth Kuti's *Treehouses* and *Departure and Arrival* by Dermot Bolger and Kazem Shahryary – as 'a series of interventions aimed at bringing to the consciousness of Irish and international audiences the plight of those many immigrants and refugees seeking a new life in Ireland' (p. 100). Pelletier observes how a number of productions of the tremendously successful *Dancing at Lughnasa* have stressed a particular nostalgia which is emblematic of 'an abiding need to celebrate what is felt to be lost': namely, the traditional world of rural Ireland (p. 103). She continues by making a sharp contrast between Friel's treatment of Africa as 'a repository of a universal sense of the sacred' and the much more realistic depiction of the continent as a realm torn apart by brutal internecine conflicts in *Asylum, Asylum* (p. 102). Despite their generic differences and the clear call for action present in O'Kelly's drama (which would perhaps seem out of place in Friel's work), however, both plays are seen to stress the benefits of the links with Africans for the Irish society. *Treehouses* and *Departure and Arrival* share O'Kelly's concern with the right of refugees and immigrants to look for a new home in Ireland. While Kuti's play is interpreted by Pelletier as a largely traditional, realistic drama dealing with a sense of 'in-betweenness' and the formation of identity between places, the collaborative effort by Bolger and Kurdish playwright (and exile) Shahryary is viewed as 'deliberately bring[ing] to the fore the parallels between Irish emigration and contemporary immigration' (p. 108), implying a 'historical as well as an ethical responsibility' (p. 111) which the Irish may quite reasonably be seen to have regarding in particular the regularly despised economic migrants to their country. Pelletier's portrayal of Ireland through a reading of these plays as a place which is 'reluctantly coming to terms with its multicultural character' (p. 115) concludes with a discussion of Friel's latest play, *The Home Place*. In this, Friel demonstrates that the roots of a still widely accepted outline of Irish national identity lie, notoriously, with eugenics, a doctrine which has been readily embraced by many a totalitarian regime; hence, there is perhaps no need to stress that the traditional concept of Irishness requires a swift and dramatic reformulation in post-Celtic-Tiger Ireland.

Notes

1 Dermot Bolger, *Druids, Dudes and Beauty Queens: The Changing Face of Irish Theatre* (Dublin: New Island, 2001), p. 12.
2 Ibid.
3 Christopher Murray, *Twentieth-Century Irish Drama: Mirror up to Nation* (Manchester: Manchester University Press, 1997), p. 224.

4 Michael Böss and Eamon Maher (eds), *Engaging Modernity: Readings of Irish Politics, Culture and Literature at the Turn of the Century* (Dublin: Veritas, 2003), p. 12.

5 Rory O'Donnell (ed.), *Europe: The Irish Experience* (Dublin: Institute of European Affairs, 2000), pp. 209–11. See also Fintan O'Toole *Black Hole, Green Card: The Disappearance of Ireland* (Dublin: New Island, 1994) and *The Ex-Isle of Erin: Images of a Global Ireland* (Dublin: New Island, 1996).

6 Peadar Kirby, 'Contested Pedigrees of the Celtic Tiger', in Peadar Kirby, Luke Gibbons and Michael Cronin (eds), *Reinventing Ireland: Culture, Society and the Global Economy* (London: Pluto, 2002), p. 35.

7 In *Modernity at Large: Cultural Dimensions of Globalization* (Minneapolis: University of Minnesota Press, 1996) anthropologist Arjun Appadurai discusses at length the roles of the media and migration in the redefinition and reimagining of culture in a globalised world.

8 Joyce McMillan, 'Ireland's Winning Hand', *Irish Theatre Magazine* 3: 15 (2003), pp. 16, 18.

9 Zygmunt Bauman, *Globalization: The Human Consequences* (Cambridge: Polity, 1998), p. 1.

10 McMillan, p. 22.

11 Tom Kilroy, 'A Generation of Playwrights', in Eamonn Jordan (ed.), *Theatre Stuff: Critical Essays on Contemporary Irish Theatre* (Dublin: Carysfort, 2000), pp. 1–7. 3. Article first published in *Irish University Review*, 1992.

12 Murray, p. 162.

13 Kilroy, p. 6.

14 Marianne McDonald, 'Classics as Celtic Firebrand: Greek Tragedy, Irish Playwrights, and Colonialism', in Jordan (ed.), *Theatre Stuff*, p. 16.

15 Harvey O'Brien, review of *A Cry From Heaven* in *Irish Theatre Magazine* 5: 24 (2005), p. 51.

16 O'Brien, p. 52.

17 *A Handful of Stars* (1988), *Poor Beast in the Rain* (1989) and *Belfry* (1991) were all first staged in the UK at the Bush Theatre and later were published together as *The Wexford Trilogy*.

18 Peter Brooks, *The Melodramatic Imagination: Balzac, Henry James, Melodrama and the Mode of Excess* (New Haven, CT: Yale University Press, 1976), p. 20.

19 Indeed, Aleks Sierz devotes a section of his pioneering study of the genre to *The Beauty Queen of Leenane*. Aleks Sierz, *In-Yer-Face Theatre* (London: Faber, 2000), pp. 219–25.

20 Helen Meaney in her review of the play discusses the ways in which 'the past is refracted through the present' and the issues raised in the play – 'the position of women in marriage; sexual politics and the related theme of colonialism and its attendant commercial exploitation; racism; photography as voyeurism; philanthropy as guilt-assuagement' – all find their counterpoints today. See *Irish Theatre Magazine* 5: 23 (2005), p. 91.

21 Declan Hughes, 'Who The Hell Do We Think We Still Are? Reflections on Irish Theatre and Identity', in Jordan (ed.), *Theatre Stuff*, p. 14.

22 Neil Wallace, 'The Four Estaits', *Views of Theatre in Ireland 1995*, p. 30. Cited in Anna McMullan 'Reclaiming Performance: The Contemporary Irish Independent Theatre Sector', in Eberhard Bort (ed.), *The State of Play: Irish Theatre in the 'Nineties* (Trier: Wissenschaftlicher Verlag Trier, 1996), p. 31.

23 McMullan, pp. 29–30.

24 Ibid., p. 31.

25 Garry Hynes, 'Accepting the Fiction of being National', *Irish Times*, 3 May 1993, p. 12.

26 Garry Hynes interviewed by Cathy Leeney, *Theatre Talk: Voices of Irish Theatre Practitioners* (Dublin: Carysfort, 2001), p. 207.

27 Beth Newhall, ''97 Years and a Day', *Irish Theatre Magazine* 4: 18 (2004), p. 13.

28 Brian Singleton and Anna McMullan, 'Performing Ireland: New Perspectives on Contemporary Irish Theatre', *Australasian Drama Studies* 43 (October 2003), p. 3.

29 Other important new books on the history and politics of Irish theatre include Mary Trotter, *Ireland's National Theaters: Political Performance and the Origins of the Irish Dramatic Movement* (Syracuse, NY: Syracuse University Press, 2001), Ben Levitas, *The Theatre of Nation: Irish Drama and Cultural Nationalism 1890–1916* (Oxford: Oxford University Press, 2002) and Chris Morash, *A History of Irish Theatre 1601–2002* (Cambridge: Cambridge University Press, 2002).

4

Women on the stage in the 1990s: foregrounding the body and performance in plays by Gina Moxley, Emma Donoghue and Marina Carr

Mária Kurdi

In the 1990s an unprecedented fermentation began within Irish society, calling traditional attitudes into question and revealing secret skeletons in secret closets. Instances of sexual hypocrisy, child abuse and domestic violence were made public and provoked debates which highlighted the need to reconsider perceptions as well as legal formulation of the links between the individual, the community and its institutions. Introducing their 1997 volume *Gender and Sexuality in Modern Ireland*, Anthony Bradley and Maryann Gialanella Valiulis argue that this 'fairly sudden social change in Ireland . . . is directly concerned with gender', and there is 'a growing intellectual awareness of the extent to which social experience, past and present, is gendered'.[1] A sign of the revisioning of Ireland's gender politics was that, in 1993, the ban on homosexuality was ended, and divorce became accessible after the 1995 referendum. As a result of a number of high-profile scandals, the Catholic Church rapidly lost its long-held grip on the conscience and moral life of the people.

Concurrently, in the world of the theatre the process of diversification that had begun earlier was gaining momentum, clearing as well as securing a space for the appearance and practice of an array of non-traditional approaches and experimental forms. Companies representing regional, local, and even quite specific interests related to class, gender or alternative sexuality provided a stage for playwrights becoming conscious that 'Ireland is not one story anymore, and we cannot expect single theatrical metaphors for it. Instead of one story and many theatrical images of it, we are moving towards a dramatisation of the fragments rather than the whole thing, the whole society.'[2] It was in this context that the 1990s witnessed a substantial enrichment and increasing critical success of playwriting activity by Irish women. Work by writers like Marina Carr suddenly reached both national and international stages, and several other female dramatists had their plays produced, a development in which the role of respective experimental groups and non-mainstream companies cannot be overlooked.

In addressing the female experience, several Irish woman playwrights chose to portray this broad thematic as intimately bound up with the socially constructed relations between men and women, and between women and institutions against the backdrop of history and dominant ideologies. Undoubtedly, a lot of measures have been implemented recently to alter the traditionally subordinate position of women in the patriarchal society of Ireland to ensure their gender equality, a positive result of EU membership in this respect. Entrenched as it is in far-reaching traditions, however, the socio-cultural construction of woman shows less flexibility. As Pat O'Connor points out, in spite of all visible improvements

> women continue to be seen, effectively, as 'outlaws' – people who are 'different', 'suspect', 'not like us', people whose loyalty to 'the system' is problematic. . . . Women in Ireland, regardless of their age, life stage, ascribed class position and participation in paid employment, are surrounded by structural and cultural cues which define their lives. These cues refer not only to their position in the economic, political, religious and domestic arenas, but also presuppose their positive experience of responsibility for child care, and the 'naturalness' of subsuming their identities in families and/or in other caring relationships. They assume their relative disinterest in the 'normal' male trappings of individuality, viz. economic independence, individual autonomy, money and power.[3]

The situation, thus, is rather contradictory. While woman is declared an equal citizen with man on the level of rhetoric and in the eyes of the law, an inquiry into the day-to-day reality of individual lives may provide evidence that the second sex is still the 'other' in certain conditions. Similar doubts are expressed by Tom Inglish concerning the liberalisation of sexuality:

> During the last half of the twentieth century Ireland became unsettled culturally, particularly in relation to sexuality, pleasure, and desire. . . . Sexually transgressive women may have been celebrated in film and literature, but in real life public trangressors were shamed and castigated.[4]

Drama has always been a genre primarily concerned with contradictory forces and unresolved problems. In the context of social transformations that involve significant improvements yet tend to bring ambiguities to the surface at the same time, Irish female playwrights are challenged by the most delicate, even troubling aspects of issues related to gender, sexual behaviour, marriage and family.

The essential role of the body in theatre across centuries of play-acting is, of course, indisputable. Paradoxically, however, until recent times the female body had been largely absent from the traditional stage as an agent performing subjective realities. As Stanton B. Garner contends, political and ideological conventions governed the representations of women, and the female appeared in the theatre refigured 'as image or fiction' at the expense of her disembodiment and dephysicalisation 'in terms of lived bodiliness'. It is contemporary women's drama, the critic continues, which has managed to liberate the female body from 'corporeal subjection' by introducing 'explorations of the politics of embodiment, addressing the theatrical body in gender specific terms'.[5] Due to these efforts women are no longer represented in the image men created of them or as the conveyors of male-centred ideological positions and ideas, but embody and stand for their distinct experiences and ambitions. Informed by her study of French feminist theory, feminism and theatre, Elaine Aston discusses the strategy of 'Speaking the body / the body speaking' on stage as an equivalent of Luce Irigaray's term 'feminine discourse', which was devised in reference to woman-authored literature. Also, as 'a touchstone in feminist theoretical writings on women's theatre' Aston cites approvingly Julia Kristeva's distinction between the 'semiotic' and the 'symbolic', the latter understood as the pre-Oedipal or presocial/maternal versus the Oedipal or social phase/realm, with the corollary that the speaking subject belongs to both.[6]

Foregrounding female corporeality in drama provides a medium through which creative ambiguity can be achieved, made possible by the duality that the body is a sign of both social positionality and cultural experience associated with the symbolic. At the same time it also reflects individual desire that remains undefined by communal discourses and retains ties with the semiotic. Subjectivity is evoked in this kind of theatre as a process rather than a fixed entity, a site of rivalling forces that ultimately defy strict categorisations of the self.

Critical accounts of the Irish theatre have highlighted the privileging, until very recently, of the verbal and literary over the physical and performative. Arguably, this may have been connected to the focus on colonial/postcolonial identity in a considerable bulk of earlier drama, a perspective the authors tended to revisit and often treat as a complex given rather than a field of contestation. In contemporary Irish culture – inviting the post-postcolonial description under the ramifying effects of globalisation, Celtic Tiger economy and the reverse migration the

country has been facing – the concept of identity is becoming, necessarily, more flexible, allowing for fluid, protean formations. The tendency fits in with comparable worldwide developments which reinforce
the notion that identity should be understood in terms of performative
behaviour that enacts changes, and not by interpreting it as a bundle
of static characteristics. Lib Taylor, writing on the recent scholarly investigation of the subject, states: 'Postmodernism, feminism and psychoanalysis have theorised identity as performative, perceiving identities
as constructed through a process of reiteration (repetition/rehearsal)
and citation (reference/quotation).' Having been imported into social
discourse from the vocabulary of the theatre, the term performance/
performative is nowadays reapplied by theatre and drama studies and
'implies a self-aware theatricality', the 'conscious use of the practices
and conventions of theatre' and the 'deliberate manipulation of citation
and reiteration' as a potential strength of the genre.[7]

In contemporary Irish drama, the renaissance of the monologue
signals a self-conscious move towards heightening the performative
element in the exploration of the self, according to revised perspectives
on identity. The monologue seems to be a dramatic subgenre practised
by male authors primarily, involving acts of performance which take
place through the medium of language, sound, and the unfolding of
multiple narrative spaces, and less so through acts of corporeality.
Characteristic examples include respective plays by Brian Friel, Conor
McPherson, Donal O'Kelly and Enda Walsh. It is mainly in the work
of new Irish woman playwrights that the performing body as a complex source of signification gains more prominence than it has since
Yeats, and renders hidden realities visible as well as reifies alternative
modes of self-construction. Their praxis exploits the representational
potential we can understand through Judith Butler's terms, who claims
that 'As an intentionally organized materiality, the body is always an
embodying *of* possibilities both conditioned and circumscribed by
historical convention'.[8] For the purposes of the present chapter the
emphasis is on 'possibilities'.

Central to the following discussion is the staging of women characters
in three plays, *Danti Dan* by Gina Moxley (1995), Emma Donoghue's
Ladies and Gentlemen (1995) and *By the Bog of Cats . . .* by Marina
Carr (1998). On the one hand, these works are found representative
of the bulk of female-authored writing in the mid- to late 1990s for
the ways they deploy, reshape and forge resources and strategies to probe
into the corporeal dimension of experience. What these texts conspicuously foreground is the socially inscribed body with its potential for
change, while they also enhance awareness of the element of performance

in the portrayal of their woman characters' 'resistance to definition'[9] and search for self-possession on their own terms. The three plays, on the other hand, are different enough in focus to offer an opportunity to explore through them the richness and novelty of the female contribution to the representation and critical revisioning of the subject of gender. The Moxley and Donoghue plays were first performed at the Project Arts Centre in Dublin by Rough Magic and Glasshouse Productions respectively, while Carr's had its première at the Abbey during the Dublin Theatre Festival in 1998.

About the thirteen-year-old female protagonist of *Danti Dan*, called Cactus – a nickname suggestive of both difference and rejection – Gina Moxley writes in her afterword to the play:

> Girls of that age are very often presented as passive victims of men's behaviour towards them and I wanted to see what happened if the reverse was the case. I'd never bought into all of that sugar and spice stuff and was interested in having a female character with an unnervingly steady gaze and who appears remorseless.[10]

By turning the tables this way, the author subverts the gender stereotypes in conventionally scripted victimiser–victim scenarios, and represents a girl/boy story from an unorthodox angle to result in a play which is ruthlessly unsentimental and disturbing. In his review of the first production, Fintan O'Toole claims that the principal merit of *Danti Dan* lies in 'the remarkable skill and unflinching determination with which Moxley pursues an uncompromising vision of the relationship between sex and power. Beneath the dull surface there is a turbulent interplay of countercurrents and reversals.'[11] My analysis relies on the proposition that Cactus's 'unnervingly' cruel and uncompromising acts of victimisation should be treated not as a manifestation of innate wickedness, but as an instance of the potential danger inherent in the prevailing gender economy of a working-class environment at the time the action is set, the summer of 1970, in rural Ireland.

Given its all-teenager cast, made up of three girls and two boys between thirteen and eighteen, the play is inevitably preoccupied with the body from the start. At the dramatic stage of transition between childhood and adulthood, the characters' hyper-consciousness of corporeal signs and changes is combined with their interest in sex in general and the expression of their emerging sexual needs in particular. The girls are obsessed with fashion, discuss the size of their growing bosoms, compare the dates when their period is due, and, in secret, initiate role-playing to act out adult sexual encounters as depicted in a syrupy novel they get hold of. At the same time the play stresses that they are regulated bodies in their society, whose values are transmitted to and imposed on them within the structure of the patriarchal family. The off-stage parents are reported to be keeping a strict, unfailing control over sixteen-year-old Ber and fourteen-year-old Dolores's movements. Their father deals the girls an occasional 'clatter' (p. 9) so that they should keep to the uncontestable rules of domestic life and observe the requirement not to stay out late.

Moxley's play succeeds in revealing the paradox which lies at the core of the dominant discourse on sexual behaviour and its restrictive implications for the developing female body. While the guarding of virginity before marriage is of paramount importance, the teenage girls are left largely ignorant of or are even misled about elementary questions of women's intimate healthcare. Tampons should not be used during menstruation as the offstage mother insists, her sanction quoted by Dolores with more than a little embarrassment: ''Cause you are not a virgin anymore after them or something like that' (p. 23). Asked by Cactus about the actual details of lovemaking and the sensations it involves, Ber, who has started to have sex with eighteen-year-old Noel, gives tentative or evasive replies, testifying to a lack of self-confidence and a personal voice to speak about sex. O'Connor claims that adolescent girls tend to value themselves less highly than boys and the fate of their relationships is often subject to 'the culturally created difficulty of treading a line between being too sexually available and not sufficiently sexually available' which are 'important elements in patriarchal control'.[12] Ber's confusion and apparent lack of interest in sexuality as a source of personal fulfilment renders her passive and negligent, since she does not bother about the possible consequences of the unsafe sex she practises. A crucial issue in the play, Ber's teenage pregnancy is represented in the context of severe regulations on the body unhappily combined with adults' failure to give the young a basic introduction into its reproductive functions. Ber thinks of herself as 'far too young' for pregnancy, and tries to lull her suspicions by the thought that 'Anyway, it [the intercourse] was only standing' (p. 23). Yet in spite of this immature view of how her own body works, she is conscious of pregnancy as a disaster for a young unmarried girl even in modern Ireland, unless a quick marriage remedies her moral status. The drama demonstrates the weight of the relevant social conditioning and the cautionary impact of reports circulating about the tragic incidents of child-murder linked with pregnancies and deliveries kept secret. When she steps on a bundle lying at her feet, Ber takes fright that the covered object may be the lifeless body of an abandoned infant.

Unmarried youngsters in a conservative Irish community are hardly granted space to enjoy sex privately and undisturbed in their parents' home and so Ber and Noel's lovemaking takes place in the fields. Yet adult restrictions on allowing the discourse of sex to be more helpful for teenagers prove inefficient and backfire in an important respect. The intimacies of Ber and Noel are on show for the vigilant eyes of the younger characters, who roam outdoors during the summer holidays, initiating them into the otherwise forbidden territory. The couple's first duet on stage constitutes a scene witnessed by Cactus from her hiding place like a spectator in the depth of the pit of the theatre, rendering her passive but voyeuristic, susceptible to and influenced by what she peeps at and overhears. Ber and Noel act out their respective positions in the relationship, which can be viewed from Butler's perspective that gender is performed and the 'mundane reproduction ground of gendered identity takes place through the various ways in which bodies are acted in relationship to the deeply entrenched or sedimented expectations of gendered existence'.[13] The series of speech- and bodily acts Ber and Noel produce present their gender identity rather conventionally, as constructed in terms of the divisive binary system. The girl proposes that they start saving, that they buy soon the nicest rings as well as decide which hotel would be the most suitable venue for the wedding reception. In contrast, the boy demands more bodily contact and strives to control the situation from the position of male authority. 'Come on down to the cornfield', he asks Ber impatiently, barely attentive to the issues preoccupying the girl, then gives the order: 'put your hand in me pocket there a minute. . . . The front one, you fucking eejit' (pp. 12–13).

Even though it defies religious teachings and parents' hints and warnings, the rebellion of teenagers in response to adult strictures regulating their sexuality, which seems to culminate in Ber's engaging in premarital sex with Noel, does not revise the conventional model of gender roles. That gender relations are basically unequal and, moreover, manifest relations of power is reconfirmed for Cactus in a later scene. In this Noel is enraged over the news that Ber wears a mock engagement ring in secret and has got pregnant, which threatens him with the prospect of having to marry her out of duty far too soon for his inclinations. He pushes the girl with such vehemence that 'she falls down the steps of the monument' (p. 50). Fearing she might lose him if she protests, Ber reacts with self-humiliation. By the acts she has witnessed and the insinuations she has been exposed to, Cactus, however, is prompted to imitate Noel's behaviour in her own sexual experimentations. She forces the mentally retarded, fourteen-year-old Dan to have sex with her, exercising power over him in a way she saw to be a salient part of Noel and Ber's encounters.

For Cactus, Dan is a partner weaker than she, whom she can abuse at will. The scenes in which their encounters are staged replay in grotesque, exaggerated, violent fashion those where Noel and Ber enact their unequal gender roles. Cactus orders her vulnerable partner to engage in kissing and in touching each other's private parts with her, imitating the manoeuvres adopted by Noel earlier. Here, however, the bodily subjection of the partner is far more pronounced:

> CACTUS: [. . .] What are you afraid of? . . . Come on, I haven't got all summer you know. Do it Danti-dan.
>
> *He kisses her, his arms stiffly by his sides. She thumps him to make him more active. He clumsily fumbles inside her shirt. She gropes in his pockets and down his trousers.*
>
> [. . .]
>
> DAN: When's the man going to give me the money? (pp. 53–4)

The relationship of Noel and Ber reinforces elements of conventional heterosexual exchange, promising to give both the parties what they wish for, which is characteristically gendered as well. On his part, the boy takes it for granted that when married, he will be entitled to 'flah you cross-eyed whenever I like' (p. 12), whereas the girl hopes she will have the chance 'to move out, to give up work' (p. 22). Similarly, Dan complies with Cactus's self-serving schemes in order to achieve his own goal. He is eager to get money through the mediation of the girl with which he could leave for the American West, a dream outdated like Ber's idea about marriage as a solution for a woman's life. By inverting the observed gender roles, Cactus acts out a kind of mimicry of masculine authority that she has seen governing Noel's behaviour toward Ber.

Mimicry is a strategy conceptualised by postcolonial, feminist and cultural studies as a means of interrogating the alterability of power relations and intervening in the hierarchical system of positions. Citing Irigaray, Marvin Carlson contends that mimicry has a disruptive power which 'lies less in its conflict of codes, . . . than its excess and exaggeration', and reveals its capacity to become subversive of the patriarchal order.[14] Cactus's manipulations are subversive, yet also destructive, entailing disruption which grows into disaster. The play's catastrophic final scene stages a frightened Dan divulging to Ber the clandestine sexual games he took part in with Cactus. This provokes a fierce fight, which ends with Cactus tossing her betrayer into the river. The vengeful act not only replicates, but magnifies to horrific proportions, the earlier scene where the furious Noel pushes Ber for her 'lies' with such vehemence that she falls to the ground. Cactus's mimicry replays gender inequity with excess, leading to a fatal outcome which exemplifies the latent danger underlying the 'original'. Unwilling to conform to the gender rules which require her to remain passive and wait to be courted, Cactus refuses to perform the role of the subordinate 'other' in the conventional way. Her acts reverse elements of the given system and, bringing about disorder and destruction, expose the oppressive tendencies lurking in the practices of gender communication and sexuality in the society. Moxley's representation of how the weaker body can be manipulated denaturalises the working of normativity, envisioning its potentially distorting impact on young individuals' personal development and nascent sexual relations. Although the action of *Danti Dan* takes place decades ago, the shocking sight of child abuse ending in tragedy provokes audiences to ask the question whether equity in gender has advanced so much since 1970.

Emma Donoghue's *Ladies and Gentlemen* is one of those recent Irish plays which, in the words of Dawn Duncan, 'move from internal examination to external vision'.[15] As such, it guides the audience further than Moxley's in both place and time, yet its links with the 1990s disputes about gender are fairly obvious. The play's principal character is Annie Hindle, a real person living in the late nineteenth century, renowned for her contribution to the American theatre, the vaudeville in particular. In the New Island edition the text is followed by excerpts from an 1891 article originally published in the New York paper *The Sun*, entitled 'Stranger than fiction',[16] a phrase which alludes enigmatically to the exceptional course of Hindle's life. Born in England in 1847, she settled down at a young age in the United States where she enjoyed a brilliant career on the stage as male impersonator. The author of the article clearly relishes reporting the unorthodox turns in her story: first Annie got married to a male actor, then to a dresser working in the theatre, a woman whose background was Irish. A few months after the wedding she separated from her husband, bearing the marks of the unhappy marriage on her body in the form of bruises and a black eye. Subsequently she remained a faithful 'husband' to her other partner until the latter's untimely death from breast cancer.

Male impersonation, the act of performance Annie excelled in, is usually discussed alongside its male-driven counterpart, the drag. Laurence Senelick contends that 'Unlike the ancient and sanctioned practice of men portraying women on stage, female assumptions of male identity appeared in the theatre as a novelty, a salacious turn, a secular

Johnny-come-lately'. Such practices were prevalent from the 1860s, a period, as Senelick observes, 'when the female emancipation movement was growing more vociferous and demanding. On stage, unruly women disguised as men were less threatening . . .'.[17] In a sense it was just the right time for Annie to enter the scene, as she could attract hundreds of women audience members who may well have cherished the secret wish to be free to dress and behave like men. Male spectators, in contrast, were probably content to see that the transgressive inclinations of woman, the 'other', were duly contained, and so controlled within the walls of a social institution, the theatre. Given the far-reaching traditions of the art, crossed-dressed males tended to achieve subtle meanings, but male impersonators had to work harder to counteract the easy discovery of their act and critics berating it as a 'sentimental, and therefore harmless reversal'.[18] Annie, however, won the battle as a result of her exceptional talent and skills. She appeared not in the stereotypical roles of 'a sailor or a farmhand or a schoolboy' that lovers of the music-hall had been accustomed to, 'but as a flash young spark, clad in natty, well fitting street-wear'.[19] In short, she impersonated a dandified male individual, a cultural icon of the Anglophone world in the period, whom many an average vaudeville fan would celebrate as a real, desirable man and not just as a good imitation.

Ladies and Gentlemen offers a unique variant of the female biography play in that it represents a life centred on role-playing on stage, thus doubling the basic situation of theatre performance and its 'potential for displaying self-conscious performativity' which 'can become the mechanism for [social] deconstruction'.[20] The very title underscores the play's metatheatrical character, which Donoghue further enhances by appointing the dressing-room as primary setting, a liminal, in-between space for actors to shed their everyday selves and prepare themselves for their next entrance on stage. Through the figure of Annie, the drama introduces the practice of female cross-dressing as a performative strategy to re-negotiate the ontological status of gender. In realising the subversive potential of the act, the protagonist reveals the gendered signification of 'men's clothes', her actual stage wear: 'They're only called that because men got a hold of them first. You bet your sweet life I like 'em; they've got pockets for everything' (p. 22). Dressed in these clothes Annie 'set[s] out to look more man than the men do' (p. 23), her version of male impersonation presenting the body as protean and herself as 'the model of modern man' according to the song, 'A Real Man' (p. 103). The self-styled strategy brings to mind Oscar Wilde, Annie's contemporary, for whom androgyny and the aesthetic provided an alternative to the limitations of identity operative in both Irish nationalist and British imperialist discourse.[21] Annie's activity of impersonation exposes as well as makes full use of the performative nature of gender. Butler argues:

> If the ground of gender identity is the stylized repetition of acts through time, and not a seemingly seamless identity, then the possibilites of gender transformation are to be found in the arbitrary relation between such acts, in the possibility of a different sort of repeating, in the breaking or subversive repetition of that style. . . . the acts by which gender is constituted bear similarities to performative acts within theatrical contexts.[22]

By acting in men's clothes, imitating male corporeal movements with ease and plausibly addressing women in songs to regard her as an eligible male, Annie succeeds in demonstrating that gender transformation is really possible. Audience reaction can be gauged from a letter from one of her admirers, which reads: 'Darling Mr Hindle, please oh please oh please leave off this pretence that you are a woman only dressed as a man. . . . I told my mother I know you are a real true man and I intend for to marry you' (p. 38). Annie's performing female body associated with authentic masculinity is a contradiction that throws light on the ambiguous nature of gender as an embodied mediator of cultural inscription and social conditioning.

That gender is not necessarily a prescribed destiny but can be lived and experienced as a 'subversive performance'[23] is also suggested by the insight the play offers into Annie's second marriage. Reciprocal love grows between her and an Irish girl, her new dresser called Annie Ryan, whom she rechristens as Ryanny, for whom Annie looks 'more of a gentleman than any man I ever laid eyes on' (p. 58). Ryanny's insistence that they should get married and have a church wedding with the usual paraphernalia must be linked to her Catholic roots and conservative upbringing. Yet the act qualifies as highly subversive, violating both age-old law and custom while constituting an early example of same-sex marriage, a much questioned option and only recognised in a few places even over a century later. The portrayal of Annie and Ryanny's life together alienates gender even further by appropriating the lesbian theatrical practice: they perform a butch–femme couple who construct their family roles outside the ideological system, a choice which enables them 'to playfully put on and take off the gendered sign-systems of appearance'.[24] One of the significant props in the play, the dummy called Miss Dimity the couple receive as a present from the dressing-room, symbolises, with her bare body ready to carry whatever kind of cover is selected for it, that woman is a signifier open to a set of potentials.

To reclaim the private life of a public idol requires a dramaturgical feat which allows the audience to see the person without the mask, as conventional expectations would have it. Donoghue, for her part, follows the Wildean precept and gives Annie the mask to tell the innermost truth about herself. The play is working across two temporal modes; its main line of action, set in 1891, presents her in the act of dressing and undressing, strapping and unstrapping the bandages to flatten her breasts as well as putting on, taking off, then resuming men's clothes again in preparation for the stage. For Annie, called back to work at the vaudeville theatre after Ryanny's funeral, the sequence of actions incarnates the pangs of hesitation, fear and self-doubt she suffers, raising the question whether art is possible after the trial of extreme trauma. Interspersed are scenes from the protagonist's memoryscape, which run a cycle between confession of love to the experience of loss through the partner's death and, thus, provide the private story with an archetypal frame. Only the language of the body is able to communicate the complexity of emotions involved, as two complementary scenes highlight:

ANNIE: What if I had something to tell you but I didn't know how?

. . .

I can't. . . . Let me show you instead. (*Kisses the side of* RYANNY's *face, kisses all the way to her mouth*) (p. 55)

. . .

RYANNY: What if I had something to tell you but I didn't know how?

. . .

I can't. Let me show you instead. (*Turned away from the audience, she undoes her nightdress.* ANNIE *looks* [at the malignant growth] *and recoils*) (pp. 83–4)

Eventually, Annie cannot but decide to wear the costume and step on the 'board' to sing and play again because, despite the torments of self-questioning, she concludes 'This is all I've got' (p. 100) – to perform is necessary. Impersonation as a gender-bending theatrical act assumes an ontological status. It appears to be equal to life, carrying a scale of memories from happiness to grief as the protagonist's story depicts while offering the opportunity to expand and multiple the self on the stage of the world.

Though set in the present unlike the plays discussed above, Carr's *By the Bog of Cats* . . . has the aura of timelessness about it, being a tragedy which loosely follows a Greek model, *Medea* by Euripides. While the resonance with ancient drama is a feature it shares with *The Mai* (1994) and *Portia Coughlan* (1996), the other parts of the writer's

Midlands trilogy, *By the Bog of Cats* . . . is unique in that it has a frame grounded in the mode of the performative. A recent article by Maria Doyle looks at the presentation of the respective female protagonists' dead body on stage in mid-action in *The Mai* and *Portia Coughlan*, 'which is, after all, not in fact dead, can be reanimated, and doing so, . . . testifies to the vitality and the malleability of the theatrical experience'.[25] Extending this direction of investigation to *By the Bog of Cats* . . . , parallels as well as differences strike the eye. At the opening of *By the Bog of Cats* . . . , it is dawn and a surrealistic scene unfolds with the protagonist, Hester, entering on a bleak and barren landscape of ice and snow, trailing 'the corpse of a black swan after her'.[26] She meets a man introducing himself as the Ghost Fancier, who turns out to have come for her. Yet, mixed up about what part of the day it is, he relinquishes his aim and leaves with the promise to return at dusk. Kind and polite, almost courting the lonely Hester, the Ghost Fancier enacts the role of lethal messenger as well as incarnating impending death, comparably to the gentle Death-figure in the poetry of Emily Dickinson, who 'kindly stopped for me'.[27] Prophecies also reinforce the idea in the initial scenes that Hester's life is doomed. Whereas displaying the heroines' dead body well into the action 'certainly forecloses escape as an option' in *The Mai* and *Portia Coughlan*,[28] escape seems to be foreclosed for Hester from the start: she is destined to die before the end of the day, the span of the play following the classical structure. Death is envisaged by Hester in two distinct ways. On the one hand, it is to be embraced rather than feared, being an end which forms part of nature's eternal cycle. After the disappearance of the supernatural visitor, she says to the choric figure, Monica: 'Swear the age of ice have returned. Wouldn't ya almost wish if it had, do away with us all like the dinosaurs' (p. 15). Her soul mate, the black swan, died in a similar fashion, its body having to be ripped out of a frozen bog hole by Hester. On the other hand, a sense of disintegration is looming as an actual threat to her identity in her discourse. Her life 'doesn't hang together' (p. 16) now that she has lost her common-law husband, Carthage Kilbride, to another woman.

Analysing *By the Bog of Cats* . . . as a transposition of the Medea-myth in contemporary Ireland, Melissa Sihra claims that the 'relationship between space, gender and the body' is crucial to its overall design.[29] A heightened corporeality in both action and language, supported by a strategic use of costume and accessories mark out the boundaries of two worlds, antithetical yet also overlapping, which can be associated with the Kristevan duality of the semiotic and the symbolic. Its centre being 'this auld bog, always shiftin' and changin' and coddin' the eye'

(p. 15), the one constitutes a liminal realm of otherness with a mysterious conjunction between visible and invisible, the living and the dead, rational and irrational, where the past keeps on intruding. It is dominated by the feminine with the Catwoman as professed Keeper of the bog, whose appearance in clothes of mouse fur and stinking of turf fuses human and animal, whereas her physical blindness, coupled with an inner vision empowering her to see into the secrets of the beyond, is a mythical feature. Opposed to this world is that of the settled community, governed by laws and rules of propriety which structure the life of its members, compelling them to comply with and inhabit their allocated place in the system. The dominant figure here is a patriarch, Xavier Cassidy, who walks about with a gun that lends weight to his peremptory orders and emphasises readiness to break those he finds rebellious in either of the two worlds. Hester lives on the margin of the two domains in a house by the bog, which for her is also a place of the maternal replete with memories of her mother called Big Josie, a traveller who was elusive like the bog itself and had 'somethin' cold and dead about her except when she sang and then . . . ya'd fall in love with her' (pp. 64–5). Losing Carthage involves a multiple trauma for Hester: she is forced to leave the bogside house and move to town, to anonymity, which would entail dislocation as 'corporeal unhomeliness',[30] dispossession of love, home and roots. In Act I Carthage, his bride Caroline and Cassidy, her father, parade in front of her in their wedding clothing, which underscores her exclusion from an event that secures socially approved ties among people. Moreover, their treatment reduces her to the stereotypes constructed in relation to travellers as others[31] when she is offered money by all to hasten her departure to 'another haltin' site' (p. 35). Hester's very identity as a human being is questioned, which Carthage even puts into words: 'Who are ya and what sourt of stuff are you made of?' (p. 34).

Plays based on foretold destiny tend to deploy repetitive patterns that permeate and cut across various levels of the dramatic composition, including visual and auditory signs to structure, and reinforce tragic inevitability. Like its counterparts within the trilogy, *By the Bog of Cats* . . . displays a web of recurrent motifs woven into its fabric to enhance the sense of entrapment as noted in Clare Wallace's discussion concerning tragic destiny and abjection in Carr's Midlands trilogy.[32] The bridal garment and images of women dressed in white trail through *By the Bog of Cats* . . . , establishing co-references to illuminate Hester's journey toward her fate with a special focus on the mother–daughter relationship in the context of women faring amid the constraints of a bifurcated world. Josie, Hester's seven-year-old daughter, comes on stage ready for her father's wedding in 'Communion dress, veil, buckled shoes, handbag, the works' (p. 41), evoking a picture of herself at seven for Hester: 'Ya know the last time I saw me mother I was wearin' me Communion dress too. . . . And I watched her walk away from me across the Bog of Cats. And across the Bog of Cats I'll watch her return' (pp. 41–2). The white communion dress is associated with initiation 'into the central ritual of Roman Catholicism and patriarchal Christianity',[33] a system of symbols and rules, and the scene from Hester's early life calls to mind the primal experience of individuals which involves separation from the mother to make entry into the symbolic possible and facilitate the achievement of subjecthood. However, Hester's obsession with waiting for her mother, which repeats Big Josie's habit of 'pausin' (p. 22), signifies that she managed to integrate into the community of the settled people only temporarily. In Sihra's opinion Hester, a marginalised 'itinerant living on the bog . . . failed to become a fully subjectified individual as she has never gained a sufficient substitute for the loss of her mother'.[34] Carthage had bought her a bridal dress, but did not fulfill his promise to marry her, having used her as an exotic sexual object for a time just as Cassidy may well have used Big Josie, only to give her up when a marriage bringing him prestige and economic gain was in sight. Disadvantaged and also existentially frustrated, Hester duplicates her mother's split nature in her restless, explosive comportment and temper: 'there's two Hester Swanes, one that is decent' while 'the other Hester, well, she could slide a knife down your face, carve ya up and not bat an eyelid' (p. 30).

The world of law, order and rules may also show its vulnerable side when, in unguarded moments, it becomes permeable to subversive forces and unruly bodies that despite its coercive power and ruthless pragmatism it fails to repress completely. Carr deploys folkloric humour, comic carnality and the performative to mock the hypocritical miming of respectability and represent the impulse to trangress institutionalised fixities and the binaries of gender and class. A hilarious little scene in Act I finds Josie dressed up to impersonate her Granny, a woman of traveller background as well, ridiculing her obsession with buying expensive clothes and her extreme greediness as signs of the effort to assimilate by overdoing the expectations of the settled community. Josie's show prefigures the grotesquely comic orchestration of the wedding dinner set in the Cassidy house in Act II, which is conceived in the traditional mode of the carnival as semiotic performance to 'resist, exaggerate, and destabilize the distinctions and boundaries that mark and maintain high culture and organized society'.[35] The Catwoman is 'lapping wine from a saucer' (p. 43) while the priest who is flirting with her wears his trousers and shirt but as a loose mask over his pyjamas and substitutes the text of saying grace with fragments of his one-time romance, incarnating and voicing the duality of social gloss and private reality. But most importantly for the present investigation, there is a strange proliferation of women in white, including the bride, Carthage's mother Hester dressed in the wedding garment she got from Carthage, and Josie wearing her communion dress. They all masquerade as the bride, producing an excess which deconstructs the conventional lustre of the wedding celebration and exposes, alongside the other carnival effects, 'Church, State, family and marriage . . . as false icons' to borrow from Enrica Cerquoni's analysis of the play.[36] The real bride, Caroline, becomes disillusioned by having to realise that marriage is not a new start, nor does it automatically bring about a happy ending. Having already 'killed' one bride, Carthage Kilbride may as well 'kill' another. On the other hand, Hester's appearance in the wedding dress can also be read as part of the larger, tragically woven structure of recurrent motifs. Her response to exclusion by claiming that this is 'my weddin' day be rigths and not wan of yees can deny it' (p. 54) only provokes Carthage's final rejection, echoing the one-time scene of loss when, also in a white dress, she was left alone by her mother. With the difference that now the people of power are ready to ostracise, even eradicate, her as a hateful intruder for her rebellious entrée, to 'make out [she] never existed' (p. 56).

In *Powers of Horror* Kristeva asserts that within abjection there looms 'one of those violent, dark revolts of being, directed against a threat that seems to emanate from an exorbitant outside or inside, ejected beyond the scope of the possible, the tolerable, the thinkable. . . . a vortex of summons and repulsion places the one haunted by it literally beside himself'.[37] The brutal deeds of Act III are committed by Hester in the state of 'beside herself' under threats of annihilation and self-loss that come not only from outside but also from inside. Meeting the ghost of Joseph, her brother, confronts her with her repressed former realisation that the cherished memory of Big Josie as a mother caring for her and worth waiting for has been an illusion, since she 'had a whole other life there – How could she have and I a part of her?' (p. 74). Hester now feels exiled from both worlds, that of the settled people as well as that of the maternal she has been clinging to. In an interview Carr has said that for Hester, a traveller and thus 'a complete outsider', '[l]osing her common-law husband, and the possibility of losing her child due to the power of society is what makes her so vulnerable'.[38] The threat of separating her from her child haunts the discourse of the Kilbrides and Cassidys throughout the drama, their recurrent phrase being characteristically physical: Josie should be got 'off of her'. With the most terrible outcome, Hester revolts against this too. Josie is still wearing her communion dress when Hester kills her out of love to save her from the trauma of losing her mother like herself, left alone also in the white outfit at the same age, and the child is taken 'off Hester' (p. 80) by Carthage only when dead.

The old black swan 'died on the wing' (p. 20), and Hester's death takes place in a similarly 'elevated' way: the Ghost Fancier reappears engaging her in a dance of death, which raises her suicide to the level of the fulfilment of destiny by linking the personal with the universal. Unlike Carr's other female suicides, The Mai and Portia, who kill themselves by drowning, Hester dies in the manner of performing agency over her own body and not letting society eradicate it; her cut-out heart, 'like some dark feathered bird' (p. 81), falls in front of the eyes of the other characters, spectators of a terrifying denouement. It is the kind of death she has envisaged for herself from the start, a reclamation of identity through reunion with nature. Bernadette Bourke extends her analysis of the carnivalesque mode in the play to Hester's death dance, which is at once 'terrifying and jubilant', 'representing renewal in a return to the great nurturing womb of nature, giver of life, death and continuity'.[39] Subversively, Hester's terrible deeds including the destruction of property, infanticide and suicide lay bare that the system of power can hardly operate by stigmatising and excluding the gendered and marginal other without wounding and paralysing itself as well. Christopher Murray's contention that in her previous work 'Carr sees pathos as more important than polemics' and is not interested 'in dramatising "issues" on stage'[40] holds true for By the Bog of Cats. . . . Pathos, however, might have the force to literally shake and stir the audience to derive those issues from the play for themselves.

The three authors show their female protagonists in the process of seeking and finding the means to appropriate agency through corporeality and performative acts, mimicry, masquerade and impersonation in particular, allowing them to sever themselves from the repetitive cycle of constructed roles which are inscribed in language and body. Agency may work to destructive ends, as Cactus and Hester testify in their own ways, yet it can still, or even more so, critique the manipulations of power when confronting the audience with pain and tragic loss happening in systems that harbour inequality, exclusion and marginalisation in however refined and concealed forms. To assess the innovative aspect of the work of new Irish woman playwrights, feminist theatre studies expert Jill Dolan's argument is worth quoting: 'If we stop considering the stage as a mirror of reality', which most of the writers undoubtedly do, 'we can use it as a laboratory'.[41] Laboratory – the term sounds illuminating. A space of experimentation where dramatic works are shaped to negotiate, transcend or alter the socio-cultural inscriptions primarily through the body as a locus of lived experience, as well as transgress the boundaries of inherited patterns of attitude and comportment while engaging their female characters in performing versions of gendered subjectivity and individual identity.

Notes

1   Anthony Bradley and Maryann Gialanella Valiulis (eds), 'Introduction', in *Gender and Sexuality in Modern Ireland* (Amherst: University of Massachusetts Press, 1997), p. 1.

2   Fintan O'Toole, 'Irish Theatre: The State of the Art', in Eamonn Jordan (ed.), *Theatre Stuff: Critical Essays on Contemporary Irish Theatre* (Dublin: Carysfort Press, 2000), p. 54.

3   Pat O'Connor, *Emerging Voices: Women in Contemporary Irish Society* (Dublin: Institute of Public Administration, 1998), pp. 4–5.

4   Tom Inglish, 'Of Irish Prudery: Sexuality and Social Control in Modern Ireland', *Éire-Ireland* 40: 3/4 (fall/winter 2005), pp. 30–1.

5   Stanton B. Garner, *Bodied Spaces: Phenomenology and Performance in Contemporary Drama* (Ithaca, NY and London: Cornell University Press), 1994, pp. 186–7.

6   Elaine Aston, *An Introduction to Feminism and Theatre* (London and New York: Routledge, 1995), pp. 51–2.

7   Lib Taylor, 'Shape-shifting and Role-splitting: Theatre, Body and Identity', in Naomi Segal, Lib Taylor and Roger Cook (eds), *Indeterminate Bodies* (London: Palgrave Macmillan, 2003), pp. 164–5.

8   Judith Butler, 'Performative Acts and Gender Constitution' in Julie Rivkin and Michael Ryan (eds), *Literary Theory: An Anthology*, second edition (London: Blackwell Publishing, 2004), p. 902.

9   Geraldine Harris, *Staging Femininities: Performance and Performativity* (Manchester and New York: Manchester University Press, 1999), p. 22.

10   Gina Moxley, *Danti Dan*, in Frank McGuinness (ed.), *The Dazzling Dark* (London: Faber, 1996). p. 73. All further parenthetical references are to this edition.

11   Julia Furay and Redmond O'Hanlon (eds), *Critical Moments: Fintan O'Toole on Modern Irish Theatre* (Dublin: Carysfort Press), 2003, p. 136.

12   O'Connor, p. 14.

13   Butler, p. 904.

14   Marvin Carlson, *Performance: A Critical Introduction* (London and New York: Routledge, 1996), p. 176.

15   Dawn Duncan, *Postcolonial Theory in Irish Drama from 1800–2000* (Lewiston, Queenston, Lampeter: Edwin Mellen Press, 2004), p. 235.

16 Emma Donoghue, *Ladies and Gentlemen* (Dublin: New Island Books, 1998), p. 104. All further parenthetical references are to this edition.

17 Laurence Senelick, *The Changing Room: Sex, Drag and Theatre* (London: Routledge, 2000), pp. 326, 340.

18 Kate Davy, 'Fe/male Impersonation: The Discourse of Camp' in Janelle G. Reinelt and Joseph R. Roach (eds), *Critical Theory and Performance* (Ann Arbor: The University of Michigan Press, 1992), p. 235.

19 Senelick, p. 329.

20 Taylor, p. 166.

21 See Éibhear Walshe, 'Wild(e) Ireland', in Scott Brewster, Virginia Crossman, Fiona Becket and David Alderson (eds), *Ireland in Proximity: History, Gender, Space* (London: Routledge, 1999), p. 68.

22 Butler, p. 901.

23 Anna McMullan, 'Gender, Authorship and Performance in Selected Plays by Contemporary Irish Women Playwrights: Mary Elizabeth Burke-Kennedy, Marie Jones, Marina Carr, Emma Donoghue', in Jordan (ed.), p. 44.

24 Aston, p. 103.

25 Maria Doyle, 'Dead Center: Tragedy and the Reanimated Body in Marina Carr's *The Mai* and *Portia Coughlan*', *Modern Drama* 49: 1 (spring 2006), p. 41.

26 Marina Carr, *By the Bog of Cats . . .* (Oldcastle: Gallery Press, 1999), p. 13. All further parenthetical references are to this edition.

27 Emily Dickinson, poem 712 *Final Harvest: Emily Dickinson's Poems* (Boston: Little, Brown and Company, 1961), p. 177.

28 Doyle, p. 41.

29 Melissa Sihra, 'Greek Myth, Irish Reality: Marina Carr's *By the Bog of Cats . . .*' John Dillon and S. E. Wilmer (eds), *Rebel Women: Staging Ancient Greek Drama Today* (London: Methuen, 2005), p. 119.

30 Anna McMullan, 'Unhomely Bodies and Dislocated Identities in the Drama of Frank McGuinness and Marina Carr', in Segal, Taylor and Cook (eds), p. 189.

31 See Sihra, 'Greek Myth, Irish Reality', p. 128.

32 Clare Wallace, 'Tragic Destiny and Abjection in Marina Carr's *The Mai, Portia Coughlan* and *By the Bog of Cats . . .*', *Irish University Review* 31: 2 (autumn/winter 2001), p. 438.

33 Lisa Fitzpatrick, 'Metanarratives: Anne Devlin, Christina Reid, Marina Carr, and the Irish Dramatic Repertory', *Irish University Review* 35: 2 (autumn/winter 2005), p. 332.

34 Melissa Sihra, 'A Cautionary Tale: Marina Carr's *By the Bog of Cats . . .*', in Jordan (ed.), p. 257.

35 Mary Russo, *The Female Grotesque: Risk, Excess and Modernity* (London: Routledge, 1994), pp. 54, 62.

36 Enrica Cerquoni, ' "One Bog, Many Bogs": Theatrical Space, Visual Image, and Meaning in Some Productions of Marina Carr's *By the Bog*

of Cats . . .', in Cathy Leeney and Anna McMullan (eds), *The Theatre of Marina Carr: 'Before Rules was Made'* (Dublin: Carysfort Press, 2003), p. 186.

37 Kelly Oliver (ed.), *The Portable Kristeva* (New York: Columbia University Press, 1997), pp. 241, 229.

38 Mária Kurdi, 'Interview with Marina Carr', *Modern Filologiai Kozlemenyek* 5: 2 (2003), p. 99.

39 Bernadette Bourke, 'Carr's "cut-throats and gargiyles". Grotesque and Carnivalesque Elements in *By the Bog of Cats . . .*', in Leeney and McMullan (eds), p. 139.

40 Christopher Murray, *Twentieth-century Irish Drama: Mirror up to Nation* (Manchester: Manchester University Press, 1997), p. 237.

41 Jill Dolan, 'Gender Impersonation Onstage: Destroying or Maintaining the Mirror of Gender Roles?', *Women and Performance Journal* 2 (1985), p. 8.

5

The stuff of tragedy? Representations of Irish political leaders in the 'Haughey' plays of Carr, Barry and Breen

Anthony Roche

Plays which deal directly with political life are rare in the Irish canon. Mostly, the emphasis is on family relations, with the direct political context placed in the background, if not almost entirely effaced. But there are those exceptional occasions when contemporary playwrights have felt the need to address the state of the nation more directly by placing politicians squarely on the stage. Brian Friel did so in his 1969 play *The Mundy Scheme*, with its mendacious Taoiseach F.X. Ryan and his scheme to repopulate the west of Ireland by filling it with the dead bodies of rich foreigners; and in 1982's *The Communication Cord* the equally corrupt Senator Donovan mouths as hypocritical pieties many of the views of Irish identity seriously promulgated two years earlier in *Translations*: 'This determined our first priorities! This is our native simplicity! Don't give me that shit!'[1] Both plays were unusual in Friel's *oeuvre* in being ferocious satires; neither did well commercially or critically, neither has been much revived (if at all) and *The Mundy Scheme* is not currently in print.

In 1982, Hugh Leonard followed his autobiographical plays of the 1970s, *Da* and *A Life*, with his black comedy, *Kill*, whose central politician Wade is a thinly disguised version of then-Taoiseach Charles Haughey. Leonard's play was neither a critical nor commercial success. With such antecedents it can hardly have been on commercial grounds that in the concentrated period of 2002–03 three Irish playwrights staged dramas which centred on a political leader who bore in varying degrees a recognisable resemblance to Charles J. Haughey (1926–2006): Marina Carr's *Ariel* (2002), Sebastian Barry's *Hinterland* (2002) and John Breen's *Charlie* (2003).[2] At the time, Haughey had been out of power for a decade and was in bad health. What brought his name back into the headlines was the series of tribunals then under way which summoned a wide range of politicians, builders and businessmen who had prospered during the Haughey era. The primary purpose of the tribunals was to inquire into the possibility of financial links between the politicians and the businessmen, either in the form of direct financial donations or of re-zoning decisions for property development which signally altered the value of land. A particular area of investigation was possible connections between Irish politicians and offshore accounts designed to evade the payment of taxes. When Haughey himself was summoned to appear before the Moriarty Tribunal, he insisted he knew little of such matters, since he left the handling of his financial affairs to his advisor Desmond Traynor. Pressed further on the matter, Haughey claimed, in Justin O'Brien's words, 'limited mental recall'.[3] In the face of this repeated assertion and Haughey's declining health (the cancer which subsequently claimed him), there was a tacit agreement not to call the former Taoiseach before any further tribunals.

This daily drama in the courts may well have prompted a degree of soul-searching on behalf of the playwrights, a decision to take the measure and probe the state of health of the body politic in the new millennium. As Sebastian Barry argued when defending his writing of *Hinterland*: 'these people [politicians] are part of us . . . It is not possible to step away from them now that they are disgraced. Even as a principle of self-preservation, we should realise we're shooting off a part of our own body. The thing has to be healed rather than cut off.'[4] By the late 1990s the unprecedented national confidence which accompanied the financial buoyancy of the Celtic Tiger prompted a greater degree of soul-searching. In deciding to establish the Tribunals, Taoiseach Bertie Ahern stated that their purpose was 'to address serious allegations of corruption in the political and business spheres', emphasising that their job was 'to get at the truth and to reveal all to the public so that faith in the political process is restored and that people can again have confidence in their politicians'.[5] Such a process of self-examination on the part of the Republic was bound to focus on the figure of Charles J. Haughey, since nobody more embodied the contradictions at the heart of the transformation of the old Ireland – the frugal comfort and rural self-sufficiency advocated by Eamonn de Valera – into the new – the thrusting economic self-confidence which finally replaced emigration with immigration. In his charisma and self-image, Haughey radiated confidence and a sense of manifest destiny; he showed that an Irish Catholic could just as easily lord it over a grand estate as any Protestant landlord and that an Irish Taoiseach could take an equal place at the European high table of the new confederation of countries. But this image of munificent success was projected by Haughey during the decades when the country itself was running up huge debt and the workers were being urged to exercise self-restraint with regard to their demand for wage increases. How, it was increasingly asked, could Haughey maintain such a life-style on a mere politician's salary? Haughey's style of leadership encouraged either unquestioning loyalty or determined opposition, not just in the country as a whole but more critically within the Fianna Fáil party itself. On the three occasions during the 1980s where he went to the country seeking an overall mandate, he never achieved it, and was always forced into some kind of political coalition to survive. But that division itself reflected a country divided between the conservative and the modernising impulses, as the roughly fifty–fifty votes in all the various referenda (on divorce and abortion) demonstrated. The advent of the Celtic Tiger posed the question most sharply: was Haughey the political visionary who made possible the growth of such prosperity or was he the ruth-less pragmatist whose vanity held back such progress until he was no longer a political force? The model which suggested itself, as much on the political as on the theatrical stage, was the figure of the Shakespearean tragic hero. Was Haughey a great man brought down by the machinations of his political enemies, a figure of great intelli-gence and talent betrayed by a singular flaw in that same nature, or a small man devoted to the street tactics of survival and deluded by his own hubris?

When Haughey stepped down from the office of Taoiseach in 1992, he did so by quoting from *Othello*: 'I have done the state some service, and they know't; / No more of that.'[6] Appropriately, therefore, all three plays make frequent allusion to tragedy, especially Shakespearean, and the Shakespearean parallel/context is one I will pursue in this chapter. The tragic overtones in which Barry's fictional Taoiseach dresses him-self are at times supported by the play, but equally at times undercut by satiric and farcical passages. Marina Carr's portrait of a contem-porary politician has distinct echoes of Greek as well as Shakespearean tragedy; its mix of the mythic and the contemporary are its most dar-ing stylistic feature, and also its most unstable. Both plays deal with their subject through an almost exclusive emphasis on the family romance. Breen in opting for a more broadly social and satirical per-spective would appear to have sidestepped some of the complications they encounter; but the more direct representation in *Charlie* of scenes from Irish political life has to contend with the wide range of archive material available to the documentary makers. All three plays depend on a degree of knowledge of events from the last forty years of Irish political life which is virtually unprecedented in the canon.

What most surprised me when I saw *Hinterland* was the extent and degree of the parallels between Barry's fictional Johnny Silvester and Charles J. Haughey. Much of the hostility the play attracted was charged to the closeness of the parallel, as being 'too personal'. Both in 2002 were men in their seventies, recent Taoisigh living in ostentatious Georgian mansions in north Dublin. Both have had a strong measure of success in their long, chequered careers but are now facing daily denunciation in the newspapers. There are repeated calls to appear before tribunals investigating ethical and legal questions relating to political leaders and their sources of income. Vincent Browne, in his time as editor of the current affairs magazine *Magill*, persistently raised questions about the means by which Haughey had acquired his vast and ostentatiously displayed wealth, particularly as he came from a family of modest means; not only did Browne keep asking it for over twenty years but he set it as a challenge to every young reporter who wanted to work for him. The same question is put to Silvester by a young UCD student who interviews him in Act II of Barry's *Hinterland*. His reply that he is not a rich man and has handled very little money leads into a sophistic speech talking about certain expenditures that were written off: 'There was, until recently, an understanding that occasional exceptional spending might go on this bill, and it was accepted that these things might now and then be quite large, especially when I was head of the country.'[7] Three other figures surrounding Silvester consolidate the Haughey parallels. To begin with, there is his wife Daisy, the daughter of a former leader, as Maureen Haughey was the daughter of the first modernising Taoiseach, Sean Lemass. When Silvester remarks '[t]hey didn't begrudge him his achievements, political and financial', Daisy replies: 'Dad was the soul of probity, Johnny' (p. 19). Another voice which regularly rebukes Silvester in the course of the play is his former friend and colleague, Cornelius. The details of Cornelius's failed attempt to become President of Ireland, losing out to 'a bloody woman president, with her selfless bloody tone' (p. 39), and of a failed kidney operation to rectify his diabetes, echo Tanaiste and Minister for Foreign Affairs Brian Lenihan to a nicety. The ghost of Cornelius appears like a Jacob Marley from beyond the grave to his former crony, to sound the note of betrayal that, when his political adversaries came looking for a head, Silvester handed them Cornelius's. Silvester's mistress, Connie, appears late in the second act to try to revive the relationship. Connie is a journalist who, when reminded that she sold their story (with incriminating photos) to the newspapers, as her prototype Terry

Keane had done,[8] remarks 'A girl has to make a living somehow' (p. 71).

But there is one key element of the play which bears no particular relationship to Charles Haughey, so far as one is aware, and that is the father–son relationship between Silvester and the manic-depressive Jack. Such evidence as we see would tend to support Daisy's contention that Silvester was never any kind of father to his young son while he was off being father to the nation. In a play generally notable for its lack of action, the arrival of Jack into the darkened drawing-room in the middle of the night and his attempted hanging appear to come from a different play. As Colm Tóibín has put it: 'In scene after scene, the connections between the Silvesters and the Haugheys had been made abundantly clear. Now the script had departed from the story of the Haugheys to tell another story, one of grief and estrangement and the damage fathers cause to their sons.'[9] All Jack's father can manage to do when he is helping to pick his son up from the floor after the failed suicide attempt is to hit him with literary quotations: 'All manner of things will be well. "The woods decay, the woods decay and fall. . . ." You remember your Tennyson, eh?' (p. 44). And when Jack responds 'After many a summer. Can't bear it, Daddy', Silvester's inappropriately humorous reply is 'Things fall apart, the ceiling cannot hold'.

The question of the play's mixed status – whether it is a dramatised version of Haughey's history or of a dysfunctional father–son relationship – is further raised by the question of genre. What kind of play is it? Silvester has no doubt that he is a Shakespearean tragic hero, muttering early on the line 'I have done the state some service' from Othello's closing speech to those who have arrested him and who intend to bring him to justice. Haughey made his own departure from the Dáil in 1992 with the selfsame lines. But Silvester goes further along the path of self-mythologisation with frequent quotations from *King Lear* and *Hamlet*.[10] The question is: to what extent are these consciously quoted lines confirmed or denied by the play? The treatment of Silvester by Barry is not so much an undermining as a complex layering. In relation to *Hamlet*, Silvester more often resembles the figure of Claudius, a usurper with a questionable claim to the throne who has to deal with a suicidal son. As he puts it, appropriating Hamlet's lines about Claudius to himself: 'I will smile and smile and be a holy villain' (p. 83). The tragic overtones and parallels with *Hamlet* are at one level confirmed by the attempted suicide of young Jack, but structurally the scene teeters on the verge of farce. The farcical tone returns with a vengeance when the mistress Connie and Silvester are surprised by the unexpected return of Daisy and Jack. He beckons her to hide in a cupboard:

CONNIE (*indignant*): In here? This is not a bedroom farce, Johnny.

JOHNNY: Well, this is not a bedroom; it is a State Papers cupboard. (p. 75)

The confrontation scene which follows clarifies why Barry has risked the tragic aura by pushing the play so much in the direction of farce. He requires that the father–son scenario reach its climax by this route, with the son (who has all along maintained that he loves his father despite his mother's accusations) being made complicit in the hypocrisy of the sexual cover-up:

Daddy, I know this woman. I met her with you. Train station, when I was seventeen. 'You are a man of the world, Jack', you said. 'Don't mention this to your mother.' (p. 77)

The one area in the play where its concerns most come together is in relation to the North of Ireland, a crucial area which any play based on Haughey must confront. In the opening moments of *Hinterland*, Silvester is writing a letter to his two aunts in Derry, 'where so many of my childhood memories reside' (p. 7). This is biographically true of the Haughey family, who moved from Derry to Dublin when Charles was a youngster. They did so for economic reasons, as so many from the North did, but also because Haughey's father had a strong Republican history. Haughey's Northern background is less well known than other aspects of his biography, in part because he rarely discussed it and because the rural area in Ireland to which he gravitated was the Blaskets, where he could live like a Gaelic chieftain in exile on his own private island. The 'Hinterland' of the title has a number of references: in the satiric mode, it is a crude metaphor for the ageing body of the Taoiseach and to the prostate problems with which he is afflicted; in the shared reminiscences of Silvester and Cornelius, it connotes the emergence from their Mercedes to the hand-pumping and tea-drinking as they campaigned through the backroads of Ireland. In more general terms, it can be taken to refer to the questionable moral hinterland Haughey inhabited in his career. But its deepest resonance, because it is the point in this discordant play where the personal and the political fuse, is the way in which Donegal functions as a hinterland for the Catholics of Derry. As Silvester puts it, 'my mind often returns to the poignant fact that Derry was once the market town for a much greater district, before partition divided the old city from her own hinterland of Donegal' (p. 7). As he goes on to remark, 'my father was hardly the same man after partition'. And though the ghost of Silvester's father does not stalk directly through this play, he is evoked in Silvester's mind by the ghost of Cornelius, tellingly in relation to the hunger strikers of 1980. Silvester retorts:

> let us have no bullshit now, here at the edge of the world, for God's sake. Alright. When the hunger strikers started to die, one by one, [. . .] I knew my heart was compromised. I felt my father turning – painfully – in his grave.' (p. 64)

In the end, looking on what he has become through all of his compromises and how he stands in relation to his departed wife and son, Silvester utters his most hollow boast: 'I will live, I will live for ever, like a fucking vampire!' (p. 83). This is not a direct quotation, as so often with Silvester, but it manages to exhume the memorable lines penned by Conor Cruise O'Brien in relation to Haughey's career-long succession of political comebacks. Reflecting on the number of occasions on which Haughey's political career was declared over before he staged yet another resurrection, O'Brien wrote: 'Even if Charles Haughey were to be laid out at a crossroads, and a stake driven through his heart – I speak metaphorically, of course – I'd still wear a sprig of garlic, just in case.'[11]

Tragic or Gothic? This is the mix which much more clearly defines Marina Carr's *Ariel*. The tragic is particularly dominant in a work where, in its account of an ambitious politician who sacrifices his sixteen-year-old daughter to gain power, there is a strong debt to Euripides' *Iphigenia at Aulis*. Carr's play covers a time-span of over ten years. It tracks Fermoy Fitzgerald from the night before the election in a tightly fought contest with his opposite Hannafin, the night of Ariel's sixteenth birthday on which her father takes her on a fatal ride in the brand new car he has bought for her, through to a period ten years later when, in a television interview, Fermoy discusses his meteoric rise to political success, his record of achievement in three government ministries, and his ambition to be Taoiseach. This is also the night on which he will be killed by his Clytemnestra, his wife Frances, when she discovers what he has done to their daughter. The third act extends the time span posthumously with the return of Fermoy's ghost, still searching for a reunion with his dead daughter. The mix of the mythic and the contemporary is the play's most daring stylistic feature, and also its most unstable, in terms of the relationship between the two. This is a recognisably contemporary Ireland, more so than in many of Carr's other plays, with a Celtic Tiger family that has prospered from the success of its cement factory, which can now afford to send its children to university and to buy them brand new cars for their sixteenth birthdays. But it is also a world where incest and murder are part of the family legacy, where the ghost of a dead child can talk to her father from the bottom of a lake, and where a contemporary politician can speak of his one-to-one relationship with God.[12] The play could be said to be probing the contemporary political unconscious here. The overt emphasis in public debate is on economic development while the sub-structure of religious belief which still underpins the Irish state remains unaddressed or even acknowledged. At this level the play is enacting a return of the repressed, of those atavistic impulses which are the more insatiable because denied.

The lengthy television interview Fermoy gives at the start of Act II is the most realistic/satiric in the play and, in the detail given of the three government ministries, provides the greatest opportunities for locating parallels in the contemporary Irish political scene. The first was Fermoy's period in Arts and Culture, a ministry that was established a bare ten years previous during a Fine Gael/Labour coalition, when the Labour Party's Michael D. Higgins was the first to occupy the newly created post. It has since been filled twice by Fianna Fáil, with Sile de Valera and currently John O'Donoghue. The Ministry of Arts and Culture has picked up more portfolios along the way, incorporating the Islands and the Gaeltacht during de Valera's period in office, and adding Sports under O'Donoghue. With each addition there has been a corresponding diminution of emphasis on the arts. When *Ariel* was premiered at the Abbey Theatre in October 2002, the closest anyone came to a one-on-one identification was to suggest some resemblance between Fermoy Fitzgerald and Michael D. Higgins. Both had been Ministers for Arts and Culture; both identified themselves as visionaries and engaged in an attack on the 'gombeen man' mentality in Irish politics. But Higgins has published several volumes of poetry and is well up on Irish writing, whereas Fermoy declares that the arts 'was an area I knew very little abouh when I took over the brief. I used look up to artists and poets before I got to know em. Ih was a greah education to realize they're as fickle and wrongheaded as the rest of us.'[13] As the interviewer notes, Fermoy went on to become Minister of Finance after Arts and Culture and, if he is to be believed, '[my] term in Finance was wan of the most successful in the history of the State' (p. 39). Those who wish to make a case for the positive political achievements of Charles J. Haughey often point to his term as Minister of Finance in the late 1960s. For it was Haughey in Finance who brought in the legislation, unique among European countries, whereby a writer deemed to be an artist may live in the country without paying taxes on their earnings from their writings, no matter how large (or small). So it remains over three decades later that every Irish playwright, whatever their views on Haughey, continues to benefit financially from his legislation. In addition, while Haughey was Taoiseach, his artistic advisor Anthony Cronin set up Aosdána, an association of artists, most of whom are able to avail of an annual tax-free salary on the basis of being writers. Charles Haughey's treatment of artists – not only in a financial sense but in the prominence and importance he attached to them as part of civic and cultural life – may be seen as an example of enlightenment. But in the context of the tribunals and of the general aura of corruption and sleaze now associated with him the question emerges as to what extent Haughey has bought off the artists of Ireland; to what extent and degree the playwrights who have benefited – and they all have – are mired and implicated in the same financial double standards which the former Taoiseach promoted. This troubling question may well lie behind the emergence of Haughey on the stages of Irish theatre in 2002 and 2003. That tax-free status which was Haughey's legacy to the writers of Ireland is under pressure from the European Union, where it is anomalous and without precedent in relation to the tax laws of all of the other member states, and has had to be vigorously defended by those writers in the run-up to recent budgets. In general, the liberal intelligentsia has welcomed the pressure brought by the European High Court on Irish legal practice in relation to such issues as the decriminalisation of homosexuality; their own tax-free status is another matter.

Traces of Haughey can be seen in Carr's *Fermoy*, not just as a former successful Minister of Finance, but in the delusions of grandeur they both share. Brendan Behan memorably defined an Anglo-Irishman as a Protestant on a horse and the iconic and much reproduced photo of Haughey, sitting on his horse outside his Kinsealy estate, shows how much he cast himself in the role of Anglo-Irish squire. In frequently having an Irish poet at his side, he clearly saw himself as a combination of an Irish chieftain and a Renaissance prince. On his foreign travels, he stood squarely beside Japanese emperors and European monarchs as equal to the best of them. In the late lamented *Scrap Saturday*, a weekly satiric radio series on RTE, the self-mythologising aspect of Haughey was brilliantly captured in Dermot Morgan's monologues, where Haughey would adapt his family genealogy to whatever country and potentate he happened to be visiting. In Haughey's political career, he frequently invoked the emperor Napoleon as examplar and equal. And so when Fermoy places himself in the company of Napoleon, as he does on more than one occasion in *Ariel* – 'Dreamt last nigh I was dinin wud Alexander the Greah, Napoleon and Caesar' (p. 14) – the resonances with Haughey are unmistakeable. There is no clear parallel for Fermoy's third government ministry, Education, except to observe that of the many incumbents over the years, not one has gone on to be Taoiseach – as clear a prophecy as any that neither will Fermoy, as he hopes.

The first act also casts considerable doubt over whether Fermoy will win the local election. His long-standing opponent Hannafin defeated him the last time out, although only by four votes, as Fermoy reiterates. Hanafin drops by and urges Fermoy to withdraw by hinting at the dirt he will sell to the papers to tarnish his opponent, not least the fact that 'there's a few inquiries to be med as to how the cement and gravel empire goh off of the ground' (p. 34). In the Act II interview, which confirms that Fermoy beat Hanafin, there's the suggestion he did so by disclosing scandal about his opponent.

> VERONA　　. . . didn't you rise in proportion to Hanaffin's fall?
>
> FERMOY　　A cuurse I did, but thah doesn't diminish divine grace. If that scandal had broken a week laher, Hannafin would've kept hees seat.
>
> VERONA　　There were suggestions at the time, Minister, that you were instrumental in the breaking of that scandal.
>
> FERMOY　　Malicious gossip. (p. 38)

Fermoy goes on to rest his case on the fact that 'I was elected fair and square by the people' (p. 39). But in the Midlands dialect Carr has made her own, the merely rhetorical 'of course' is transformed into 'a cuuurse', a more potent form of word magic. Even in the short extract just quoted, Fermoy refers to his belief that 'divine grace' was operative.

There is a huge area of this play to be explored in terms of its belief systems; and having concentrated on the political side of the play for the purposes of this chapter, I can do no more than touch on it. But if Fermoy claims that he is merely following God's plan in sacrificing his daughter Ariel, the question remains: what God? The theistic issue is raised by his wife Frances when she accuses Fermoy of the murder in Act II. But it emerges even more powerfully in Act I, when he is still contemplating the deed and is discussing it with his brother, the monk Boniface. There is some suggestion that in a Yeatsian sense the Christian dispensation is at an end and what will succeed is the 'rough beast', when Fermoy invokes a 'blood-dimmed tide':

> FERMOY　　. . . I'll give him [God] whah he wants for ud's hees in the first place anyway.
>
> BONIFACE　And whah is ud he wants?

FERMOY   I tould ya, blood and more blood, blood till we're dry as husks,
          then pound us down, spread us like salt on the land, begin
          the experiment over, on different terms next time.
BONIFACE We've moved beyond the God a Job, Fermoy. (p. 19)

This invocation of Job is the only Old Testament reference in *Ariel*;
but in a biblical context where Abraham is called upon to sacrifice his
son Isaac the reference provides a worldview in which human sacrifice
to the deity can be considered. The primary reference would appear to
be the Greeks where, even though the play retains the singular reference, what is being talked about is 'the gods', those figures who take
a particularly delight in intervening in human affairs and toying with
the destinies of human individuals. But it is quite a task to translate
these concepts into contemporary Ireland and I am not sure the play
succeeds in doing so. If there is no endorsement of Fermoy's views
by the play, then he is a raving megalomaniac, a psychotic creature beyond
the reach of the other characters and our belief or sympathy. If there
are gods to whom contemporary Irish politicians have sacrificed in
order to achieve their worldly success, then I am not convinced that
addressing them in borrowed Greek robes, in terms that are not fully
translated into the post-Catholic Ireland of the twenty-first century, is
the best or most dramatically effective way to present them.[14]

In 2003, the year following Sebastian Barry's *Hinterland* and Carr's
Ariel, the dramatisation of the life and career of the former Taoiseach
was taken a stage further by playwright John Breen in *Charlie*. As the
play's title indicates, there is no longer a fictional veneer or melange of
identities in the representation of the title character. From the outset,
the names and references indicate that this is a play about Haughey. In
the play, as in life, he is surrounded by the politicians who aided him
in his efforts to become party leader of Fianna Fáil and who are readily identifiable by their last names: Padraig Flynn, Sean Doherty, Albert
Reynolds, Brian Lenihan. A ubiquitous presence is Haughey's press secretary, P.J. Mara, the original spin doctor, whose tendency to refer to
Haughey as 'Boss' owes as much to the mythologising of the satirical
series *Scrap Saturday* as it does to fact. Breen's play is not a family play,
as were those by Barry and Carr; the political narrative is not being
filtered through the family tragedy. Instead, *Charlie* concentrates on the
dimension of Haughey's life and career that were singularly absent from
the other two plays: the public life, the campaigning for political office,
the backstage intrigue. Karen Fricker remarked on the difference in
her *Guardian* review: 'Wisely, Breen focuses exclusively on Haughey's
political life (it was dramatising the man's personal affairs that got Barry

into hot water).'[15] The retrospect on his career is framed by a visit
Haughey makes in the present of 2003 to the Mayo farm of a man
called Michael, whose uncle he had known some decades before. In a
play where every character seems to have a real-life prototype, this scenario does not immediately suggest one. The uncle who was forced to
back off from taking a legal case against the local Fianna Fáil TD stands
in for any number of anonymous plain people of Ireland who felt betrayed
by Haughey's failure to deliver on his promises of supporting them against
the vested interests; he is also used to evoke Haughey's treatment of
his close friend Brian Lenihan when he dismissed him from public office.

The retrospect on Haughey does not go back to the beginning of his
political career: the period in the 1960s when he first came to prominence as an enterprising minister in several portfolios in Sean Lemass's
government. Instead, it kicks off with the immediate aftermath of the
Arms Trial debacle in 1970, a low point from which there would seem
to be no recovery. *Charlie* benefits from the lateness of its composition
by fully addressing the Tribunals of the late 1990s where the mysterious
sources of Haughey's wealth were placed under sustained scrutiny.
Between these two low points the play charts in a number of key scenes
the upward trajectory and process by which Haughey fought his way
back from the political wilderness to become leader of Fianna Fáil
and to head up several government administrations. The decade from
1970, when he was fired from Jack Lynch's government, to 1980, when
he replaced Lynch as party leader and as Taoiseach in an internal putsch,
were characterised in the RTE/Mint Productions four-part TV documentary, *Haughey*,[16] as the years of the 'chicken and ham' circuit. During
those years, Haughey travelled the length and breadth of the land in
order to attend innumerable local party dinners, to press the flesh and
to build a countrywide network of personal allegiances and support
that would back him in the subsequent heave for power. The process
is wonderfully crystallised in a scene in *Charlie* where he is primed by
P.J. Mara as he works the room:

CHARLIE: Where are we?

P.J.:   Ballyokane. This is Richard Murphy. Runs a piggery. Wife's
               a singer with the musical society.

CHARLIE: Richard, good to meet you again. How're the pigs?
               Remember, Ireland will always need bacon. Did I see your
               wife on the television?

CHARLIE *moves around the room.*[17]

He then encounters a man who is identified with the Jack Lynch camp
and whose son has been barred from playing hurling. Charlie promises

the man something he has not asked for – that his son will get to play in the hurling final – and thanks him for 'taking a risk' by coming out to support him – something the man has not declared. We are deep in the political land of wink and nod, or (as the play calls it elsewhere) the territory 'of implication and innuendo' (p. 41), where the absence of outright statement opens up the rich possibilities of ambiguity. Breen's play is alert to how language and its manipulation were central to the Haughey years and is at its best when it exploits this awareness.

The play is also alert to Haughey's contradictions as the title character undergoes a series of metamorphoses. Through the 1970s, by working the 'chicken and ham' circuit, Haughey consciously identified himself with the rural core values of the Fianna Fáil party, and in particular the farmers. But Haughey had made his mark in the 1960s and come to national attention as a moderniser, one of the new breed of Young Turks who were resolutely urban and forward-looking, who based their appeal (and their bid for power) on their alliance with Sean Lemass, an alliance cemented in Haughey's case by his marriage to Lemass's daughter, Maureen. The 1970s saw him build a contradictory rural persona, a role ironically more akin to the tradionalism of de Valera than the modernising of Lemass, as he toured the country and increasingly came to be photographed against the natural beauty of County Kerry and the island he purchased off its coast. It was inevitable that when he was returned to power those rural values would be betrayed; and this is the burden of Michael's charge against him in the play's present. If Haughey can claim (as he does) that he regarded Michael's uncle 'as the pulse of the Party, of the Nation' (p. 36), then the accusation when it comes has all the more moral force: 'He [the uncle] said last year that you were wrong to fire Brian Lenihan. . . . You fired your best friend as Taoiseach' (p. 62).

Another contradiction that Breen's play is well placed to explore, given the evidence of the tribunals, is the increasing gap between Haughey's modest origins and the grandiose lifestyle while in office, the Charvet shirts and Le Coq Hardi restaurant. Throughout *Charlie*, and particularly when he is out of office, Haughey has scenes with his bankers, who insist that he come to terms with his ever-accumulating debts while he persists in borrowing ever larger sums. The first banker points out that Haughey's 'debts are spiralling out of control' and that he 'is living beyond his means' (p. 11), while the second offers the defence (Haughey's own) that he 'is a very popular politician' who 'has connections with some of the wealthiest individuals in this state' (p. 12). Haughey's financial affairs run through the play, bringing in a supporting cast of financial advisers, wealthy businessmen and bankers. The final pay-off is the large sum donated by supermarket magnate Ben Dunne to Haughey, the only donation given as a direct cheque and therefore traceable. When Dunne's solicitor points out that the money ended up in Haughey's bank account, Haughey's defence speaks equally of manifest destiny and dodgy hubris:

> I was the Taoiseach, I didn't receive money like a vagrant. . . . I was running the country, the European Union. I couldn't be walking around without an arse in my trousers. . . . I was the Taoiseach. History is going to judge me. Ben Dunne is a fucking shopkeeper. (p. 74)

If Haughey spent the 1970s cultivating his role as man of the people, he displayed his wealth in the guise of an Anglo-Irish grandee, inhabiting the 'Big House' at Kinsealy, riding to hounds, buying expensive artworks and breeding greyhounds. Here was one of the colonised asserting his independence by mimicking the dress and behaviour of the former colonising power. This role-playing reached some kind of apotheosis when as Taoiseach he presented a Georgian silver teapot to the then British Prime Minister, Margaret Thatcher, at their first meeting. The scene is memorably represented in *Charlie*. Mara objects to the gift as a token of abject forelock-tugging, since it looks as if Charlie is 'going cap in hand' (p. 36). Haughey's defence is that the gesture betokens equality rather than colonial mimicry. But he goes further by charging P.J. that he does not understand women. Margaret Thatcher is the only female character in the play. With the domestic eliminated, neither Haughey's wife nor his mistress gets a dramatic look-in. But Breen plays up the extent to which Haughey is casting this meeting between the prime ministers of two sovereign states in heavily gendered terms as the romantic wooing of a woman by a man. As he declares to an adviser who suggests he brings index cards on the subjects he and Thatcher are to discuss, 'I have never needed help creating the right atmosphere with a woman' (p. 38). It is not the first time that Anglo-Irish relations have been figured as those between a man and a woman, but significantly Haughey here reverses the traditional identifications by casting Ireland in the role of the male. The musk generated by their encounter may well help to explain the subsequent debacle when their non-exchange on the future of Northern Ireland was translated afterwards by spokesman Brian Lenihan into the claim that 'the north's constitutional position was [now] up for discussion' (p. 41) and that 'it could mean a united Ireland in ten years' (p. 43). If there are contradictions between the urban and the rural in Haughey's persona (or personae), between the man of the people and the Anglo-Irish gentleman, the most confounding element of all is the most deeply buried: the Republican passion about the fate of the North bequeathed by his Derry origins and his father's politics. Haughey's relationship with Thatcher foundered on the fact that 'I always thought that I, I was the man that would sort out the North. From the start of it' (p. 44). When Thatcher and Taoiseach Garrett Fitzgerald brokered the Anglo-Irish Agreement in 1985, Haughey opposed it and was bitterly criticised for so doing.

When the Ben Dunne revelations (which Haughey had persistently denied) forced him to leave office and resign, he did so by quoting from Othello's closing speech; 'I have done the state some service, and they know't; / No more of that.'[18] But the context hardly seems applicable. Othello has just murdered his wife. To those surrounding Haughey in the Fianna Fáil party, the threat he posed was not so much to their lives as to their livelihoods, as TD Charlie McCreevy (one of the non-supporters) put it in the *Haughey* documentary. His self-consciously theatrical exit speech is consciously recalled in the closing moments of Breen's play. His Charlie glosses the act of identification with Shakespeare's tragic hero as follows: 'Othello was a great man brought down by his baser instincts' (p. 79). Michael, who says he has read the play for his Leaving Certificate exam, ripostes that he 'was thinking of Iago' and the admonition 'Put money in thy purse' as the more apposite. But the Shakespeare play which most proliferates intertextually in *Charlie* is *Julius Caesar*. Charlie himself, in recalling his meeting with Margaret Thatcher, invokes the figure of Caesar and his 'great campaigns' (p. 43) to lament the fact that 'I would never be tested on a great stage'. The references to the play itself are most prominent when he and his backers are considering the heave against Jack Lynch. To P.J. Mara's query as to whether it is too soon, Haughey responds: 'There is a tide [in the affairs of men,] which taken at the flood leads on to Fortune' (p. 17). The lines are spoken by Brutus, not early in the play, as the context might suggest, but late. When the assassination of Julius Caesar is first being canvassed, the 'noble' Brutus is the one who has to be persuaded, not the one who is doing the persuading. Haughey himself did quote a version of these lines from *Julius Caesar* when deciding to call a snap election in 1989. Addressing the faithful at the Fianna Fáil Ard-Fheis, he declared: 'Our spirits are high; let us take the tide at the flood.' And so he went to the people for the third time in a decade, seeking the overall majority which had all along been denied him (and Fianna Fáil under his leadership) and which he thought was his and the party's God-given right. Had he considered the dramatic context and consequence of Brutus's lines, Haughey might have thought twice – and decided not to call the election. Brutus is urging Cassius not to hold back in the face of the forces advancing on them but to march and meet them at Phillipi. The outcome is the defeat of their forces and the self-slaughter of both men. The result for Haughey of the 1989 election was coalition with the Progressive Democrats, the party founded by former Fianna Fáil politicians unhappy with his leadership; and it is they who would finally walk away in the face of the various scandals that emerged. Haughey was never tempted to fall on his sword, as the two Romans (and indeed Othello) had done. Instead, he liked to quote the example of the Chinese emperors who stayed in power until they were ninety. Mara warns Haughey in the play that he 'shouldn't have made that joke . . . about going on till you're ninety like the Chinese. It made people nervous' (pp. 69–70). The remark reflected Haughey's determination not to step down, and instigated a putsch against him which ironically was stage-managed by many of the same people who had first worked with him to oust Jack Lynch.

For it is in these ongoing internal struggles that the greatest relevance of Shakespeare's *Julius Caesar* to the career of Charles Haughey is to be found. The play opens with Caesar returning to Rome in triumph: those who rush to greet him are reminded that they have done exactly the same with Caesar's predecessor Pompey and are asked: 'And do you now strew flowers in his way, / That comes in triumph over Pompey's blood?'[19] This mode of overthrow and replacement of a leader is taken a step further by the conspirators when they actively plot Caesar's assassination on the Ides of March. To do so, they have to engage in the kind of internal political canvassing that became endemic in the Fianna Fáil camp during the Haughey era, soliciting support for a move against the leader by urging the greater good of the party. As Cassius relates, 'I have mov'd already / Some certain of the noblest-minded Romans / To undergo with me [this] enterprise' (I, iii, 121–2). But the biggest catch of all, that which would draw the wider support of the people to their cause, is Brutus. Cassius builds on Brutus's unease at Caesar's moves to have himself declared leader by stressing the ambition of the deed and how the kinship all three have shared is threatened by it. When Caesar falls at their hands, he singles out – in the well-known line '*Et tu, Brute*' (III, i, 77) – the one he least expected to oppose him. The pattern of recurrence suggested by the play creates the expectation that no leader will be secure in the future. The same process worked its way through Fianna Fáil. In turn, Haughey was replaced. On that final day in the Dáil, the air was thick with Shakespearean references. The figure who saw him off, Labour Party leader Dick Spring, cast himself in the role of Mark Antony and opened by saying that he came to bury Haughey, not to praise him (even though, as he observed of the date, it was not the Ides of March). And when Bertie Ahern, the loyal deputy described by his boss as 'the most cunning and devious of them all', became Taoiseach and sought to distance himself from Haughey, the line 'Et tu, Bertie' was heard from more than one pair of lips. *Julius Caesar* does not offer the absolute identification with the great (if flawed) tragic hero that a political leader would desire; it shows instead the realities of political change, with the poisoning of former loyalties and the overthrow of hitherto acclaimed leaders by those politically closest to them.

At the end of the RTE *Haughey* documentary, Declan Kiberd offered the valedictory comment: 'Perhaps the tragedy is that there was no tragedy, because he wasn't really as great as he looked.' He also spoke of all of the different and conflicting roles played by Haughey in his career as so many layers of the onion – and that they are peeled away to reveal an essential hollowness at the core. There is a suggestive re-sonance here for the ideological construction of 'modern' Ireland, and for many cherished icons and ideas. Charles Haughey did not contribute directly to the *Haughey* documentary – a singular absence amid family, friends (and enemies), and former colleagues, a case of *Hamlet* with-out the prince. He is unusual among former Taoisigh in that he wrote no memoirs. When P.J. Mara was asked about Haughey and the Arms Trial, he replied that Haughey never spoke of it. Haughey, citing his ill health, finally refused to testify any further before the tribunals that were inquiring into the sources of his wealth. The enigma of Charles Haughey has opened up a gap of possibility for Ireland's playwrights to conjure with the man and his contradictions. As I write these con-cluding lines, I do so the week after Charles Haughey has died – on Tuesday 19 June 2006 (from cancer). In the aftermath of his death, fulsome tributes were paid by many (though not all). The lines he quoted from Shakespeare received frequent airing. As Eileen Battersby pointed out in *The Irish Times*, the Shakespearean figure who most came to mind during this period was not Othello but Richard III, another politician who stopped at nothing to gain power but when he had it did not know what to do with it. As she writes, 'even Haughey must have suspected he had more in common with Richard III.'[20] But he may not have done so. After all, unlike *Julius Caesar*, *Othello* and *Hamlet*, *Richard III* has never been on the Junior or Leaving Certificate exams. Not one of Shakespeare's history plays is to be found in the syllabus of the Irish educational system. Their lines are not lodged in the memory of the citizenry and hence are not available for ready quota-tion (and recognition) in political speeches. Perhaps they are excluded because the parallels they might suggest to Irish political life would prove more immediate and less flattering than the tragedies.

Notes

1 Brian Friel, *The Communication Cord* (Oldcastle: Gallery Press, 1989), p. 75.
2 Marina Carr's *Ariel* was produced by the National Theatre in association with Fiach MacConghail and first presented at the Abbey Theatre during the Dublin Theatre Festival in October 2002; Sebastian Barry's *Hinterland* was co-produced by Ireland's and England's National Theatres with the UK touring company Out of Joint and opened at the Octagon Theatre, Bolton, in January 2002 before touring to Dublin, London and elsewhere; John Breen's *Charlie* was produced by the Yew Tree Theatre, Ballina, Co. Mayo in a touring production and was first presented at the Pavilion Theatre, Dun Laoghaire, Co. Dublin in April 2003.
3 Justin O'Brien, *The Modern Prince: Charles J. Haughey and the Quest for Power* (Dublin: Merlin Publishing, 2002), p. 168.
4 Cited in O'Brien, *The Modern Prince*, p. 2.
5 O'Brien, *The Modern Prince*, p. 164.
6 William Shakespeare, *Othello*, in *The Arden Shakespeare Complete Works*, ed. Richard Proudfoot, Ann Thompson and David Scott Kastan (Walton-on-Thames, Surrey: Thomas Nelson and Sons Ltd, 1988), p. 975. The reference is to Act V, scene ii, lines 539–40.
7 Sebastian Barry, *Hinterland* (London and New York: Faber and Faber, 2002), p. 54. All future references to the play are to this edition and will be incorporated into the text.
8 Colm Tóibín, in an essay on *Hinterland*, confirms the identification: 'For an Irish audience, this would have been instantly accepted as a reference to the journalist Terry Keane, who published a series of articles in *The Sunday Times* about her long affair with Charles Haughey and who made no secret of the affair in her column in *The Sunday Independent*.' Colm Tóibín, '*Hinterland*: The Public Becomes Private', in Christina Hunt Mahony (ed.), *Out of History: Essays on the Writings of Sebastian Barry* (Dublin: Carysfort Press; Washington, DC: The Catholic University of America Press, 2006), pp. 204–5.
9 Colm Tóibín, '*Hinterland*', p. 205.
10 One example among many that might be cited is when Silvester self-consciously describes himself in the following terms: 'Enter Lear dressed fantastically in wild flowers' (p. 40).
11 This Gothic representation was first employed by Conor Cruise O'Brien in his column in *The Irish Times* in 1982, after one of Haughey's frequent falls from power. He repeated the Haughey/Dracula comparison in the columns he wrote when Haughey resigned. See Conor Cruise O'Brien, 'Don't write him off just yet', *Irish Independent*, 25 January 1992, and also 'Diary: Clove of Garlic', *The Times*, 24 January 1992.

12 American politicians are given to this, but it is extremely rare in an Irish context.

13 Marina Carr, *Ariel* (Oldcastle: Gallery Press, 2002), p. 38. All future references to the play are to this edition and will be incorporated in the text.

14 For an essay which addresses just these aspects of *Ariel*, see Cathy Leeney, 'Marina Carr', in Anthony Roche (ed.), *The UCD Aesthetic: Celebrating 150 Years of UCD Writers* (Dublin: New Island Press, 2005), pp. 265–73. See also J. Michael Walton, 'Hit or Myth: The Greeks and Irish Drama', in Marianne McDonald and J. Michael Walton (eds), *Amid Our Troubles: Irish Versions of Greek Tragedy* (London: Methuen, 2002), pp. 3–36.

15 Karen Fricker, review of *Charlie*, *The Guardian*, 25 April 2003.

16 *Haughey*, a four-part television documentary (2005), co-produced by Radio Telefis Eireann and Mint Productions, directed by Niamh Sammon, co-produced by Steve Carlson and Miriam O'Callaghan.

17 John Breen, *Charlie*, unpublished script, p. 8. All future references to the play are to the script and will be incorporated in the text. I am grateful to John Breen for supplying me with a copy of the script and the reviews.

18 Shakespeare, *Othello*, in *The Arden Shakespeare*, p. 975.

19 Shakespeare, *Julius Caesar*, in *The Arden Shakespeare*, p. 335 (Act I, scene i, lines 51–2). All future line references to the play are to this edition and will be incorporated in the text.

20 Eileen Battersby, 'Haughey was an Opportunistic Pragmatist', *The Irish Times*, 24 June 2006.

6

'New articulations of Irishness and otherness'[1] on the contemporary Irish stage

Martine Pelletier

Though the choice of 1990 as a watershed year demarcating 'old' Ireland from 'new', modern, Ireland may be a convenient simplification that ignores or plays down a slow, complex, ongoing process, it is nonetheless true to say that in recent years Ireland has undergone something of a revolution. Economic success, the so-called 'Celtic Tiger' phenomenon, and its attendant socio-political consequences, has given the country a new confidence whilst challenging or eroding the old markers of Irish identity. The election of Mary Robinson as the first woman President of the Republic came to symbolise that rapid evolution in the cultural, social, political and economic spheres as Ireland went on to become arguably one of the most globalised nations in the world. As sociologist Gerard Delanty puts it, within a few years, 'state formation has been diluted by Europeanization, diasporic emigration has been reversed with significant immigration and Catholicism has lost its capacity to define the horizons of the society'.[2] The undeniable exhilaration felt by many as Ireland set itself free from former constraints and limitations, waving goodbye to mass unemployment and emigration, has nonetheless been counterpointed by a measure of anxiety. As the old familiar landscape, literal and symbolic, changed radically, some began to experience what Fintan O'Toole has described as 'a process of estrangement [whereby] home has become as unfamiliar as abroad'.[3] If Ireland changed, so did concepts of Irishness. The term 'Irish diaspora' gained increasing currency in that decade, encouraged no doubt by Mary Robinson's own emphasis on the Irish nation as expanding well beyond the geographical confines of the island to include all those who had emigrated to the various corners of the world, and for whom she kept a lighted candle in a window of her official residence in Phoenix Park. By the end of the 1990s, emigration had been replaced by immigration as a burning issue in public debate. Ireland's new-found wealth and well-advertised labour shortage led to the influx of numerous immigrants, an unprecedented and unexpected situation which took Irish people and their government by surprise. Between 1996 and 2002 over 153,000 people moved to the state; the 2002 census returned 5.8 per cent 'non-nationals' and there was a 600 per cent rise in the number of work visas granted between 1999 and 2004. In 2003 alone, 47,000 employment permits were issued.[4]

One major Irish problem that remained to be solved was the continuing violence in Northern Ireland. By 1994, with the help of the USA, an IRA ceasefire had been brokered, soon followed by a similar cessation of violence on the part of the loyalists. In spite of numerous difficulties a fragile peace has been established thanks to the constitutional arrangements contained in the 1998 Good Friday Peace Agreement, opening in Seamus Heaney's words 'a space – and not just in the political arena but in the first level of each person's consciousness – a space where hope can grow'.[5] In the wake of the Agreement, Irish people were asked to vote in a referendum to modify the two articles of the Constitution which laid claim to Northern Ireland. The new version of article 2, enthusiastically ratified by the voters, enshrined in the Constitution a different conception of citizenship according to which the link between individual and territory was now less strong than that between individuals:

> It is the entitlement and birthright of every person born in the island of Ireland, which includes its islands and seas, to be part of the Irish nation. That is also an entitlement of all persons otherwise qualified in accordance with law to be citizens of Ireland. Furthermore, the Irish nation cherishes its special affinity with people of Irish ancestry living abroad who share its cultural identity and heritage.[6]

While it would be naive and still premature to say that no return to violence need be feared and that the Northern Ireland problem has found a definite political solution given that devolved government is yet to be restored, there is no denying that a huge sense of relief now prevails, allowing both parts of Ireland to re-imagine themselves as peaceful societies. This evolution, together with the economic boom and attendant Americanisation and globalisation of the Republic, has brought about a reassessment of the paradigms of Irish identity in which the relationship with England/Britain features far less prominently. Such deep and sweeping changes have led to a re-energising of critical discourse in and about Ireland, with a shift away from colonial/postcolonial models of analysis towards globalisation as the core issue demanding elucidation.

In this process, the image of Ireland as sharing some of the characteristics of the Third World as well as of the First World, one of the tenets
of post-colonial theory, has come under much strain. Michel Peillon
has argued persuasively that this Third World perception had to be
reviewed so as to acknowledge that Ireland today enjoys the agency of
a First World power, not the alleged passivity of a colonial victim.[7]

One particularly striking characteristic of the recent analyses propounded by scholars and observers has been a new focus on immigration, also notable in public discourse and in creative works, most
particularly in theatre. A number of recent Irish theatrical productions have engaged with this new phenomenon and its implications for
Ireland's identity and self-image and these have, in turn, become the
object of critical inquiry. In what follows, I would like to look at a
number of plays that engage, directly or indirectly, with the experience
of immigration as translated for the stage. I will deliberately frame this
study with two plays by the most famous and acclaimed Irish playwright,
Brian Friel, in order to show how under the surface of the deceptively
'traditional' subject matter of both *Dancing at Lughnasa* (1990) and
The Home Place (2005) can be found very topical concerns that testify
to the playwright's awareness of the seismic shift affecting Ireland,
and to his ability to engage, on his own terms, with the new Ireland's
anxieties, hopes and challenges. Beside Friel's two works, other plays
under scrutiny will be, in chronological order, *Asylum! Asylum!* (1994)
by Donal O'Kelly with reference to other work by Calypso productions,
Treehouses by Elizabeth Kuti (2000) and *Départ et Arrivée* (*Departure
and Arrival*) (2004), the latter being a collaborative venture involving
Dermot Bolger, Kazem Shahryari (an Iranian-born, Paris-based director),
and French translator Emile-Jean Dumay, who had introduced
Shahryari to Bolger's work. Taken together, these plays by writers of
different generations, genders, geographical origins and aesthetic sen-
sibilities amount to a series of interventions aimed at bringing to the
consciousness of Irish and international audiences the plight of those
many immigrants and refugees seeking a new life in Ireland. They bear
out Jason King's contention that 'more than any other literary or
performing art form, the Irish theatre has proven highly receptive to
the experiences of immigrants in Ireland'.[8] Some of these works also
bring to light the literal and symbolic interconnections between the
journeys of the new migrants and those undertaken by several generations of Irish men and women who emigrated to more or less distant
and hospitable lands, thus establishing links between a traumatic part
of Ireland's past and the challenges and responsibilities it faces in the
present.

Brian Friel's *Dancing at Lughnasa* arguably brought the 1980s to a close and set the tone for the new decade, as Terence Brown suggests by beginning his chapter on Ireland in the 1990s ('Revelations and Discoveries') with a discussion of the play in the updated version of his seminal *Ireland. A Social and Cultural History: 1922–2002*. While the play ostensibly deals with Ireland in the 1930s, a number of its ingredients point to more contemporary issues and concerns: modernisation and urbanisation, the emphasis on repressed female sexuality, the challenges to the Catholic Church, the parallels with Africa, the foregrounding of music and of the body on stage, all either anticipated or set the pace for future developments in Irish theatre and society. The retrospective form, as the story of the Mundy sisters is recounted through the consciousness of an adult narrator – Michael, Friel's exact contemporary and a mere child of seven in 1936, the time of the dramatic action – perfectly captures that movement of the mind between past and present while endowing the past with an undeniable 'presence'. Declan Kiberd's insightful and balanced analysis of the play in *The Irish Review* succeeds in pinpointing its many strengths, elucidating how the shifts in rhythm, the acceleration in Michael's narrative, perfectly mirror the acceleration Irish society was being subjected to:

> The clinging of the sisters to the present moment is their response to being hurtled into the future at breakneck speed and the uneven pace of the narrator and dramatisation perfectly render the reality of lives lived at different speeds. It is as if the older Michael is impatient to give history a forward shove, while the actual dramatis personae do their utmost to retard it.[9]

The play is too well known and much studied to deserve a lengthy discussion here. For my purpose however I will focus on two related aspects, namely the place afforded to women and the 'elsewheres' of the play, Africa, Wales and London. In the Ireland portrayed and remembered by Michael, the place of women is in the home, tending children and looking after their husbands' needs. As the countryside is rapidly losing its population to emigration, marriage opportunities have become rare in Ballybeg, though marriage is one of the few forms of fulfilment for women officially sanctioned by Church and state. All five sisters have remained and will remain single and it is no wonder that they should break out into a manic dance in the privacy of their kitchen, releasing for one short moment all their pent-up energies and frustrations to the sound of Irish music on the wireless. The respectability of the Mundy household, already challenged by Chris's having had a child out of wedlock, is put to further test by the return of Father

Jack from his mission in Ryanga. Father Jack comes home in disgrace, having 'gone native',[10] a sin that will cost Kate, the bread-winner of the household, her job as schoolteacher. As a result of their failure to procure either husbands or jobs, now that home-knitting will be super-seded by machine-knitting at the new factory since the industrial revolution has caught up with Ballybeg and caused casualties, Agnes and Rose feel compelled to leave and seek their fortune in London, as did countless others before and after them. This sacrifice brings little good, though, as the two sisters face anonymity, hard work, homelessness and death in destitution, away from the familial love and solidarity that had made their hard lives bearable, a familiar Friel motif. While Gerry, Chris's lover and father to Michael, seems able to commute between Ireland and Wales, where he has another family (as Michael will dis-cover much later), Agnes and Rose's departure proves final. While London comes to mean erasure and death, and Wales is equated with betrayal, Africa is endowed by Jack with life-affirming possibilities, thanks to its continued link with the sacred, its paganism that has resisted all efforts at Christianisation, his own included. The Irish Catholic Church has sought to repress the pagan rituals of the ancestral Celtic culture, represented in the play by the Lughnasa festival and its bonfires and animal sacrifices, but in Ryanga, pagan rituals and ceremonies still permit a spiritual communion which does not deny the body. Jack's tales of African customs – in which dancing, polygamy and love-children fea-ture prominently – holds out an image of a world in which the sexual energy of women is neither feared nor frustrated, though that image itself may owe as much to Jack's imagination as to fact, as Michael's own memories of that golden summer of 1936 do. It is nonetheless strik-ing that Friel should pit the sterility of Irish culture, deprived of any continuity with its pagan Celtic roots, against the joyous celebrations and dances of Africa perceived as a repository of a universal sense of the sacred. Africa though, is beyond the reach of the sisters, whose only choice appears to be either a frugal, lonely life in Ballybeg or emigra-tion to London. A culture that offered such a bleak alternative to five intelligent and energetic women still in their prime had clearly become unsustainable, and failed the legitimate aspirations of its population.

By 1990, however, Ireland had embarked on a transformative jour-ney, and theatre would record those transformations; more than a few members in the audience of the original production, and of subsequent revivals, may have been willing to make theirs Michael's comment 'I had a sense of unease, some awareness of a widening breach between what seemed to be and what was, of things changing too quickly before my eyes, of becoming what they ought not to be'.[11] In the play, Friel catches one of those moments of transition and succeeds in conveying with great subtlety and force both the failure of the traditional rural world the Mundy sisters inhabit, and the loss and anxieties entailed in its supersession by a materialistic, increasingly technological modern world that risks destroying the last connection with ritual and the sacred. The play treads a fine line between nostalgia for a culture that had its beauty and value, and a harsh, unsentimental recognition of the inevitability of that culture's demise, a line a number of productions of *Dancing at Lughnasa* have crossed, deliberately or not, usually to err on the side of nostalgia, a temptation that may also tell us something about an abiding need to celebrate what is felt to have been lost.

Africa reappeared on the smaller Peacock stage of the National Theatre with Donal O'Kelly's *Asylum! Asylum!* in 1994, in a changing context just as the new phase of prosperity, soon to be dubbed the 'Celtic Tiger' phenomenon was gathering momentum. In O'Kelly's play, Africa is not the place where contact with the numinous and the sacred has been preserved, but a continent in the throes of violent, internecine conflicts, where barbarous acts of torture and murder are committed. *Asylum! Asylum!* is based on a real horrific event, reported in the 1991 Amnesty International Report. As rewritten by O'Kelly, it becomes the tale of a miraculous conversion, as well as the sad story of a failed escape from the threat of torture and death.[12] Joseph Omara (the name sounds deliberately Irish – O'Meara – to suggest a proximity that the difference in the colour of the skin conceals) is applying for asylum in Ireland, having fled northern Uganda. He must convince the authorities, represented on stage by Pillar Boylan and Leo Gaughran, two Irish immigration officers, that he is not an illegal economic migrant but a genuine refugee. Leo's sister Mary, a newly qualified lawyer, takes up his case and Bill, Leo and Mary's father, offers him shelter while his application is being processed. Thus the whole family becomes implicated in Omara's story.

There is clear, physical, evidence Joseph has been tortured, but Leo refuses to believe his tale of being brutalised by the army because he had refused to set fire to a pit in a village; the flaw in the story is revealed as Joseph, on bail from Mountjoy prison while his case is being examined, attends, at Mary's invitation, the family barbecue organised to mark Leo's promotion to Europol. Leo's eagerness to leave an Ireland he despises as backwards counterpoints Joseph's desire to gain admittance to the country. While Leo dreams of self-fulfillment and better career prospects, in tune with the country's embrace of materialism and of Europe as the exit route, Joseph's only ambition is to make a home in a place where he need not fear for his life. In what might appear as a somewhat crude parallel, the sight of the barbecue leads Joseph to relive and tell the full tale of what happened in Bucoro, of how the pit he dug was not empty when it was set on fire, but contained five local men, including the local schoolmaster, his own father, about whom he has told so many moving stories and for whom he has expressed much love and admiration. It was Joseph's refusal to light the fire himself which led to his punishment at the hands of the soldiers. His guilt and horror – he could not acknowledge his dying father for if he had, he would have been thrown in the pit himself – which were initially repressed can now be put into words. While Mary and Bill are shocked by the account, it elicits only jeers and applause from Leo who refuses to accept the veracity of Joseph's story. Such callousness causes Bill and Mary to ask Leo to leave: 'Get out! Go to Europe, go to Europol and take your hatred with you'.[13] Joseph's subsequent acceptance into Bill's home and life is presented as both an instance of genuine Christian hospitality and an opportunity for Bill to mend the fence with his daughter Mary, whom one understands he had neglected as a child because of his wife's premature death. As father and daughter are drawn closer, Bill finds the courage to speak about his wife Helen, herself a refugee of sorts as her parents' home in Dublin was burnt in a 1941 bombing, and recounts that it was thanks to his own parents' invitation to the young girl to stay in their home that their romance blossomed. Meanwhile, Mary and Joseph are increasingly attracted to one another, suggesting a tentative inter-racial romance which Boylan and Leo find distasteful but which Bill condones. In the third act, another few months have elapsed and Joseph's last chance to appeal a deportation order has been exhausted. As Pillar Boylan comes to the house to take away a disbelieving and desperate Joseph who begins to suspect Mary of betrayal, Leo reappears, not in the guise of the heartless law enforcer, but as a man who has been transformed. He explains that, while in Germany a few days before, he witnessed the burning of a hostel full of immigrants by a racist crowd and saw the man he did not believe in, Joseph's father, 'tall like a giant, thin like a leaf'. He stood alone in one of the rooms, uttering the phrase Joseph had seen him utter in the pit, a favourite quotation of his taken from Winston Churchill's *African Journey*, before being engulfed by the flames. Leo's conversion – what Boylan mockingly refers to as a road to Damascus experience – gives him the strength to encourage Joseph and Mary to flee; to no avail, as the African is soon captured and sent back to an uncertain fate in Uganda. Mary, Bill and Leo now share a common purpose: they are all ready to fight an unfair immigration system that relies on fear and allows racism to fester.

While the number of asylum applications was extremely limited in Ireland in the early 1990s, it rose dramatically within a few years, as Terence Brown explains: 'From 39 persons applying for refugee status in 1992 those seeking such status rose to 7,724 in 1999. Forbidden to work, subsisting on small state handouts, often forced to wait years before their cases could be heard, asylum seekers in the 1990s faced hostility in the popular press as they were branded as "fake" applicants'.[14] Shortly before *Asylum! Asylum!* was produced, O'Kelly translated his own commitment to the defence of human rights by setting up Calypso Productions with playwright Kenneth Glenaan. Its mission statement reads:

Calypso's mission is simple, practical and humble. We want to change the world . . . the change we want to effect is small, significant and possible . . . By our future world family, we will be remembered in one of two ways. We will either have been caring guardians who nurtured their inheritance – social, political, artistic, environmental and sacred – or we will have been the parasites who depleted some of the hope and possibility from their lives; we are all world citizens; some of us are lucky enough to have inherited life saving rights, life enhancing social opportunities and life affirming creative possibilities. With those rights and privileges comes a responsibility to defend them for ourselves and for others.[15]

Thus Calypso's mission is to 'produce theatre as an intervention in contemporary political and civil life, and to envisage in a new way, the world as a stage, or site of contestation of choices made in the political sphere'.[16] *Asylum! Asylum!* perfectly embodies that desire to move from the actual to the possible and the belief that theatre is the right art form, because of its collaborative, public nature and its capacity to generate empathy, to enact that transformation of hearts and minds. The play was rightly deemed flawed, even by sympathetic observers and critics like Fintan O'Toole. The latter thought the play brave and passionate, in the Shavian tradition of argumentative theatre,[17] but questioned its adherence to realistic conventions which are partly at odds with the contents. Victor Merriman, who has written on various occasions on Calypso's work, also directed a production of the same play in 1997 which tried to eschew the naturalistic trap by using an in-the-round design to bring into sharper focus the strange, magic realist ending.[18] For his part, O'Kelly went on to explore non-western forms of theatre and by 1998, with *Farawayan*, he offered a piece that returned to the central concern of *Asylum! Asylum!*, the plight and fear of the stranger in a strange land. He did so moving beyond language and narrative to make full use of music, sounds and images in what he described as 'a non-Irish form of theatre' before correcting himself and suggesting that Calypso could be, in their own modest way, part of those 'generating a new Irish form of theatre'.[19] The programme notes outlined Calypso's belief in the need to change Irish attitudes towards asylum seekers: 'Asylum seekers and immigrants are not burdens to be borne or invaders to be repulsed. They are human beings with life stories and human rights, with abilities and energies, and with a range of contributions to make. They are to be welcomed'.[20] By extension, they also come from countries and cultures with different theatre traditions that are also to be made welcome on the Irish stage as they can help revitalise a theatre reaching its limits after over a century of verbal, naturalistic plays. What is more, as Merriman contends, some forms of experience cannot be conveyed in the language of western drama and need their own, appropriate forms in order not to betray the otherness of lives lived outside the western centre.[21]

In 2000, the same Peacock stage saw the first production of Elizabeth Kuti's *Treehouses*.[22] In this play, a young writer of English–Hungarian origin now based in Ireland 'explores the dilemma of those whose identity is formed between places',[23] as Anna McMullan puts it. To convey this sense of in-betweenness, Kuti opts for a largely realist setting with a difference, as she interweaves three stories, each with their own time and space, each featuring a woman at a different stage in her life, adolescent, middle-aged and ageing. The focus shifts constantly from the Irish nursing home where old Magda lives and recalls her past, to the story of her younger self she conjures up, and to a third story, location unclear, which features Eva, whose father has just died and whose thoughts, undramatised but narrated with a stream of consciousness technique, constantly waver between her childhood memories and her current grief and bereavement. The link between Magda's and Eva's stories will become manifest only in the ending. Kuti's fluid to-ing and fro-ing between different times and places as well as between narrative and dramatic enactment of the memories on stage may bring to mind Friel's *Dancing at Lughnasa*, though there is no single controlling viewpoint but rather a range of female subjectivities.

Old Magda recalls her adolescence on a farm in Eastern Europe. Her father's decision to give shelter to Joseph, a young Jewish boy whose parents have been deported, marks Magda's entry into a harsh world from which her father's love had insulated her. Magda takes increasingly seriously her role as the boy's protector, though she is unsure what she is protecting him against; as he reveals to her that deportation is but another word for execution, afraid that her father will ask the boy to leave since hiding him has become terribly dangerous, she decides to run away with him so that his chances of escape may be greater. But Stephen, the young attractive schoolmaster, is in love with Magda and has asked for her hand. He is increasingly jealous of Magda's relationship with the Jewish boy. A mixture of jealousy and concern for Magda's safety motivate his holding her back and ultimately fear and weakness will induce Magda to stay behind, leaving the boy to flee the farm alone. Magda married Stephen and left Eastern Europe to settle in a strange land, but the thought of the boy she failed to save, of the promise she could not keep, has never left her.

Eva's tale is one of filial love for a father, abandoned by his wife, who constructed a treehouse for his beloved child. The treehouse is a symbol of their intimacy and mutual dependence as no outsider was to be allowed in. The arrival of a new neighbour, bearing the Jewish name of Miriam, and the relationship that develops between her and the father, shatter the child's dream of being her father's 'one and only'. On the day the pair got married, Eva remembers, her younger self burnt the treehouse. Now that her father has died, she is left to make her peace with his memory and to come to terms with her feelings:

> to say it was a betrayal is too strong too strong of course you reached for what you loved and reached towards the shape of your desire I was not your burden you didn't let me stop you and now I know I'm grateful for that though then I did not could not know it you never promised protection against everything you never promised protection from the dark from alone from death that was not in your gift.[24]

Thus the inability of Eva's father to protect his teenage daughter echoes Magda's rash promise to protect and keep safe the boy, a promise she failed to keep. Old Magda remains haunted by what she sees as her failure to keep her word and keep the boy safe, returning to the biblical image of Pharaoh's daughter and the baby in the ark. In an ending that is both poetic and deeply moving, our own doubts and fears, if not those of Magda, are finally assuaged as we discover that Eva's father was none other than that same Joseph who had given young Magda the key to his mother's musical box as a keepsake. As Magda rummages through her room with the help of kind-hearted nurse Ger, retrieving the key she feared had got lost, Eva, looking through her father's personal effects, comes upon a musical box that she cannot open as the key is missing. So the boy did escape and made his own way to some hospitable shore, one tale holding the key to the locked world of the other tale. A story of love, filial and romantic, selfish and generous, of secrets and guilt, of promises kept and broken, *Treehouses* invites the audience to empathise imaginatively with those who have found a new home in a new country, though the ghosts of their past may still haunt them. Kuti's play subtly conveys the horror of the Holocaust and its impact on the survivors. The play repeatedly makes use of the inter-connected symbols of the ark and the treehouse. Both evoke sanctuaries, ways of hiding and/or escaping from threats/others. But as Anna McMullan rightly perceives, these interrelated symbols are highly ambiguous as Eva and Magda also use their respective treehouses to keep the others out, to exclude. This prompts her warning:

> As Irish society becomes more diverse and new stories, traditions and histories are introduced into the fabric of our culture, the traditional bound-aries of the realist room can no longer accommodate the layered and com-plex experiences of home and identity that inhabit contemporary Ireland. The playwrights whose work has been discussed above have articulated fragmented, splintered identities, which must be patched together if agency is to be recovered, but whose visions and voices offer alternative perspectives and identities questioning the concept of a homogenous, shared world or audience which traditional realism assumes.[25]

While both O'Kelly's and Kuti's plays foreground the immigrant's experience and difficulties upon getting access to the promised land or the guilt felt by those who left others behind, *Départ et Arrivée* delib-erately brings to the fore the parallels between Irish emigration and con-temporary immigration. In his article, Jason King underlines the role theatre has played, serving 'to provide both a vehicle and a venue for the enactment of this imaginative space, and the staging of spectacles of intercultural contact, in which the interconnections between immig-rant perceptions and Irish historical memory have become dramatized as a recurrent narrative conceit in a number of recent Irish theatrical productions'.[26] While he does not discuss *Départ et Arrivée*, this play undoubtedly confirms King's sense that such a connection should be seen as central to the way theatre could address immigration in Ireland, whilst also offering evidence both of the potency and relevance of this parallel, and of its dangers, in terms of the conflation of too disparate experiences.

The genesis of the play is somewhat unusual in that the two play-wrights did not share a common language and Dumay, the translator, had to act as go-between, translating Bolger's English into French and Shahyari's French into English. The French version, *Départ et Arrivée*, has been both staged and published, drawing largely positive critical reactions.[27] Dermot Bolger, unhappy with the result of their efforts, has so far refused to allow the English version of the play to be staged, though an unpublished version of the script exists and Bolger's 'half' of the play, 'Departure', originally written as a monologue and then cut up and interspersed with Shahryari's 'Arrival', was broadcast as a one-act play on RTE Radio 1 in December 2004. *Départ et Arrivée* hinges on a device reminiscent of that used by Bolger in the successful *Finbar's Hotel* series of short stories, and consists of two intertwined monologues that should, but do not always, amount to a dialogue across time and cultural barriers. A living pregnant Kurdish woman and the ghost of an Irish pregnant girl share a space, a small room in a B&B in Dublin. Susan's arrival in the room awakens the ghost/memory of Maureen who also occupied that room on her way to England in the 1960s. The image of the ghost is recurrent throughout Bolger's work, and is used in *The Passion of Jerome*, for example, also staged in French by Shahryari. The starting point of the play for Bolger may well have been an incident involving the tragic death of eight Kurdish stowaways found suffocated in a container in Wexford. That Shahryari, who had directed two of the French productions of his plays, should be of Kurdish origin and a refugee from Iranian persecutions prompted Bolger's offer to pen this piece together.

Bolger's character, Maureen, left small-town Ireland after 'getting in trouble' with Michael, a young local man who has migrated to England and has come home for a holiday. The romance involves a dark secret and a crossing over of boundaries. Michael's uncle, branded an informer, was supposedly killed by Maureen's uncle during the civil war. Together the lovers plan Maureen's departure to join Michael in England, but Maureen soon hears of his death on an English building site. Her mother discovers her pregnancy and forces her to leave home rather than face the shame of being branded 'a slut' by the intolerant villagers. Given that all of her many brothers and sisters have also left Ireland for England and America, her going away would only be natural. Yet, rather than enter one of the infamous Magdalene Laundries or follow her parents' advice to go to the Catholic Protection Agency, where her child would be taken from her at birth, Maureen decides to use the money her father has given her, her mother's untouched dowry in fact, to take a boat for England and face up to the challenges of a new life as a single mother in Manchester, the town where the father of her child had worked and planned a future for them. In deference to her love for Michael she will not have the child born of their love grow up unaware of who his parents were. Her departure is thus both an escape from an Ireland that rejects 'fallen women' and an act of affirmation, though her fate in Manchester may be uncertain.[28]

Shahryari's Susan lives in Turkey but is of Kurdish descent; her encounter in the neighbouring woods with Vedat, a non-violent militant

of the Kurdish cause, enables her to gain access to a whole memory of
cultural and political oppression and suppression from which her
father had protected her. Susan's decision to accompany Vedat into exile
in Paris thus involves an embracing of the cause he defends. It signals
a rediscovery of her origins, not an escape from shame or dishonour,
as there is no suggestion that her loving father might force his pregnant daughter to leave the house. However, Vedat is killed by Turkish
soldiers as he returns to the village where Kurds were murdered and
left unburied. The place will be flooded to create an artificial lake, also
causing Susan's father to go and make a new home elsewhere. Rather
than follow him in his new exile, the young woman chooses to go and
look for her elder sister, Kudret, who has settled in Ireland. As the
sad stories of the two young women unfold before our eyes, parallels
and connections are established for and by the audience, confirming
that cultural differences cannot obliterate our shared humanity and the
universality of love, filial and romantic, of desire and hope.

As both Emile-Jean Dumay and Victor Merriman have argued,[29]
Sharhyari's almost 'magical realist' optimism jars with Bolger's darker
realism for reasons that may go beyond individual aesthetic choices.
Shahryari places himself on the side of life and survival, endowing his
Susan with a resourcefulness and optimism translated through her song
of hope and the final image of the dancing girl. Where Shahryari, understandably given his own life story, can portray emigration as a personal
liberation which may herald a future collective liberation, Bolger seems
unable to embrace such a positive vision and sees Ireland as still dependent upon its former coloniser for economic survival and in denial of
its own limitations and failures.

Meanwhile, the future of the real-life counterparts of Susan and
her child were closely bound up with evolutions in Irish legislation on
emigration. As Ronit Lentin, a specialist in sociology observes angrily:
'In 2003 96% of all asylum applications were rejected, and according
to the Irish Refugee Council, in 2003, 90 people each week were refused
entry to Ireland to present asylum applications – no wonder there was
a 32% fall in applications in 2003'.[30] In line with European directives,
Ireland put in place stricter immigration controls, though pressure for
limitation of the granting of citizenship to children of non-nationals largely
came from within the country. Following upon a Supreme Court decision in January 2003, non-national parents no longer had a case to reside
in Ireland to bring up their Irish-born children. A referendum held on
11 June 2004 and carried by a huge majority reversed its *jus soli*
citizenship access and removed the birth right to Irish citizenship of those

same children. By establishing parallels between economic migration from Ireland in the 1950s and 1960s[31] and current immigration to Ireland, the play also suggests that the country has a historical as well as an ethical responsibility to remember and act humanely, generously: a much needed reminder, it seems.

During a panel session on 'Irish Theatre and Globalisation' at the Prague 2005 IASIL conference, two of the participants, Karen Fricker and Patrick Lonergan, argued that Friel's *The Home Place* (2005) raised issues very relevant to today's concern with what constitutes Irish national identity, in the days of asylum seeking and immigration, so that the somewhat clichéd opposition between native Irish and English settler, far from being obsolete, had attained a new importance if one was willing to move beyond the obvious and broaden the spectrum; following upon this insight, I would like to read the play precisely in that light. *The Home Place* is, arguably, Friel's most substantial play for a number of years and a return home to Ballybeg after his recent forays into foreign, mainly Russian/Chekhovian territory. It is worth examining the use the playwright makes of anthropology and anthropometry as a metaphor and to examine how *The Home Place* can be read in terms of contemporary concerns with globalisation, genetics and new markers of identity, as well as the more visible ongoing interrogation of Anglo-Irish relations in the wake of the Good Friday Agreement and the amendments to the Irish Constitution. The play is set in the fictional and emblematic village of Ballybeg in Donegal, the time is 1878, on the eve of the outbreak of the Land War, at a time when the fear of a new Famine caused agrarian violence to resurface on a larger scale; it is also the eve of the formation of a National Land League (August 1879) and its alliance with Parnellism and Fenianism: in short, another of those transitional phases in Irish history that Friel regularly chooses as a backdrop for his plays.

The Home Place shows signs of an indebtedness to the Beckett of *Waiting for Godot*[32] and to Chekhov's *The Cherry Orchard*[33] but it is also closely related to several other pieces in the Friel canon; it self-consciously both looks back to *Translations* (1980), set in the 1830s when Baile Beag became Ballybeg, and forwards to *Aristocrats* (1979) with its 1970s setting. It can also be linked to *Making History* (1988) by suggesting a parallel between the partly anglicised Hugh O'Neill and the partly hibernicised Christopher Gore, and the difficulties attendant upon this hybridised condition. Like *Aristocrats*, *The Home Place* is strongly indebted to Chekhov and deals with the family, love, loyalty, and the fate of a social group that has become isolated, through wealth and status when that assumed superiority (political, economic and social) disintegrates. In *Aristocrats*, the key metaphor was the writing of a family biography by an American professor eager to put in writing the truth about the O'Donnell family as representatives of the Catholic upper classes in Ireland. The playwright had stopped short of making his land-owning family Protestants and Anglo-Irish, a step he takes in *The Home Place*, for obvious historical reasons and the sake of verisimilitude. *The Home Place* is also, on another level, a companion piece to *Translations* as the arrival of the two Englishmen, Richard Gore and Perkins, mirrors the arrival of Yolland and Lancey with the British Army. But whereas the earlier play surveyed the situation from the vantage point of the hedge-school, *The Home Place* gives us direct access to the Big House in a radical shift of perspectives. The clearest instance of a deliberate crossover between the two plays is the character of Clement O'Donnell who shares with his ancestor, Hugh, the responsibility of a school, a marked pomposity and a fondness for drink.

The central metaphor for the England/Ireland relationship and ongoing misunderstanding in *The Home Place* is anthropometry, the measuring of man's physical characteristics. This 'scientific' approach will prove as ineffective, in fact as destructive, as the map-making in *Translations* or the academic thesis on upper-class Catholics propounded by Hoffnung in *Aristocrats*. The character of Dr Richard Gore seems partly inspired by the real-life Alfred Cort Haddon (1855–1940). As David McConnell explains in the programme notes, Haddon, a graduate from Cambridge University, was appointed Professor of Zoology at the Royal College of Sciences in Dublin in 1880: 'A follower of Galton he became interested in distinguishing races and sub-races by measuring the shapes of skulls (craniology), and in relating these physical qualities to behaviour'.[34] The Gallery Press edition of the playscript features both an extract from 'Studies in Irish Craniology: The Aran Islands, Co Galway', a lecture Haddon gave to the Royal Irish Academy in 1892, and a reproduction of a black and white photograph subtitled 'Anthropometry in Aran'. The photograph shows a person, presumably Haddon, sitting on a chair outside a whitewashed cottage, making notes while in front of him a man in a bowler hat measures the skull of a 'volunteer' as two locals, a man and an elderly woman look on. Unlike Haddon, the fictional Dr Gore has not taken up residence in Ireland but, like Haddon, he is a follower of Galton, an explorer and a cousin of Darwin's, who initiated and coined the term 'eugenics' in 1883. Galton's abiding interest was the hereditary transmission of intellectual capacity, which he studied through anthropometry. To quote McConnell,

Galton postulated that natural selection acted on groups within the human population, favouring the breeding and success of certain races, nationalities, social classes and even families. Such theories became the talk of the great houses in England and Ireland. Notions of genetic, racial superiority reached their awful nadir in Nazi Germany and still reappear from time to time. They were, and are, of course distasteful and in their extreme forms horrible, but they were also scientifically wrong.[35]

Friel stresses the links between anthropometry as practised by the likes of Richard Gore and colonialist, racialist mindsets which led to Victorian suspicion of the Irish, and which have found a new relevance today in the xenophobic discourse of far-right parties. As sociologist Steve Garner reminds us, race is about more than the colour of the skin: 'Races have without fail been constructed as a set of hierarchies, reflecting the dominant relations in the social and political domains',[36] a point exemplified by the racialisation of the Irish in Victorian Britain. Friel's Richard Gore is, according to the stage directions, 'a man of resolute habits and Victorian confidence'. Speaking about his earlier visits to the Aran Islands, he comments: 'An awesome place inhabited by a truly remarkable tribe. You must see them. Handsome, wild, courteous and vengeful (because Irish). Extraordinarily long faces and black eyes. And of course addicted to the most extravagant supersti- tions. A primeval people really'.[37] Though he believes his widowed cousin ought to remarry, he has qualms about the suitability – both social and racial one surmises – of a possible union between Christopher and his housekeeper. Yet, his repulsion at what he construes as an inter-racial union and miscegenation is tempered by his admiration for Margaret's physique: 'Pity to see Kent vanish – if he does marry her. Bigger pity though if she were to be diluted. Wouldn't it?' (p. 34). Bringing to mind the mass emigration that resulted from the Famine, he compares the photographs that he will take and give to each subject to glass beads, gratefully accepted by thrilled natives who send them off 'as special trophies to their relatives in America'. As both David and Christopher seem to find his comparison of the Irish to primitive African tribes crude, Richard goes on to elaborate the purpose of his research, claiming that 'a combination of physical features might constitute an ethnic code we can't yet decipher' and that 'an enormous vault of genetic information is only just beyond the reach of our understanding'. Cracking the code 'will reveal to you how a man thinks, what his character traits are, his loyalties, his vices, his entire intellectual architecture'. Fired up by his own dream of total control, he exclaims 'If we could break into that vault, David, we wouldn't control just an empire. We would rule the entire universe'. Here is the ultimate dream of power, and a reminder that eugenics could prove dramatically attractive to dictatorial, racist regimes like Hitler's Germany. It is an equally potent warning about contemporary abuses as the phrases 'genetic information' and 'crack the code' suggest a very modern understanding and environment, including cloning and work on the human genome, as well as the age-old racist fear of miscegenation and the 'contamination' of the white race.[38]

Richard Gore's 'measuring business' is brought to an abrupt halt by the intrusion of Con O'Donovan, a local youth with links to the agrarian/political activists, who demands that Gore and Perkins leave. Faced with a direct threat to his life and that of his guest, Christopher gives in. In this short but violent clash between two ideologies, British imperialism and Irish nationalism, Gore's claims are matched by O'Donovan's, and the latter's confidence that he is entitled to say who is Irish or merely entitled to live in Ireland and who must leave or die is as chilling as Gore's imperialist stance. Violent exclusion generates violent rejection. O'Donovan's are no empty threats since he is responsible for the assassination of another landlord, Lord Lifford, a neighbour of the Gores. Though born and brought up in Donegal, Christopher spent his childhood summers in Kent: 'And the truth is I hated being shipped over to the home place every damned summer', he recalls, before admitting 'And I love this place so much, Margaret. This is the only home I've known'. Now, looking at the estate, he becomes lost in the golden memories of the 'home place' in Kent before awakening to the reality of his fate: 'I'm an exile from both that memory and this fact now, amn't I?' (p. 63). Impetuously, he asks Margaret to marry him and make a new life with him somewhere else, 'anywhere where roles aren't imposed on us – where we'll be free of history and heritage and the awful burden of this [house]' (p. 65). Margaret gently refuses him and denies his definition of her as an exile too, though to a large extent she has also crossed borders and ended up in the no-man's land in between Planter and Gael, in between her social origins and the role of chatelaine Christopher would have her play. Margaret will marry neither Christopher nor David, choosing instead to leave the Lodge and return 'home', to her father, in what remains a highly ambiguous move open to different interpretations. As he angrily confronts his situation, any illusion of being 'at home', irrevocably shattered, Christopher expatiates on the plight of his class:

> The planter has to be resilient, hasn't he? No home, no country, a life of isolation and resentment. . . . And that resentment will stalk him – and never forget it – down through the next generation and the next and the next. The doomed nexus of those who believe themselves the possessors and those who believe they're dispossessed. (p. 68)

There lies the crux of a play that begs to be read in the context of early twenty-first-century, post-Good-Friday agreement, global, multicultural Ireland.

To conclude, the plays analysed here, in all their diversity, show characters striving to find a place they could call home in the full sense of the word since, as O'Toole reminds us, 'One of the things that culture reminds us of is that home is much more than a name we give to a dwelling place. It is also a whole set of connections and affections, the web of mutual recognition that we spin around ourselves and that gives us a place in the world'.[39] Whether globalisation, with its emphasis on the nomadic and its contempt for nostalgia and traditional forms of belonging, can do away with any sense of home or whether it merely translates older allegiances in new terms remains to be seen. In an Ireland that is, albeit reluctantly, coming to terms with its multicultural character, playwrights and artists generally have an important role to play as they explore subjectively, imaginatively the consciousness of others, and produce contact zones[40] where changing concepts of Irishness and otherness can co-exist and be articulated in meaningful ways.

Notes

1 I borrow the phrase 'new articulations of Irishness and otherness' from Ronit Lentin's article, 'Black Bodies and Headless Hookers: Alternative Global Narratives for 21st Century Ireland', *The Irish Review*, 33 (2005), p. 2.

2 Gerard Delanty, 'Irish Political Community in Transition', *The Irish Review*, 33 (2005), p. 16.

3 Fintan O'Toole, *The Ex-Isle of Erin* (Dublin: New Island Books, 1997), p. 173.

4 Figures given by both Terence Brown in *Ireland. A Social and Cultural History: 1922–2002* (London: Harper Perennial, 2004), and Ronit Lentin.

5 Seamus Heaney, *Finders Keepers. Selected Prose* (London: Faber, 2002), p. 47.

6 Quoted in Brown, p. 395.

7 See Michel Peillon, 'Agency, Flows and Post-Colonial Structure in Ireland', *The Irish Review*, 30 (2003): 'The connections between an Irish and a global culture cannot be subsumed under a structural model, which only accounts for the ability of "colonial centres" to constrain and shape Irish culture. It occludes the other side of the story: that Irish culture has contributed, and not only in a subordinate way, to the culture of the "centre", that many cultural forms in Ireland are thriving and occupying the centre. This argument relates to another weakness of the post-colonial

approach: it does not allow for the possibility of cultural agency, other than unspecified resistance' (pp. 78–9).

8   Jason King 'Interculturalism and Irish Theatre: The Portrayal of Immigrants on the Irish Stage', *The Irish Review*, 33 (2005), p. 25. King's article examines Donal O'Kelly's *Farawayan* (1998), Roddy Doyle's adaptation of *Guess Who's Coming for the Dinner* (2002), Maeve Ingolsby's *Mixing in on the Mountain* (2003), Paul Mercier's *Native City* (1998), Joe O'Byrne's *It Come Up Sun* (2000), Charlie O'Neill's *Hurl* (2003), and the work of African Voices in Ireland theatre company (2003).

9   Declan Kiberd, 'Dancing at Lughnasa', *The Irish Review*, 27 (summer 2001), p. 30.

10 Father Jack's improprer conduct – there is a hint he may have entertained a close relationship with Okawa, his houseboy and mentor – may echo the various scandals that affected the Irish Catholic Church in the 1990s and contributed to the Church's loss of moral authority.

11 Brian Friel, *Dancing at Lughnasa* (London: Faber and Faber, 1990), p. 2.

12 For an interesting analysis of the play, see also Paul Murphy, 'Inside the Immigrant Mind: Nostalgic Versus Nomadic Subjectivities in Late Twentieth-Century Drama', in *Performing Ireland*, special issue of *Australasian Drama Studies*, 43 (October 2003), pp. 128–47.

13 Donal O'Kelly, *Asylum!Asylum!* in *New Plays from the Abbey Theatre*, ed. Christopher Fitz-Simon and Sanford Sternlicht (New York: Syracuse University Press, 1996), p. 145.

14 Brown, p. 386.

15 Quoted in Victor Merriman, 'Songs of Possible Worlds: Nation, Representation and Citizenship in the Work of Calypso Productions', in *Theatre Stuff*, ed. Eamonn Jordan (Dublin: Carysfort Press, 2000), p. 280.

16 Victor Merriman 'Cartographic Connections: Problems of Representation in Calypso Theatre Company's The Business of Blood', *The Irish Review*, 22 (summer 1998), p. 29.

17 Fintan O'Toole, review for the *Irish Times*, 9 August 1994, reprinted in *Critical Moments*, ed. Julia Furray and Redmond O'Hanlon (Dublin: Carysfort Press, 2003), pp. 126–8.

18 Merriman in Jordan, p. 290.

19 O'Kelly, 'Strangers in a Strange Land', *Irish Theatre Magazine*, 1: 1 (autumn 1998), p. 12.

20 David Storey, quoted in Merriman, 'Songs of Possible Worlds', p. 288.

21 See Merriman in Jordan.

22 Elizabeth Kuti, *Treehouses* (London: Methuen, 2000).

23 Anna McMullan, 'Unhomely Stages: Women Taking (a) Place in Irish Theatre', in *Druids, Dudes and Beauty Queens*, ed. Dermot Bolger (Dublin: New Island, 2001), p. 88.

24 Kuti, *Treehouses*, p. 49.

25 McMullan, p. 90.

26 King, p. 14.
27 *Départ et Arrivée* (Paris: L'Harmattan, 2004); performed in November 2004 in Art Studio Théâtre, Paris.
28 In many ways, Maureen's story ends where Felicia's begins in William Trevor's 1994 novel, *Felicia's Journey* (Harmondsworth: Penguin, 1995).
29 At a conference held in Caen (France) on 'Theatrical Adaptation in Ireland since 1970', in September 2007. See also Lara Marlowe, 'Lost in translation', *The Irish Times*, 17 November 2004, p. 14. I am very grateful to Emile-Jean Dumay for giving me access to material relating to *Depart/Arrivée* and to the unpublished script in English.
30 Lentin, pp. 4–5.
31 Bolger himself emigrated to Germany as a young man and worked in a factory, an experience that influenced the writing of his first successful stage play, *The Lament for Arthur Cleary*.
32 See in particular the relationship between Dr Richard Gore and his assistant, the bowler-hatted Perkins, which recalls on a lighter mode that between Pozzo and Lucky. Lucky's barely comprehensible 'speech' on science and metaphysics (among other things) includes a reference to the 'unfinished labours of Testew and Cunard crowned by the Acacacacademy of Anthropopopometry of Essy-in-Possy' and mentions 'the skull in Connemara', already taken up by McDonagh of course in his own Leenane Trilogy, and here, no doubt, one of those skulls Richard Gore is so eager to measure on the Aran Islands.
33 The set of *The Home Place* features 'a crescent of trees' whose symbolic value becomes the subject of the somewhat belaboured final scene which concentrates on the 'doomed trees' marked out for destruction.
34 Programme notes to *The Home Place*.
35 Ibid.
36 Steve Garner, 'Guests of the Nation', *The Irish Review*, 33 (2005), p. 78.
37 Brian Friel, *The Home Place* (Loughcrew: Gallery Press, 2005), p. 31. All further references to the play will be to this edition and will be given in the text.
38 In 'The Unbidden Ireland: Materialism, Knowledge and Interculturality', *The Irish Review*, 31 (2004), pp. 3–10, Michael Cronin advances the hypothesis that current scientific evolutions (robotics, genetic engineering) should prompt discussions about the 'posthuman' rather than post-nationalism or post-colonialism.
39 O'Toole, *The Ex-Isle of Erin*, p. 136.
40 Mary Louise Pratt, *Imperial Eyes: Travel Writing and Transculturation* (London: Routledge, 1992).

Part III

Poetry

7

Scattered and diverse:
Irish poetry since 1990

Jerzy Jarniewicz and John McDonagh

I

In the introduction to *The Penguin Book of Contemporary Irish Poetry*, first published in 1990, editors Peter Fallon and Derek Mahon note that Irish poetry 'speaks for itself in one or another of the many voices which have evolved over the years'[1] and this crucial acknowledgement in an important and popular anthology points clearly to the disparate, polyvocal and chimerical nature of a good deal of contemporary Irish poetry up to 1990 and beyond. Ranging from Cathal O'Searchaigh's homoerotic odes to his gay lover to Paul Durcan's laments over the crass materialism of contemporary Ireland, Irish poetry since 1990 has been clearly marked by the notable absence of a dominant voice and an eclectic, surprising and challenging *mélange* of subject matter. Light has been shone on almost every manifestation of contemporary Irish life by poets displaying, in Louis De Paor's wonderful phrase, an 'agitated intelligence'[2] in the wake of widespread social and economic changes. What can be said with some certainty is that contemporary poetry in the Republic is marked by a broad range of confident voices articulating a tentative recognition of the complex nature of major shifts in the traditional markers of Irish identity. In the North, a changing social and political landscape is equally reflected in the discontinuous narrative of the major poetic voices, including Ciaran Carson, Paul Muldoon and Medbh McGuckian, an uncertainty captured by Carson in 'Belfast Confetti' when his self-image reflects a national questioning: 'My name? Where am I coming from? Where am I going? A / fusillade of question marks'.[3]

In the Republic, the economic boom of the 1990s continues unabated in the 2000s, heralding unparalleled prosperity, increased urbanisation and large-scale immigration, factors which place pressure on accepted models of a collective national perspective. Ironically, the very lack of a predominant school or voice places greater pressure on critical reflections of the nature of contemporary Irish poetry in that the diffracted nature of poetic expression makes it resistant to categorisation. What can be said is that there are few, if any, areas of contemporary experience that lie beyond the scope of the poetic. This confidence in the future, and a tacit recognition of the resonance of the past, is summed up by Micheal O'Siadhail, one of the most accomplished and accessible poets to emerge in recent times:

> Given riffs and breaks of our own,
> Given a globe of boundless jazz,
> Yet still a remembered undertone,
>
> A quivering earthy line of soul
> Crying in all diminished chords.
> Our globe still trembles on its pole.[4]

O'Siadhail's work illustrates the nature of contemporary Irish poetry, particulary south of the border. Collections such as *Hail Madam Jazz* (1992), *A Fragile City* (1995) *and Love Life* (2005) showcase a poet at home in his own fragile sense of humanity, sensitively aware of the everyday concerns that consume so much time, and refreshingly free from any sense of an over-arching theme or agenda. His poetry is that of almost instant recognition, often unadorned, eschewing complex imagery yet crafted with a sharp eye on the unity of form and subject. Contemporary life in Ireland is shown to be something that cannot be grasped in its totality, but this frenzied cultural climate demands direct intellectual and emotional engagement.

During a visit to Poland, made at the start of the new millennium, Seamus Heaney gave an interview in which he defined the change that occurred in his understanding of the role of the poet and the practice of poetry:

> I guess my own situation now is more scattered or diverse. I said to you the other night that if I were to choose a pseudonym now I would chose the name *Sartor*, and I do think more and more of the great grandfather tailor. The poems begin with digging with the spade, digging into the centre, but I think now I would use the image of the needle, perhaps, unpicking the stitches, and restitching it into a different shape and moving around like a tailor, the tailor moving around with the needle, rather than the guy with the spade. That's just the symptom of some kind of change, loosening of the roots.[5]

Heaney alludes here to his early poem 'Digging'. Published at the outset of his poetic career, on the opening page of his first collection, and usually read by the poet at the beginning of his readings, even now, four decades after it was composed, this poem can be taken to stand for the poet's manifesto. The central metaphor of the title suggests the process of going deep, layer after layer, into the rich depth of the soil, to the hidden foundation which serves as the postulated, hypothetical starting point for the poet's work. But going *down* to the deep roots soon acquires a different meaning, that of going *back* in time, of digging into history, and more specifically into the poet's private and collective past. The process of writing poetry, grounded in the vertical geological/historical toil, is seen as a natural continuation of the useful work of the poet's fathers and grandfathers.

This significant change of metaphor from digger to tailor that Heaney talks about in this interview is resonant in a number of ways. Although the poet remains still with the heritage left to him by his *male* ancestors, the stitching which replaces digging is much less a male profession, and indeed might more readily be associated with the feminine. Whereas digging suggests consistent movement in only one, vertical, direction, with each generation contributing to the effect achieved by their predecessors, stitching may turn against itself and wander around: it is a work of doing, as well as of undoing. Significantly, Heaney's first image in the passage quoted above is that of 'unpicking the stitches', which points to the negative, critical or deconstructive aspect of the poet's work. It is only later, when the stitches have been unpicked, that the tailor can re-stitch them, thus linking in one image the dual act of negating and affirming, questioning and reassessing, dismantling and creating. The poet, as *sartor*, the tailor, tests the creative possibilities of various designs and arrangements, and in this way acknowledges the tentative character of each composition and each narrative his work may produce.

Another crucial difference that emerges in this shift of metaphor, from digging to stitching, is that in the tailor's work we no longer deal with an activity of going down for what is hidden, yet fundamental. The tailor works with surfaces, with flat materials which can be organised and composed in a variety of shapes and in numerous arrangements, which shows the tailor's ability to stitch most heterogeneous elements together. If flatness is characteristic of maps, Heaney's transition can be interpreted as the replacement of archaeology by cartography, history (genealogy) by geography, hence the search for the centre which supposedly lies at the bottom, at the roots of things, by a renewed acceptance of the simultaneity and multiplicity of the phenomenal world. The authoritative, essentialist concept of depth is exchanged for the fascination with the incessant processes of metamorphoses and differentiation.

It is significant that the two words uttered at the beginning of the quotation, 'scattered' and 'diverse', can serve as key terms in the characterisation of the paradigmatic shift that Heaney talks about and which is not untypical of contemporary Irish poetry more generally. The stitching metaphor opens the world of poetry to the realm of the flux, the many, and the heterogeneous. It cannot pass unnoticed that Heaney's description of his work – and, by extension, of poetry – fits perfectly well in any discussion of contemporary writing. The poet's words illuminate changes that have occurred not only in his own work, but also in a substantial amount of Irish poetry written at the end of the century. In historical terms, the changes seem to signify the shift away from various forms of modernist legacy towards a postmodern aesthetics and sensibility. In her study of A.R. Ammons's poetics, Diana von Finck claims that the American poet is representative of a development 'that has taken place in breaking away from a common impulse to find an encompassing order of reality – as it is put forth for instance in the poetics of W.C. Williams, Wallace Stevens and T.S. Eliot – to a general preoccupation and enforced interest in exploring the possibilities of disorder'.[6] By disorder she understands 'extremely complex information rather than an absence of order'.[7] Whether or not all three modernists mentioned here were equally interested in searching for order is a debatable issue. Nevertheless, the general reorientation from the one to the many, from the fixed to the ephemeral, from the patriarchal to the feminine, can be seen as characterising contemporary poetry, including poetry written in Ireland.

It is not by chance that one of the Irish poets whose debut collection appeared in the last decade of the century, Paula Meehan, also opens her work with an act of establishing her private genealogy and invoking the idea of the inherited design in the poem called 'The Pattern'. Yet, in *her* backward glance, Meehan looks to her mother rather than, as Heaney did, to a father figure, and introduces the image of knitting or embroidering – significantly closer to stitching than digging. The much more problematic and ambiguous relationship with the mother is described in terms that suggest both her acknowledgement of the parent's formative presence in her life and its ultimate, unconditional rejection. Meehan simultaneously invokes the pattern in which her mother tried to include or confine her, and revolts against it, exposing it as an emblem of violence, a repressive power that perpetuates historically motivated submission and self-denial. The poem ends with mother's words addressed to her daughter: 'One of these days I must / teach you to follow a pattern', but this seemingly innocent, innocuous statement, referring literally to the art of knitting, belongs to a scene in which the daughter has to assist her mother in a submissive position, suggestive of enslavement, with wool around her hands resembling handcuffs:

Sometimes I'd have to kneel
an hour before her by the fire,
a skein around my outstretched hands,
while she rolled wool into balls.[8]

Though it would be inaccurate to see Meehan's 'The Pattern' simply as a direct polemical response to Heaney's 'Digging', its imagery invites comparison between the two poems, underlining their analogies and differences, ones which disclose many of the changes in Irish poetry in recent decades. The lines 'Her steel needles sparked and clacked, / the only other sound a settling coal / or her sporadic mutter / at a hard part in the pattern' invoke Heaney's description of his father's and grandfather's work similarly rich in visual, aural and tactile imagery. And yet whereas Heaney's poem ends with a declaration of the speaker's readiness to follow 'men like them' by digging with a pen, in Meehan's poem the daughter, uncomfortably wearing a dress made by her mother, resolves to watch 'the Liffey, for hours pulsing to the sea / and the coming and going of ships, / certain that one day it would carry me / to Zanzibar, Bombay, the Land of the Ethiops'.[9] One could risk elaborating on and extending Meehan's image, and claim that the Liffey indeed carried many poets of her generation, as well as her younger colleagues, if not to Zanzibar, then to Paris, Princeton, Prague and Warsaw, where – scattered and diverse – they would feel at ease to stitch and unstitch the various patterns they had inherited, and so 'by transforming that past / change the future of it'.[10]

II

The election of Mary Robinson to the office of President in 1990 is an event that has, in the 20–20 vision of hindsight, been heralded as a seismic shift not only in the political outlook of the Republic but in the self-perception of an entire generation. Robinson defeated Brian Lenihan, the Fianna Fáil candidate who was a shoo-in for the position at the start of the campaign, after a series of blunders and lies that allowed a rank outsider to enter Aras an Uachtaran as the first woman President. Paul Durcan, arguably the emblematic southern Irish poet of the 1990s, published *Greetings to Our Friends in Brazil* in 1999, a collection that encapsulates many of the changes represented by Robinson in her tenure as Head of State. For Durcan, Robinson's Presidency was an unambiguous symbol of the collective desire for change, a tangible instance of a country prepared to accept voices from the margins and heralding a more pluralistic outlook on a variety of social, cultural and political fronts. In a poem entitled 'The First and Last Commandment of the Commander-in-Chief', Durcan notes her election as a crucial displacement of the predominant values that held sway in the south since the foundation of the state:

> By 1990 in Ireland we'd been adolescents for seventy years
> Obsessed with the Virgin, automobiles, alcohol, Playboy, Unity.
>   The Commander-in-Chief issued her first and only
> Commandment:
>   First and last you must learn to love your different self.[11]

While Durcan can be accused of over-stating the optimistic response to Robinson's election, it serves as a useful marker for the emergence of a polyphony of voices on the poetic scene in the Republic. Durcan's targets frequently include the Catholic Church along with what he perceived to be the creeping philistinism of Irish society. A critic can easily trace the contours of Ireland's economic, social, cultural and religious development in Durcan's satirical and surreal verse. What also marks him out for special attention is the fact that he is one of the few southern poets to make Northern Ireland a significant poetic concern, and his collections from the 1980s and 1990s frequently contain poems that confront head-on the tragic human consequence of paramilitary violence on both sides of the sectarian divide. His 1998 poem, simply entitled 'Omagh', is a haunting catalogue of the names of the twenty-nine victims of the Real IRA bomb that exploded there on 15 August 1998. It later emerged that one of the victims, Avril Monaghan, was heavily pregnant with twins which, by Durcan's calculation, brings the death toll to thirty-one. The implied irony of the death of two unborn children by those claiming to uphold the ideals of a republic that constitutionally acknowledges the right to life of the unborn gives this poem its particular power.

Another important, often overlooked poet producing major work during this period is Brendan Kennelly, whose great epics *The Book of Judas* (1991) and *Poetry My Arse* (1995) addressed in a most mischievous way the twin pillars of history and religion in the construction of Irish national identity. His development as a poet could be seen as indicative of the shifting paradigmatic boundaries of that decade. If Seamus Heaney can confidently describe his poetic mission as 'digging', then Kennelly's Judas could be accused of bobbing along upon the backwash created by the 'relentless, pitiless, anecdotalism of Irish life',[12] sure only that he is a cipher of often vicious vicarious expression. The implied confidence that Heaney enjoyed in the mid-1960s with his 'snug' pen contrasts sharply with Judas' rhetorical question in the very first poem of the collection entitled *Lips*, in which he mulls over how often he had been betrayed by his words: 'They slave for me, ask nothing in return. / The harder they work the more I wonder / If I believe them.[13] Kennelly sustains his exploration of the myriad manifestations of betrayal over 584 poems, the disjointed chronology unwittingly held together by the isolated, irredeemable figure of Judas, an outsider who embraces and absorbs both the forces that exclude and the consequences of that exclusion. He emerges from Kennelly's text as a complex exemplar of contemporary Ireland, dazed and confused by the ever-shifting markers of his diffracted identity. In many respects it would be more accurate to refer to what Kennelly identifies in the introduction as the 'Judasvoice' (p. 11), an often miasmatic articulator of vituperative anger, misogyny, greed, tenderness and denial. As well as his varied contemporary manifestations, Judas also appears in his historical guise, albeit pursued by – amongst others – film crews, journalists and talk-show hosts. It is in the poems in which Jesus and Judas engage in an often surreal dialogue that the collection achieves its sharpest focus and historical critique. Iconic historical moments are cleverly contemporised by the abrupt appearance of recognisable social stereotypes, characters whose narrative function is to bring the historical into sharp contemporary relief. The absurdity of the moment, both the historical and the contemporary, is highlighted by their strange parallel expression, the past and the present finding mutually informing moments of both intense illumination and simultaneous farce. One such moment arrives at a defining originary moment in Christianity when Jesus is stretched on the cross waiting to be nailed. However, no one can be found to 'finish the job' (p. 88), despite advertisements in the national newspapers and 'on the telly'. Finally, however, the ubiquitous Irish labourer appears on the scene, ready and willing to complete any job if the price is right. Flanagan nails Jesus to the cross with competent ease, pockets his money and vanishes, 'eschewing all displays of bravado or glamour', a professional job well done. The desacralising of Jesus's final moments purports the normality of the crucifixion at the time, leading us to infer that its sacred status is one that has accreted over the centuries. Flanagan epitomises the concept that individuals have no control over what history will do to them and actions carried out for purely pragmatic reasons will be wholly reinterpreted by succeeding generations. Equally, the time vortex through which the characters in the poem travel dislocates both the actuality of the historical event, inasmuch as it can have actuality, and the contemporary re-reading of that event.

Flanagan's appearance as a recognisable contemporary jobber hints at contemporary moral values driven by a desire for profit at the expense of the moral outcome of that action. Time is distended in the poem, the human tragedy of Jesus' final humiliation overshadowed by a cute Irish 'apparition' who elides the significance of the moment with his casual profiteering, a chronological conflation that Lucy Collins adroitly identifies in the poetry of Eiléan Ní Chuilleanáin. Kennelly's epic sequence is a powerful indicator of the changes afoot in 1990s Ireland, where many of the social and cultural certainties were crumbling under the weight of their internal contradictions.

III

One of the most interesting manifestations of the reconfigurations that have taken place in contemporary Irish poetry is the special place occupied by translation. Just as the art of stitching works by juxtaposition and extension, rather than by removing the layers and getting down to the centre, so does translation, extending horizontally, open poetry to the juxtapositioning of diverse voices, forms and viewpoints. As Bernard O'Donoghue has demonstrated, translation, particularly from Irish into English, has always been an invigorating factor in the history of Irish poetry, to the extent that 'what has come to be called the *voice of Irish poetry in English* was partly developed by the translators'.[14] O'Donoghue has in mind specifically the work of the two Celtic revivalists Douglas Hyde and Augusta Gregory, and consequently sees translations as one of the three main categories of Irish poetry, apart from 'poems in Irish' and 'poems in English'. These translations 'brought into English poetry formal qualities that are at one entirely foreign to it and totally successful within it, and which therefore remained a permanent option within English'.[15]

Yet although translations from Irish to English played a very special role in the history of Irish verse, marking English poetry with characteristically Irish prosodic qualities, translations from other languages also exerted and are still exerting strong influence. The growing popularity of central and eastern European poets that can be observed since the late 1960s were in part sparked by the famous Penguin Modern European Poets series, which introduced into the English language the works of such authors as Zbigniew Herbert from Poland, Miroslav Holub from Czechoslovakia, Janosz Pilinszky from Hungary or Vasko Popa from Serbia. The influence these poets exerted was political, aesthetic and ethical. Their voices were enabling because they embodied an art that faced up to fundamental political and moral questions. For poets from Britain and Ireland these writers from the other Europe became exemplary figures because of their readiness to confront history in its barest, ugliest forms, and to accept the role of witness. In Ireland the most evident *hommage* to the significance of translation for native poetic traditions can be found in Heaney's essay 'The Impact of Translation' (1988), where the poet famously asked: 'Might we not nowadays affirm that the shortest way to Whitby, the monastery where Caedmon sang the first Anglo-Saxon verse, is via Warsaw and Prague?'[16] More a declaration than a question, Heaney's words refer to English poetry, but can well be applied to poetry written in Ireland, if the emphasis is put specifically on translation – the way to Whitby via Warsaw is the way of translation as opposed to the Tara via Holyhead route, which implies leaving the country and looking at it from a distance.[17] If Heaney's essay is a theoretical elaboration of the theme, then his collection *The Haw Lantern* (1987), influenced by Eastern European parabolic tradition, provides evidence of translation affecting the very practice of writing.

Heaney, however, is by no means the only Irish poet open to the possibilities offered by translations from Polish, Czech or Romanian poetry. Just before the period focused on this book, a collection of poems was published providing ample evidence that Irish poets acknowledged the importance of translations from Eastern European poetry. Marin Sorescu's *The Biggest Egg in the World* (1987) was, as the blurb revealed, 'hatched in Belfast' and includes English versions by, among others, Heaney, Michael Longley and Paul Muldoon, all introduced by Edna Longley. These various literary enterprises, which rediscover the importance of translation for the practice of poetry towards the end of the 1980s, determined the way in which Irish poetry developed in subsequent decades. Since 1990 Heaney has continued his involvement in Eastern European poetry, producing with Stanisław Barańczak a joint translation of *Laments* (1995) by the sixteenth-century Polish poet Jan Kochanowski, and conducting a poetic dialogue with Czesław Miłosz, and Zbigniew Herbert, two of Poland's foremost poets.

Though, arguably, interest in Eastern European writing was partly the side effect of the Cold War and so might well have waned with the fall of the Iron Curtain, the period covered by the present volume has in fact been marked by the continuation and intensification of cross-cultural and cross-linguistic links. In the light of this process, possibly the most important single translation was Heaney's rendering of *Beowulf* in 1999, which became one of the key texts in contemporary Irish poetry of the last decade. If, as O'Donoghue points out,[18] English renderings of Irish verse made a permanent mark on English, translations meant a gradual emancipation of Irish English and its elevation from the status of a dialect to that of a legitimate, sovereign language, one that can engage itself directly as an autonomous source and resource in a reciprocal relationship with British English and its literary tradition. Heaney attempted a reversed transition when he took an Old English epic and rendered it not into modern standard or 'established' English, but quite consciously and systematically into Irish-English, the poet's original vernacular. The general orientation of his project becomes clear with the very first word of the poem, 'So!', as the Hiberno-English equivalent of 'Hwat!', evoking as it does the way in which the Irish storytellers start their narratives. This modelling of the language of his translation into the language spoken by his Northern Irish relatives is, as Heaney admits, 'one way for an Irish poet to come to terms with that complex history of conquest and colony, absorption and resistance, integrity and antagonism, a history that has to be cleverly acknowledged by all concerned in order to render it ever more 'willable forward / again and again and again'.[19]

Many other Irish poets were equally quick to explore imaginatively the aesthetic, cultural and political implications of the art of translation. Among the books shortlisted for the 2005 T.S. Eliot Poetry Prize was Tom Paulin's *The Road to Inver*. This consisted of 'translations, versions, imitations' of works by an astonishing variety of authors, including Sophocles, Horace, Goethe, Pushkin, Brecht, Ponge and Pessoa. Ciaran Carson, after publishing *The Alexandrine Plan* (1998) – a bilingual collection of his versions of sonnets by Baudelaire, Rimbaud and Mallarmé – set on a much more daring task of adapting into Irish-English Dante's *Inferno* (2002). In *Adaptations* (2006) Derek Mahon collected his free translations from French, German, Italian, Greek and other languages.

Younger-generation Irish poets have also been drawn to translation, acknowledging the impact the translated author has on their own work. One of the most recent examples is Justin Quinn's English versions of poems by the Czech poet Petr Borkovec. A separate category includes translations from Irish. In 1993 Heaney produced an abridged English version of Brian Merriman's eighteenth-century Gaelic poem *The Midnight Verdict*, adding in a later edition in 2001 two of his translations from Ovid's *Metamorphoses*. Merriman's poem has been translated also by Ciaran Carson and published as *The Midnight Court* (2005). Paul Muldoon's translations of Nuala Ní Dhomhnaill's Irish-language poems (*The Astrakhan Cloak*, 1992) have been rightly praised, significantly helping to establish Ní Dhomhnaill as one of the major voices in Irish poetry to emerge since the mid-1980s.

While translation studies shed revealing and challenging light on the nature of the development of contemporary Irish poetry, an overview of this progression cannot ignore the vitality and range of poetry written in the Irish language. Throughout the 1990s, many Irish-language poets, including Michael Hartnett (1941–99), Michael Davitt (1950–2005), Nuala Ní Dhomnaill (b.1952), Cathal Ó Searchaigh (b.1956) and Gearóid MacLochlainn (b.1966) have written poetry in Irish that is every bit as socially and culturally challenging as its English-language counterparts. The principal difficulty facing Irish-language poetry is obviously the thorny issue of translation into English, and many prominent contemporary poets have used the kind offices of fellow poets to bring their Irish language poetry to an English-speaking audience. Indeed, that audience is principally an Irish one in that the readership for Irish language poetry is very small. A classic example of this linguistic exchange can be found in the work of Michael Hartnett, who famously turned his back on English in 1974 only to return triumphantly a decade later with his *Inchicore Haiku*, one of which beautifully summed-up his linguistic dilemma: 'My English dam bursts / And out strolls all my bastards / Irish shakes its head.'[20]

While most Irish-language poets eventually succumb to the irresistible attraction of translation, some notably resist, the most prominent of these being Biddy Jenkinson, whose resistance to translation has become something of a *cause célèbre* in Irish-language circles. Of the poets who have been translated, Ó Searchaigh remains the most subversive. The 1996 publication of *Na Buachaillí Bána* deals unambiguously with homosexual love. The fact that the poems are often set against the backdrop of a remote part of rural Ireland only serves to heighten the feeling that his poetry is attempting to redefine, or at least reshape, the traditional landscapes of Irish poetry. In a poem entitled 'Caoineadh (i gcuimhne mo mháthar)', translated by Seamus Heaney as 'Lament (in memory of my Mother)', Ó Searchaigh expresses a profound regret over the inevitable decline of Irish, while English is portrayed as a language picking the bones of its Celtic counterpart:

> To-day it's my language that's in its throes,
> The poets' passion, my mothers' fathers'
> Mothers' language, abandoned and trapped
> On a fatal ledge that we won't attempt.
> She's in agony, I can hear her heave
> And gasp and struggle as they arrive,
> The beaked and ravenous scavengers
> Who are never far. Oh if only anger
> Came howling wild out of her grief,

> If only she'd bare the teeth of her love
> And rout the pack. But she's giving in,
> She's quivering badly, my mother's gone
> And promises now won't ease the pain.[21]

Many of Ó Searchaigh's translated poems are also a clear indicator of the broadening perspective of contemporary Irish poetry. His homoerotic poems celebrating sexual union are unambiguously explicit, allowing 'the love that dare not speak its name' a clear expression in the context of a society far more at ease with competing models of sexual orientation, recognised by the decriminalisation of homosexuality in the Republic in the early 1990s. This legal recognition of homosexual partnerships only came about after a tortured legal wrangle in the European Court of Human Rights. Ó Searchaigh's erotic celebration is a marker of the degree to which contemporary Ireland can no longer point to the axis of heterosexual/Catholic/married as a secure repository of an imagined national identity. The fact that these poems originally appear in Irish further enhances the perception of a shifting linguistic paradigm where the national language becomes the carrier of cultural change rather than a perceived repository of traditional values.

IV

If so much space above has been devoted to the presence of translation in contemporary Irish poetry, it is because it seems, along with the emergence of women poets, the most important development in the most recent Irish verse. The special role of translation reflects the changing attitudes to language and poetic diction, as well as to issues of cultural identity, authorship and originality. Irish poetry since 1990 has become 'more outward-looking and open to developments going on elsewhere',[22] more truly multilingual. For example, *The New Irish Poets* anthology by Selima Guinness includes poems with quotations in French, German and Polish.[23] The term 'multilingual' is used here not only because so many Irish poets have been practising as translators of foreign verse, but also because of the concomitant diversification of the languages of contemporary Irish poetry. Nowhere is this tendency better demonstrated than in the work of Ciaran Carson.

Perhaps one of the other most significant features of the development of contemporary Irish poetry since 1990 has been the emergence of a variety of women poets ready and willing to challenge the old orthodoxies, although it is as difficult to identify a predominant school amongst contemporary woman poets as it is amongst their male counterparts. The more established figures of Eavan Boland, Nuala Ní Dhomnaill,

Medbh McGuckian and Eiléan Ní Chuilleanáin have been joined by a wave of interesting poets with a broad range of interests, including Sinéad Morrissey, Vona Groarke, Paula Meehan, Kerry Hardie and Colette Bryce. In her chapter in this volume, Lucy Collins perceptively traces the significance of the home in the poetry of Ní Chuilleanáin and Groarke. She highlights the refreshing instability of contemporary perceptions of personal and national identity as she points to the simultaneity of past and present in the work of both poets. Collins argues that they inscribe the home as a place of creative inhabiting, at once secure and unstable, ripe for annotation. In his chapter, Michael Parker sets his sights on the work of two other poets born in the 1970s as exemplars of a new poetic hermeneutics. His study of the poetry of Sinéad Morrissey and Nick Laird points to a recurring theme of the 1990s, namely a pervading and palpable sense of local and personal displacement, and Parker particularly identifies what he refers to as a 'sense of restless, continuing motion' in Morrissey's and Laird's work, again a characteristic that could easily be applied to their southern counterparts.

Equally the poetry of Rita Ann Higgins might have been cited as particularly resonant of the brasher manifestation of contemporary Ireland. Her work is as evocative and resonant of contemporary life in the Republic as McGuckian's poetry is of the North. Higgins's Ireland is a place of social and cultural disillusionment, populated by a tranche of individuals who have, unwittingly and otherwise, missed the bus of the economic boom. Her satirical and lacerating critiques of the pretensions of 'the chattering classes' are laced with a biting humour. Her harassed characters act as a wonderful counterbalance to a culture that prides itself on an unwavering confidence. Higgins unflinchingly deals with the darker side of life in the Republic, ranging from the epidemic of suicide to the unrelenting death tolls in road accidents. Her poetry is a barometer of the many casualties of Ireland's social and cultural development. Indeed, the witty, surreal cover to her 2001 collection, *An Awful Racket*, features the late Pope John Paul II preaching to a flock of penguins on an iceberg in the Arctic, an image indicative of the drift away from clerical authority that is so characteristic of 1990s Ireland.

V

One of the most prolific and certainly the most protean of contemporary Irish poets is Ciaran Carson, whose reputation continued to grow in the last years of the old and early years of the new century. Building on the phenomenal success of *The Irish for No* (1987) and *Belfast*

Confetti (1989), Carson took diverse routes and detours, developing the possibilities that the new poetics offered him. He approached the nearly Ashberyean non-referentiality and free play of signifiers in *First Language* (1993) and *Opera Et Cetera* (1996), experimented with the form of a sonnet in *The Twelfth of Never* (1999), changed his poetic alliances – from C.K. Williams to W.C. Williams – in *Breaking News* (2003), and ventured very successfully into the realm of prose with a sequence of books.[24]

Of special significance for his work, as well as for the discussion of the language of poetry, is his T.S. Eliot Prize-winning collection, *First Language*. The book's very title invites polemical debate.[25] Does it mean one's mother tongue, the language with which, or into which, one is born and which one learns first? Or does it refer to the myth of the Tower of Babel and stand for the first language ever, the one people spoke before they tried to erect the Tower, before their language was confounded? The first language in that second, mythological sense is the *Ursprache*, the root of all other tongues. To alert his readers to its central significance, Carson decided to reproduce on the cover of the book a painting of the Tower of Babel. Symptomatically, as one can discover from the reproduction of the painting, the work is neither Irish nor English, but Polish. The Tower of Babel figures in *First Language* in a Polish phrase as 'Wieża Babel'; the poet bought the painting from a street artist whom he came across during a visit to Warsaw. The polylingual character of the whole collection, both in its subject matter and in its very material, is introduced in the opening poem written in Gaelic, yet with a French title 'La Je-Ne-Sais-Quois' (sic). In 1998, in a conversation with Jerzy Jarniewicz, Carson spoke about his linguistic background, saying that he *thinks* Irish was his first language. He talked about his parents who had accepted Irish as their tongue for ideological reasons, as a sign of their Irishness and Catholicism. Hence, their family language was not their first language, but an adopted one. Carson, having been born in a family where Irish was spoken, treated it as his first language, although it was the language in which he could not communicate in the street: 'I realise everyone spoke English'.[26] And if today Irish can be heard in Belfast it is English Irish, spoken again for ideological reasons, the language infused with English structures and rhythms. 'Is it Irish?' Carson asks, and evades the question, as he has to.

Language is, after all, never pure, but a protean phenomenon, or a process. George Steiner claimed that 'language is the most salient model of Heraclitean flux. It alters at every moment in perceived time'.[27] Interpreted in the context of such views, Carson's use of foreign tongues in his poetry raises the question of the possibility of a pure language, pure Irish, pure English, and demonstrates that no such language is possible. This inherent impurity of language – something that many Irish poets examine today – allows for the noise, the verbal commotion, the sprawl of linguistic items which even native speakers of a given language find incomprehensible: language is set loose, liberates itself, as abstract art, from the subjection to meaning and starts acting with its phonic quality and distant, often non-verbal, associations.

It can be argued that Carson's examinations of the possibility of a first language brought him to inspect not only his first tongue, i.e. Gaelic, but, perhaps more interestingly, the foreignness of English. The foreignness that Carson tries to uncover in *First Language* makes English strange to all those who claim it is their mother tongue:

> English not being yet a language, I wrapped my lubber-lips around my thumb;
> Brain-deaf as an embryo, I was snuggled in my comfort-blanket dumb.
>
> Growling figures campaniled above me, and twanged their carillons of bronze
> Sienna consonants embedded with the vowels alexandrite, emerald and topaz.
>
> The topos of their discourse seemed to do with me and convoluted genealogy;
> Wordy whorls and braids and skeins and spiral helices, unskeletoned from laminate geology.[28]

Ostensibly, the poem recalls the poet's acquisition of English as his second tongue, starting from the stage when it was not yet a 'proper' language. But the multifarious vocabulary, suffused with foreign terms, makes the text difficult even to many native English-speaking readers, who could find its fragments incomprehensible without the aid of a comprehensive dictionary. What, for example, are 'carillons' and 'helices'? The seemingly obvious claim that the poem is written in English has been severely questioned: how *English* is the Italian noun 'campanile', or the adjective 'Sienna'? How English are the Greek 'helices' or Latin 'lamina'? And such words and phrases taken from the poem as 'Araphoes', 'Nimrod', 'I-Ching', 'Ad altare Dei', 'che sera', 'fleurs-de-lys', 'Pharaonic unguents', make the poem look like a multilingual collage, an example of the post-Babelian confusion of the tongues, exploding any possibility of a homogenous and pure diction, and unveiling the essentially hybrid nature of English.

First Language, unavoidably perhaps, finds room for poems which are translation, from French (Baudelaire) and Latin (Ovid), but it also includes a poem called 'Tak, Tak'. This un-English title is taken, again, from Polish (the poem is dedicated to Piotr Sommer, the Polish poet, translator and Carson's friend). The story of Babel continues: firmly set tongues become confounded,[29] words change their meanings, sometimes surprisingly so. The title phrase with the repeated affirmation, 'tak, tak' means 'yes, yes', but also, as Sommer explains it to the speaker, it may mean 'Of course' and 'Is that so?' The twice repeated word may affirm something and express great disbelief: it is a paradoxical, self-contradictory statement that is both positive and negative, that claims and disclaims at the same time.

Heaney has remarked that the language of *Beowulf* gave him an opportunity of moving 'into some unpartitioned linguistic country, a region where one's language would not be simply a badge of ethnicity or a matter of cultural preference or an official imposition, but an entry into further language'.[30] Carson's vibrantly multilingual *First Language* may be considered such an unpartitioned country, in which language rather than delimiting or confining those who use it (language as 'a badge'), opens its doors and leaves its essentialist definition behind, confronting 'further language' and second tongues, language itself as 'an entry'.

The widely defined notion of translation as discussed above allows for the introduction of the poetics of the many and the heterogeneous, of the scattered and the diverse. In the wake of the Good Friday Agreement, former inherited boundaries and strict categories of exclusion lose their legitimacy, with the growing number of translations as cross-boundary and cross-cultural shifts making their mark on contemporary poetry. Most conspicuously, perhaps, the former divisions into the poetry from the North and from the Republic have become increasingly problematic, ever since the apparent disappearance of the physical frontier between the two territories and the acceleration of the processes of political and economic unification in Europe. Furthermore, the old label of Ulster poets, which in most cases meant Belfast poets, lost its meaning when the key figures of that literary phenomenon changed places: Heaney, Mahon, Gerald Dawe, all formerly associated with the North and Belfast, have been living now in Dublin for many decades, while Muldoon is now an American citizen.

The process of invalidating or at least problematising the old division is due also to the increasing traffic observable between the poets from the North and from the Republic. Symptomatic of these ties is Nuala Ní Dhomhnaill's poetry, which has been translated from Irish into English by the two outstanding poets from the North: Paul Muldoon and Medbh McGuckian. The Irish-into-English translation is dominant, but movement in the opposite direction also takes place.

Ní Dhomhnaill, for example, has written Irish-language versions of McGuckian's poems.[31] This rapprochement finds assistance in the politics of many poetry publishers, such as Gallery Press, whose lists include poets from both parts of Ireland. Though in the period under discussion there were attempts to anthologise separately poets from Ulster (most recently in *Magnetic North. The Emerging Poets*, edited by John Brown) or from the Republic (*The Inherited Boundaries. Younger Poets of the Republic of Ireland*, edited by Sebastian Barry),[32] it seems that in post-Troubles Ireland these categories become blatantly extra-literary, reflecting no intrinsic formal or thematic qualities of the poetries in question, nor defining any significant aspects of literary life associated with the two geographically labelled regions. Such a division looks more like an imposition of schematic political categories on the phenomena which exceed, if not openly subvert them.

Yet the gradual dissipation of the well-established North–South divide which we are now witnessing does not imply that the poetry written in Ireland today is uniformed and subsumed best under the one totalising heading 'Irish'. On the contrary, in the place of the two main politically defined centres Irish poetry has now many more specific and focalised centres, defined by divergent, though often overlapping, literary and cultural criteria. In the time of accelerated social mobility the question where one was born and lives loses its former significance in determining one's stance in various literary debates. Poets would rather declare themselves with respect to their attitude to the many contending programmes (such as formalism, open form, performance poetry) and to larger cultural issues (feminism, gay culture, multiculturalism). It is symptomatic of the changes discussed, that the greatest divide now is between the poets of the 'mainstream' tradition(s) and the modernist, or neo-avant-garde revisionists, like Randolph Healy, David Lloyd, Maurice Scully, who 'propose Brian Coffey, Denis Devlin and Thomas MacGreevey as alternative avatars to Kavanagh and Clarke'.[33]

What contributed to this dispersal or decentralisation of the poetic scene in Ireland since 1990 is certainly the unwillingness of the poets to form poetic groups, schools, or announce poetic manifestos, though this was precisely what helped to create the concept of Ulster poets of the 1960s: Heaney, Mahon, Longley, Simmons, who bound by poetic friendship wrote poems to one another, and were mistakenly seen from afar as representatives of one single literary movement. Similarly, a few years later, the equally individual voices of Medbh McGuckian, Paul Muldoon, Ciaran Carson or Tom Paulin were lumped together as representative of the second, or 'postmodern', generation. The rest of Ireland seems not to have had then, nor to have now, an equivalent to Hobsbaum's seminar, *The Honest Ulsterman* or the Troubles as a collective experience that helped critics to label and identify the movement. The tendency, persistent especially outside Ireland, to assume that it is poetry from the North that stands for the whole of contemporary Irish verse was further strengthened by anthologies published in Britain which focused exclusively on the few canonical poets of the Ulster group, such as Heaney, Mahon or Muldoon.

Yet though the group has ceased to be perceived as such – and many new poetic voices, including Paula Meehan, Sinéad Morrissey, Vona Groarke, Catriona O'Reilly, Tom French and Justin Quinn, have since emerged – the poets of the two Ulster generations have all been producing an important body of work in the period since 1990. As with Heaney and Carson, the last decade of the century was particularly fruitful for Michael Longley, who broke his long silence with a sequence of exciting new collections: *Gorse Fires* (1991), *The Ghost Orchid* (1995), *The Weather in Japan*, winner of the T.S. Eliot Prize (2000), and *Snow Water* (2004). Paul Muldoon opened the decade with an astounding genre-defining project of *Madoc. A Mystery* (1990), which was followed by collections which further affirmed his reputation as one of the most original voices in modern poetry: *The Annals of Chile* (1994), *Hay* (1998) and *Moy Sand and Gravel* (2002), and now *Horse Latitudes* (2006). For Derek Mahon the 1990s meant the publication of *The Hudson Letter* (1995) and *The Yellow Book* (1998), two collections marking a radical departure from his previous tightly formal style. Medbh McGuckian has been consistently extending the territory of her work, addressing, for example, the bicentenary of United Irishmen with commemorative poems from *Shelmalier* (1998) and *Had I a Thousand Lives* (2003). As McGuckian's most recent work reveals, the concern with history, always an ambivalent hallmark of Irish poetry, has by no means disappeared.[34] And yet contemporary Irish poets tend now to travel more often in space than in time. The theme of dislocation, 'the importance of elsewhere', leading to the redefinition of home and national identity, has been severed from the traditional, highly politicised theme of exile. Travelling or living abroad, no longer tied to economic or political necessity, have contributed to the linguistic and imaginative diversification of poetry. The 'elsewhere', not surprisingly the title of one of the more recent collections by an Irish poet,[35] provides poets with an opportunity to look at the home in a critical, comparative manner, which often results in what John Brown aptly called 'mobile poems', 'bifocal visions'.[36]

Apart from the familiar dislocations, to America (Muldoon) or England (Tom Paulin), there is a conspicuously growing number of 'translated' poets who chose as their temporary or permanent habitat countries associated much less, if at all, with traditional Irish migrations. Justin Quinn has produced a series of poems set in Prague, where he has been living since 1994. Cathal McCabe has spent over a decade in Poland, translating modern Polish poetry and opening his own verse to his Polish experiences,[37] Sinéad Morrissey has lived and taught in the Far East, which affected a sequence of poems 'Japan' from her second collection, *Between Here and There* (2002). Harry Clifton, who lived first in Italy, then in France, with intervening periods in Africa and Asia, has, in Derek Mahon's words, 'taken the world as his province'.[38] Nick Laird, having spent some time in Poland, included 'A Guide to Modern Warsaw' in his debut collection *To a Fault* (2005). Leontia Flynn wrote of herself as living 'on the beaten track, the sherpa pass, between Kraków / and Zagreb'.[39]

Affected by the rapid economic and social changes in the Ireland of the Celtic Tiger boom and in the political order in the North following the Good Friday Agreement, with no single group or coherent movement that would dominate the scene and inform its identity, it is a nomadic art of many voices, equally prone to probe into local traditions as to take on the risks of unstitching the patterns and looking for inspiration elsewhere, in 'further languages', in 'Zanzibar, Bombay, the Land of the Ethiops'.

Notes

1 Peter Fallon and Derek Mahon (eds), *The Penguin Book of Contemporary Irish Poetry* (London: Penguin, 1990), p. xxii.

2 Louis de Paor, 'Contemporary Poetry in Irish: 1940–2000', in *The Cambridge History of Irish Literature*, ed. Margaret Kelleher and Philip O'Leary (Cambridge: Cambridge University Press, 2006), p. 349.

3 Ciaran Carson, *The Irish For No* (Oldcastle: Gallery Press, 1987), p. 31.

4 Micheal O'Siadhail, from *Tremolo*, in *Globe* (Tarset: Bloodaxe Books, 2007).

5 Quoted in Jerzy Jarniewicz, *The Bottomless Centre. The Uses of History in the Poetry of Seamus Heaney*, Łódź University Press, 2002), p. 173.

6 Diana von Finck, 'A.R. Ammons's Poetics of Chaos', in *Freedom and Form: Essays in Contemporary American Poetry*, ed. Esther Giger and Agnieszka Salska (Łódź: University Press, 1998), p. 120.

7 Ibid.

8 Paula Meehan, *Mysteries of the Home* (Newcastle-upon-Tyne: Bloodaxe, 1996), p. 13.

9 Paula Meehan, 'The Pattern', in *Mysteries of Home*, p. 13.

10 Paula Meehan, 'Fist', in *Dharmakaya* (Manchester: Carcanet, 2000), p. 13.

11   Paul Durcan, *Greetings to Our Friends in Brazil* (London: Harvill, 1999), p. 236.
12   Brendan Kennelly, *The Book of Judas* (Newcastle-upon-Tyne: Bloodaxe Books, 1991), p. 11.
13   Ibid., p. 15.
14   Bernard O'Donoghue, 'Poetry in Ireland', in *The Cambridge Guide to Modern Irish Culture*, ed. Joe Cleary and Claire Connolly (Cambridge: Cambridge University Press, 2005), p. 178.
15   Ibid., p. 180.
16   Seamus Heaney, *The Government of the Tongue* (London: Faber, 1988), p. 41.
17   Stephen Dedalus notes in his diary: 'The shortest way to Tara was via Holyhead', James Joyce, *A Portrait of the Artist as a Young Man*, ed. Seamus Deane (London: Penguin Books, 1992), p. 273.
18   Bernard O'Donoghue, 'Poetry in Ireland', in *Modern Irish Culture*, ed. Joe Cleary and Claire Connolly (Cambridge: Cambridge University Press 2005), pp. 173–89.
19   Seamus Heaney, Introduction, *Beowulf. A New Translation* (London: Faber, 1999), p. xxx.
20   Michael Hartnett, *Inchicore Haiku* (Dublin: Raven Arts Press, 1985), p. 9.
21   Cathal Ó Searcaigh, *Ag Tnúth Ieis an tSolas 1975–2000* (Cló Iar-Chonnachta Teo., 2000), p. 150.
22   Justin Quinn, 'The Irish Efflorescence', *Poetry Review*, 4: 91 (winter 2001/02), p. 46.
23   Selina Guinness (ed.), *The New Irish Poets* (Newcastle-upon-Tyne: Bloodaxe Books, 2004).
24   Ciaran Carson, *Last Night's Fun* (London: Cape, 1996), *The Star Factory* (London: Granta, 1997), *Fishing for Amber* (London: Granta, 1999) and *Shamrock Tea* (London: Granta, 2001).
25   The following part of the chapter is based on Jerzy Jarniewicz, 'After Babel. Translation and Mistranslation in Contemporary British Poetry', *European Journal of English Studies*, 6: 1 (2002), pp. 87–104.
26   Interview with Ciaran Carson and Michael Longley, *Literatura na Świecie*, 4–5, Warsaw, 2000, pp. 251–68.
27   George Steiner, *After Babel. Aspects of Language and Translation* (Oxford: Oxford University Press, 1998), p. 18.
28   Ciaran Carson, 'Second Language', in *First Language* (Oldcastle: Gallery Press, 1994), p. 10.
29   'And the Lord said, Go to, let us go down, and there confound their language, that they may not understand one another's speech'. *Genesis* 11: 7.
30   Seamus Heaney, Introduction to *Beowulf* (London: Faber, 1999), p. xxv.
31   *The Southern Review. A Special Issue: Contemporary Irish Poetry and Criticism*, 3: 31 (summer 1995), 444–9.

32 John Brown (ed.), *Magnetic North: The Emerging Poets* (Derry: Verbal Arts Centre, 2005); Sebastian Barry, *The Inherited Boundaries. Younger Poets of the Republic of Ireland* (Mountrath: Dolmen Press, 1986).

33 David Wheatley, 'Irish Poetry into the Twenty-First Century', *Cambridge Companion to Contemporary Irish Poetry*, ed. Matthew Campbell (Cambridge: Cambridge University Press, 2003), p. 253.

34 Another example being Tom Paulin's book-length poem on the origins of the Second World War, *The Invasion Handbook* (London: Faber, 2002).

35 Michael Murphy, *Elsewhere* (Nottingham: Shoestring Press, 2003).

36 Brown, p. 12.

37 It was in Poland that his first poetry books were published.

38 Derek Mahon, Foreword to Harry Clifton's *The Desert Route* (Oldcastle: Gallery Press, 1992), p. 9.

39 Leontia Flynn, 'The Furthest Distances I've Travelled', in *The New Irish Poets*, ed. Selima Guinness (Newcastle-upon-Tyne: Bloodaxe, 2004), p. 101.

8

Architectural metaphors: representations of the house in the poetry of Eiléan Ní Chuilleanáin and Vona Groarke

Lucy Collins

Feminist criticism frequently employs metaphors of space to interrogate the position of women within society and their ability to articulate that position to a wider world. The idea of 'clearing a space' from which to speak suggests that for women freedom of expression can only be achieved in 'empty' space, space that is unmarked by ideological and aesthetic convictions. Yet such emptiness is impossible, since the speaking self must be meaningfully located. Space, both public and private, is closely related to the construction of identity and to its textual representation. This chapter examines the representation of the house by two contemporary women poets, arguing that the relationship between the speaking subject and the space of dwelling – and of writing – is a complex and contingent one. By examining poems from collections by Eiléan Ní Chuilleanáin and Vona Groarke published since the early 1990s, the differing responses that the established poet and the younger writer have to concepts of house and home can be developed. As a site of exploration of self, and of the relationship between self and other, the house cannot be perceived as a fixed space. Like the poem itself, the house in its accretion of layers of meaning, in its ghosts of previous inhabitants and remembered experiences, facilitates the inter-relationship of past and present. It foregrounds issues of enclosure and freedom and raises questions concerning kinship and sexual relationships. Furthermore, it opens debates on identity and belonging that are central to any consideration of the dynamic between individual and national identity, both culturally and politically. It is this relationship between house and home, between the space and its emotional constructs, that will be the particular focus of this chapter.

Ideas of belonging have considerable political and cultural importance for the Irish writer, yet they also have larger implications for the act of writing itself:

> Distinctions between home and exile (or alienation) have signified, variously, distinctions between silence and speech, writing and speech, the literal and the figurative, and, ultimately, the temporal and the divine.[1]

In this way the dynamics of house and home affect the relationship between the speaking (or writing) subject and language. Whether speech or writing are possible, and what form such expressions may take, are issues of particular importance for the contemporary woman poet who often negotiates the difficult relationship between subject and object in her poems. By situating the self using a voice that can be identified and located the woman may gain power both through the act of self-articulation and through the assumption of a recognisable identity. Yet at the same time she surrenders the freedom of movement and self-definition that accompanies imaginative representations. The relationship between the speaker and the material world of the poem often reflects the contingent nature of 'home' for these poets: one interpretation sees the house as a space of security and sheltered intimacy; another, as a place of disenfranchisement for women. This double perspective problematises the act of representation, since it positions the home as both *of* the world and a shelter *from* the world (my italics). Gaston Bachelard argues that the house is experienced 'in its reality and in its virtuality',[2] which is significant here. For Irish women poets the house represents a material site, where their own roles as women can be explored, and an imaginative one, allowing them to structure the psychological explorations in their poems.

In the Ireland of the 1990s attitudes towards traditional social structures and roles underwent considerable change. At the beginning of the decade Mary Robinson was elected the Republic of Ireland's first female president and her liberal pluralist perspective, together with a committed attachment to human rights reform and feminist causes, reflected the forward-looking attitudes of a younger generation. This was a decade during which long-running debates on divorce and abortion paved the way for new legislation that weakened the influence of the Catholic Church on matters of state and offered women more control over their private lives.[3] This change marked a radical shift in how younger women especially perceived and represented their sexual identities and their domestic commitments. For an older generation these issues were still marked by difficult negotiations and ambiguous feelings; for those born from the late 1960s onward unquestioned personal independence was often the norm. As a result of this accelerated transition, much of what made Ireland 'home' had begun to change, though for those who had left Ireland to live and work abroad during the 1980s and 1990s the country often remained fixed in the past. Discussing writing of the diaspora, Justin Quinn asks 'What is the sell-by date of the "Ireland" that is being exported? One year? Or twenty? When does it stop being a true picture of the country or region the poet comes from?'[4] For many Irish women poets, engagement with a changing Ireland meant rethinking the nature of their private and public selves. This is less true of poets emerging now, such as Leontia Flynn and Leanne O'Sullivan, whose negotiations of self are not restricted by these particular cultural dilemmas. At the beginning of the twenty-first century the house may enclose not a clearly defined unitary family but a series of relationships, some lasting, some transitory. Through the image of the house the poet may explore a concept of belonging necessarily altered – and further alterable – by the disintegration of traditions and by social mobility.

Ideas and ideals of the home have been central to nation-building in Ireland throughout the twentieth century, and are implicated in complex debates on origins and on belonging both north and south of the border. In the Republic the traditional primacy of the family both legislatively and socially had imbued the concept of home with a moral significance – through this ordering of human behaviour and relationships, a larger social order could be maintained. The operation of community could be seen in microcosm in the home and in its mediation of crucial forms of personal relationship. Thus Irish women experienced the house both practically and symbolically, much as the larger idea of home/land could be set against the actual experience and emotional construct of exile. Such ideas of home are necessarily inflected by problems of definition: borders become important in clarifying the difference between self and other, between those who belong and those who are excluded. Politically, these are linked to nationalist and revisionist debates on the meaning of Irish identity, but by the 1990s these positions had extended in scope and complexity:

> An Ireland without frontiers is obviously an Ireland without borders. This does not, however, entail a 'united Ireland' in the traditional sense of the term. For the Nation-States of Britain and Ireland, which constitute the very basis for the opposing claims of nationalist and unionist ideologies, would be superseded by a European constellation of regions.[5]

The extent to which the European context would alter this dynamic is far from simple but the dramatic expansion of identity to include what was once outside its bounds is a feature of the newly cosmopolitan Ireland that has implications for the experience of the individual. It is a development that creates complex emotional responses to identity as well as new readings of community. A sense of place remains strong among Irish women poets, in spite of the changing nature of the relationship between the individual and both cultural and domestic space. In confronting this relationship these poets use differing strategies to investigate singular and collective positions, from Eavan Boland's use of a landscape marked by history in 'My Country in Darkness'[6] to Sinéad Morrissey's account of traversing a divided Belfast by taxi in 'Thoughts in a Black Taxi'.[7] Just as the experience of the individual opens a larger debate on identity, so the house is associated not only with the interior space but with a greater relationship to place that is intensified by historical and political factors, which may include consideration of gender and class, geographical location and religious affiliation. Each representation must thus be placed in its cultural moment, yet must also be seen as part of the individual poet's development.

Heidegger viewed the home as an important site of spiritual unity between people and things: 'dwelling itself is always a staying with things'.[8] The significance of things and of their contextual implications in Heidegger's work bears an interesting relation to the centrality of specific cultural factors for many of these poets. The house as both an actual and symbolic space began to resonate in different ways, depending both on social circumstances and on attitudes towards the newly contingent nature of belonging. Such distinctions find particular expression in the work of Eileán Ní Chuilleanáin, one of the finest and most complex poets to emerge in Ireland in the late twentieth century.[9] She is not prolific and the careful progress of her work over almost four decades, together with the subtleties of the poems themselves, are indicative of the reflective quality of her process. Her poetry affirms the strength of her emotional connection to place and her understanding of the subtle tensions between different locations and cultures, between exile and belonging. 'For me, exile was the definition of isolation', she has said in interview; yet her concepts of 'home' invoke complex attitudes towards the relationship between the individual and the group.[10] Her interest in religious communities can seem at odds with an increasingly secularised Ireland, yet it investigates historical realities that have had a significant shaping force on contemporary society. It foregrounds the intersection between lived experience and spiritual meaning, as well as exploring the ways in which tradition can be maintained and examined. In spite of its complexity, her poetry is never wilfully abstract but instead finds significance in the connections between experience and ideas:

Ní Chuilleanáin's poetry shows a strong interest in questions of an existential dimension, where the speaking subject is seen as an embodied subject, firmly situated at the point where the mind is inseparable from our bodily, physical nature and the poetic voice gives utterance to the interconnectedness of the physical and spiritual dimensions of human existence.[11]

This level of interconnectedness has a further effect on the speaking subject in her poems. Ní Chuilleanáin establishes a voice that neither articulates an unequivocally singular experience, nor lays claim to a coherent shared narrative, but instead negotiates the shifting ground between these extremes.[12] From her earliest work the qualified nature of personal experience and observation has been important; one of the hallmarks of her poetry is its attention to what is only partially, or fleetingly, seen. Thus the house or home is not a space of assurance but one of tentative exploration. Her representation of Cork, the place of her birth and upbringing, emphasises the idea of 'home' as one that does not necessarily yield readily to either speaker or reader: 'Just visible, a glass window, / Blackness beyond / Half veiled by a net curtain'.[13] This fleeting glimpse is a refutation of expected ideas of significance; instead place becomes an act of observation and a state of mind. Ní Chuilleanáin neither sentimentalises the city of her birth nor attempts to trace a secure domesticity. The periods of time she has spent abroad and her attachment to other cultures accords with the experience of many of her generation for whom a return to the home place can never be a simple one. This new mobility, both within Ireland and beyond its borders, alters ideas of belonging, often substituting an anonymous or rootless existence for an identifiable role in the community. Ní Chuilleanáin investigates this nuanced relationship between space and meaning by combining personal and cultural awareness in subtle ways.

A number of Ní Chuilleanáin's early poems, such as 'The Lady's Tower', negotiate the relationship between nature and human habitation: 'my thatch / Converses with spread sky, / Heronries'.[14] It is a dynamic that is reminiscent of Heidegger's fourfold: ' "on the earth" already means "under the sky." Both of these *also* mean "remaining before the divinities" and include a "belonging to men's being with one another" '.[15] These ways of placing the self, of asking what it means to exist, become more complex in the poetry of the 1990s, where the origins of the poet's images and ideas are harder to trace. In 'A Glass House' from *The Brazen Serpent* (1994) Ní Chuilleanáin again explores these perspectives, showing the solid structure of the house becoming transparent and giving way to a watery scheme:

In the clear salty pool
Open to the tides, I am sinking

Past open globes of eyes.
I can see where the sandy floor
Brushes away; a cloud floats
Puffed into the shape of myself[16]

The pool is open to the tides, suggesting an enclosed space that is affected by magnetic forces. The relationship between the house and its surroundings is intensified by this transparency while the nature of concealment and visibility is highlighted, especially by the speaker's ability to see into previously hidden spaces. The speaker is open to the gaze of others and can herself engage in observation: the cloud of sand disturbed from beneath may also be the floating cloud of the unsettled day. This reflection upward and downward causes the sense of structure and fluidity to merge and disturbs our spatial sense of reading, so that the location of meaning here is always relational. It also contradicts any assumption that the house as an object must be fixed and contextualised. The final image of the poem, the crate of racing pigeons, conjures with ideas of displacement from home and the possibility of return there. The concept of home itself, whether it may indeed be recoverable, is interrogated in this way. This problem is finally connected to language, and to the difficulties that beset interpretation, since language is not always 'clear' but may be 'clouded' by its own forms and conventions, as well as by cultural accretions: 'It is language that tells us about the essence of a thing, provided that we respect language's own essence.'[17] Here the poet implies that we may be required to move into another realm, to travel some distance, in order to interpret words meaningfully.

Vona Groarke's first collection, *Shale*, also published in 1994, is prefaced by a quotation from Elizabeth Bishop's 'The Riverman': 'I waded into the river / and suddenly a door / in the water opened inward'.[18] Some of Bishop's ambiguous treatment of the movement between water and land, between different states of being, informs this book. The first five poems engage directly with bodies of water: the fourth of these, 'Sunday's Well', explores the relationship between individual identity and domestic space in ways that also disturb the clear establishing of boundaries. The poem opens with an apparent disruption of logical space: the open skylight admits the river – more probably the sound of the river – into the space of the room and the poem. Paradoxically, the river contains the *silence* of the city. This relationship between sound and silence becomes important, not only in the delicate contest that is established between these but in the reminder that this, in many ways, is the stuff of which poetry itself is made. This poem resonates with mental disturbance; the dispersal of the self that results is metaphorically represented through the fear of being engulfed by water, yet it is not the speaking self but her books and letters, her texts, that risk this dispersal:

> What will happen when morning has come
> and my books and letters are washed up in the park?
> Who will find my clothes and take them home?
> How will I ever know my life again?[19]

The second part of the poem shifts perspective: the speaker becomes a dreamer who imagines the body of a woman 'washed up in the park'. Now her separation from meaningful objects – 'a row of books, / a lover's photograph' – renders her unidentifiable. The poem's title, though it names an area of Cork City, manages also to invoke a lonely descent into watery oblivion. Yet this could also be the wellspring of life, suggestive of the idea that language itself can be renewed. Set against the slippage into anonymity and death is the ordered space of the room, an enduring image at the close of the poem.

The loss of self and the uncertainty of its renewal is a preoccupation of many women poets. Traditional roles of wife and mother and their conflict with artistic aspiration can account for some of this concern. Yet the rapid pace of change in late twentieth-century Ireland which offered new freedoms to women also brought challenges: choices that were difficult to reconcile; values that contradicted existing ways of living. This situation accords with the sense of hesitation or disruption of continuity that many women poets express both thematically in individual poems and in the shape of their writing lives.[20] These tendencies become integral to the act of poetic interpretation itself: while textual strategies may be apprehended cumulatively by the reader through lengthy engagement with an individual poet's work, there is often a sense that new and varied perspectives are essential to recent writing projects, since social and aesthetic change is wrought by means of shifts in space and time that must find analogues in the act of poetic representation. The sense of being between places and states often occurs in the work of these two poets. For Ní Chuilleanáin this may be marked by perspectives shifting to yield new insights into the relationship between self and world. A dynamic and sometimes uneasy relationship between inner and outer is also a hallmark of Vona Groarke's representation of the house in her work. It was such a predominant trope in *Shale* that her second collection, *Other People's Houses* (1999), used it as a unifying device.

Her approach has both flexibility and range, though, and moves easily from childhood memories, through historical reflections to consider ideas of subjectivity and relation to others. 'Outdoors' interrogates the last of these subjects, drawing attention to the passage of time in the formation of knowledge of self and other. The speaker in the poem articulates the shared experience of waiting for night to fall, of waiting for the moment 'when we might call it a day / and settle for the night'.[21] Putting on the interior light becomes an act of separation of outer and inner, yet also one in which the spaces are merged. In this case the window reveals a reflection not just of the speaker, but of her partner. He is simultaneously in the same space as her 'where we can draw the curtain and talk of tomorrow' and also 'confronting [her] from the garden'. Even affirmations of commitment and love are shadowed by separateness, so that the house itself loses its fixity of structure. Through the power of reflection and the strong tension between inside and outside, between finite and infinite space, it drifts outwards beyond its own boundaries – 'our kitchen at sea on the lawn . . . / . . . our faces marooned in stars'.

The extent to which the house can be the particular focus of imaginative states reveals its importance not just as a space of memory but of possibility – it does not just anchor the woman in a recognisable context but allows her a framework for speculative enquiry. The issue of imaginative recognition surfaces in poems by many contemporary Irish women, and could be argued to be an important aspect of any poetic impulse: the extent to which the world of the poem can be both transformed and familiar at the same time. Nuala Ní Dhomhnaill renders this in her combination of ancient and modern contexts; Caitríona O'Reilly in her dream-like engagement with the natural world. In theorising place and identity, house and body are often metaphorically connected:

> The house and the body are intimately linked. The house is an extension of the person; like an extra skin, carapace or second layer of clothes, it serves as much to reveal and display as it does to hide and protect . . . Moving in ordered space, the body 'reads' the house which serves as a mnemonic for the embodied person. Through habit and inhabiting, each person builds up a practical mastery of the fundamental schemes of their culture.[22]

This 'ordered space', which is also the space of the poem, is often disturbed by contemporary women poets, for whom a more complex interrogation of the domestic is required. That this can be done in the language of dreams, as Ní Chuilleanáin herself has remarked, signifies

the creative importance of this act of re-imagining as well as its fundamentally allusive quality.

'The Dream House', another poem from *Other People's Houses* (1999),
explores this act of transformation in the trajectory of the work itself.
Here the speaker's relationship with the house alters as the rational
co-ordinates that define it inexplicably change. The opening stanza is
the most regular in rhythm and rhyme, in keeping with the order of
the rooms, 'all civility and grace'. The stillness of the place and its imper-
viousness to human interference – 'nothing stirs for any move of mine'
– reflects its quality as a form of historical artefact, rather than an inhabited space. The speaker is, paradoxically, silent and compelled to be so,
permitted only to follow the guide and listen to his commentary: 'I am
following my guide, as I must do, / in silence, while he talks me through
the plan'.[23] Her failure to recognise the house only changes when it
becomes less orderly and when its human dimension begins to be
expressed through the twin images of the family portraits and the
mirror reflecting the speaker herself. Groarke's handling of this kind of
trope is deft. It is suggestive both of the ways in which the house has
integrated her presence among its own forms and of how it has become
a metaphor for her own tentative self-exploration. Just as the 'mood
of certainty' falters, so does the rhythm of the poem, becoming more
uneven and giving the repeated impression of a sudden halting of movement. The process by which the speaker 'begin[s] to see for [her]self'
can be identified when the house becomes 'readable' by her and is seen
as a place she could inhabit, containing clothes that she might wear
and books she might read. The poem concludes:

> The house is all beyond me; the room recedes.
> I begin to lose the sense of what I saw.
> In all this detail, one apparent flaw:
> my unlost earring crumpled on the sheets. (p. 25)

The dream-world of the house can express processes of recognition
and understanding at the same time as it can represent what is ration-
ally impossible – that her earring can be simultaneously worn by her
and lying on the bed. The warping of time that this suggests draws the
uncanny into the poem and complicates readings of it that might
equate the dream with a mildly distorted memory. Here the boundaries
between the house and the body become unstable: the curtains are the
colour of the speaker's eyes '[i]n certain light' and the earring, expressive
of sexuality, is found on the bed describing the sheets' own crumpled
state. In the dream the movement is towards the private spaces and also
towards the intuitive and experiential, as the guide's presence becomes

shadowy and his knowledge less necessary. The house too, though initially a place of order and permanence, is ultimately no more than glimpsed, becoming a vivid yet transient imaginative space at the close.

For Groarke the home is the place where human emotions and memories can be negotiated with both directness and subtlety. In the title poem 'Other People's Houses' the space of relationship is deconstructed by the passage of time so that the shape of the house – and of the poem itself – is radically altered: 'There's been a fire and the roof's caved in'; 'The ceiling of the sitting room is upended / on the floor' (p. 52). Whereas 'The Empty House' depicts the place taking on a life of its own – 'When we are gone, the house will close over us / as though we'd been swimmers in an unmoved sea' (p. 51) – in 'Other People's Houses' the home bereft of human energy cannot stand. Yet ultimately both poems trace the relationship between dynamic emotional states and fixed space. The speaker acknowledges her creative development, referring to the 'flowery poems' she wrote formerly, and we are reminded that this is not just a personal past for the speaker, but a means by which she can chart her changing awareness through language. This engagement with the shifting spaces of memory and imagination seems deliberate; the speaker 'walked to a house' where she and her lover once lived, as though in an act of deliberate reclamation. Her initial reflections give way to an inventory of objects – sofa, radio, mattress – asserting the meaningful nature of what is lost and the possibilities for transcending such feelings.[24] So here there is both a wistfulness concerning this lost connection and a recognition that it represented a phase of transition, a time spent in 'other people's houses' as a kind of preparation for having a 'stake in a place of our own / which keeps us steady and tied'

> halfway between the In- and the Outdoors,
> where one time, looking two ways at once,
> I saw you stranded in both and thought
>
> I would throw in my lot with yours.[25]

This is a form of the image that also provides the core to the poem 'Outdoors' and it is an acknowledgement of the contingent nature of love and intimacy, the extent to which they represent slow and fruitful transitions for the human individual.

The act of pausing 'between the In- and the Outdoors' has earlier found expression in Ní Chuilleanáin's work. Poems such as 'The Hill Town' and 'MacMoransbridge' from *The Magdalene Sermon* (1989) use this form of spatial representation to explore complex family dynamics, established over long periods of time. Where Groarke's work often deals with the past crystallised into a memorable image or encounter, Ní Chuilleanáin's involves slower, more painstaking evolutions and juxtapositions difficult to reconcile without further clarification. Often the boundaries between spaces are themselves hard to detect, or seem to be undone by the force of past or present circumstances. 'The Party Wall' from *The Brazen Serpent* (1994) explores how the historical division of land brought to the speaker's attention by an uncanny happening – the arrival of a drift of 'stiff white feathers' in the garden: 'We were not shocked at all until the next day / When the aerial photographs were published / Showing the house that backed against ours / . . . / Visited the same'.[26] Many of Ní Chuilleanáin's poems contain strange or inexplicable phenomena and here this involves a re-interpretation of the space of ownership. The security of the house with its 'tall iron gates' and 'fancy grilles' is threatened in the most unexpected of ways, by a visitation that seems partly natural and partly divine. Indirectly, the questions of land ownership so prominent in Irish history emerge in the present, in the aunt's story 'About all the trouble over building the party wall' (p. 40). Yet the division here is also of the self, as the tenants in the adjoining house 'had my grandfather's name'. By centring this exploration on personal property, Ní Chuilleanáin concerns herself with the local effects of larger historical questions and in particular of the ways in which the individual is brought to awareness.

For Vona Groarke such spatial divisions are also placed in a specifically familial frame, though one that has a more clearly recognisable context. In particular she uses interior or domestic space as a means of investigating the relationship of self to others and of exploring where the individual can fit in the social arrangements of the world. 'Oranges', from *Flight* (2002), is a poem that engages directly with the representation of boundaries: here the poem itself enacts the uneasy emotional drifts in lines that part in the centre and shift to each side.

> Say you approach   your house in winter
> home from work   or in from the shops.
> The light is on   in your living room
> and the blind   still up.[27]

The separateness that enables the speaker to look at her family from a distance, yet closely, also creates apparently contradictory feelings of belonging and being excluded. These feelings, rather than being simultaneous, may indeed be separated as one moment is from the next; much of Groarke's poetry thrives on this kind of hesitation between emotional states and it is one of the aspects that makes the dialectic between her poetry and that of other women so fruitful. As in the poem 'Outdoors', dusk provides the temporal frame ideally suited to this exploration. Here, in the movement between day and night, between light and darkness, it is the brilliance of the lived life that is important: 'Your life shines without you. / The keys blaze in your palm' (p. 26). This illumination is an important aspect of the act of observation itself, where the thing observed gains special meaning in the process. It is particularly apt given the evocative power of Groarke's work and the watchfulness of her poetic persona. Yet the poem ends in hesitation, as its structure has suggested all along, and the emotional resonance returns to the speaker herself.

To be a distinct observer of the family home foregrounds individuality and permits the speaker to explore a connection to others as well as to represent a unique perspective. The speaker in Ní Chuilleanáin's 'Sunday' from her 2001 collection *The Girl Who Married the Reindeer* reflects the home life of others – the chaos of romping children and preoccupied parents – as an inevitability: 'I can't go there, but I know just how it will be'.[28] Here the 'but' might almost read 'because', since the speaker has witnessed this scene before and seems repelled by the disconnected energy expressed in it. The lack of boundaries evident in the children's movement and the merging of the spaces of house and garden show Ní Chuilleanáin handling this dynamic in different ways to Groarke. The speaker here is impelled neither to engage with such a relationship, nor to probe its implications through the act of writing itself. Meaning, it seems, is elsewhere and the weight of the poem's significance lies in its last stanza: 'I have to hear the chestnut choir' (p. 13). She will spend this particular Sunday in autumn in an isolated place with strangers:

> They won't remember
> me there,
> But all the same, this autumn,
> I am going to hear the office they sing on that Sunday
> At vespers, before the longest vigil of the year. (p. 13)

The momentum of her intention is cleverly enhanced by the subsequent poem 'The Chestnut Choir' in which the journey to the convent and the experience of hearing the singing finds expression. Often Ní Chuilleanáin's poems enact such disengagement and re-engagement and demand similar processes from the reader. It is at this stage in her career that the tenuous, drifting nature of human connection seems most fully acknowledged and the use of the house as a means of engaging imaginatively with difficult forms of relationship becomes most pronounced.

Many of the debates concerning the representation of home involve the tensions between finding an existing space and creating a new one. Early in her writing career Ní Chuilleanáin engaged perceptively with this theme in her portrayal of Odysseus, who, in 'The Second Voyage', abandons the dangers of the journey in favour of a place in which he can create a home. As the poem progresses it becomes clear that what he longs for is *his* home, a place of memory rather than imagination, and the difficulty of repossessing the past becomes the poem's subtle theme. Though Ní Chuilleanáin uses personal material obliquely in her latest poetry, links between private and public concerns afford her opportunities to explore important cultural issues through the shaping of individual perspectives. 'In Her Other House', also from *The Girl Who Married the Reindeer*, invokes a return to childhood with which the representation of the house often engages. Rather than emphasising the passage of time, the poem suggests the imaginative simultaneity of past and present. To return endlessly to the past is not to render that past explicable but to alert the reader to the inseparable nature of moments of intense experience: as Bachelard argues, 'we are unable to relive duration that has been destroyed . . . memories are motionless, and the more securely they are fixed in space, the sounder they are'.[29] Many women poets problematise the nature of memory by exploring the unfixed nature of all positions. For a poet like Medbh McGuckian the past becomes a site of personal and cultural recollection, of imaginative creation and textual engagement. The contextual shifts observable in her work refute the possibility of being fixed in space, testing the reader's ability to locate the self meaningfully. Ní Chuilleanáin's work enacts a more gradual movement, while also challenging the notion of a singular perspective. The poem 'In Her Other House' invokes this straight away; the place is 'other' from the start. The 'her' of the title becomes 'my' and the focus of the poem shifts to a dreamlike memory. The otherness in this poem seems to interrogate the very notion of home but it may indicate the immediacy of the lived and imagined past, where the vision is selective, even deliberately limited and '[t]he table is spread and cleared by invisible hands'.[30] In this home books are the distinctive feature and supersede the domestic detail, becoming the nurturing centre of the household together with the fire and the meal. The imaginative power of the home is a textual one, so that the role of language in reclaiming this space is crucial: it is a house of books and letters, where past, present and future are there to be read, as much as to be experienced. Again Ní Chuilleanáin resists simple domesticity, engaging instead with the act of representation itself. Reclaiming this past involves present creativity: to be at home is to be among written words.

The poem's final lines are especially significant in this regard: 'In this house there is no need to wait for the verdict of history / And each page lies open to the version of every other' (p. 20). Here chronological time is disturbed by the presence of the dead. These books seem to refute the logical progression of meaning in favour of a freer engagement, and in doing so suggest that acts of poetic interpretation need to remain alive to the dynamic range of influences that shape the writing process.

The inter-relationship of texts, especially within a single volume, is clearly becoming increasingly important to Ní Chuilleanáin. As well as providing a memorable image in this poem, the idea of one page lying 'open to the version of every other' also illuminates the sequencing of poems in the collection. Again the relation of one poem to the next is important: on the opposite page to 'In Her Other House' lies 'In Her Other Ireland' which makes its location explicit in its title and in addition gives a specifically female viewpoint from which to interpret the material of the poem. Yet even this level of certainty is problematised by the notion of 'otherness' that is so explicitly addressed, and the links between the poems suggest that each cannot be seen simply as a self-contained unit. 'In Her Other Ireland' moves outward from the personal dimension of the preceding poem, yet retains both the experiential quality and the slightly distanced perspective that is so characteristic of this poet's work. Here the desolate nature of the landscape can be read both literally and metaphorically, so that it evokes a sensory experience for the reader at the same time as it speaks of the inevitability of hardship and struggle. Ní Chuilleanáin is always acutely aware of the settings and surroundings of the house: from such early poems as 'The Lady's Tower' this concern has been evident and the built environment of her more recent poems is also culturally contextualised. Often the building may be a church or convent rather than a house. Throughout Ní Chuilleanáin's work, religious institutions are seen to offer the security and support more usually associated with the family home and her sense of the religious community is one of female opportunity rather than limitation. 'In Her Other Ireland' sees the austerity of religious life bizarrely placed alongside (or within) the world of the seaside fairground, creating two opposing time-frames, both under siege by the same strong winds.[31]

> The mistress of novices has sent all the novices
> Upstairs into the choir to practise
> The service for deliverance from storms and thunder.
> Their light dapples the sharkskin windows,
> The harmonium pants uphill,
> The storm plucks riffs on the high tower.[32]

The retreat upstairs is one that both protects and exposes the novices in the face of the coming storm, yet they only 'practise' the service, postponing the fullest test of the power of prayer. Both high tower and merry-go-round – opposing structures of spiritual and material, of safety and carefree leisure – are subject to the elements. In this small seaside town the sand blows onto the streets and the flagstones are wet: here the boundaries cannot be secured, neither can the space be abandoned – there is '[n]owhere to go when the wind blows'.

The problematic dynamic of staying or leaving has inflected Ireland's political and social history in different ways. Accompanying the pattern of invasion that has shaped the country's history is the question of settlement – whether the land and its people offer a hospitable space for the outsider. To inhabit involves a level of acceptance of the exist-ing cultural space: '[t]o dwell, to be set at peace, means to remain at peace within the free, the preserve, the free sphere that safeguards each thing in its essence'.[33] The strange, undomesticated environment of 'In Her Other Ireland' offers a new perspective on the experiential nature of geography, and invites reflection on what it is to fully inhabit a space. The ruined or abandoned house is a significant trope in Irish cultural representation because of the prevalence of acts of disposses-sion in Ireland's history. Vona Groarke has already enacted a return to a former home; Ní Chuilleanáin for her part rewrites the famous Irish-language poem 'Kilcash' in a coda to *The Girl Who Married a Reindeer* and in doing so makes such an act of return one of historical and poetic significance. The dynamic of loss and renewal that 'Kilcash' traces has particular resonance for Ní Chuilleanáin's own pursuit of such themes in her work; more importantly it can be linked to the Irish lan-guage itself. 'No word of Kilcash nor its household, / Their bell is silenced now'[34] marks the fame and social significance of the place once but also shows how it is quelled by colonial rule. The wish for the house to be 'built up anew' gains in potency by being repeatedly expressed; yet that expression is in English, an irony in the historic scheme as a whole: 'And from now to the end of the story / May it never again be laid low' (p. 52). Ní Chuilleanáin herself grew up in a household where both Irish and English were spoken, as well as a smattering of other languages, but she has chosen to write exclusively in English. The presence of other languages is significant in freeing her from the constraints of a single tradition, though: 'I feel now that I write English rather as if it were a foreign language into which I am constantly translating.'[35]

The revival of the house as an emblem of cultural survival reveals its potential as a repository of emotional meaning, especially in con-nection with forms of self-determination in language. In the private context, the house also provides an essential creative space within which to think and write. For a poet orientated towards home and family it is inevitable that Vona Groarke should explore the home as a specifically creative space. In her most recent collection *Juniper Street* (2006) she includes a poem 'The Annotated House' in which the space is demarcated by the process and technical elements of writing. If the house has been a particular inspiration to Groarke, it also brings creative expectations: 'The window is flush with words, but my page / hangs limp as the snow cloud slouching over / Carlo's house'.[36] It is the form of the house that engages her; first its boundaries – window, sill and porch screen; next its internal structure – stairs, basement, the hall, the kitchen. In this scheme every object indicates language, so that the movement through the house becomes the trajectory of the line and the missed beat a physical stumble:

> The treads and risers
> of every line return me to a carpet scheming
> with print. One wrong foot, and there's
> no telling what month heaped in the basement –
> like laundry thinned by colour – will reveal. (p. 55)

The matter of the house itself becomes a reproach to tentative creativity yet its representation is evidence that these hesitations have been overcome. The poem depends on this extended metaphor and on the potential wordplay that comes with it: every term is mined for its linguistic connotations and form is of the utmost importance. Nature, in all its dynamic formlessness, causes most trouble in this process, from the first slouching clouds to the tangle of branches and drifting smoke of the final stanza. Yet it is the tension between the natural and the man-made, between 'getting on' and having 'nowhere to go from here' that is productive of the poem itself and important in establishing its meanings. At the core of the poem is the act of creative inhabiting; the human sensibility capable of observing and naming this space. This is, after all, an 'annotated house', where the initial structure is expanded and clarified through interaction with the thinking mind.

The significance of the house for these two poets is both a cultural and a creative one. Its role in the interrogation of definitions of home and belonging allow the personal and the political to be linked in subtle and complex ways. Perhaps most important of all are the issues it raises about the nature of representation itself, about poetic composition as a structured and contextualised process. Both Eiléan Ní Chuilleanáin and Vona Groarke explore important dimensions of their observing and writing selves by means of this fascinating matrix of images.

Notes

1 J.D. Law, 'Joyce's "Delicate Siamese" Equation: The Dialectic of Home in *Ulysses*', *PMLA*, 102: 2 (March 1987), p. 197.

2 Gaston Bachelard, *The Poetics of Space*, trans. M. Jolas (Boston: Beacon Press, 1994), p. 5.

3 Divorce legislation in Ireland was prohibited by the Constitution of 1937. A referendum seeking to amend this position was decisively defeated in 1986, but in 1995 a narrow majority voted to permit divorce for couples that had lived apart for four years. The Constitution's prohibition on abortion was challenged by referendum in 1983 but, while the amendment was enacted, the absence of appropriate regulations has made the practical effects limited. The debate came to prominence again in 1992 when the Supreme Court overturned a High Court decision banning an under-age rape victim from travelling abroad to procure an abortion.

4 Justin Quinn, Introduction to *Metre* 3 (autumn 1997), pp. 5–6, p. 6.

5 Richard Kearney (ed.), *Across the Frontiers: Ireland in the 1990s* (Dublin: Merlin, 1988), p. 18.

6 Eavan Boland, *The Lost Land* (Manchester: Carcanet, 1998), p. 13.

7 Sinéad Morrissey, *There Was Fire in Vancouver* (Manchester: Carcanet, 1996), pp. 19–20.

8 Martin Heidegger, 'Building Dwelling Thinking', in *Basic Writings*, ed. David Farrell Krell (London: Routledge, 1993), p. 353.

9 Eiléan Ní Chuilleanáin was born in Cork City in 1942 to an intellectual family with a Republican lineage. Educated at University College Cork and at Oxford, she is a Fellow of Trinity College Dublin. Her first collection, *Acts and Monuments*, was published in 1972. This was followed by *Site of Ambush* (Dublin: Gallery Press, 1975), *The Second Voyage* (Dublin: Gallery Press, [1977] 1986), *The Rose Geranium* (Dublin: Gallery Press, 1981), *The Magdalene Sermon* (Dublin: Gallery Press, 1989), *The Brazen Serpent* (Dublin: Gallery Press, 1994) and *The Girl who Married a Reindeer* (Dublin: Gallery Press, 2001). She is one of the founding editors of the literary magazine *Cyphers*.

10 Leslie Williams, 'Interview with Eiléan Ní Chuilleanáin', in *Representing Ireland: Gender, Class, Nationality*, ed. Susan Shaw (Gainesville: University of Florida Press, 1997), p. 32.

11 Irene Gilsenan Nordin, ' "Betwixt and Between": The Body as Liminal Threshold in the Poetry of Eiléan Ní Chuilleanáin', in *Metaphors of the Body and Desire in Contemporary Irish Poetry*, ed. Irene Gilsenan-Nordin (Dublin: Irish Academic Press, 2006) pp. 224–42, p. 225.

12 Guinn Batten, 'Boland, McGuckian, Ní Chuilleanáin and the Body of the Nation', in *The Cambridge Companion to Contemporary Irish Poetry*, ed. Matthew Campbell (Cambridge: Cambridge University Press, 2003), p. 186.

13 Ní Chuilleanáin, *The Rose Geranium*, p. 14.

14 Ní Chuilleanáin, *The Second Voyage*, p. 1. Originally from *Site of Ambush* (1975), this was chosen as the opening poem for *The Second*

Voyage (1986). Patricia Haberstroh argues that it is a riposte to the intellectual, masculine environment of Yeats's Thoor Ballylee and compares it to the austere environment of 'A Gentleman's Bedroom', the last poem in *The Second Voyage*.

15 Heidegger, p. 351.
16 Ní Chuilleanáin, *The Brazen Serpent*, p. 21.
17 Heidegger, p. 348.
18 Vona Groarke was born in Edgeworthstown in 1964 and was educated at Trinity College Dublin. Her first collection, *Shale*, was published by Gallery Press in 1994 and won the Brendan Behan Memorial Award the following year. Subsequent volumes are: *Other People's Houses* (Dublin: Gallery Press, 1999), *Flight* (Dublin: Gallery Press, 2002) and *Juniper Street* (Dublin: Gallery Press, 2006). She was shortlisted for the Forward Prize in 2002. She lives in North Carolina where she teaches at Wake Forest University.
19 Groarke, *Shale*, p. 15.
20 Poets such as Eavan Boland, Nuala Ní Dhomhnaill and Mary O'Malley use aspects of the past to illuminate the roles of women in contemporary Ireland. Patterns of publishing are also significant: some women poets publish no poems for long periods; others only begin to publish late in life.
21 Groarke, *Other People's Houses*, p. 54.
22 Janet Carsten, and Stephen Hugh-Jones (eds), *About the House: Levi-Strauss and Beyond* (Cambridge: Cambridge University Press, 1995), p. 2.
23 Groarke, *Other People's Houses*, p. 24.
24 It is interesting to consider Heidegger's linking of object and human purpose in this regard. The things that Groarke recalls are objects of use, and as such they evoke experiences. The idea that objects refer to one another, thus constituting a realm of significance, also fits with Groarke's imaginative recovery of the interior of her former house. See M. Inwood, *Heidegger: A Very Short Introduction* (Oxford: Oxford University Press, 2000), pp. 35–6.
25 Groarke, *Other People's Houses*, pp. 52–3.
26 Ní Chuilleanáin, *The Brazen Serpent*, p. 40.
27 Groarke, *Flight*, p. 26.
28 Ní Chuilleanáin, *The Girl who Married a Reindeer*, p. 13.
29 Bachelard, p. 9.
30 Ní Chuilleanáin, *The Girl who Married a Reindeer*, p. 20.
31 Persistent clerical scandals emerged in Ireland in the 1990s with allegations of physical and sexual abuse undermining respect for those in the religious life. These difficulties, together with an increasing sense of the anachronistic nature of religious orders, inflects Ní Chuilleanáin's treatment of this material.
32 Ní Chuilleanáin, *The Girl who Married a Reindeer*, p. 21.
33 Heidegger, p. 351.
34 Ní Chuilleanáin, *The Girl who Married a Reindeer*, p. 51.
35 Williams, 'Interview with Eiléan Ní Chuilleanáin', p. 31.
36 Groarke, *Juniper Street*, p. 55.

9

'The places I go back to':[1] familiarisation and estrangement in Seamus Heaney's later poetry

Joanna Cowper

It is possible to detect within Seamus Heaney's poetry recurring patterns of alternating 'familiarisation' and 'estrangement'. By poems of familiarisation I mean ones in which he strives towards an accurate portrayal of the places, events or individuals that his poems 'st[an]d in for',[2] overcoming 'otherness' with a diligent scrutiny. Cycles of estrangement invariably follow those of familiarisation, as Heaney seeks to recapture something of the 'outsider's' perspective in order to revitalise the poetic energy that familiarity saps from the world around him. In lyrics that re-examine the familiar from a new perspective or re-imagine it in a new context, he re-invents his conditions and renews the world's capacity to surprise. In his 1990 lecture, 'Joy or Night', Heaney declares that

> it is essential that the vision of reality which poetry offers should be transformative, more than just a print-out of the given circumstances of its time and place. . . . an act of writing that outstrips the conditions even as it observes them.[3]

This is the agenda behind Heaney's poetry of estrangement, in which he consciously strives to transform the quotidian into the fantastic. Such poetry can be subdivided into two groups, the first of which might be termed 'artificial', in that it achieves estrangement through the deliberate assumption on Heaney's part of a stance or persona calculated to offer a new perspective. This type of estrangement is typical of Heaney's earliest attempts to 'make strange'. The second mode of estrangement is 'organic', in that a transformative new perspective is thrust upon the poet by events or changes in the world around him, so that his environment becomes estranged from itself without any deliberate effort on his part. Heaney's most recent poetry of estrangement is predominantly organic in style, as it sees him re-examining familiar territories through older eyes, discovering that the world itself has become a different, emptier place, at once identical to and light years away from that in which he had grown up. His later poetry therefore reflects a new-found alienation from places and objects once imbued with the comfort of the familiar.

His most recent volumes, *Electric Light* (2001) and *District and Circle* (2006), combine to present a complete cycle of organic familiarisation and estrangement. *Electric Light* witnesses a return to the mode of familiarisation. Prior to that volume, Heaney had spent three poetry collections and fourteen years perfecting a mode of writing originally developed in response to the experience of bereavement, a poetry whose energies derived from the potentialities of empty space. By 2001, the sense of loss with which he struggled in *The Haw Lantern*, and whose emotive impact he had harnessed so successfully in the estrangements of *Seeing Things* and *The Spirit Level*, had grown familiar to him. His subsequent repositioning in *Electric Light* therefore reflects not a renunciation of the wisdom of *The Spirit Level*'s manifesto, but a recognition on the poet's part that he is entering a new phase of life. He declares in the opening poem of *Electric Light* that 'negative ions in the open air / Are poetry to me. As once before / The slime and silver of the fattened eel',[4] and in so saying, closes his most recent cycle of estrangement by taking for granted that which had once seemed raw and shocking. These closing lines of 'At Toomebridge' place Heaney's two previous modes of poetry, that of physical proximity and that of reverberating emptiness, in the remembered past alongside the checkpoint and the hanged rebel boy.[5] The sibilance and rattle of the final line, and the airy lightness of the declaration that precedes it, gesture towards Heaney's perfected ability to write in either mode. In this line he signals that both are now mastered arts, and that a new creative cycle must begin.

Electric Light leaves Heaney's preoccupation with loss behind, because loss has ceased to be his predominant sensation. The long-accustomed sense of emptiness is replaced by the comfort of homecoming, as *Electric Light* finds him rediscovering people and places familiar from his childhood, which are assimilated in the form of memories. Eugene O'Brien observes of *Electric Light* that it 'embraces the ordinary, endowing it with a significance of memory and hindsight'.[6] This collection begins a new cycle of familiarisation as Heaney explores a new state of being, whereby 'home' is no longer located outside the self, but within it.

The concept of assimilation of place and experience into self is central to *Electric Light*, and it is the resultant concept that 'home' exists both as a physical location and as an interiorised state that enables Heaney to travel in Greece, France, Spain and into the remembered past, without the need to dislocate himself from the landscape of his first world. In this collection, Heaney proposes that one's physical location is not one's only location, that each individual carries the memories of those places and events that have affected them, and it is in the security of these memories that the self can repose. The milker, John Dologhan, acquires an air of mystery on account of having been 'in Montana once', a transformative fact that sets him apart from those who have not travelled so far. By contrast 'the horse pistol', with its resonances of 'the Great North Road', Bob Cushley and Ned Kane, is a thing 'out of place' (*EL*, p. 17) in the Heaney household. Despite its physical presence in rural Ireland, its essence resonates with a sense of 'elsewhere'. In 'Ten Glosses', meanwhile, Heaney enumerates and evaluates the places, people, ideologies and literature that have influenced him and, in so doing, have combined to compose his own portable sense of self.

It is this newly acute consciousness of the composite nature of the self that leads Heaney to write of 'The very "there-you-are-and-where-are-you?" / Of poetry itself' (*EL*, pp. 80–1), and the duality of being suggested by his compound 'adjective' becomes one of the driving preoccupations of *Electric Light*. Jonathan Bolton has observed that, in Heaney's later poetry, he

> has come to view memory and the space–time continuum in terms of the relation between absence and presence, and he has come to acknowledge that certain things, presences that exist in the here and now, uncover or disclose absences that exist in past time.[7]

This link between current and remembered phenomena is keenly felt in *Electric Light*. Heaney's 'Sonnets from Hellas' look out not only onto a Greek landscape, but also onto Harvard and the Bellaghy GAA Club; his travels towards Piedras Blancas open up vistas of the 1950s Gaeltacht; his experience of Belgrade is decoded in the context of remembered images of Ireland in years gone by. In these poems, Heaney affirms that the ostensibly new is rendered familiar through its relationship to that which is already assimilated. By relating recent trips to Europe to experiences that belong to different places and times, he examines the extent to which one can be simultaneously 'here' and 'there', located in the 'now' and the 'then', and, once more, 'away', 'lost' from one's origins and 'at home'. 'The Gaeltacht' addresses the question central to these dualities, musing that 'it would be great too / If we could see ourselves, if the people we are now / Could hear what we were saying' (*EL*, p. 44).

This reverses the conventional conceit that wonders what the earlier self would think of the later. In challenging the presumption that 'the people we are now' can in fact recall the concerns and experiences of the people we once were, Heaney hints at the unwitting falsification inherent in the differentiation between interiorised memory and historical fact. This concern does not preoccupy *Electric Light* to the same extent as it troubles *District and Circle*, as will be seen below, but this is the collection in which Heaney familiarises himself with the notion that life as it is remembered has the power to overwrite and ultimately even to obliterate life as it was lived. John Taylor has criticised *Electric Light*, saying that

> The Irish poet's particular way of looking back merits attention. One wishes that he had produced a more unified collection devoted to recovering vanished objects from his past.[8]

What Taylor fails to acknowledge is that Heaney's 'way of looking back' in *Electric Light* deserves attention precisely because of the extent to which it questions the very possibility of 'recovering' anything intact from the past. In 'Known World', Heaney remembers how 'Caj Westerburg / A Finnish Hamlet in black corduroy / Sweated "on principle" (or was that my projection / Of a Northern tweed-wearer's contrariness?)' (*EL*, p. 19). The humorous aside prefigures a more serious address of the same issue, and later in the poem Heaney asks, 'How does the real get into the made-up?' and finds himself outfaced by the question, brushing it aside with 'Ask me an easier one' (*EL*, p. 21). His suspicion that the process of forging or 'making up' memories from the 'real' world may not be under the control of the remembering mind is a disconcerting one. Eugene O'Brien remarks that Heaney's most recent poetry recognises 'memory, in its fullest sense, [a]s the bringing to bear of complex influences that were never operative on the original scene',[9] and in *Electric Light* Heaney is conscious that inherent in each of his 'double looks' is not only here and there, now and then, but also the real and the fabricated.

The publisher's blurb on the front flap of *Electric Light* speaks of 'the poet's calling to assign things their proper names', and Heaney's interest in doing so in this collection is driven by his increasingly acute sense of the tenuous nature of remembered identity; the concern that, if proper names and real-life identities are not firmly coupled, original identity may be lost and replaced by the mind's 'projections'. Whilst acknowledging the human compulsion to draw meaning from experience, comparing new with old and reorganising memories to achieve coherence, Heaney suggests in *Electric Light* that the first, simple 'look' at an experience might well be the most revealing. Remembering a mass celebrated in the mountains, Heaney recalls that 'I had been

there, I knew this, but was still / haunted by it as by an unread dream'
(*EL*, p. 22). In likening the perplexity generated by this memory to that
left by a troubling dream, he highlights the disquieting impact of those
recollections to which 'meaning' cannot be attributed, and at the same
time airs the possibility that experiences, like dreams, may be devoid
of discernible argument or meaning.

Electric Light, with its exploration of the differences between memory
and fact, ultimately persuades Heaney to doubt the integrity of the compound self. If the accrued memories of which the self is constructed are
inaccurate in their representation of the 'originals' upon which they are
based, the self is revealed by implication to be unstably founded. This
collection betrays Heaney's longstanding 'temperamental disposition
towards an art that [is] earnest and devoted to things as they are',[10]
within which the highest approbation is reserved for things that simply
'are', ineffably themselves, like the goatherd whose simple life sets him
'beyond eclogue and translation' (*EL*, p. 38). In 'Real Names', Heaney
maps a two-way process of assimilation between individuals and their
histories, as Shakespeare's characters are taken on by a schoolboy cast.
In their short hours on the stage, the boys become part of a literary
tradition greater and more enduring than any of the individual actors
or productions that have contributed to it, immersing their schoolboy
selves in the service of Shakespeare's glorious character fabrications. Yet,
even as he recalls the young actors in their borrowed identities, Heaney
reminds himself of the ability of truth to trump fiction. In a double look
that elevates the tangible reality of the boys' real lives above and beyond
the scope of the roles they play, he diminishes the significance of the
production, recasting it as one of many minor episodes that make up
the boys' personal histories. Assuming new identities for the duration
of the play, the young actors leave something of themselves imprinted
on their audience's appreciation of the characters portrayed, whilst at
the same time absorbing something of the characters into the complex
medley that makes up their own projected identities.

In this preoccupation with processes of assimilation and change in
people and things, Heaney in *Electric Light* is sending 'an early warning
/ From myself to be more myself' (*EL*, p. 40). Although he must assimilate experiences, he must nevertheless strive to remain unadulterated,
unassimilated and with his integrity intact. 'Norman Simile', one of the
'Ten Glosses' placed at the centre of the collection, offers an imperative
to Heaney in *Electric Light*, urging him to keep open to experience,
regardless of the prevailing conditions, 'To be marvellously yourself like
the river water / Gerald of Wales says runs in Arklow harbour / Even
at high tide when you would expect salt water' (*EL*, p. 56).

The *Haw Lantern*, with its agenda of 'sift[ing] the sense of things from what's imagined',[11] saw Heaney coming to terms with an increasingly cerebral world in which the tangible commands no greater weight of reality than the ethereal. As such, it formed the foundation from which he could embark upon the imaginative flights of *Seeing Things* and *The Spirit Level*. By 1998, Heaney was ready to acknowledge the possibility that 'the truth may be bounded by different *tearmanns*, that it has to take cognizance of opposing claims' (*HL*, p. 51), and it was this acceptance of multiple 'truths' that gave him the confidence that he needed to begin 'making strange' once again. *Electric Light* performs a similar role in preparing the ground for *District and Circle*, since it is a collection in which the poet familiarises a challenging new outlook, establishing the basis from which forays into the 'strange' can be conducted. The concept of the compound self is sustained throughout *District and Circle*, but where *Electric Light* was largely positive in its outlook, allowing the assimilation of experience to be equated with assurance and stability, this latest collection projects a darker mood in which assimilation is ever more strongly associated with worldly loss. As the poet finds himself confronted by the realities of life in a global community scarred by the events of 11 September 2001 and haunted by the personal tragedies of friends and family lost to death and illness, the joyful assurance that characterised Heaney's acts of assimilation in *Electric Light* is replaced by the fear that assimilation may have become a habit of self-deception designed to ward off despair. *District and Circle* sees Heaney beginning to suspect that there is no alternative but to interiorise and to cherish the past as the tangible world becomes ever more insecure and loveless in outlook, no longer offering the comfort and succour that it once promised. This shift in perspective triggers a new urgency in Heaney's interest in 'Real Names', and his new drive towards estrangement is concerned with the paring apart of memories, separating the real from the made-up in an attempt to restore the lines of differentiation between the qualities that are inherent in people, places and objects, and those that are ascribed to them by the remembering mind. Heaney's agenda of estrangement in this volume has as its focal point the restoration of original identity to the things of the world. He recognises his 'private mythology' for the partial fabrication that it is, and, without denying the human drive to attach personal meanings to memories of people, places and experiences, attempts to strip away the layers of memory to confront an empirical truth. This restoration of original 'otherness' necessarily leaves Heaney in a colder world than was portrayed in *Electric Light*, for where that collection placed the self at the centre of its universe, this confronts the possibility of personal irrelevance as encroaching mortality becomes a haunting preoccupation.

In working towards this position, Heaney draws distinctions between what is lasting in the face of history, and what is lasting in the remembering mind. Looking at 'Wordsworth's Skates', he is most acutely aware not of the 'bootless runners', poor, lifeless objects gathering dust in a display case, but of 'the reel of them on frozen Windermere'.[12] This sharper vision is one that Heaney himself has never witnessed, but he recognises here that it has informed his perception and memory of the skates more profoundly than the actual 'perished bindings' and dust, which he explicitly excludes from his appreciation of them. The echo of 'real' in their imagined 'reel' highlights the distinction drawn between that which was experienced, and that which is remembered. The same preoccupation is present in the twin forge poems, 'Midnight Anvil', described by Heaney as one of the 'tuning forks for the poems that appear in the early pages'[13] of *District and Circle*, and 'Poet to Blacksmith'. These poems look back to 'Digging', the poem in Heaney's first collection in which the poet's 'labour' was likened to that of the farmer, and to 'The Forge' in *Door into the Dark*. Where the earlier poem established reality as the standard against which poetry should be judged, approving the act of writing only insofar as it could be compared to that of digging the earth, these poems reverse the argument of 'Digging' to assert that the poet's celebration of his world is in fact not concerned with the actual, but with his own transformative vision of it. The poet in the translation 'Poet to Blacksmith' concludes that the 'best thing of all' about a well-made spade is 'the ring of it, sweet as a bell' (*DC*, p. 25) – not the tangible product of the blacksmith's labour, but the quality of the spade that comes closest to spoken poetry. 'Midnight Anvil' reverses the scenario of 'Poet to Blacksmith'. Where the first poem told the story of a poet commissioning a spade from Seamus MacGearailt, the blacksmith, the second imagines blacksmith Barry Devlin asking the poet Seamus to 'make' him a poem. In both cases, the quality most highly esteemed by the commissioner is very different from – even at odds with – the criteria on which the maker's skill is traditionally judged. The original poet, ambassador of a world of concept and simile, wants a practical, physical object not for its conventional purpose of digging the earth, but to fulfil his desire for a true note more commonly sought in the church or the concert hall. The modern blacksmith, embodiment of tangible reality, wants poetry that is both accountable and factual, equal to the given conditions and capable of recording them with the faithful accuracy of photography. 'Midnight Anvil', the poem that Heaney distils from these disparities, responds to the modern blacksmith's imagined request with the story of the long-ago poet and blacksmith. In this masterful circularity, Heaney shows that poetry is born not out of history, but out of the interpretative machinations of the poet's remembering mind. None of the 'subjects' of the poem he creates – the millennial chimes, Devlin's request for a poem and the earlier request for a spade 'sweet as a bell' – are drawn from Heaney's first-hand history: they are all stories that he has experienced only in imagination. His poetry therefore transcends his situation, and instead of recording a physical, factual world, transforms an imagined world of folklore and stories into something fresh and new.

The differential between the bare facts that constitute the conditions of life, and the temptation of the interpreting consciousness to transform given conditions into something 'more', is addressed again in 'Saw Music', with the observation that oil painting 'is a paltry thing / Compared with what cries out to be expressed' (DC, p. 51).

The double-look that sees oil painting reduced to lifeless daubs and simultaneously recognised as the attempted expression of the ineffable essence of the world it depicts is typical of District and Circle. The epigraph to 'Saw Music' quotes a response sequence from the Catechism, 'Q. Do you renounce the world? / A. I do renounce it', but the poem itself concludes that art and music, 'however paltry' (DC, pp. 50–1), defy renunciation. Heaney's struggle to separate 'the real' from 'the made-up' stems from the recognition that even when the real world is cold and uncaring, the constructions of art and memory have power to transform objective experience and to offer the irresistible promise of meaning. As such, the poet cherishes them above the inconstant world they immortalise.

In his efforts to differentiate between the 'thing' and the emotive constructions that surround it, Heaney apprentices himself to the art of Rilke. The German poet is a new presence in Heaney's work, and the inclusion of translations of two of his poems in District and Circle reflects Heaney's growing interest in the concept of the 'einfache Schaue' (childlike simplicity of vision) propounded in Rilke's Der Neuen Gedichte. The elegant simplicity of these two translations helps Heaney to clarify his growing sense of the difference between 'feeling and . . . feeling recollected' (DC, p. 68), and it is to some extent thanks to the example of Rilke's 'The Apple Orchard' that Heaney, by the end of District and Circle, comes to accept the separation of memory from experience, identifying and celebrating the attempt to compose sense from life as the means by which mankind learns to accept the inevitability of death. This sense of acceptance is characteristic of the last poems in the collection, but comes only at the conclusion of a painful cycle of estrangement and reconciliation with worldly loss. Heaney's other translation of Rilke, 'After the Fire', is placed much earlier in the collection and recounts how a young boy is changed in the eyes of his peers by the loss of his childhood home:

> For now that it was gone, it all seemed
> Far stranger: more fantastical than Pharaoh.
> And he was changed: a foreigner among them. (*DC*, p. 16)

In the boy's position Heaney parallels with his own. *Electric Light* saw the poet define himself in relation to the people and places that populated his memory: *District and Circle* takes a closer look at the more challenging question of how the self continues, when the people and places that once helped define it are gone. Heaney questions the validity of a personal identity premised upon things that no longer exist.

Early in the collection, Heaney recalls one day by the old aerodrome when 'Wherever the world was, we were somewhere else' (*DC*, p. 11): a physical impossibility that introduces a growing interest in the separation of modes of 'being' from bodily presence. This is a theme that persists and develops throughout *District and Circle*. In the same poem, Heaney recalls that when the aerodrome itself was knocked down and repurposed he found that the memories he had associated with it had grown independent of the need for physical verification, and that its presence or absence no longer played a part in what it 'meant' for him:

> Hangars, runways, bomb stores, Nissen huts,
> The perimeter barbed wire, forgotten and gone (*DC*, p. 11)

In a recent interview, Heaney asserted, 'I want a hand-to-hand engagement with myself – self-forgetfulness rather than self-consciousness',[14] and, in order to attain this new perspective, in *District and Circle* he seeks 'a bird's eye view of [him]self' (*DC*, p. 76). The self is no longer centre stage, as was the case in *Electric Light*. Instead, it is reduced to a small repository of memory amidst a plethora of larger external forces. Michael Parker has identified in Heaney's mature poetry an uncertainty

> as to whether his whole perception of 'the first kingdom' from which he had derived his sense of himself, was merely the product of a wild and flawed imagination[15]

This uncertainty is probed more exhaustively than ever before in *District and Circle*. In order to see himself afresh in relation to his origins, Heaney strips away layers of memory in poems whose acts of de-familiarising renunciation stand directly opposed to the possessive urge that drove the young naturalist-poet. In *The Spirit Level*, Heaney prophesied that his 'last things [would] be first things slipping from [him]',[16] and *District and Circle* can be viewed as the beginning of just such a process of letting go, stripping the comfort of familiarity from early memories. Where Heaney's first poetry presented a rural mindscape composed of acts of 'making' – thatching, forging iron, churning butter – *District and Circle* looks back on the same formative period and physical locus through a darker lens, with the focus on reduction and even death: we see a barber cutting hair, a butcher parcelling meat, a 'turnip snedder' pulping vegetables and a group of locals slaughtering pigs. The theme of 'whole' things being acted upon in such a way as to become less than the original sum of their parts preoccupies Heaney in *District and Circle*, as the accepted notion of a 'cycle' of life gives way to a new vision of existence inevitably compelled to end in an emptying-out of energy into nothingness.

Within the context of this collection the attempt to read meaning into fate is foiled from the outset. 'A Shiver', the second poem in the collection, likens the destructive force behind a contemplated sledgehammer blow to 'a long nursed rage' (*DC*, p. 5). The comparison exemplifies the human tendency to comprehend devastation in relation to attributed emotional motivation, and simultaneously exposes a complete absence of rancour from the action described, setting it in a new and chilling context of simple fact. 'Anything Can Happen', the translation from Horace that Heaney identifies as one of the two 'tuning forks' of the first part of *District and Circle*,[17] is explicit in its depiction of a universe in which destruction and violence are without motive, neither preventable nor foreseeable.

District and Circle's blunt refusal to indulge the human desire to read 'meaning' into inconsequential fate was prefigured in *Station Island*, in the resignation with which Heaney concludes his bitter tirade against 'everything / that made me biddable and unforthcoming'.[18] This new-found resignation leads Heaney to reflect upon the pride and futility of 'the tribe whose dances never fail / For they keep dancing till they sight the deer' (*SI*, p. 86). The tribal belief system that attempts to impose causality upon the relationship between human action and human fate becomes the emblem for all that is self-deceiving and hopeless, yet at the same time as using their behaviour as the metaphor for a futile wish of his own, Heaney identifies the particular absurdity of attributing meaning where none is inherent as the practice of uneducated others, stopping short of relating it to his own life. That he does so is unsurprising, as the concept of an existence bounded by unassailable and 'unreadable' absolutes – glimpsed in the heartbeats of his dying friend that 'scared me the way they stripped things naked' (*SI*, p. 81), and lurking beneath the accusations of his murdered cousin, 'you saw that, and you wrote that – not the fact' (*SI*, p. 83), is the terror from which Heaney finds himself constantly shying away in this poem. 'Station Island' makes the tacit acknowledgement that perhaps neither poetry nor the human perception of reality can hold its own in the face of incontrovertible historical 'fact', but makes no attempt to explore or to confront the implications of this possibility. Rather than face up to his un-looked-for glimpse of 'naked' reality, the Heaney of *Station Island* attempts to re-clothe it in banter before retreating, unreconciled. In *District and Circle*, he finally acknowledges this force of cold reality around him and begins his exploration of a strange new world that has been 'hosed-down', 'cleaned-up' (*DC*, p. 69) and denuded of all that experience and imagination had appended to it.

For much of *District and Circle*, Heaney is held uncomfortably in thrall to the empty chill of his de-humanised world. 'The Turnip Snedder' opens the collection in a Mossbawn location that will be familiar to readers of Heaney's earlier poetry, but offers an estranging new view by adopting the perspective of the snedder itself, which declares that ' "This is the way that God sees life" ' (*DC*, p. 3). Regardless of any argument as to whether Heaney intends the voice of the snedder to echo his own, the positioning of this statement at the beginning of the collection necessarily influences our reading of the poems that follow, and the notion of an impervious, unreasoning God whose vision of death leaves no scope for resurrection haunts the early poems in *District and Circle*.

This collection sees Heaney's old horrors – fears of malignant energies in the natural world, manifested in suspected presences in the barn, at the flax dam and amidst the pea drills – replaced by the more rational, adult dread that the world may be free from malice simply by virtue of being free from motive. A creeping, glacial coldness threatens to paralyse Heaney: 'cold smooth creeping' (*DC*, p. 34) steel, 'dawn stone-circle chill' (*DC*, p. 54), 'frozen shore' and 'rimed horizon' (*DC*, p. 44) contribute towards an atmosphere of impervious frigidity within which warmth is dismissed as 'unseasonable' (*DC*, p. 15). 'Höfn' imagines an apocalypse of ice, setting cold in opposition to life and poetry as the glacier threatens to 'deepfreeze . . . every warm, mouthwatering word of mouth' (*DC*, p. 53). This vision is sustained throughout 'On the Spot', where Heaney's 'adoring' of nature is arrested by the shock of finding coldness where warmth should have been, and the positioning of this poem immediately after 'Höfn' makes a compelling case to suggest that the same unappeasable, unreasoning nothingness is 'what conspired to addle / Matter in its planetary stand-off' (*DC*, p. 54). The sinister construction, 'of what conspired', is prefigured in the earlier poem 'Polish Sleepers', where no hint is given as to what the conspiring forces may be. By repeating it in 'On the Spot', Heaney retrospectively embeds the inevitability of future cold into the childhood memory, sapping the summer heat of the earlier poem as he estranges his memory from itself to bring it in line with a new agenda of anaesthetised deep freeze.

Had *District and Circle* closed with 'On the Spot', its outlook could have appeared very bleak indeed. Just as the donkey portrayed in 'Out of Shot' wanders free at the end of the poem, unmoved by the events in which it has played a part and now 'lost to its owner, lost for its sunlit hills' (*DC*, p. 15), so the places and objects that had been assimilated into Heaney's life are restored to their original states of otherness until the poet stands alone. All that had once seemed comforting and familiar is rendered strange through the bold attempt to recapture the unassimilated essence of things, and the poet is left staring into a future of godless emptiness. Yet amidst this newly hostile world, Heaney begins to formalise a personal creed of regeneration, drawing upon the lexicon of conventional religion that has been latent in his poetry for many years. In 'Like everybody else . . .' Heaney refers explicitly to his long-standing attachment to the language of his Catholic upbringing, admitting meaning has been drained from the concepts it once embraced, leaving behind nothing more than a shell of long-cherished words: 'The loss occurred off-stage. And yet I cannot / disavow words like "thanksgiving" or "host" / or communion bread' (*DC*, p. 47). Just as it has become more difficult for Heaney to renounce the fictions of art than the indifferent reality of the world that inspired them, so the poet finds that the power of the words that once signified the core values of his religion have outlived that of their meanings. He says of these words that 'they have an undying / tremor and draw, like well water far down' (*DC*, p. 47), and in so saying he detaches – estranges – them from their original connotations, repurposing them as he binds them to a new pseudo-religion of nature. Within the context of *District and Circle*, warmth, germination and flowing water are set on the side of life, whilst all that is frozen, hard or unimpressionable sides with death. The regenerative potential that Heaney has always recognised in the act of 'making strange' redeems him at the point when it had seemed bound to betray him into hopelessness, as the Tollund Man, a figure long dislocated from his native place and time, reappears to assume a position at the centre of a new world order.

Heaney recalls how 'this Iron Age revenant was . . . "discovered" in a new setting', and

> In a new start that was both unexpected and exhilarating, I returned to a figure who had given me rare poetic strength more than 30 years earlier . . . the convention is to call such a figure a 'persona', but in this case he felt more like a transfusion, and I found myself writing poems about glacier melt and river flow, crab apples and fiddlehead ferns, birch groves and alder trees.[19]

'The Tollund Man in Springtime' brings the first hint that the winter of *District and Circle* may not prove endless, representing a renewal of hope. This renewal does not undermine the agenda of estrangement that runs throughout the collection, for the Tollund Man remains unassailably 'strange' in his otherness. His power lies in the fact that he has remained unchanged throughout the cycles of life around him; his physical endurance has grown into a kind of spiritual strength. Outlasting his long-ago death, he is 'neither god nor ghost / Not at odds or at one, but simply lost / To you and yours' (*DC*, p. 55). He stands against the threat of cold emptiness simply by continuing to exist, representing an unfailing constancy that outstrips his transportation out of context and out of time. Equally indifferent to the demands of his one-time peers as to the significations that history has thrust upon him, he acknowledges 'Faith placed in me, me faithless as a stone / The harrow turned up when the crop was sown' (*DC*, p. 56).

Within *District and Circle*, the Tollund Man stands for transcendence of individual mortality, and through him Heaney finds the faith and inspiration that enables him to translate his empty world into a series of concentric life cycles. Heaney's success in restoring 'otherness' to the objects in his world gave him the power to separate 'actual' people and places from the weight of meaning appended to them in memory, and in doing so he came close to dislocating himself from all that he held dear. Through the Tollund Man, he reminds himself that the 'actual' and its appended meaning are not necessarily bound to the same life cycle. Just as the 'reel' of Wordsworth's skates outlasts their perished bindings whilst the bindings themselves outlive their wearer, so the Tollund Man's existence and significance outlasts his lifespan, transcending death and offering a modern, godless image of immortality through 'self-forgetfulness'.

This discovery enables Heaney to overcome his sense of growing chill, and he affirms with the Tollund Man, '"The soul exceeds its circumstances". Yes' (*DC*, p. 56). In this bold acknowledgement and in the eloquent certainty of that 'Yes', Heaney asserts that the unassailable facts of history, which dictate that human life is short, death is forever and well-loved places may not last, does not necessarily outweigh the vision of immortality achieved through memory, art, literature or simple love. This conviction spurs him on into a final, triumphant act of defamiliarisation as he defies the coldness of fact and history, turning instead towards a new world of possibility in which the past can once more be re-imagined and reshaped to fit the demands of the present. He remarked in a recent interview that, within *District and Circle*, 'the Tollund Man releases me into pleasure . . . more personal stuff . . . more spontaneous',[20] and the poems that follow 'The Tollund Man in Springtime', whilst retaining the preoccupation with mortality that characterises the collection, are newly optimistic in their outlook. In the closing poems of *District and Circle*, Heaney dares to carve out a new, as-yet-unfamiliar place in which to live and write that lies 'Between what happened and was meant to be' (*DC*, p. 56), that relies neither upon unforgiving history nor the now-discredited notion of an interested God to endorse or underwrite its reality.

In 1991, embarking upon his post-*Haw-Lantern* cycle of estrangement in *Seeing Things*, Heaney recognised that 'The places I go back to have not failed / But will not last' (*ST*, p. 101). *Seeing Things* and *The Spirit Level*, in their acts of re-imagining those places, and *Electric Light*, with its assimilation of place into self, are preoccupied with a search for ways in which well-loved people and places can be made to 'last'. Throughout these collections, Heaney's allegiance moves increasingly away from the places of the world and towards the places of the heart. *District and Circle*, with its agenda of recovering the original essence of the world itself, estranging Heaney from the matter of his own memories by looking afresh at the raw material out of they were composed, represents the beginnings of a repositioning on Heaney's part in relation to the places he has known. With a new-found acceptance of inevitability, Heaney faces up to the changing, and even the loss, of people and places that remain important to him, looking afresh at external reality and no longer focusing exclusively upon his construction of the world.

In common with *Electric Light*, *District and Circle* seems at first glance to show Heaney deserting well-known places in favour of more distant territory. The title poem looks towards London and the tube bombings of 7 July 2005, whilst others conjure images of New York's fallen towers, war in Afghanistan and global warming. Tobias Hill, reviewing the collection for the *Observer*, observed that Heaney has now 'gone global'.[21] A closer reading, however, will reveal that these far-flung settings do not represent a change of focus on Heaney's part. The poet himself suggested that 'On second thoughts, a reader might realise, "Ah, yes, in spite of the London poem, in most of the others, he's circling his own district"',[22] adding that the title 'had the virtue of unexpectedness . . . At the same time, it signalled an inclination to favour a chosen region and keep coming back to it'.[23]

Critics of *District and Circle*, in common with critics of the collections that preceded it, charge Heaney with a failure to 'move on'. Clive Wilmer dismissed the new collection as the work of one 'cornered by his own genius: writing too many poems that emulate past successes, and shutting off routes to discovery',[24] whilst Stephen Knight finds that Heaney 'replaces surprise with deliberation' in a collection that suffers from 'a lack of edge . . . [and is] nothing like as immediate as his earlier work'.[25] These critics fail to appreciate that, in Heaney's most significant poetry, we should look not for new and unfamiliar places and preoccupations, but for regenerative new ways of estranging the familiar, 'freshening your outlook, beyond the range you thought you'd settled for' (*ST*, p. 99). In a feature in *The Times* at the time of publication of *District and Circle*, Heaney betrayed his awareness of the tendency to find fault with his practice of returning to old ground in retorting to an unspoken criticism with the protestation, 'Not that there's anything wrong with revisiting earlier themes and settings'. He went on to explain, 'such a return can produce a wonderful re-creative charge'.[26]

It is just such a 're-creative charge' that transforms 'The Blackbird of Glanmore' from a simple revisiting of a known environment and a known theme – Glanmore Cottage, and the subject of 'Mid Term Break' – into something unfamiliar and new. The estranging influence in this poem is provided by Heaney's own changed perspective, as he looks towards a new phase of life and writing. In an interview, Heaney named 'The Blackbird of Glanmore' as his favourite poem in *District and Circle*, explaining 'the reason I like the last poem . . . [is that] it's a kind of different stage in life. You're beginning to be aware of the underground journey a bit more'.[27] With reference to poetic composition in general, and *District and Circle* in particular, he observes that 'you have to surprise yourself, if possible', saying that he finds himself perpetually 'either surprised, or obsessed. There's no halfway house.'[28] 'The Blackbird of Glanmore', in common with much of Heaney's later poetry of estrangement, draws together the qualities of surprise and obsession. Well-known sites are compulsively, 'obsessively' revisited, either in their remembered states, as is predominantly the case in *Seeing Things* and *The Spirit Level*, or in their current, physical states as in *District and Circle*, and each return revives 'surprise' as Heaney continues to discover thoughts and approaches that are new in settings that have long been familiar.

Notes

1 Seamus Heaney, *Seeing Things* (London: Faber, 1991), p. 101. Hereafter given in the text as *ST*.
2 Seamus Heaney, *Crediting Poetry* (Oldcastle: Gallery, 1995), p. 12.
3 Seamus Heaney, 'Joy or Night: Last Things in the Poetry of W.B. Yeats and Philip Larkin', *The Redress of Poetry* (London: Faber, 1995), p. 159.
4 Seamus Heaney, *Electric Light* (London: Faber & Faber, 2001), p. 3.
5 A reference to Roddy McCorley, executed in Toome on Good Friday 1799 for his involvement in the 1798 Rising.
6 Eugene O'Brien, *Seamus Heaney: Creating Irelands of the Mind* (Dublin: Liffey Press, 2002), p. 159.
7 Jonathan Bolton, '"Customary rhythms": Seamus Heaney and the Rite of Poetry', *Papers on Language and Literature*, 37: 2 (spring 2001), pp. 205–22.
8 John Taylor, review of *Electric Light*, *Poetry*, 179: 5 (February 2002), pp. 296–8.
9 O'Brien, p. 128.
10 Heaney, *Crediting Poetry*, p. 12.
11 Seamus Heaney, *The Haw Lantern* (London: Faber & Faber, 1987), p. 51.
12 Seamus Heaney, *District and Circle* (London: Faber & Faber, 2006), p. 22.
13 Seamus Heaney, 'One Poet in Search of a Title', *The Times* (Books Supplement), 25 March 2006, p. 7.
14 Ben Naparstek, 'Notes from the Underground', *The Times* (Books Supplement), 25 March 2006, p. 6.
15 Michael Parker, *Seamus Heaney: The Making of the Poet* (Basingstoke: Macmillan, 1993), pp. 205–6.
16 Seamus Heaney, *The Spirit Level* (London: Faber & Faber, 1996), p. 6.
17 Heaney, 'One Poet in Search of a Title'.
18 Seamus Heaney, *Station Island* (London: Faber & Faber, 1984), p. 86.
19 Heaney, 'One Poet in Search of a Title'.
20 Sam Leith, 'Return of the Naturalist', *Daily Telegraph* (Telegraph Magazine), 2 April 2006, www.telegraph.co.uk/arts/main.jhtml?xml=/arts/2006/04/02/boheaney.xml (accessed 6 October 2008).
21 Tobias Hill, 'Arms around the World', *Observer* (Review), 2 April 2006, p. 21.
22 Naparstek, p. 6.
23 Heaney, 'One Poet in Search of a Title'.
24 Clive Wilmer, 'Down to Earth', *New Statesman*, 17 April 2006, pp. 48–9.

25 Stephen Knight, '*District and Circle*: The bog man cometh (again)', *Independent*, 9 April 2006, www.independent.co.uk/arts-entertainment/books/reviews/district-and-circle-by-seamus-heaney-473470.html (accessed 6 October 2008).

26 Heaney, 'One Poet in Search of a Title'.

27 Leith, 'Return of the Naturalist', np.

28 Robert McCrum, 'From Cattle to Battle', *Observer* (Review), 2 April 2006, p. 21.

10

Neither here nor there: new generation Northern Irish poets (Sinéad Morrissey and Nick Laird)[1]

Michael Parker

'Skies change, not cares for those who cross the sea'[2]

Confirmation that a new generation of talented poets is beginning to re-shape the face of Irish and Northern Irish literature can be found in two recent anthologies: Selima Guinness's *The New Irish Poets* (2004) and John Brown's *Magnetic North: The Emerging Poets* (2005).[3] Amongst the defining characteristics of the new poetry, according to Guinness, are a postmodernist distrust of grand narratives, an alertness to wider geopolitical concerns, and a preoccupation with domestic and family, rather than national history. For Brown, whose focus is exclusively on Northern poetry, the coming poetic generation displays a high degree of mobility and disparity in their work, a determination to cross borders, break silences and proffer 'bifocal or comparative visions' (p. 12) of changing private and public terrain. While not wishing to question the validity of these assertions in relation to a substantial number of the younger poets, I would suggest that many traits identified by Brown and Guinness are equally demonstrable in the writing of their literary forebears, the Heaney–Mahon–Longley and Muldoon–McGuckian–Carson generations. Indeed, Brown himself recognises continuities in content, form and style, and how poets from each generation developed different strategies in facing up to a common imperative, the need to address the appalling evil that destroyed so much of, and in, the province from the late 1960s onwards: 'Darkness remains both a felt, elemental or metaphysical presence . . . the image of poetry as a "door into the dark" is with us more than we care to acknowledge' (p. 12). As he also rightly points out, while altered political and social conditions since the ceasefires may have led to a diminution in the political pressures and expectations placed on the poets, the imprint of the recent past – of 'ancestral', communal and family memory – is still clearly visible in their work.

Rather than offer a broad, potentially fleeting survey of a range of writers from this new generation, this chapter will focus instead on the début collections of two writers, Sinéad Morrissey and Nick Laird, whose work exemplifies many of the attributes identified by Guinness and Brown. Other fine young poets born in the late 1960s and early 1970s, such as Frank Sewell, Colette Bryce, Leontia Flynn or Allan Gillis, might have equally been selected for scrutiny and enabled me to contrast distinctive, individual perspectives from the last and first decades of the twentieth and twenty-first centuries. Born respectively in 1972 and 1975, Morrissey and Laird came of age at a turning point in the province's history, the time of the first ceasefires, after a childhood and adolescence dominated by near-continuous political violence. Despite prolonged absences from the North, both are beneficiaries of the relative normality[4] that has existed there since the ceasefires of 1994 and 1997, and the cultural and economic transformations that have accompanied them. Their particular geographical and cultural relocations have clearly enriched their work and enabled them not just to look back on both their own and their parents' experiences, but also to look upwards and outwards to engage with other cultures, places and times.

With three volumes to her credit, Sinéad Morrissey has perhaps the most substantial profile to date among the new generation of poets. Born in Portadown on 24 April 1972, and educated at Belfast High School, she lived in the province until 1990. In a recent interview, she explains that since her parents were atheists, she was not culturally aligned to 'either community . . . so I think that's given me a degree of impartiality'.[5] At eighteen, she became the youngest ever recipient of the Patrick Kavanagh Award for Poetry, and went on to study English and German at Trinity College, Dublin. She returned to Belfast in 1999, and in 2002 became Writer-in-Residence at the Seamus Heaney Centre for Poetry at Queen's University. From its outset, *There Was Fire in Vancouver* (1996), her first collection, negotiates the intersections of private and public spaces in the North. The 'double vision' of the opening poem's title refers simultaneously to this conjunction as well as to unspecified differences in perspective between the speaker and her unidentified addressee. The poem's initial descriptions of Belfast occupying 'a *shallow* bowl of light' or of the Black Hill constituting 'a *power failure* / touching the sky' (my emphasis) have obvious political resonances. 'Double Vision's main focus, however, is on another kind of failure. Whereas her visual and political experiences of Belfast emphasise accessibility and excess ('I've seen it all'), the narrator's personal relationship with her partner reveals an absence of both qualities: 'the places in your head / Stay shut to me', 'with me none the wiser'. Socially, intellectually, geographically, the pair may have much in common ('You've travelled up as I have'), but in their perceptions of the place and the situation they seem miles apart: inside his head there is 'None of what I saw'. For him, it would appear, Belfast is somewhere amenable to scrutiny ('gone into') yet somehow devoid of presence ('gone'). Yet in the closing stanza the city's road signs and street-lamps are invested with power, and seem almost to be conspiring together to mock the reluctant exile's return: '*You're back*', they chorus, 'Glimmering with victory'.[6]

Threats of erasure, images of dissolution[7] recur in many of the North-based poems that follow. Set in the Thatcherite–Reaganite 1980s, 'CND' starts with another double-take, the grinning face of a nine-year-old activist juxtaposed with the grim caption on a balloon, 'I want to grow up, not blow up!'. The poem traces the girl's journey from 'innocence' to 'experience', evoking in stanza two her naïve plea-sure at signing hate mail to the American President, collecting stickers, tasting beer. It is only when confronted with the macabre picture of two bomb victims ('two skeletons / Scared of the sky') that the fear of 'being nothing too soon and too suddenly'[8] strikes her, silencing her 'for the day'. This last phrase stresses the temporariness of the blow delivered to her political enthusiasms, and encourages us to see the poem itself as a rejection of silence.

In contrast to 'CND', 'Ciara', 'Europa Hotel' and 'Belfast Storm' voice sorrow and anger at devastation close to home. 'Ciara' is another poem that arises from a childhood act of witness, and segues cleverly between times and perspectives. Like the focaliser's, our initial response to the image of a woman 'crying over potatoes' is incomprehension. Deftly, economically, Morrissey evokes the child's self-centred viewpoint. Her disappointments ('There would be no walk', 'Ruined Christmas') give way to something on a grander scale, the conflation in her ima-gination of 'boiling potatoes' and 'catastrophe'. Towards the close, a maturer voice intervenes to explain their symbolic function, standing in for a son 'who had his knees blown somewhere else'. That image of physical disintegration is repeatedly being re-run in his mother's 'shattered', 'fraying' mind, stranding her on the margins ('edge') of life. Metaphors of repleteness serve as an ironic counterpoint to the 'mess' the poem makes present, the 'frightening rain, pouring out / Of the Armagh sky' (p. 12) a sign of the fall-out[9] and psychological 'legacy' of the Troubles. The reader's line of vision is directed upward again in 'Belfast Storm', which fancifully attributes the atmospheric effects to the angels' rage and distress, as they look down on the city 'heads in hands and howling it out all over us'.[10] A first-person narrator suddenly materialises at the beginning of line four, one who, after expressing surprise at the angels' reaction, sardonically acknowledges a difference brought about by the 'peace dividend':

> I can't think what they haven't got used to by now
> The great gap in the street where his knees hit the wall
> Meant wheelchairs, rather than coffins. (p. 17)

Such black, mordant humour is not untypical of Belfast people from both communities, and surfaces again in another short poem across the page from 'Belfast Storm'. Lighter in touch and tone than Ciaran Carson's elegy for the bombed-out Smithfield Market,[11] 'Europa Hotel' generates empathy for a building targeted repeatedly by republican paramilitaries during the poet's childhood and teenage years. She imagines the hotel waking up to find its windows around its 'ankles' and smoke 'billowing' from its head. The Europa will have to continue in this 'impaired' state for the next fortnight, denied sight 'Of the green hills they shatter you for' (p. 16). This last line hints at the blinding absurdity of the militant republicans' bombing campaign, the mismatch between their idealised vision of 'Ireland' ('the green hills') and the destruction they wreak on their 'motherland'.

In a three-part sequence entitled 'Thoughts in a Black Taxi', Morrissey depicts her own return to Belfast and her problematic, liminal position as one who is neither/nor. Absorbed, watching loyalists preparing for the twelfth, she thinks about questioning 'the bare-chested men swanking about' high up on the bonfire. In time she recalls how her curiosity might be received:

> One 'What are *You* called?' from them, and it would all go black.
> I'd have to run to stay whole. (p. 19)

This prompts part two's recollections of earlier gaffes, such as demonstrating an unfamiliarity with loyalist paramilitary acronyms,[12] or laughing at German visitors disparaging Ian Paisley while travelling in a black UVF-run taxi heading into East Belfast. Most tellingly, she remembers her father urging her to conceal her identity, lest she be taken for a Catholic: 'Never say Morrissey again'. The closing stanzas take her back to her schooldays and the constant fear of being misidentified by nationalists. Going daily along the Grosvenor Road in Belfast High School uniform was 'like having *Protestant* slapped across your back':

> I always walked with my heart constricting,
> Half-expecting bottles, in sudden shards
> Of West Belfast sunshine,
> To dance about my head (p. 20)

Ostensibly, a third of the way into this first collection, attention switches to other locations and situations, yet not surprisingly the North and Morrissey's upbringing there remain a constant background presence. 'Bosnia' recalls a specific incident in the mid-1990s, when an anti-war protestor set fire to and killed himself in the grounds of the Palace of Westminster. The poet's critique of Western indifference at atrocities committed in areas of little or minor strategic importance arises in part one suspects from her experience of media coverage of the North in the 1970s and 1980s. Her imagery stresses the temporariness of the impact the man's suicide makes, comparing it to a 'short circuit', to a firework and spark which quickly slips from view. Instead of persuading the British and European governments to intervene in the Balkans, his gesture affects only 'the wrong people', those who recognised that 'it meant giving a damn' (p. 23). Fire reappears as the subject of the title poem, again as an object of spectacle. Paying no heed to the human cost, physical, psychological or financial, the watchers regard the conflagration as a theatrical performance, 'marvelled' at its visual effects, 'wondered' where it would next 'bestow its dance'. By conveying so strikingly the narrator's aestheticisation of violence, her translation of it into something sublime or epiphanic ('bright crusade', 'we watched with Moses') Morrissey displays the morally dubious position of the artist and citizen in the twentieth and twentieth-first centuries, the dangers of becoming desensitised to catastrophe, natural and man-made.

America's West Coast proves to be one of many stop-over sites in what turns out to be a remarkably assured, increasingly expansive quest for individuation. Recurring images and motifs – allusions to sea, light, colours, weather, windows, rooms, music, art – lend a measure of continuity to her wanderings, as a six-part sequence entitled 'Mercury' attests. This opens in an extremely restricted space, a 'Bottom Drawer', with a speaker riffling through the texts (diaries, letters, photographs) that collectively give 'testimony' to another's life. Selecting a metaphor to sum up the deceased woman's 'intricate', contained existence, Morrissey opts for a Chinese vase, 'painted in / By time', 'brittle as bone' (p. 33). In 'Nomad', she dwells upon the role of place in identity, concluding that 'where you are' necessitates 'facing the road'. Reflecting on her short lifetime, in which villages gave way to cities, 'scarecrows to gantries', she recognises that she now has 'No space to hold', that her past (the walled-up room?) is 'Somewhere you can't get back to' (p. 34). Although 'Gull Song' talks of flight and an achieved self-sufficiency ('I . . . come clear', 'I have nothing to fear in weather and distance'), a counterpoint to song is the heart's 'own crumpled urges' and the magnetic pull of her defiled homeland, a 'torn monastery', with 'open altars' (p. 35).

'Finding her Feet', part four of the sequence, steps into magical realist territory to depict conflicting impulses within the human psyche and specifically within the artist's imagination. In the opening stanza, its narrator describes diving into the sea to rescue one of the feet.[13] Its attraction to 'coral' and preference for 'inward' journeying might suggest the draw of family and of literal and literary sites of origin; in these lines Morrissey may well allude to Ariel's song in *The Tempest* ('Full fathom five your father lies; of his bones are coral made') and to Seamus Heaney's 'Bogland', which compares Ireland's artists to 'pioneers' who 'keep striking / Inwards and downwards'.[14] The other foot, meanwhile, was swanning around Bangladesh, 'In raptures with the stars' and his own success. In attempting to put a distance between himself and his 'roots' ('running away'), ironically this foot had run 'out of room'. At the close, irreconcilable differences between the feet – 'here' and 'there', local and international? – are resolved as a result of decisive authorial intervention. Poetry itself will serve as the home, room or structure where an accommodation can be reached with her poetic 'feet', and their contrary, competing tendencies.

In Mercury's fifth part, 'Leaving Flensburg', the winged feet bear her to a city on the German–Danish border, in the historically contested state of Schleswig-Holstein.[15] The place provides her with a temporary 'grounding', but also visual and emotional experiences which she can draw upon 'for years'. With its dank, cold climate, the shipyard with its 'sad men welding steel' (p. 37), it inevitably evokes thoughts of what she has left behind and will return to. 'No Need to Travel', the sequence's final lyric, seems to mark a repatriation, followed as it is by poems dedicated to close family members. The tulips in a local garden blazon a resilience that has endured despite everything, a 'knowing how to thrust colour skywards / Flaunting the unlikely, shocking through bloom' (p. 38).

The destabilising effects of family division and loss are central to the next cluster of texts, which maintains the book's linked preoccupation with the problematic nature of identity and art's assuaging, restorative possibilities. 'Hazel Goodwin Morrissey Brown' records a final visit to the family home, which is the process of being disassembled. In an act which sets in motion the poem's creation, the narrator plucks from the débris an old photograph of her mother in her 'GDR-Worker phase', placing it alongside a recent business card, thus conjoining her times as a communist fellow-traveller and entrepreneur promoting 'Nu Skin' products in New Zealand. Cosmetic renewal gives way to reincarnation myth in stanza two, when the daughter in the poem 'discovers' – thanks to an antipodean psychic – that in a previous existence she had been her mother's mother. The neatly arranged rhymes of the final verse ('fight'/'flight', 'space'/'race', 'airport'/'last resort') underline ideas of cycles of recurrence, her mother's journeying eastwards and southwards in pursuit of freedom presaging the poet's own. Later poems ('My Grandmother Through Glass', 'Losing a Diary') are unable to recapture the affirmation of this response to bereavement; departure generates an 'awful hush' (p. 45) in the former, while the latter locates the author 'in open sea', neither 'moored' nor 'married'. Her craft cannot recreate 'the sad, fixed honesty of how it was' (p. 46), she ruefully acknowledges.

Yet as *There Was Fire in Vancouver* concludes, a series of short lyrics praising light radiates a late sense of benison. This *fiat lux* begins with 'September Light', which delights in the sun's alchemy, 'rareness making gold' (p. 49). 'Twenty-One', a coming-of-age poem, picks up where that left off, thanking God for the gift of the world. An objective correlative of the print she wants to take, the poem celebrates 'blown blossom' and 'receding colours of the day', and concludes with a declaration of aesthetic intent, an envisioning of widening horizons. This is immediately followed by another self-reflexive piece, 'Guardians', which resonates with a psalm-like, lyric authority

> Light is their element, they make waves
> In the world with the force of their rays. (p. 51)

The immanent, Blakean spirits of the title are guarantors of stability ('Making sure the earth holds'), guides overseeing our ascent into a better state, a plateau 'where minerals dazzle', a place of transfiguration.[16]

Morrissey's light display reaches its climax in 'The Juggler' and 'Restoration'. Like the young Heaney in his eulogies to the skills of the ploughman, the diviner, the smith, the thatcher, Morrissey stresses initially the quotidian, humble origins of the juggler's art; she pictures him practising for hours between bins and mattresses in 'a rented back yard'. What she does not replicate, however, is Heaney's deployment of a child's perspective, opting instead for the standpoint of a somewhat cynical, world-weary narrator. 'God knows what / Anachronism he took up before', she comments, dismissing the juggler's act as merely 'a sideshow', a rather crass attempt to turn back time. A more nuanced reaction begins to emerge in stanza three, with a recognition of the therapeutic effects the spectacle creates, providing – like the poet? – an escape from 'the *drain* / Of things modern' (my emphasis). From this point onwards the juggler, rather than the narrator, becomes *the* focal point ('we ring / Him with faces'), a figure imbued with understanding, resolve, resilience:

He knows
How we anticipate failure
And that what he owes

His audience is a defiance
Of breakdown.

Accumulating references to 'magic', 'radiance', 'weightlessness' signal
how much the speaker's perception has been transformed, while the
repeated use of first person plurals indicates how he has whirled the
audience into a collective entity. Ultimately, his role is perceived as
comparable to that of an artist or priest, since he cajoles 'improbables
. . . / Into truth', and leaves us 'not so far out / From faith as we were'
(p. 56).

The concept of faith as something fixed or grounded contrasts, of
course, with Matthew Arnold's vision in 'Dover Beach' (1867), which
imagines it as a sea in retreat. Morrissey clearly has Arnold's poem
in her sights in 'Restoration', the book's closing poem. In locating and
dating its two parts, 'Achill, 1985' and 'Juist, 1991', the poet invites
us to see the distinction between her worldview at thirteen and
Weltanschauung six years later. Desolation appears at first to be the
dominant note in the first poem, whose narrator recalls watching, along
with a single gull, a beached dolphin being ripped 'Of all its history',
by an apparently indifferent 'Easter wind'. 'Abandoned', 'washed up',
'on the edge' of things, it might have seemed to mirror the teenager's
own exposed condition, facing a sea 'wide and emptied of love'. Yet
the memory of how 'its body / Opened in the sun', and re-use of the
verb 'Caught'[17] to reveal her captivation, seem anticipatory, making us
re-read the experience as a moment of epiphany. The positioning of 'Juist,
1991' immediately after 'Achill, 1985' results in the collection ending
as it began with double vision, a sense of here and there. From the date
in the title one assumes that the poet visited this small East Friesian
island while taking her degree in German and English at Trinity.
Whereas Arnold's elegy opens in tranquillity, with a calm North Sea
and white chalk cliffs glimmering in the moonlight, Morrissey's poem
'booms' at its outset and remarks on a complete absence of light on
the beach and in the sky. The sea, however, is a revelation in light, of
light; touched, 'the water explodes / In phosphorescence' (p. 59).
There, on Juist, here on the page, the sudden discharge of energy is
illuminating, not life-destroying. The last lines seem possessed by an
evangelical zeal, passing from uncertainty ('No one knows') into
mystery, or rather *the* mystery of *creatio ex nihilo*:

Let there be light in this world
Of nothing let it come from
Nothing let it speak nothing
Let it go everywhere (p. 60)

Like the sceptical audience watching the juggler, some readers may recoil from this apparent throwback to an earlier time and state; others might maintain that genesis is an entirely appropriate place for an emerging poet to set off from. Yet tensions remain despite the uplift in this resolution. Amid the assertions that light should simply 'be', a prohibition appears: 'let it speak nothing'. This seems to indicate a recognition of the limitations of, even a distrust of, the very medium she is employing.[18]

When Edna Longley writes that 'The speech or eloquent silence of the father is an important motif in Northern Irish poetry',[19] she may have been thinking primarily, though not exclusively, of male poets. In contrast to Morrissey, whose book contains only one passing reference to her father (in 'Thoughts in a Black Taxi'), Nick Laird's *To a Fault* begins with a series of glimpses of his father, a figure who comes across as simultaneously present and remote. He first features in 'Cuttings', a poem whose title is entirely appropriate given its setting (a barber's shop) and Laird's clipped, highly visual technique. Signs that the location is Northern Ireland are immediately apparent, as the sunlight highlights 'a patch of *paisley* wallpaper'.[20] Although there is something theatrical about the barber and the way he whips off the cape 'with a matador's flourish', at the same time he is depicted as deft and diplomatic with the customers. Avoiding dangerous topics like 'the troubles or women or prison', he confines the conversation to safer substitutes, 'parking or calving or missing'. The idea of absent and repressed narratives is developed further in the narrator's subsequent focus on his father and, midway through the poem, on the calendar portraying the 'glories of Ulster'. This latter, bright aesthetic object is isolated in the mundane dullness of its surroundings (amid the utilitarian beige lino, red chair, and brown ceramic sink), its positive images subverted by the disclosure that it is merely advertising 'JB Crane Hire or 'some crowd flogging animal feed'. The penultimate verse consolidates the notion of the hairdresser's shop as an emblematic space within the province, a 'bandaged' place where diverse individuals – 'Eelmen, gunmen, the long dead, the police' – temporarily find common ground. Into this unprepossessing frame, an initially unidentified male figure appears, 'my angry and beautiful father'. The ambivalent feelings and 'contradictory awarenesses'[21] compressed in that phrase are maintained in the concluding images, which present him negatively ('his eyes budded shut') and positively ('expectant and open'), his head filled with 'lather' and 'unusual thoughts'. The father remains for the reader – as for the speaker perhaps – an elusive, enigmatic figure; what makes him so angry, we never discover. What Laird does present at the close is a man curious enough to reach for something beyond the quotidian and parochial, capable of engaging with the strange and the sublime.

Laird, like Morrissey, proves to be deeply engaged by the relationship between family and identity, conscious both of the need to belong and to break rank.[22] Something of this anxiety can be seen in 'The Layered', one of *To a Fault*'s lighter offerings. This finds the poet playing games with his name and depicting, somewhat cryptically, three family members. First up is Matthew Thomas or, as the poem has it, 'Empty Laird' (p. 28), a man who in his last years lamented a dearth of opportunities (educational, political?). His son, 'Laird Jnr', is unflatteringly represented as 'a nit-picker . . . a hair splitter', yet also as someone who felt terror at his own insubstantiality. Contrasted to these flawed males is the future Mrs Laird, whose physical presence, repleteness and confidence made an impression immediately on 'see-thru' Junior. The bizarre line with which the poem ends ('into my grave into my grave into my grave she was laid', p. 29) alludes to *Hamlet*, reinforcing the image of the son as a lack or absence which she – and textmaking – filled.[23]

Fecundity and criminality seem to be characteristics of the extended family portrayed in 'Pedigree' (pp. 35–7). Having established that the bloodline includes a shoplifter, a cattle-smuggler, a rustler-turned-killer, it is hardly surprising that the family blazon proposed by the narrator should be 'an enormous unruly blackthorn hedge', rather than a yielding willow. Trying to determine his own place in the family tree, the narrator – who shares a passing resemblance to the lawyer author – describes himself, understandably, as 'out on a limb'. When, mid-way through, the spotlight moves on to his more immediate forebears, an element of bathos enters in. The portrait of his father as a young man contains nothing of the dramatic, heroic, illicit or adventurous, only their absence; he is pictured fishing away his boyhood, longing for a Davy Crockett hat, polishing the medals of 'his legendary uncles' all of whom had perished at the Somme.[24] Having disclosed the fact that neither of his parents left school with qualifications, the narrator lays emphasis on his mother's subsequent endeavour to remedy that lack. His use of the adjective 'each' and the verb 'heave' convey her determination, commitment and energy, qualities seemingly absent in the father:

Each evening after work and dinner,
she'd do her OU course
and heave the brown suitcase of books
from out beneath the . . . bunks. (p. 36)

In delivering his verdict on the relationships within his family –
father–mother, brother–sister, but not father–son or mother–son – the
speaker employs a strangely cheerless word: 'There is such a shelter in
each other'. Home, thus, appears to be associated with protection and
proximity, but not with emotional warmth or intimacy.

Directly after this, the narrator switches his attention to a very different location and entity, when its primary addressee is introduced and
takes centre stage. He describes his lover padding from the bathroom,
'gentled with freckles and moisturized curves'. She is presented as an
iconic figure, the embodiment of physical, linguistic and syntactical grace
('perfect in grammar and posture'). In yet another self-reflexive touch,
he identifies her as a kindred mark-maker in referring to her 'singing
. . . footprints'. In the middle of his eulogy, a call from the past breaks
in, suddenly compelling him to confront the gulf between his present
and that past. He is made uneasy by the tone his partner adopts in
speaking to his family from 'across the water'. Although the poem's
closing statement ('this is a charge not a pleading') seems to be an indictment of *her* for her inability to relate to them, one detects also feelings
of guilt on his part, a fear perhaps that he can no longer 'hear them
right' (p. 37), that *he* has forged a distance from his point of origin.

Subsequently Laird moves beyond the family circle to provide a
number of highly evocative portraits of the province in the wake of the
1990s ceasefires. The aptly titled 'Remaindermen' contemplates initially
the survivors of the Troubles' years; praising their 'weathered' resistance
and endurance ('their ability to thole'). Theirs have been lifetimes
taken up with deaths and emigration, watching

their cemeteries filling up
like car parks on a Saturday,
their young grow fat for export (p. 9)

Contrasted with these solitary, passive, pacific figures are the intransi-
gent in the community, who the narrator characterises as preferring an
'ice-bound'[25] world than one involving fluidity and compromise. In what
proves to be one of many self-reflexive moments in *To A Fault*, the
speaker notes how 'someone' charged with transcribing 'the last fifty
years of *our* speech' (my emphasis) has yet to encounter the word 'sorry'
or employ a question mark, an indication that truth might be plural.
The poem ends with a wry, unconscious sign of the contrariness of the

local townspeople who, in erecting a triumphal arch, inadvertently encouraged visitors to leave; those arriving were greeted with a 'Safe Home Brethren', while those departing were wished a 'Welcome'.

'The Signpost' maintains the collection's focus on the violent semiotics of the North, and starts with a punishment beating carried out on a loyalist paramilitary by two former drinking-companions. In its narrative, demotic style and sardonic humour it anticipates *Utterly Monkey* (2005), Laird's first novel, in which one of the leading characters, Geordie Wilson, is subjected to an identical ordeal, having to wait for his attackers to bring a second gun to knee-cap him after the first one jams.[26] The damage to his legs, the speaker observes drily,

> put paid to plans for ascending Everest,
> and playing for Rangers. . . .
> (though it left open Glentoran, as his father suggested). (p. 10)

Splayed out on the ground after the shooting, his body is described as resembling a signpost, a pointed warning to others of the toll exacted for transgression. The closing stanzas find the paramilitary/ victim in a bed at the Royal, gazing out over the Belfast skyline. At a remove now from the two 'stringy cunts' and guns which put him there, he observes two massive cranes, 'their *arms* low over the city / *as if*' (my emphases) in a gesture of benediction.[27] As in 'Cuttings', the poem ends in an expression of wonder, how 'all that gathered weight' remains 'upright'. The irony, of course, is that East Belfast is hardly or simply a place of benison, restraint and moral rectitude. Significantly, when he manages to locate 'his father's house'[28] – a metonym no doubt for the province – he notes that it is in a state of darkness.

One of the most accomplished and complex of the early poems is 'The Length of a Wave' (pp. 6–7), which illustrates how effectively Laird is able to switch from domestic, familial and local preoccupations to larger concerns, such as politics and the function of art. This sense of restless, continuing motion is signalled in the poem's opening line, which juxtaposes 'the mythic coast' and 'the kitchen stove'; phrase-structures and word-sounds echo each other. The dominant presence in the early stanzas is again that of the narrator's father, this time as an increasingly disturbed, disturbing figure. Although initially depicted indulging merely in a little *schadenfreude* – talking 'of floods / riptides, the boy drowned in Bundoran' as he warms himself beside the stove – the speaker then alludes to tidal mood-swings ('dependent on the moon'), before informing us how twice he 'broke the light-switch . . . punching it'. Outside the house, his father's voice resonates still, yet loses in power both as a result son's intellectual advances ('I could judge', 'by knowing') and shift of concern, his desire for news from the poem's unidentified addressee, presumably a lover back in England.

The poem's second movement monitors a sequence of alternative sound-effects, beginning with the waves rippling out from a bomb-blast (perhaps that in Omagh in 1998?) 'to the corpses in the mortuary awaiting recognition'. Turning from the horror of that devastated scene, he attunes himself to noises closer to home, like the clatter made by a barley machine, a ball 'gonging' against a garage-door, the sound-swell created by speech, an 'adult' bird in flight, his sleeping beloved's 'tidal breathing', this last image transporting us lyrically into an unthreatening seascape, and far from the morgue's stillness.

In the third section the auditory imagination switches to frequencies particularly associated with Northern Ireland. Mention of 'the droning Chinook' reminds one of how often images associated with surveillance figure in poems by Carson, McGuckian and Zell. In evoking the sound of a rifle shot – he compares it to a 'domestic slap' – he hints at how common violence has become both outside *and* inside the domestic sphere. Initially 'the embassies of Home' with their 'quartered flags' appear as if wreathed in light, associated with sanctuary, stability, the assertion of individual identities. In the pivotal tenth line of this section, however, it emerges that they are a place where one struggles 'to stay intact'. What troubles the narrator's own sense of home is the verbal aggression exhibited by his father, whose final question ('Are you coming in or out?') encodes a demand for allegiance to family and origins. Although the young man's answer seems at first equivocal ('I'm still not sure'), the closing stanzas bespeak a deep commitment to originary locations, specifically the liminal beauties of Donegal. There he imagines watching 'light complicate the water', wading out into the 'stinging cold saltwater', which, like poetry, possesses transformative power. Its waves are credited as capable not only of restoring silver, but also, tellingly, of 'disinfecting wounds'.

Although it frequently alludes to continuing violence back home, *To A Fault* demonstrates the extent to which the decade since the ceasefires has freed up Northern Irish writers from the younger generation to engage with wider, global and historical concerns. The most striking illustration of this new breadth and confidence in Laird's collection is 'Imperial', an intricately fashioned parable about war and power-politics spanning the centuries, bearing its readers from ancient Mesopotamia to present-day Iraq. In this poem, whose appearance in the *London Review of Books* coincided with the beginning of the US campaign to topple Saddam,[29] Laird sets up a Saidian[30] analogy between nineteenth-century, early twentieth-century and contemporary colonial adventurism; like Shelley's 'Ozymandias',[31] the poem invites us to reflect on the transience of empire and the monumental follies political leaders continue to commit. At the same time, it should be added that Laird's perspective is itself ineluctably 'compromised' since it regards the east through western eyes.[32]

Its first two parts portray the working practices of the archaeologist Sir Austin Henry Layard (1817–94), whose surname resembles the poet's own.[33] As a result of successful excavations at Nineveh and Babylon and the books in which he recorded his 'discoveries', Layard achieved celebrity status in early Victorian Britain. In Laird's poem he comes across as a contradictory figure. The early stanzas depict him in hostile mood, 'scattering' anyone who threatens his occupation. Anticipating the colonial administrators who would follow in his wake, he has arrived at certain conclusions about those whose cultural legacy, not to mention rights and territories, he has helped to appropriate ('the male Musselman is naturally this or commonly that', p. 11).[34] Fearful that 'his' relics might be pilfered, he has no qualms about carrying out 'summary punishments' from time to time *pour décourager les autres*. When it comes to artefacts, however, he is delicate in his labour, easing 'pieces out from the flesh of the earth / as a midwife might' (p. 11), so that they can be delivered intact 'to the *pale* hands in the *cool* basement of the British Museum', and their new, surrogate owners.

The three subsequent sections of the poem move into pastoral terrain, placing the archaeologist – and readers – in the role of observers of nature. Oxen plodding along beside the riverbanks become symbols of timelessness, like the old horse in Hardy's 'Breaking of Nations' poem.[35] What disturbs the tranquil, companionable mood, generated by images of cattle lying down 'in each other's shadows' or 'ambling . . . / . . . between milking and darkness', are the monstrosities Layard uncovers by the north-west walls of the palace in Nineveh.[36] Monuments to imperial might, these part-human, part-lion, part-avian[37] figures were created to instil fear, to warn those contemplating opposition or transgression of the swift and vicious retribution they could expect. Having established the predatory nature of the indigenous imperialist régimes (ancient Assyrian, modern Ba'athist), the narrator's focus turns to the *external* agents out to topple them. The 'voice from the south' which over-confidently predicts 'Nineveh's imminent demise is *simultaneously* that of the biblical prophet Jonah and the current American President, George Bush.[38] In contrast, the Old Testament original stresses the humiliations and deprivations the Ninevite king and people endure in order to ward off destruction,[39] which prompts Yahweh to deal with them compassionately.[40] Laird's poem foregrounds those who make a swift profit from crisis: 'Stripped of sackcloth, the saved resume their businesses / . . . buying and selling' (p. 12). The 'saved' here might be identified as locals who have managed to survive the onslaught or, conceivably, Republican-backing, American entrepreneurs and their companies, rewarded with reconstruction contracts by a grateful administration. The term is clearly one associated with Christian fundamentalism.

In part three, the cattle reoccupy centre stage, their passive demeanour contrasted with the frenetic comings and goings of the empowered – money-men, prophets, warriors, an unnamed 'white man on horseback' (Layard?) and 'the slip of a cowherd who keeps them'.[41] Docile, resigned, 'pool-eyed' watchers, they are themselves a recurrent object of the narrator's observations. The answer to his own question ('Can they remember?') has the effect of humanising them, but also of registering them in the long history of cruelties inflicted by humans on their own kind and kine. 'They catalogue hurt' (p. 12).

Imperialist discourse, then and now, privileges its own and rarely recognises the need to differentiate between the natives. Underlining this point, the poem's closing section, like its first, begins naming another interloper, following in the wake of Jonah and Layard. A successor to the latter, and beneficiary of his project, Gertrude Bell (1868–1926) served in the Arab Bureau during the Great War and subsequently as 'Oriental secretary to the British military high command in Iraq'.[42] First-world intervention in the Middle East is characterised as a casual affair. After 'a pleasant afternoon' riding in the desert, Bell is seen trailing 'a walking stick behind her', marking out the frontiers for the 'new countries' the victorious western powers brought into being. Yet their attempts at inscribing their presence in the region face repeated resistance, which Laird renders primarily in nature imagery. By moving 'under the borders', the rivers subvert them. Pitted against the 'kingdom of here', its 'relics', 'oilfields' and 'satellites', is an older, elemental technology, 'the machinery of the wind / which starts up and ticks over' (p. 13), and erases man-made lines in the sand. Momentarily, at this critical juncture, the narrative shifts from third to first person, implicating its readers in the recurring history of intervention it decries: 'We are *again* among these ruins and the dying' (my emphasis). This, like the allusion to 'oilfields' and the reworking of one of T.S. Eliot's most famous phrases,[43] brings us very much into the twenty-first century and current 'grief' in Iraq. In speaking of 'Satellites mistaken for portents', the poem hints at the part faulty intelligence played in the justification for the coalition invasion. Broken into its component parts, prefix and root, the participle epitomises much that has gone before in the poem and in history.[44]

Politics and the abuse of 'legal' processes feature prominently in the 'The Given', a nightmarish parable reminiscent of Auden's 'O What is that Sound', H.G. Wells's 'The Country of the Blind' and Kafka's entire oeuvre. It details the progressive encroachment of the State into the most private of private domains, the human body itself; in each of its succeeding stanzas force and the law are deployed to snatch or confiscate one of the five senses. Yet the poem is as much an indictment of the passivity in the populace as it is of the authorities, since it is only after 'they came for sight' that any token resistance is mounted:

> The door we've blocked with books now shakes.
> We play them tapes we had prepared
> then hiss and mouth our tongueless chorus. (p. 4)

Like C. Day-Lewis's 'Newsreel', it warns of the dangers of sleeping too long.

A concern with texts, textuality and intertextuality is apparent from the outset of Laird's volume. 'Poetry' (p. 5) sets the self-reflexive agenda. Here the art-form is primarily envisaged as observation, the recapturing of fragmentary images and spots in time. In the first of a sequence of analogies, the speaker compares his art to the view in the 'big window / on the top deck of the number 47', in which everyone and everything is envisioned 'through my own reflection'. There is something distinctly Kavanaghesque in the way Laird intercuts the secular and the religious, and finds transformative potential in the everyday. There is poetry in

> opening my eyes when everyone's praying.
> The wave machine of my father's breathing,

> my mother's limestone-fingered steeple,
> my sister's tiny fidgets, and me, moon-eyed, unforgetting (p. 5)

The poem closes with a form of release, with an image of two unwieldy oak doors flapping open 'to let us out'. Like the building from which they leave (a church?), the poem resembles 'some great injured bird trying to take flight'.

'The Riddles of the Ardcumber Book' sees the poet donning a scholarly persona, as well as indulging in a little post-structuralist play. At the outset its speaker informs us that he has spent the previous twenty years of his life on a recently discovered theological text which incorporated in its margins a sequence of riddles composed 'in a rustic Latin'. The fact that it is the marginalia which has fired his passion is, of course, highly significant, especially given Laird's own cultural 'provenance'. Interspersed in the academic's discourse are tantalisingly short, enigmatic fragments from the Dark Ages. Thus, in the midst of a comprehensive dismissal of previous scholarship on the riddles as either scant or slip-shod, he slips into the text in brackets and italics quotations from his fictional primary text, '(*the fish is a quiet guest*)' (p. 32) and '(*the quill is the joy of the sparrow*)' (p. 33). Despite dismissing others' speculations on the anonymous author's identity, he is prepared to offer his own, picturing him as 'a cowherd bedded in heather / watching the shifting cross-hatching of shade / in the valley' or perhaps as 'a chieftain' – a Gaelic laird? – an escapee from the massacre, 'waiting out time / far from the burning and bloodshed'. That the riddler's word-games have had a salutary, even salvatory effect on the academic is suggested by his cryptic comment that 'They prevent me from falling'. Like myth, and like art,

> the riddle springs from the need to vest life
> in the garb of the coldly fabulous. (p. 33)

Having listed a delightfully disparate range of alternatives, the speaker asserts that 'the final solution' to the conundrum is not as 'Williams' claims 'God', but rather 'riddle', but then immediately attacks the idea of there ever being a definitive answer. Poetry lies in the 'seeking', he concludes, and readers should shun those making dogmatic statements as to its meanings.

John Redmond's assertion that *To a Fault* is uniformly 'depressing' is wide of the mark,[45] though he is right to be critical of its occasional stylistic drifts downmarket, into what he terms 'newladspeak'. Since the dust-jacket's biographical notes draw attention to the fact that Laird 'has lived in Warsaw and Boston', one might have expected a more substantial representation in the poetry of both. Neither poem located in Poland suggests that he gained much insight into a culture as complex as his own. 'A Guide to Modern Warsaw' reduces the city to a limited cluster of signs, contrasting the huge Sony logo which lords it over the site where the Great Synagogue once stood with the flimsy flyers 'at pavement level', offering sexual services, sessions in the martial arts', and voicing 'pleas for missing dogs'. A little earlier in the collection Laird had included a poem about Auschwitz, but by misspelling its Polish name (Oświęcim) rather undermines his historical and cosmopolitan credentials. 'Oświęciem' begins with a bee swarm encountered on a visit to the camp, and ends with a conceit linking the 'end-stopped histories' of the drones and the inmates. The analogy depersonalises the victims, leaves them as anonymous as the cattle in 'Imperial'. A restorative manoeuvre, borrowed from Michael Longley's 'The Linen Workers', is attempted at the close, when the narrator talks of opening the prisoners' cases and replacing in them the various objects confiscated by the Nazis and now displayed in the camp's museum. In a sinister final twist, he imagines leaving the cases in lockers in each of Europe's major airports, where they would sit alongside other signs of crime, 'stolen goods / and photographs in envelopes, and bombs' (p. 38). The intention may well have been to draw a parallel between the race crimes of the Nazis and atrocities committed by today's terrorists, but the scale and magnitude of the killing routinely carried out by the former make such a conflation deeply flawed.

At times 'pitched closer to anger than wonder' ('An Appendix', p. 56), *To a Fault* is nevertheless a book which delights and impresses much of the time. Poems like 'Imperial', 'The Length of a Wave' and 'The Riddles of the Ardcumber Book' will not look out of place in future anthologies, and reflect, like Morrissey's three volumes, the continuing strength in depth of Northern Irish poetry. This is evident in many other début collections published since 2000, such as Leontia Flynn's *These Days*, awarded the Forward Poetry Prize for the best collection of 2004, and Alan Gillis's *Somebody, Somewhere*, which received the 2005 Rupert and Eithne Strong Award for a best first collection and was short-listed for the prestigious *Irish Times* Poetry Now Award. Like so many of her peers in the new generation, Leontia Flynn is a highly self-reflexive writer, frequently given to 'baring the device'. Midway through *These Days*, for example, she wheels out a dream poetic mentor, who is forthright about what it takes to coin success. Abrasiveness sells well, he suggests: 'If you can fashion something with a file in it for the academics / to hone their malicious nails on – you're minted'.[46] The acute sense of displacement registered in Morrissey's 1990s poetry, composed while violence was still raging, is largely absent from Flynn's work, much of which appears to circle around family, domestic spaces, every-day objects, albeit 'under a ticking', intermittently 'bewildered.sky'.[47] Significantly, 'Naming It', the opening piece in *These Days*, transports us from 'the gloomiest most baffled / misadventures'[48] into a sudden 'clearing' where the unfamiliar can be relished. Mercurial, lyrical, street-wise and wry, her poetry exemplifies a quality she praises in an ex-partner, the ability to 'take the clockwork out of things', to strike 'a new sound from a dud motor'.[49]

Equally impressive is Alan Gillis's first foray into poetry. One of many highpoints in *Somebody, Somewhere* is 'Progress', a wry but moving reflection on not-so-distant times in Northern Ireland, and one worth quoting in full. Its initially somewhat uncertain, tentative narrator imagines the traumatic, devastating violence since the late 1960s being suddenly, miraculously put into reverse. As so often in Laird's and Flynn's poems, register and diction veer between the informal/conversational ('it's great now', 'So I guess') and formal/lyrical ('explosively healed', 'coalescing into the clarity'):

> They say that for years Belfast was backwards
> and it's great now to see some progress.
> So I guess we can look forward to taking boxes
> from the earth. I guess that ambulances
> will leave the dying back amidst the rubble
> to be explosively healed. Given time,
> one hundred thousand particles of glass
> will create impossible patterns in the air
> before coalescing into the clarity
> of a window. Through which, a reassembled head
> will look out and admire the shy young man
> taking his bomb from the building and driving home.[50]

The poem deploys a simple idea, one which so easily might have descended into embarrassing and tasteless whimsy.[51] Yet like Morrissey's and Laird's, Gillis's control of his material is exemplary, compelling readers to contemplate once more the devastation and horror which so recently afflicted somewhere which is and is not 'home'.

Notes

1 Much of this chapter previously appeared in *Northern Irish Literature 1956–2006: The Imprint of History* (Basingstoke: Palgrave Macmillan, 2007). My thanks to the publisher for allowing the material to be reprinted here.

2 Horace, *Epistles*, I, xi, 27 ('Caelum non animum qui trans mare currunt'), as rendered by Seamus Heaney in 'The Flight Path', *The Spirit Level* (London: Faber, 1995), p. 24. The same line from Horace had been deployed by Derek Mahon twenty-five years earlier in 'Homecoming', *Ecclesiastes* (Manchester: Phoenix, 1970), p. 10.

3 Selima Guinness (ed.), *The New Irish Poets* (Newcastle-upon-Tyne: Bloodaxe, 2004); John Brown (ed.), *Magnetic North: The Emerging Poets* (Derry: Verbal Arts Centre, 2005).

4 Violence had diminished, but not ceased. Months after the signing of the Good Friday Agreement, a bomb planted by dissident republicans claimed the lives of 29 people in Omagh, Co. Tyrone. Punishment beatings continued, along with sectarian attacks and intimidation.

5 Interviewed by Annamay McKernan, *Tatler Woman*, 24 June 2002 www.carcanet.co.uk/cgi-bin/reframe.cgi?app=cipher&index=author.

6   Sinéad Morrissey, *There Was Fire in Vancouver* (Manchester: Carcanet, 1996), p. 9.

7   This pattern reappears in later poems such as 'After the Hurricane', p. 48.

8   There may be an echo here of Ted Hughes's 'Crow's Account of the Battle' (from *Crow* (London: Faber, 1970), pp. 26–7), which similarly envisages a nuclear apocalypse: 'Blasting the whole world to bits / Was too like slamming a door / . . . / Too like being blown to bits yourself / Which happened too easily / With too like no consequences'.

9   This image linked to nuclear war occurs once more in 'Thoughts in a Black Taxi', p. 19.

10   Later in the volume, in 'My New Angels', she returns to this theme: 'My new angels are howling, hard, / . . . / For every snuffed out light on a back road' (p. 52).

11   Ciaran Carson 'Smithfield Market', *The Irish for No* (Oldcastle: Gallery, 1987), p. 37.

12   The UYM cited in the poem stands for Ulster Young Militants. The CAIN website identifies the group as the youth wing of the Ulster Defence Association (UDA), which probably dates from 1974. In April 2001 members of the UYM were charged with the murder of Trevor Lowry (49), a Protestant civilian, whom they misidentified as a Catholic: http://cain.ulst.ac.uk/othelem/organ/yorgan.htm#ym

13   Significantly the feet in the poem are gendered male.

14   *The Tempest*, Act I, scene ii, lines 394–5; Seamus Heaney, *Door into the Dark* (London: Faber, 1969), p. 56.

15   Flensburg, along with the state, passed from Danish to Prussian control following the war between the two kingdoms of 1864.

16   Morrissey composed the poem in the summer of 1993 in the Swiss Alps, returning there the following summer when news of the ceasefires came through.

17   The word appears at a critical moment in 'The Juggler', p. 56.

18   Earlier evidence of this unease about language comes in 'If Words' (p. 55), which depicts words as 'unfortunates'. Their lack of fixity is commented on later when she describes how they 'spill like sewage and dismay'.

19   Edna Longley, *The Living Stream* (Newcastle-upon-Tyne: Bloodaxe, 1994), p. 65.

20   Nick Laird, *To a Fault* (London: Faber, 2005), p. 3.

21   A phrase of Seamus Heaney's 'A Pilgrim's Journey', *Poetry Society Bulletin* 123, (winter 1984), p. 2.

22   Morrissey uses the image twice in 'My Grandmother Through Glass' (pp. 42–5), once in relation to herself (II), once in relation to her mother (IV).

23   When Polonius asks Hamlet if he will 'walk out of the air', the Prince replies with this mordant quip. *Hamlet*, Act II, scene ii, line 209.

24   A further reminder of the continuing significance of the Somme within the imaginations of the preceding generation of Northern Protestants.

See Fran Brearton, *The Great War in Irish Poetry* (Oxford: Oxford University Press, 2000), pp. 27–37, 257–60.

25 Images depicting Northern Ireland as trapped in an ice age are a recurring feature in early Troubles' poems, including Seamus Heaney's 'Tinder' (*Wintering Out*) and Paul Muldoon's 'Macha' (*Knowing My Place*). Ice images feature also in Trevor McMahon's 'Breaking', which speaks of how now 'Only the snow exists / fractured, / remaining through the breaking of / tribes' (*The Wearing of the Black* [Belfast: Blackstaff, 1974], p. 2) and in Michael Longley's poem 'The North', from *Lares* (Woodford Green: Poet & Printer, 1972), p. 13: 'There are no landmarks round here, / Only immeasurable shifts / Of the snow, frozen eddies / To guide us home. Snow and ice / Turn us into eskimoes . . . / We die walking in circles'.

26 Nick Laird, *Utterly Monkey* (London: Harper, 2005), pp. 16–18.

27 This image of the famous Belfast shipyard cranes, Samson and Goliath, which imagines them blessing the city is a surprising one. More typically they might be associated with masculinity, industrial might and sectarian aggression. Reference to their 'arms' serves as a reminder of what has happened to the limbs of the man who views them in this positive light.

28 Laird here makes a coded allusion to the gospel according to St Luke, 16: 27.

29 *London Review of Books*, 25:6 (20 March 2003). The American campaign began with missile attacks on various Iraqi sites in the early hours of that day.

30 In the opening chapter of *Orientalism* (London: Penguin, 1991 [1978]), pp. 42–3, 76–83, Edward Said details the massive investment in scholarship that accompanied Napoleon's Egyptian Expedition of 1798–99, 'an invasion which was in many ways the very model of a truly scientific appropriation of one culture by another' (p. 42).

31 Several of the observations made by David Pirie about 'Ozymandias', in *Shelley* (Milton Keynes: Open University, 1988), p. 59, could be equally applied to Laird's poem. Amid the 'elaborate network of ambiguities' the poem contains stands one central 'monumental irony'. The structures depicted in both poems are 'a lasting statement' to the 'inevitability of change and the ultimate helplessness of all . . . megalomaniac dictators'.

32 I am grateful to my co-editor, Scott Brewster, for this insight.

33 A later poem, 'The Layered' (p. 28), finds the poet again playing name-games.

34 Said, in *Orientalism*, p. 227, maintains that westerners like Kipling, Layard and Bell fell easily into 'the culturally sanctioned habit of deploying large generalisations' in order to categorise 'reality', 'each category being not so much a neutral designation as an evaluative interpretation'.

35 Thomas Hardy, 'In Time of "The Breaking of Nations" ', *The Complete Poems* (London: Palgrave, 2001) p. 543.

36 With the head of a lion and body of a man, physiologically one such carving Layard describes is the exact opposite of Yeats's 'rough beast' in 'The Second Coming'.

37 From 1965 onwards Saddam Hussein used an eagle as an emblem for the Iraqi state.

38 The reference to 'a preacher repeating his God' may be an allusion to Palestinian leaders' claims that President Bush had told them in 2003 'that God guided him in what he should do . . . and led him to Iraq to fight tyranny': http://news.bbc.co.uk/1/hi/world/americas/4320586.stm. See also 'Bush puts God on his Side', by BBC Washington Correspondent, Tom Carver, 6 April 2003: http://news.bbc.co.uk/1/hi/world/americas/2921345.stm.

39 *Jonah*, 3, vv. 7–9.

40 Ibid., v. 10. Somewhat imprudently, Jonah rebukes Yahweh for showing mercy and is subsequently taught a lesson. Jonah's angry response, according to one leading biblical scholar, illustrates a xenophobic tendency in 'postexilic Judaism', a 'narrowness' which 'frequently expressed itself in a hate of foreign nations' and a 'desire for their destruction'. See John L. McKenzie, *Dictionary of the Bible* (London: Chapman, 1968), p. 451.

41 This might be an allusion to the former Iraqi president, though Saddam Hussein's father was a shepherd, rather than a cowherd.

42 Juliet Gardiner and Neil Wenborn (eds), *The History Today Companion to British History* (London: Collins and Brown, 1995), p. 73.

43 'Signs are taken for wonders', from 'Gerontion' (1919), *The Complete Poems and Plays of T.S. Eliot* (London: Faber, 1969), p. 37. The post-colonial theorist Homi Bhabha appropriated the phrase for the title of a key essay in *The Location of Culture* (London: Routledge, 1994).

44 'The Evening Forecast for the Region' (pp. 53–4) includes further allusions to the war in Iraq. At its close, the speaker decries how 'the white so loves the world it tries to make a map of it / exact and blank'.

45 John Redmond, *Tower Poetry* (February 2005), www.towerpoetry.org.uk/poetry-matters/february2005/laird.html (accessed 6 October 2008).

46 Leontia Flynn, 'My Dream Mentor', *These Days* (London: Cape, 2004), p. 20.

47 Ibid., p. 14.

48 Ibid., p. 1.

49 Ibid., p. 14.

50 Alan Gillis, *Somebody, Somewhere* (Oldcastle: Gallery Press, 2004), p. 55.

51 Two of Gillis's precursors in depicting reverse versions of history are Kurt Vonnegut in *Slaughterhouse Five* (New York: Dell, 1991 [1969]), p. 74, and Martin Amis in *Time's Arrow* (London: Vintage, 1992).

Part IV

Fiction and autobiography

11

'Tomorrow we will change our names, invent ourselves again': Irish fiction and autobiography since 1990

Liam Harte

[B]oomtime Ireland has yet to find its Oscar Wilde or its Charles Dickens or even its Evelyn Waugh. The strange place we now inhabit does not seem to yield up its stories easily. . . . What has happened, essentially, is that the emergence of a frantic, globalised, dislocated Ireland has deprived fiction writers of some of their traditional tools. One is a distinctive sense of place. To write honestly of where most of us live now is to describe everywhere and nowhere: system-built estates, clogged-up motorways, a vastly expanded suburbia, multinational factories, shopping centres such as Liffey Valley where the food court is called South Beach and is decked out with stray bits of Florida like an Irish pub in Germany is decorated with newly-minted old authentic Irish street signs. With an English high street here and a bit of America there, the passage to a distinctive Ireland is strewn with obstacles.[1]

It is simply not possible to write purposefully, let alone comprehensively, about the swirling abundance of themes and trends in contemporary Irish fiction and autobiography in the space allotted to me here. Every *tour d'horizon* must be hedged about with qualifications and hesitations, every typological gesture thwarted by the fact of thematic and stylistic diversity.[2] In short, the closer one looks for continuities and correspondences, the more one becomes aware of kaleidoscopic variety. Indeed, the motifs of fragmentation and incompletion are themselves among the most recurrent in recent Irish writing, being especially marked in the contemporary short story, a genre which has proved highly effective in rendering the discordant juxtapositions of post-1990 Ireland. Collections such as Anne Enright's *The Portable Virgin* (1991), Mike McCormack's *Getting it in the Head* (1997) and Keith Ridgway's *Standard Time* (2001) show how the short story's combination of lyric compression and novelistic amplitude, coupled with its preference for the particular over the cumulative, make it ideally suited to capturing prismatic fragments of the radically disjunctive consumerist society which Fintan O'Toole describes above. In looking for a Dickens rather than a Maupassant, however, both he and critics such Declan Kiberd, who has lamented the absence of a 'Trollopian *The Way We Live Now*, much less a Tom Wolfe-style *Bonfire of the Vanities* even among our younger writers',[3] appear to be still in thrall to the very anachronism which O'Toole invokes: the Great Irish Novel. If that mythical beast stalks contemporary Irish writers less intimately than it did earlier generations, it may well be because they rightly recognise the futility of the quest for definitive calibration of a national culture and self-image experiencing a prolonged refashioning under a plethora of pressures and modalities. Even John McGahern, hailed as 'the best cartographer of the physical and metaphysical landscape our generation, and Ireland as whole, has moved across over the past sixty years',[4] remains primarily committed to the local, albeit with a keen, Joycean awareness that 'In the particular is contained the universal'.[5]

In an important sense, the period under review begins and ends with the work of McGahern, a novelist who, by general consensus, has produced 'the most impressive body of work of any Irish writer in the second half of the [twentieth] century'.[6] His death in March 2006 brought forth a welter of tributes which portrayed him variously as 'a poet of ordinary days',[7] 'the voice of a generation',[8] 'a true stoic',[9] 'a moralist, a historian and commentator'[10] and a reluctant revolutionary who 'never wanted to break down the doors, just to pick the locks'.[11] In the last fifteen years of his life McGahern published four small masterpieces in three different genres: *Amongst Women* (1990), *Collected Stories* (1992), *That They May Face the Rising Sun* (2002) and *Memoir* (2005). This quartet inscribes subtle patterns of repetition and reprise, recapitulating not only themes and motifs but also phrases, idioms and scenarios in ways that mirror the circadian cycles and seasonal rhythms that frame so much of his work. Indeed, when *Amongst Women* appeared in May 1990, reviewers were quick to note the extent to which it recast characters from the earlier fiction. Michael Moran is an archetypal domestic tyrant in the mould of Mahoney in *The Dark* (1965), a father whose hold over his family is 'pure binding'. As a veteran of Ireland's separatist struggle he has an obvious affinity with Sergeant Reegan in *The Barracks* (1963), whose bitter disenchantment with independent Ireland he savagely echoes: '"What did we get for it? A country, if you'd believe them. Some of our own johnnies in the top jobs instead of a few Englishmen. More than half of my own family work in England. What was it all for? The whole thing was a cod."'[12]

Other narrative details – Moran's second, childless marriage to a middle-aged spinster, his Catholic devotion, his capricious violence – reinforce the impression of the novel as a summative achievement. Yet *Amongst Women* is also a work of powerful originality which contains one of the most fascinating and intimately drawn portraits of destructive, charismatic fatherhood in modern Irish fiction.

Moran has forcefully realised Reegan's elusive dream of becoming master of his own house, Great Meadow, which stands, like its owner, separate and proud in the Leitrim landscape. Having failed to cut a figure in the Free State army, Moran has retreated to this domestic fortress where, as Antoinette Quinn puts it, he 'directs his frustrated drive for power into a diminished form of home rule'.[13] As this phrase suggests, the novel is a critical exploration of the workings of power, fear and devotion within a rural Catholic family which is also a metaphor of post-colonial Irish society. By masterful use of militarist language and imagery, McGahern shows the ex-guerilla leader deploying the tactics which served him well in wartime in his campaign to establish emotional sovereignty over his wife and daughters, who respond by devising flexible strategies of resistance and appeasement of their own. Yet as the daughters' collective governance of their father increases as he ages, so too does their emotional dependency upon him. Their continual homecomings are not just a mark of Oedipal attachment; they also signify their need to reconnect with the hallowed ground that reaffirms their uniqueness. Even Michael, the wayward youngest son, 'looked to Great Meadow for recognition, for a mark of his continuing existence'.[14] The sole dissenting voice is that of Luke, whose defiant assertion of autonomy through exile is both a permanent rebuke to this cult of family solidarity and a reminder of the dissonant centrality of the migrant in McGahern's novels and in contemporary Irish fiction more generally.

Robert Garratt has recently observed that *Amongst Women* is preeminently a novel about memory and history, yet there is a contrapuntal movement imaged in the fact that the narrative begins and ends with the future made incarnate by Moran's daughters, who are at once carriers of their father's complex legacy and harbingers of a new, semi-feminised social order.[15] The conclusion deftly evokes the ambiguous emotional repercussions of Michael Moran's charismatic brand of patriarchal parenting. Although the actual moment of his death is conspicuously anti-climactic – he 'slipped evenly out of life'[16] – its impact is shown to be potentially seismic. His physical interment in the Leitrim clay is eclipsed by the attenuated transmittance of his patriarchal essence to his wife and daughters, each of whom 'in their different ways had become Daddy'.[17] This closing vision of emergent androgyny anticipates a future of manly daughters and womanly sons, as Sheila's contemptuous backward glance transforms the male mourners into frivolous women. The ending also casts new light on the novel's opening line – 'As he weakened, Moran became afraid of his daughters'[18] – by suggesting that the dying despot foresaw the awful, human legacy of his autocratic will in his own, female flesh and blood, and with it, the adulteration of a hypermasculine paternalism.

Eamonn Hughes is one of several critics to read Great Meadow as 'a metonym for Ireland: the displacement of Moran by his daughters and the complex gender play of the novel from its title to its final words is almost a fictional preparation for the 1990s Ireland of Mary Robinson's Presidency'.[19] Almost, but not quite, since that Ireland remains in shadow in *Amongst Women* as it does in *That They May Face the Rising Sun*. McGahern's treatment of contemporary social change seldom moves beyond the oblique in either novel and is always subordinate to the dialectic which pervades his entire oeuvre: the testing of fragile human relationships against the inexorable bass rhythms of nature and planetary time. Great Meadow exists in a 'changeless image of itself' where 'Nothing but the years changed'.[20] Only when he is on the threshold of death is Moran granted the intuition to contemplate with wonder his own mortality against the radiantly durable life force that suffuses his flourishing fields: 'To die was never to look on all this again. It would live in others' eyes but not in his. He had never realized when he was in the midst of confident life what an amazing glory he was part of.'[21] *That They May Face the Rising Sun* embodies a more sustained sacramental vision. The lake, the novel's central protagonist, enfolds the community in its redemptive elemental embrace and the natural world subsumes all to its relentless pulsion, such that the characters seem to be mostly engaged in 'turning each day into the same day, making every Sunday into all the other Sundays'.[22] Thus, linear time shades into cyclical time, which mutates in turn into a kind of transcendent timelessness of the kind McGahern found so exemplary in Tomás Ó Criomhthain's *An tOileanách* (1929):

> If the strong sense of the day, the endlessly recurring day, gives to the work its timeless quality, it is deepened still more by the fact that people and place seem to stand outside history. There is no sense of national pride. The rumblings of the new Ireland are brushed aside as distant noise, O'Malley's Ireland, or Parnell's or Redmond's or Yeats's or Pearse's.[23]

It takes little critical ingenuity to apply this analysis, *mutatis mutandis*, to McGahern's final novel, which remains resolutely focused on the inner rhythms and densely woven social codes that bind a community 'marooned'[24] in time, existing at one remove, somehow, from the spirit of accelerated socio-economic, technological and attitudinal change that has come to define the new Ireland, a country which boasts the most globalised economy in the world. McGahern's influence can be discerned in Patrick O'Keefe's novellas which, as Vivian Valvano Lynch's chapter demonstrates, also reveal the intense complexity that underlies the seeming banality of life in rural Ireland.

Yet in affirming a version of Irish pastoral that is at once consoling and increasingly anachronistic, *That They May Face the Rising Sun* also carries the germ of its own critique. A pivotal scene shows Patrick Ryan mocking the arcadian tranquillity so cherished by Joe and Kate Ruttledge, before launching into a 'burlesque of listening and stillness'[25] with Johnny Murphy. His acerbic overture – ' "Will you listen to the fucken quiet for a minute and see in the name of God if it wouldn't drive you mad?" '[26] – might serve as an epigraph for the many recent fictional portraits of rural and small-town Ireland as places of scarifying dysfunction and maddening, even murderous, tedium. Indeed, the inflection of Ryan's mordant remark resonates with the vocal cadences of Patrick McCabe's prodigal protagonists, who are among the most memorably lurid in the contemporary canon. Whereas McGahern's last novel elegises a fading world of 'broken-down gentlemen',[27] McCabe's neo-Gothic fantasies chart the grotesque frolics of sociopathic 'bony-arsed bogmen' in whose unhinged minds the forces of antimodernity and postmodernity commingle and clash. From one perspective, McCabe's jaundiced portrayals of provincial alienation echo and update earlier dissections of rural traditionalism found in the novels of John Broderick, Edna O'Brien and indeed McGahern himself. From another, however, his novels mark a definitive break with this realist tradition, not least in the way they remorselessly subvert antiquated fictional stereotypes, cultural clichés, political shibboleths and past social ritual. Widely hailed as master of the so-called 'bog Gothic' sub-genre,[28] McCabe's novels have been convincingly read alongside the plays of Marina Carr, Martin McDonagh and Conor McPherson as part of a burgeoning aesthetic trend conceptualised as neo-naturalism by Joe Cleary and as 'black pastoral' by Nicholas Grene.[29] Certainly, McCabe's fiction deals not so much in social realism as in asocial irrealism, which is not to say that his guignolesque narratives don't calibrate the drastic consequences of lovelessness or contain sharply analytical satire. Rather, the socio-economic inequities and psychosexual neuroses of late twentieth-century Ireland are filtered through a phantasmagoric lens to create a fiction of the gleeful macabre. Here is the very thing O'Toole called for: 'a new way of writing about the place with a rhythm which matches the angular, discontinuous, spliced-together nature of contemporary Irish reality'.[30]

What is strikingly new in McCabe's fiction is the degree of pathological trauma and destructive psychosis on display, and the mixture of comic exhilaration, tinged by pathos, with which such dysfunctionality is narrated. From Francie Brady in *The Butcher Boy* (1992) to Redmond Hatch in *Winterwood* (2006), McCabe's shape-shifting protagonists embody a post-colonial society in a state of chronic fragmentation, restless self-interrogation and profound dis-ease. As critics have noted, his novels expose the disabling residual effects of colonial and neocolonial modes of thought as they are manifested in varieties of psychic, social and institutional deformation.[31] Chief among his persistent concerns are the disquieting consequences of unprocessed historical and personal traumas and the troubling relations they engender between self, place and community. McCabe frequently deploys the Gothic trope of the returning revenant to represent the continuing anxieties that fester behind Ireland's brash façade of new-found capitalist modernity. His novels are permeated by figurations of national history as a precipitating cause of pathology, such that escalating anxieties about the stability of social, psychic and domestic order in the present appear as symptoms of a profoundly brutalising and unresolved past which, having never been fully assimilated as it occurred, returns incessantly in monstrous forms. Thus, Patricia Horton persuasively reads Francie Brady as the personification of 'the repressed legacy of De Valera's Ireland which surfaced so shockingly in the 1980s',[32] and Laura Eldred concurs, interpreting the pathologised society depicted in *The Butcher Boy* in terms of Julia Kristeva's definition of abjection: 'Francie is not just the community's Other, but also the community's abject and its monster. . . . McCabe suggests, however, that the ultimate source of abjection, and the ultimate monster, is the Irish nation itself'.[33] *The Dead School* (1995), *Breakfast on Pluto* (1998) and *Call Me the Breeze* (2003) further extend this coruscating critique of toxic nationhood by anatomising the psychotic borderline identities produced by the interplay of multiple and competing ideologies, while *Winterwood* dramatises the lethal effects of repressed historical memory through the spectral persona of Redmond Hatch/Ned Strange/Dominic Tiernan. This mutating monster is at once abused child and abusive adult, doting father and psychopathic paedophile, custodian of 'the authentic spirit of heritage and tradition'[34] and harbinger of a vacuous postmodernity. Such slippage between identities is the mark of a society trapped between the worlds of yesterday and tomorrow, which can neither sustain nor surrender the illusion of itself as unified. The nation's failure to add up to a readable totality is figuratively condensed in Hatch's television documentary *These Are My Mountains*, hailed as 'an anatomy of a society in flux, a magnificently detailed view of the journey from the almost medieval atmosphere of 1930s rural Ireland to the buoyant postmodern European country as it is today'.[35]

The haunting repercussions of sublimated memory and unprocessed history run like a dark thread through the fabric of contemporary Irish fiction, making the wounded, traumatised subject one of its most representative figures. According to Cathy Caruth, the traumatised 'carry an impossible history with them, or they become themselves the symptom of a history that they cannot entirely possess' but which possesses them.[36] This pathological condition is bound up with a profound crisis of historical truth which asks how we 'can have access to our own historical experience, to a history that is in its immediacy a crisis to whose truth there is no simple access'.[37] Caruth might be describing here the crisis that afflicts the protagonists of so many contemporary Irish novels, from Robert McLiam Wilson's *Ripley Bogle* (1989) to Colm Tóibín's *The Heather Blazing* (1992) to Roddy Doyle's *A Star Called Henry* (1999) to the nameless narrator of Seamus Deane's *Reading in the Dark* (1996), one of the texts discussed by Stephen Regan in his chapter for this section. Trauma in this novel-cum-autobiography is experienced both as a catastrophic knowledge that cannot be articulated and as a memory that simultaneously resists assimilation and demands constant iteration. The boy-narrator's desire to witness himself in the darkness of history, to do what his father fails to do – 'make the story his own'[38] – inscribes an analogous circularity, in that his quest for palpable knowledge amidst whispers culminates in an apprehension of his own impalpability: 'Now the haunting meant something new to me – now I had become the shadow.'[39] Paradoxically, ghostliness is reified at the very moment when consolation seems at hand. The nameless narrator wakes up from an impossible history only to find himself still trapped within history's nightmare.

As Regan's analysis makes clear, *Reading in the Dark* is essentially an abortive autobiography, a novel about the failure of self-representation and the frustration of narrative revelation. As a chronicle of gapped subjectivity it is an exemplary Irish autobiographical text, the boy-narrator's quest for enlightenment being emblematic of a ceaseless struggle for mastery over a mutinous, possibly fictive, history. This struggle engenders in turn chronic feelings of homelessness and homesickness, interlinked themes which resonate through much recent Irish autobiography, the profusion of which led one acclaimed memoirist, Nuala O'Faolain, to assert that 'Ireland, at the end of the twentieth century, was beginning to allow self-knowledge'.[40] Yet many of the more self-reflexive Irish autobiographies of recent years, including O'Faolain's *Are You Somebody?* (1996) and *Almost There* (2003), testify to a deficiency of self-knowledge, what Deane has spoken of as 'a radical privation' or 'missing agency'.[41] This deficiency is often suggested by the figure of the displaced double or twin which causes a self-generative tear in subjectivity. Thus, in *The Village of Longing* (1987) George O'Brien recalls the frisson of alterity that issued from his uncle renaming him 'Mike' in preference to 'Seoirse', the Irish form of his birth name, and Dermot Healy's *The Bend for Home* (1996) registers a similar sense of self-deferral which was literally and metaphorically reflected in a large domestic mirror:

> That mirror had given my family and me a second identity. We ate look-
> ing at ourselves in it. We were never fully ourselves, but always possessed
> by others. . . . Always there were two of you there: the one in whom con-
> sciousness rested and the other, the body, which somehow didn't belong
> and was always at a certain remove. . . . This distance between my mind
> and my body has always remained and is insurmountable.[42]

Both *The Village of Longing* and *The Bend for Home* are suffused by a muted revisionism which is partly to do with telling stories in ways that disrupt the normative relationship between self, community and nation.[43] They also testify to the difficulties that attend the post-colonial subject's claim to autobiographical agency, as shown by the narrators' repeated acts of decentring and recentring the self. As such, these works properly belong to the performative mode of autobiography in which 'the self is a series of masks and public gestures rather than a function of essence'.[44] Self-improvisation is also one of the governing themes of John Walsh's *The Falling Angels: An Irish Romance* (1999) and Hugo Hamilton's *The Speckled People* (2003), both of which Regan discusses alongside *Reading in the Dark*. Walsh and Hamilton's shared concern with experiences of cultural hyphenation, both within and outwith Ireland, lead them to construct home as a mythic place of no return, a space between absence and recuperation where the pull of deterministic identity paradigms are complicated by more pluralistic lived forms of belonging. Walsh's title neatly encapsulates the ambiva-lent fidelities of his second-generation Irishness; the Synge-inspired main title reflects the experience of being 'eternally in transit between one place and another, deprived of a sanctuary, denied a final refuge, never finding a real home',[45] while the subtitle evokes the seductive appeal of a mythologised past that is imagined as a repository of rooted belong-ing. His 'neither-one-thing-nor-the-otherness'[46] resonates strongly with

Hamilton's speckledness, which is purged of its stigmatic associations to become the signifier for an emergent post-national identity in which dissonance and hybridity are regarded as normative, progressive elements:

> He said Ireland has more than one story. We are the German-Irish story. We are the English-Irish story, too. . . . We don't just have one language and one history. We sleep in German and we dream in Irish. We laugh in Irish and we cry in German. We are silent in German and we speak in English. We are the speckled people.[47]

Whereas *The Speckled People* seeks to valorise new, braided identity formations, its sequel, *The Sailor in the Wardrobe* (2006), encodes a parallel impulse in contemporary Irish writing, one which is perhaps most marked among writers from the Republic: the longing to break free from the wearying binaries and mystifications of nationalism. Fork-tongued young Hugo's plaintive desire to rupture the Joycean nets – 'I want to have no past behind me, no conscience and no memory. I want to get away from my home and my family and my history'[48] – speaks to a persistent concern of writers such as Dermot Bolger, Roddy Doyle, Colm Tóibín, Sebastian Barry and Anne Enright to redraft received versions of the nation as a homogeneous imagined community by dramatising the manifold ambiguities and contradictions that have been elided from the dominant purview. As early as 1986 Bolger complained about an 'idea of nationhood which simply could not contain the Ireland of concrete and dual-carriageway (which is as Irish as turf and boreens) that was a reality before our eyes'.[49] Much of his literary output since then, as novelist, poet, playwright and editor, has been devoted to challenging the dominance of this nationalist aesthetic by re-imagining history from the perspective of disenfranchised social groups: emigrants, the suburban working class, the Protestant minority. In the process he has become one of the leading literary sponsors of a liberal post-nationalism predicated on the need to incorporate cultural difference within an expanded definition of Irishness. Bolger's most recent novel, *The Family on Paradise Pier* (2005), shows him extending his critique of the concept of a historic Irish identity through an exploration of the conflicting forms of ideological affiliation and alienation that attended the birth of the state. In this, his most sustained exercise in historical fiction to date, he traces the fortunes of three members of the Goold Verschoyle family, one of whom was the prototype for the former Big House mistress who offers Hano and Cáit sanctuary in *The Journey Home* (1990). But whereas that novel invites us to read this *déclassée* matriarch metaphorically as a renovated version of Cathleen Ni Houlihan, *The Family on Paradise Pier* presents her as a flesh-and-blood woman whose story, and that of her brothers, force-fully repudiates the notion that history is destiny.

Bolger's desire to give voice to Ireland's multiple cultural and sexual identities as means of counteracting nationalism's perceived homogen-ising tendencies is further amplified in the work of Enright, Barry and Tóibín. As Heidi Hansson demonstrates in her chapter, Enright's fond-ness for postmodern strategies such as non-linear narration can be read as the stylistic analogue of a demythologising aesthetic which seeks to renegotiate received meanings of nationality and community in ways that foreground fracture, contradiction and contingency. Both Barry and Tóibín, meanwhile, return repeatedly in their writings to the pressing question of how the past should be remembered and interpreted, unsealing the voices of those whose singular choices and stigmatised identities unsettle authorised narratives of belonging, be they common soldiers, exotic dancers or gay men. 'Barry's people are the footnotes, the oddities, the quirks of history', claims O'Toole,[50] and the writer him-self has commented:

> Most of the adjectives that traditionally make up a definition of Irishness I can lay scant claim to. So I have been trying to rearrange those adjec-tives to give me some chance in the lottery of citizenship. It's a hopeless task, but the hopelessness gave me the journey.[51]

As this statement suggests, Barry's imagination is typically drawn to sites of ambiguity, anomaly and dissent, as is Tóibín's, who has been a staunch critic of the exclusivist rhetoric of republican nationalism and conservative Catholicism since his bold journalism of the 1980s.[52] Indeed, Barry's elliptical comment about his practice as a playwright – 'I am interested not so much in the storm as the queer fresh breeze that hits suddenly through the grasses in the ambiguous time before it'[53] – cor-responds with Tóibín's contention that 'ambiguity is what is needed in Ireland', expressed in his 1993 review of Roy Foster's *Paddy and Mr Punch*, tellingly entitled 'New Ways of Killing Your Father'.[54] In this polemical essay Tóibín, the son of a nationalist Wexford local historian, sketches his intellectual formation as a liberal revisionist, central to which was his study of Irish history at University College Dublin in the early 1970s. 'Outside in the world there were car bombs and hunger strikes', Tóibín recalls, 'done in the name of our nation, in the name of history. Inside we were cleansing history, concentrating on those aspects of our past which would make us good, worthy citizens who would keep the Irish 26 county state safe from the IRA and IRA fellow-travellers.'[55] His reading of an essay by Joseph Lee, which challenged the notion that Henry Grattan's 1782 parliament constituted Irish self-government, elicited a moment of quasi-epiphanic enlightenment. Rarely, indeed, can a piece of dry historiography have engendered such liberatory euphoria:

> I remember feeling a huge sense of liberation. I photocopied the piece and made everyone else read it. I was in my late teens and I already knew that what they had told me about God and sexuality wasn't true, but being an atheist or being gay in Ireland at that time seemed easier to deal with as transgressions than the idea that you could cease believing in the Great Events of Irish nationalist history. No Cromwell as cruel monster, say; the executions after 1916 as understandable in the circumstances; 1798 as a small outbreak of rural tribalism; partition as inevitable. Imagine if Irish history were pure fiction, how free and happy we could be! It seemed at that time a most subversive idea, a new way of killing your father, starting from scratch, creating a new self.[56]

There are few more succinct articulations of the sense of betrayal and victimisation by history that has proved creatively vital to an adversarial Irish literary revisionism, which has at its ideological centre a deep suspicion towards nationalism in general and a profound repudiation of IRA violence in particular.

Neither Tóibín or Barry is naive enough to believe in the myth of the end of history, however. Tóibín's debut novel, *The South* (1990), dramatises the tensions between his alienated protagonist's desire to be free of the past and her countervailing need to understand it more fully, while Barry's *A Long Long Way* (2005) imaginatively recuperates the deeds of marginalised historical actors – Catholic Irishmen who fought in the British Army in the First World War – only to reveal their vanquishment by the zero-sum imperatives of Anglo-Irish politics. Both novelists would therefore recognise the validity of Terence Brown's assertion that 'the historical itself remained as a crucial category of Irish self-understanding, even in a period of rapid social and cultural change'.[57] So too would Roddy Doyle, whose fiction, as Jennifer Jeffers observes, continually rehearses stories of marginalisation and victimisation in order to challenge the strategic forgetting practised by affluent, 'multicultural' Ireland. Jeffers's chapter focuses on the reconfigurations of identity, and the complex intersections of nationality, gender and race in contemporary Ireland, and shows how Doyle's return to the repressed gives articulation to those left behind by globalisation. Similarly, in Patrick O'Keefe's short fiction the nostalgia for rural life is undercut by its recrudescent secrets, leaving his exiles haunted by a culture that cannot be fully recovered or relinquished. Questions of memory and forgetting are posed most acutely by the aftermath of conflict in the North, and Neal Alexander's chapter examines the ways in which post-Agreement Northern fiction negotiates its bitter legacies. Writers such as Glenn

Patterson and Eoin MacNamee acknowledge both the importance and difficulties of remembrance in a moment of political and social transition, when unresolved issues from the past can overshadow or jeopardise the forward-looking present.

These writers' fictional engagements with the past calls into question the categories by which it can be examined, at the same time as they refuse to simplify or mythicise complex experiences for the sake of a well-made story. For other contemporary writers, it is the emergence of a post-historical Irish consciousness which is largely indifferent to the national past and its received meanings that compels. The faultlines between inherited mind-sets which valorise Irishness and a new cosmopolitan individualism are beginning to be mapped fictionally with varying degrees of seriousness and levity. In Harry Clifton's short story, 'A Visitor from the Future', for example, the depthlessness of Ireland's globalised culture perturbs Ann, a disaffected university tutor. Her attempt to interest her students in an older Ireland, 'where people were continuous with themselves, and everything could be named', exposes deep attitudinal and generational schisms, leaving her with a 'strange sense that the country she came from was levitating into a weightless, valueless space where everything equalled everything else. These things – disintegration, discontinuity – are not threatening but good, the best of them told her. Tomorrow we will change our names, invent ourselves again.'[58] Anne Haverty's *The Free and Easy* (2006) offers a more caustic critique of this Tóibínesque vision of a present – and, by implication, a future – from which history has been evacuated. The novel, which satirises the narcissism and venality of the Dublin *nouveaux riches*, stages a contest between those who want to preserve – and opportunistically reinvent – the nation's heritage as a saleable commodity and those who wish to jettison tradition completely. What unites these seemingly polarised positions is a view of the past as an agreed-upon fiction. Affluent Irish modernity, the novel suggests, is underpinned by a wilful amnesia and a pernicious effacement of history, traits personified by Seoda Fitzgibbon, the glamorous wife of a corrupt businessman, for whom the perpetual present is the primary ground of personal and socio-economic success. Her pithy annulment of two centuries of history provides an appropriate endpoint for this brief survey of contemporary Irish fiction and autobiography, as well as offering a possible point of departure for future reviews:

> 'You can forget the last century. And you can definitely forget the century before. Ireland as we know it – and let's thank whoever or whatever – was born some time around nineteen ninety-four. Or ninety-six?' She smiled. 'Let the historians fight about the year. Historians like to have something to fight about.'[59]

Notes

1 Fintan O'Toole, 'Writing the boom', *Irish Times*, 25 January 2001.

2 For an informed and commendably brisk survey of the fictional landscape, see Eve Patten, 'Contemporary Irish Fiction', in John Wilson Foster (ed.), *The Cambridge Companion to the Irish Novel* (Cambridge: Cambridge University Press, 2005), pp. 259–75.

3 Declan Kiberd, *The Irish Writer and the World* (Cambridge: Cambridge University Press, 2005), p. 276.

4 Eamonn Grennan, '"Only What Happens": Mulling Over McGahern', *Irish University Review*, 35/1 (spring/summer 2005), p. 26.

5 James Joyce to Arthur Power, quoted in Richard Ellmann, *James Joyce* (Oxford: Oxford University Press, 1983), p. 505.

6 Colm Tóibín, *The Penguin Book of Irish Fiction* (London: Penguin, 1999), p. xxxi.

7 John Banville, quoted in Shane Hickey and John Spain, 'Politics and the arts pay homage to "voice of a generation"', *Irish Independent*, 31 March 2006, p. 10.

8 John O'Donoghue, quoted in Hickey and Spain, 'Politics and the arts pay homage', p. 10.

9 Nuala O'Faolain, 'He was already embarked on a life of heroic honesty. He already knew what he meant by being a writer', *Sunday Tribune*, 2 April 2006, p. 18.

10 Denis Sampson, 'An Irishman's Diary', *Irish Times*, 8 April 2006, p. 17.

11 Fintan O'Toole, 'Picking the lock of family secrets', *Irish Times Weekend Review*, 1 April 2006, p. 3.

12 John McGahern, *Amongst Women* (London: Faber, 1990), p. 5.

13 Antoinette Quinn, 'A Prayer for my Daughter: Patriarchy in *Amongst Women*', *Canadian Journal of Irish Studies*, 17/1 (1991), p. 81.

14 McGahern, *Amongst Women*, p. 147.

15 Robert F. Garratt, 'John McGahern's *Amongst Women*: Representation, Memory and Trauma', *Irish University Review*, 35/1 (spring/summer 2005), p. 130.

16 McGahern, *Amongst Women*, p. 180.

17 Ibid., p. 183.

18 Ibid., p. 1.

19 Eamonn Hughes, '"All That Surrounds Our Life": Time, Sex, and Death in *That They May Face the Rising Sun*', *Irish University Review*, 35/1 (spring/summer 2005), p. 151.

20 McGahern, *Amongst Women*, pp. 174, 168.

21 Ibid., pp. 179.

22 John McGahern, *That They May Face the Rising Sun* (London: Faber, 2002), p. 41.

23 John McGahern, 'What is My Language?', *Irish University Review*, 35/1 (spring/summer 2005), pp. 5, 6. This is a revised version of an essay first published in 1987.

24 McGahern, *That They May Face the Rising Sun*, p. 51.

25 Ibid., p. 77.
26 Ibid.
27 Ibid., p. 2.
28 See, for example, 'John O'Mahony, 'King of Bog Gothic', *Guardian*, 30 August 2003.
29 Joe Cleary, *Outrageous Fortune: Capital and Culture in Modern Ireland* (Dublin: Field Day, 2006), pp. 75–6; Nicholas Grene, 'Black Pastoral: 1990s Images of Ireland', *Litteraria Pragensia*, 20/10 (2000): www.komparatistika. ff.cuni.cz/litteraria/no20-10/grene.htm (accessed on 1 March 2007). Grene explains: 'Traditional pastoral idealises another space, a prior time, a pristine source of being, measured against the implied present place occupied by its readership or audience. These black pastorals invert such a norm by representing a brutally unidyllic Ireland of the past'.
30 O'Toole, 'Writing the boom'.
31 See Tim Gauthier, 'Identity, Self-Loathing and the Neocolonial Condition in Patrick McCabe's *The Butcher Boy*', *Critique* (winter 2003), 44/2, pp. 196–211.
32 Patricia Horton, '"Absent from Home: Family, Community and National Identity in Patrick McCabe's *The Butcher Boy*', *Irish Journal of Feminist Studies*, 3/1 (December 1998), p. 76.
33 Laura G. Eldred, 'Francie Pig vs. the Fat Green Blob from Outer Space: Horror Films and *The Butcher Boy*', *New Hibernia Review*, 10/3 (2006), pp. 65–6.
34 Patrick McCabe, *Winterwood* (London: Bloomsbury, 2006), p. 16.
35 Ibid., p. 233.
36 Cathy Caruth, *Trauma: Explorations in Memory* (Baltimore: Johns Hopkins University Press, 1995), p. 5.
37 Caruth, *Trauma: Explorations in Memory*, p. 6.
38 Seamus Deane, *Reading in the Dark* (London: Vintage, 1997), p. 10.
39 Ibid., pp. 10, 217.
40 Nuala O'Faolain, *Almost There: The Onward Journey of a Dublin Woman* (London: Michael Joseph, 2003), p. 59.
41 Seamus Deane, 'Autobiography and Memoirs 1890–1988', in Seamus Deane (ed.), *The Field Day Anthology of Irish Writing* (Derry: Field Day, 1991), vol. 3, p. 383.
42 Dermot Healy, *The Bend for Home* (London: Harvill, 1996), pp. 73–4. The motif of human doubles is not confined to recent works of Irish autobiography. Twins and doubles punctuate Irish novels from Bram Stoker's *Dracula* (1897) to Anne Enright's *What Are You Like?* (2000) and also feature in films, as exemplified by the recent *dopplegänger* melodrama *The Tiger's Tail* (2006). See Jeanett Shumaker, 'Uncanny Doubles: The Fiction of Anne Enright', *New Hibernia Review*, 9/3 (2005), pp. 107–22.
43 For more on autobiographical configurations of this relationship, see my edited volume *Modern Irish Autobiography: Self, Nation and Society* (London: Palgrave Macmillan, 2007).

44   Ruth Robbins, *Subjectivity* (London: Palgrave Macmillan, 2005), p. 167.
45   John Walsh, *The Falling Angels: An Irish Romance* (London: Flamingo, 2000), p. 30.
46   Ibid., p. 70.
47   Hugo Hamilton, *The Speckled People* (London: Fourth Estate, 2003), p. 283.
48   Hugo Hamilton, *The Sailor in the Wardrobe* (London: Fourth Estate, 2006), p. 7.
49   Dermot Bolger (ed.), *The Bright Wave/An Tonn Gheal: Poetry in Irish Now* (Dublin: Raven Arts Press, 1986), p. 10.
50   Fintan O'Toole, 'Introduction: A True History of Lies', Sebastian Barry, *Plays 1* (London: Methuen, 1997), p. xiii.
51   Mária Kurdi, ' "Really All Danger": An Interview with Sebastian Barry', *New Hibernia Review*, 8/1 (2004), p. 46.
52   For a sense of Tóibín's journalistic style and subject matter, see his *The Trial of the Generals: Selected Journalism 1980–1990* (Dublin: Raven Arts Press, 1990).
53   Sebastian Barry, 'Preface' to his *Plays 1* (London: Methuen, 1997), p. xv.
54   Colm Tóibín, 'New Ways of Killing your Father', *London Review of Books*, 18 November 1993.
55   Ibid.
56   Ibid.
57   Terence Brown, *Ireland: A Social and Cultural History 1922–2002* (London: Harper Perennial, 2004), p. 409.
58   Harry Clifton, 'A Visitor from the Future', in David Marcus (ed.), *The Faber Book of Best New Irish Short Stories 2006–7* (London: Faber, 2007), p. 173.
59   Anne Haverty, *The Free and Easy* (London: Chatto & Windus, 2006), p. 112. It is generally accepted that 1994 was the year in which the term 'Celtic Tiger' was coined to describe the unprecedented growth of the Irish economy. See Kiberd, *The Irish Writer and the World*, p. 271.

12

Anne Enright and postnationalism in the contemporary Irish novel

Heidi Hansson

Anne Enright has been hailed as one of the most exciting contemporary Irish writers, praised for her lyrical, evocative language and her original style. Her collection of stories, *The Portable Virgin* (1991), was shortlisted for the Irish Times/Aer Lingus Irish Literature Prize and won the Rooney Prize in 1991, her first novel, *The Wig My Father Wore* (1995), met with widespread critical acclaim and her subsequent novels, *What Are You Like?* (2000) and *The Pleasure of Eliza Lynch* (2002), have attracted much interest, as attested by reviews in the *Times Literary Supplement*, the *London Review of Books* and the *New York Review of Books*. Her account of pregnancy and becoming a mother, *Making Babies: Stumbling into Motherhood* (2004), addresses some of the themes in her fiction from a more personal perspective. Although Enright's art is the focus of several ongoing postgraduate projects, her works have so far rarely appeared in studies of contemporary Irish literature. One reason for this may be the preoccupation with issues of national identity and the state of Irish society that informs so much of current criticism, which means that literature that ostensibly avoids these themes or addresses them only obliquely easily gets overlooked. Another explanation may be Enright's fragmented storytelling, which means that themes are not always easily detected or obvious. It seems difficult to find a place for Enright in contemporary Irish criticism, though the primary reason for this appears to be the rather narrow concerns of the critics, not any reservations about the quality of her work.

The story of nation is of course one of the most fundamental narratives in western culture, and foundational myths can be found for almost every society. As Richard Kearney observes, '[o]ne cannot remain constant over the passage of historical time – and therefore remain faithful to one's promises and covenants – unless one has some minimal remembrance of where one comes from, and of how one came to be what one is'.[1] The national narrative is a means of producing communal memory and uniting people who may have little more in common than their residence within a certain set of borders. 'The development of a national literature is always an important dimension of the modern state-building project', as Joe Cleary points out, and this is particularly important in communities under pressure or in a state of transition, where Ireland would qualify on both counts.[2] The problem arises when a nation begins to take its roots for granted and denies the presence of counter-narratives or the indeterminacy of the past. 'Whenever a nation forgets it own narrative origins it becomes dangerous', Kearney cautions, because the result of this is too often 'totalitarianism, fascism and fanaticism'.[3] The story of nation then becomes a monolith, a grand narrative of the kind questioned in postmodern literature and thought.

When the nation is recognised as a narrative construct, on the other hand, it can be constantly reinvented and reconstructed, and this is to a great extent what is being done in contemporary Irish literature, at least as it is described in works of literary criticism. Studies of literature and nationhood have dominated the scene since the early 1990s, with examples like David Lloyd's *Anomalous States: Ireland and the Post-Colonial Moment* (1992), Declan Kiberd's *Inventing Ireland: The Literature of the Modern Nation* (1995), Gerry Smyth's *The Novel and the Nation: Studies in the New Irish Fiction* (1997), Seamus Deane's *Strange Country: Modernity and Nationhood in Irish Writing since 1790* (1997), Joe Cleary's *Literature, Partition and the Nation State: Culture and Conflict in Ireland, Israel and Palestine* (2002) and Ray Ryan's *Ireland and Scotland: Literature and Culture, State and Nation, 1966–2000* (2002). The final example, incidentally, is the only one that includes also a longer discussion of postnationalist writing. Numerous articles about how literature relates to, questions or shapes the national story can be added to the list. The mainstays of the most common critical perspective are consequently place, nation, region and state and the problems surrounding these concepts, and as far as criticism is concerned it would seem that every Irish novel is about nation or at least that every Irish novel should be read in a national context.

The rapid rate of change in late twentieth-century Ireland has certainly created a need for a literature that substitutes descriptions of present-day experience for former, idealised images of the country, and as Ray Ryan sees it, the canon now emerging from the Irish Republic:

> creates the context in which its own work is understood, guaranteeing the naturalness and representativeness of the experience chronicled by establishing a post-mythical landscape; that is, a landscape where meaning is, necessarily, never premature, because no pre-existing or inherited literary tradition has ever accounted for this experience. The absence of a 'natural' and representative Irish identity means that questions of identity, the nation, are subordinate to an examination of the structures of power, the state.[4]

Nevertheless, to replace romanticised versions of the nation with the more detached concept of the state is only to recalibrate the lens somewhat and carry the search for a national identity into the present. The basic pattern remains the same if images of nation are simply transformed into images of state. The question is whether the issue of nationhood is so central in present-day Ireland that every writer has to engage with it, at least at some level, or whether this is a Procrustean bed that relegates other themes to the background. What is striking, moreover, is the dominance of male writers discussed in this type of criticism, and another question that presents itself is therefore how far national or postnational writing is perceived as an exclusively male domain.

At first glance, Anne Enright's 2000 novel *What Are You Like?* does not appear to be concerned with nation or nationality at all. In a series of loosely connected chapters a number of characters ponder the question 'what they are like', which in the Irish idiom is a phrase with several double meanings, expressing the anxious or proud 'how do I look' and the admonishing 'what a mess you are' as well as the more conventional meaning. For Maria, who is the closest to a main character, this question takes on particular significance when she finds a picture of what she first believes to be herself in her boyfriend's bag. The photograph is of a girl who looks like Maria but wears clothes Maria has never worn and has a slightly different facial expression. The photograph becomes a symbol of Maria's unstable sense of self and emphasises the search for identity that is the novel's main theme: 'Maria looked at her and wanted to laugh. She had always felt like someone else. She had always felt like the wrong girl.'[5] The explanation is that she has a twin sister, separated from her at birth and brought up in England. For Maria, however, the photo becomes a visible sign of her own uncertainty and lack of self-esteem. It proves to her that she has no identity, that she is 'nothing' as she repeatedly thinks throughout the novel.

In the national story, the search for identity can usually be satisfied through information about genetic – and by extension ethnic – background and identification with the nation, but Enright demythologises many of the staples of older Irish fiction, such as rural farm life, family relationships and the moral superiority of nuns, and she does not replace these old stabilities with a new belief in genetics, which could have been logical, since the story concerns twins. Instead of showing the primacy of heredity, Enright argues, like so many postmodern writers, that identity is in constant process. Such a view is at odds with a vision of nationality founded on ethnic origin, and as a consequence both the characters' personal search for selfhood and Enright's deconstruction of common Irish myths can be linked to a postnationalist position. Hence, the novel *What Are You Like?* can be regarded as a 'postnationalist' text and Enright's narrative strategies as well as the themes she tackles can be linked to a position beyond nationalism. Reading the novel as a postnationalist text is of course to accept the centrality of 'nation' in Irish literature, albeit in a slightly different way, and since every theory is to some extent reductive, privileging the framework of postnationalism will inevitably overlook other aspects of the novel, such as its relationship to feminism or how early separation may affect the lives of twins, which is, after all, the most obvious theme. But given the preoccupation with questions of nation in present-day Irish literature and criticism it is important to include also women's writing in this context and to add expressions of postnationalism to the equation. Thus, it is valuable to consider the elements in *What Are You Like?* that can be related to a postnationalist outlook.

Postnationalism can be interpreted as both a temporal and a political concept and it can be related to a rather vague concept of 'nation' as well as to the political position of 'nationalism'. In its temporal meaning, 'postnationalism' would simply mean that which succeeds either nation or nationalism and does not necessarily imply any interrogation of these as previous stages of development. As a political idea, however, postnationalism would primarily be a challenge to nationalism as an ideology. For Ray Ryan the first definition seems to be foremost when he describes Dermot Bolger, Thomas McCarthy and Colm Tóibín as 'prominent postnationalists' because 'each has engaged with the problem of representing post-Independence Ireland when the mythic sources of Irish identity have been drained first by economic stagnation, then by the astonishing pace of modernization since the 1960s'.[6] Postnationalism for these writers would then be the representation of a society no longer informed by the ideals of nationalism. The works are set in a society after nationalism, as it were. In his introduction to the anthology *Soho Square* Colm Tóibín writes that the writers included

> have nothing in common except a beginning under the same sky, the same
> uncertain weather. And there is no collective consciousness, no conscience
> of our race, no responsibilities, no nation singing in unison. Instead diver-
> sity, the single mind and the imagination making themselves heard.[7]

This declaration indicates that for Tóibín, at least, there is no post-nationalist programme. Instead, postnationalism is defined by dissonance and divergence in contradistinction to the uniformity of nationalist thought. Discussing contemporary Canadian novels, Frank Davey defines postnationalism as an attitude that veers between the transnational and the local, where sites are either interchangeable or resolutely confined and political issues are constructed on ideological grounds that have little to do with questions of nation or history, such as aestheticism, feminism or liberal humanism.[8] For Davey, postnationalism seems to be characterised primarily by its avoidance of national politics. Richard Kearney, on the other hand, is more willing to invest postnationalism with active, not only reactive, meanings and clearly views the political definition as the most important when he emphasises, in his *Postnationalist Ireland: Politics, Culture, Philosophy* (1997), that 'the attempt to advance a postnationalist paradigm is equally, in the Irish–British context, an effort to adumbrate a postunionist one', indicating that postnationalism may be the way out of political trench wars.[9] For Kearney, postnationalism would thus be the term for a political ideology that attempts to reach beyond polarisation. In some ways this position could be seen as a response to the understanding that a politics that only reverses the hierarchy also leaves the terms of opposition in place. As Edward Said puts it, 'we begin to sense that old authority cannot simply be replaced by new authority, but that new alignments made across borders, types, nations and essences are rapidly coming into view, and it is those new alignments that now provoke and challenge the fundamentally static notion of identity that has been the core of cultural thought during the era of imperialism'.[10] In this light it might even be possible to interpret the English–Irish marriages that often conclude nineteenth-century sentimental novels as expressions of postnationalism, though they are generally viewed as conveying a Unionist position. In the context of practical Irish politics postnationalist literature could, however, play a role in breaking up the logjam of sectarianism, but remarkably few writes have chosen to deal with both Northern and Southern Irish society. 'The state divide conditions the imaginative horizons of Irish novelists on both sides of the border', as Joe Cleary observes, and both nationalism and postnationalism have become connected with the states, not the island.[11]

To question 'nationalism' must at some level also include a questioning of 'nation' as its basis, and the problem is that 'nation' is by no means a stable concept. Kearney cites five common meanings of the word, the legal, the territorial, the ethnic, the migrant and the cultural, but in the Swedish language, for instance, the words 'nationality' and 'citizenship' are usually seen as exact synonyms, which means that only the first two meanings are present.[12] A migrant nation like the nineteenth-century Jews would have given precedence to ethnicity or religion, and the numerous small states of nineteenth-century Germany defined the embracing German nation in terms of culture and linguistic unity. These divergent definitions of nation obviously give rise to a correspondingly divergent selection of nationalisms, and Kearney lists the varieties civic, ethnic, romantic, economic, separatist, sectarian and cultural national-ism.[13] No doubt the list could be expanded. In relation to Enright's novel I will use 'postnationalism' as the label for a political attitude that rejects both 'nation' and 'nationalism' in all their varieties as insufficient tools for the analysis of contemporary urban and global experience. This does not mean that postnationalism should be understood as merely reactive. On the contrary, Irish writers today may embrace postnationalism as a means to imagine new social relationships, and different histories and futures both inside Ireland and beyond. Though the interrogation of nationalist ideology is not new in Irish literature, postnationalism in this sense can be regarded as predominantly a late modern or postmodern attitude.

Since the national narrative is intended to naturalise the state and shape communal identities, it is usually coherent and linear. The fact that nationhood was a fraught question in nineteenth-century Ireland has sometimes been used to explain why the Irish tradition of the realist novel is comparatively weak. As Cairns Craig puts it, there are obvious parallels between 'the modern nation, with its implication of all the people of a territory bound together into a single historical pro-cess, and the technique of the major nineteenth-century novels, whose emplotment enmeshes their multiplicity of characters into a single, over-arching narrative trajectory'.[14] Though this is to ignore the workings of Bakhtinian dialogue in traditional novels, it is nevertheless true that a steady, linear progression is characteristic of such texts and that there is generally a sense of closure. Anne Enright, in contrast, deploys a dis-junctive narrative style that foregrounds the complexity of the past and prevents any sense of linear causality. The novel begins in Dublin 1965, but the next chapter is set in New York 1985 and the following in Dublin 1971, with different protagonists in each. 'For Enright', Penelope Fitzgerald comments in relation to *The Portable Virgin*, 'the recognis-able dimensions of time, speech and thought (though not place) are fluid and interchangeable, while metaphors often become the things they stand for'.[15] This is the case also in *What Are you Like?* Although places retain their individual character and New York remains distinct from London or Dublin, Enright dismantles the unities of time, place and narrative focus by moving between settings, and there is a tension between the main plot element which concerns a mystery of birth – a staple of nineteenth-century fiction – and the fragmented narrative technique which seems to preclude the possibility of a final answer. The novel has no plot in the usual sense of the word, and this postmodern subversion of conventional storytelling can be linked to a postnationalist position through its replacement of a single centre with multiple locations, time zones and foci. There are occasionally Irish inflections in the language, but there is no attempt to represent Irish speech patterns *à la* Roddy Doyle, which could be taken as another indication that Enright advocates a position beyond the narrowly national. Her disjointed narrative art could also be seen as a reaction to Irish storytelling traditions which would further support a postnationalist interpretation, since Irish myths are persistently connected with a nationalist perspective and an unstable text questions the explanatory function of myth.[16] This is of course not a new idea. As Richard Kearney points out, Irish literature has constantly 'displayed two different attitudes to the nationalist idea of myth' with Yeats and other literary revivalist championing it and cosmopolitan modernists like Joyce, Beckett and Flann O'Brien rejecting it.[17] According to Colm Tóibín, at least, Enright 'has taken up and refined the legacy of Sterne and Flann O'Brien and placed it in a Dublin which, for the first time in its long life in fiction, has become post-Freudian and post-feminist and, of course (three cheers!) post-nationalist'.[18] Postnationalism could consequently also be seen as an always present counter-current to the mythologising tendencies of nationalism, which would make Anne Enright part of a long-standing tradition rather than the representative of something new.

Though an important attribute of the postmodern aesthetic is that meaning resides as much in the mode of telling as in what is told it is obviously not enough to use matters of style alone to suggest a postnationalist outlook. Nevertheless, since the 'postmodern theory of power puts the "modern" concept of the nation-state into question', a postmodern literary style becomes a logical expression of postnationalism, especially when it is applied in a work that also interrogates prominent nationalist myths.[19] The ideology informing the texts of the Irish Literary Revival is an obvious target, since these works were elevated and institutionalised as the foundational literature of the Irish Free State. According to Richard Kearney, 'Yeatsian mythologizing was so imposing that it soon became part of a new cultural orthodoxy', and thus demythologisation becomes an important task for postnationalist literature.[20] When Enright destabilises common props of Irish nationalism such as the family, rural life and Catholicism this can consequently be seen as another indication of a postnationalist perspective.

The 1937 Irish constitution emphasises the role of the family in the state-building project, producing an idealised picture of family life that

Irish writers have struggled to shatter ever since. In the first chapter of *What Are You Like?* Enright describes family as very much a matter of coincidence and a solution to practical problems. Maria and her twin sister are taken out of their dead mother's womb, and, although this is not revealed until later, their father Berts decides that he can only take care of one of the girls. He also realises that he will have to marry again to be able to cope, and when his new wife Evelyn goes downstairs to heat milk for the baby the first night after their honeymoon Enright comments that '[t]hey were a family'.[21] There seem to be no feelings involved, simply practical necessity, and Enright describes Berts's decision to make Evelyn pregnant in the same emotionless terms. There is no comfort or warmth in the family, with Berts perceiving his daughter as a monster that has been given birth by a dead woman, the child Maria's eyes saying 'things that cannot be unsaid about her dead mother and her living father and the child he had conceived to supplant her',[22] Evelyn desperately wanting to find a way to make friends with her children but having to realise that they remained strangers to her, and Berts having an affair with a woman from work partly because of the lack of physical closeness in his marriage.[23] The novel's epigraph from the *Book of Job* 38 highlights the themes of procreation, parenthood and family but also raises questions about the meaning of origin: 'Has the rain a father . . . What womb brings forth the ice?' (n.p.). God as the Creator is speaking in the extract, which seems to emphasise and solemnise the matter of origin, but, on the other hand, since the Bible verses are about creation, about entities that were never born, the epigraph also seems to suggest that once something is brought into the world it has no family except, perhaps, for the similarity that exists between siblings like water and ice.

The clearest indication that family ties are not automatically strong is Berts's choice to give up one of the twins for adoption. Marie, as the hospital nuns call her, is renamed Rose by her new parents and grows up in England. For her, family and nationality are obviously even more of a coincidence, especially since the household is also filled with a succession of fostered boys who belong to the family for a short while and then leave. Anton, who carries the photograph of Rose that Maria finds, is one of these boys. But even though all the families that appear in the novel are in some manner dysfunctional Enright also shows the importance of knowing your background. Rose is shown to be constantly searching for information about her birth parents. Everywhere she goes she studies the faces of the people she meets, silently asking if one of the strangers might be her mother.[24]

While Maria has eyes 'in which the generations that made her regressed like opposing mirrors', Rose is unable to trace her origins in her face since her physical resemblance is to people she does not know.[25] She has no link to her past and no way of finding out what her heredity might be, but becomes obsessed with the idea that knowledge about her background will explain her talents, looks and behaviour and provide her with stability: 'This was why she played, because she was musical. Because somewhere out there, her real, musical mother was listening'.[26] At the same time Enright suggests that there is an endless variety of reasons for people's characteristics and behaviour and that only some of them are related to genetic heritage. Rose picks at her food 'because she was a Capricorn, because when she was a baby she had choked on a spoonful of puréed parsnip, because she had a famine gene, or a food-picking gene, or because when she was young her mother told her to sit up straight and not wolf her food. She picked at her food because she was middle class.'[27]

A central question for Rose, however, is what it means to be Irish, and her feeling of disconnection becomes acute when she is reminded of her Irish origin and attempts to produce a list to define herself, but manages only to register contradictions:

> She was Irish.
> Her favourite colour was blue.
> Her favourite colour was actually a deep yellow, but she couldn't live with it.
> She was English.
> She was tidy. She was polite. She hated Margaret Thatcher.
> She was a mess.
> She was someone who gave things up.
> She was someone who tried to give things up and failed all the time.[28]

Whereas the descriptions of Maria largely show that genetic background is no valid source of identity, the descriptions of Rose consequently demonstrate the importance of knowing one's roots. There is a tension in the text between this need for family connections and the alienation from their families most of the characters experience. Ray Ryan notes that in Dermot Bolger's work adoption and absent parents are tropes that 'sponsor a civic identity that counters [Patrick] Pearse's ethnocultural identity' because adoption 'ruptures any apostolic ethnic linkage to the past, announcing instead the beginning of a new symbolic order whose integrity is faithful, above all, to the present'.[29] If the national is conceived as a matter of ethnicity, the postnational then needs to reveal the arbitrary meanings of genealogy and genetics and show that ethnic origin has little to do with identity. The meaning of adoption is not quite so straightforward in Enright's novel. To some extent, Rose's adoption may be seen as an expression of a postnationalist attitude, since it represents a break with both ethnic origin and history. It is certainly a way of showing that ethnicity loses some of its meaning in a world of international adoptions and immigration. But there is also the real sense of loss that permeates Rose's life and makes her feel that there are no certainties against which her identity can be defined. Her question about what it means to be Irish is not related to civic identity but to exactly the kind of ethno-cultural identity that Bolger challenges, and her tragedy is that it can no longer be found in a society after nationalism.

Where Maria is concerned, Enright rather exposes the limits of genetic heritage which in a postnationalist paradigm suggests a critique of nationhood as founded on ethnic origin. In contrast to Rose, Maria knows the identity of her birth mother, but when she is taken to meet her grandparents there is no automatic sense of belonging. Instead, she feels that she is among strangers. Her connection with the past has been severed by her mother's death, and, like Rose, she experiences the effects of a broken lineage. Her grandparents' farm is incomprehensible and meaningless to her and the biological ties are not enough to make her fit in. In Revivalist literature the rural image represents 'a tested, endured solitude and the generous supportiveness of community; the patient effort of labour and the nobility of suffering; the ideal of dedication and the reward of courage'.[30] This 'richly ceremonious national idea' underlies much nationalist rhetoric and poses an opposition between the rural as authentic and true and the urban as false and opportunistic.[31] The Irish countryside has no such deeper meaning for Maria, however:

> Maria is just bored. All she wants to know is how to become less bored as she feeds the calves in the haggard, hitting them on the skull with a chair leg when they've had enough. All the wrongness of the farm does not strike her, the calves sucking each other's ears, the cows who mount each other as they crush together in the gateway of the yard. She wants to know something, but it isn't this. She doesn't know what she wants to know. They're just cows, that's all. She is so bored she can hardly speak.[32]

Life on the farm is a frozen moment where nothing new happens. Everything has always already happened and is a memory even before it occurs. Rural Ireland is a lost world that exists only as a remembrance even when it is visited, and it provides no sense of identity for the Dublin-born Maria. Alone in the barn she realises that the places and buildings of the farm only cause her to feel alienation and insecurity. Outside, she 'would have been a girl from Dublin caught in the rain, but here in the barn she was anything at all'.[33] There is no sense of liberation in Maria's unstable farm identity, only loss and confusion.

Nevertheless, when she is asked about her background by one of her New York employers Maria resorts to the nationalist myth of rural Ireland, because she expects this to be what her employer wants to hear. Instead of describing the suburb of her childhood, she invents a story about a farm with a view of distant mountains.[34] The old myths will not give way without resistance. Nationalist images are still what define Ireland in other people's eyes, as Maria sees it, and the reality of city life cannot measure up to their expectations. Just like Rose's constantly thwarted hope that there might be an explanation for what it means to be Irish, this juxtaposition of mythic and real 1980s Ireland acknowledges the tenacity of nationalist imagery at the same time as it shows how inappropriate it is for descriptions of contemporary conditions.

The fact that she was born in Ireland has had little impact on Rose's upbringing, except for through religion. 'But that's why we went to Mass, all those years', her mother says, viewing Catholicism as a matter of birth, something that is inbred in Rose because of her Irish origin.[35] The conflation of religion and nationality is an important facet of cultural nationalism, and by questioning the meaning of religious rites and offices Enright challenges a central aspect of nationalist thought. Religion in *What Are You Like?* is depicted as a series of empty gestures, as when the nun Misericordia goes through her prayers 'in jig time', both unable and unwilling to reach out to the God she prays to, or when Maria's class for First Communion learns the drill '[t]he body of Christ. Amen. Tongue', their instruction focused completely on their behaviour.[36] Faith becomes solely a matter of how to comport oneself in church. 'Anne Enright is not fond of nuns', Gabriele Annan concludes in her review of *What Are You Like?*, and 'her snide takes on them are among the most enjoyable passages in the book'.[37] Ruth Scurr comments that Enright 'draws on the full comic potential of the Church'.[38] To make fun of dignified and elevated phenomena takes away their sacred and exalted status, and Enright's postnationalist Ireland is also post-Catholic, a country where Catholicism has lost its function as definition and support of national identity.

In her review of *What Are You Like?* Penelope Fitzgerald points out that in 'women's fiction women often go slightly or quite mad'.[39] There is a long tradition of this, from Charlotte Brontë's madwoman in the attic through Dorothy Perkins Gilman's woman in the room with the yellow wallpaper and Sylvia Plath's woman in the bell jar (whom Gabriele Annan, incidentally, also uses as a reference point in her review).[40] The reason for these women's madness is inability to live up to the identities prescribed for them, a need to break out of a cage that is thwarted and results in madness instead. In Enright's novel both Maria and Rose suffer nervous breakdowns, but the reason is rather that there is no role available to them. When Maria returns to Ireland after her breakdown she has lost her sense of connection both to her family and her country. Christine St Peter cites Enright's novel *The Wig My Father Wore* as an example of a type of women's exilic fiction that presents 'narratives of women who depart from and then return to Ireland, a process that leaves them feeling strange in, or even estranged from, their natal land'.[41] Though the notion of 'exile' probably presupposes a stronger attachment to the homeland than what can be found in *What Are You Like?*, this feeling of estrangement is certainly present in the novel. At the same time, there are attempts to replace the haunting figure of the exile with global citizens who move freely between locations. Most of all Maria wants to work in an airport, but can only find a job as a fitting-room attendant which she regards as the next best thing.[42] Both airports and fitting-rooms are liminal places where change is always imminent, but they are also examples of the 'denationalized and deterritorialized realm that transcends rather than engages, observes rather than participates in the social'.[43] Instead of the value-loaded places from Irish nationalist history – the countryside, the church, the home – Enright suggests that present-day urban life takes place in in-between places that can never become symbols of nationality because they only exist from moment to moment. The fitting-room – like mirrors, photos, dress-making patterns and clothes – becomes a metaphor for how identity and its representations are always transitory. Clothes are described as 'other selves', as more real than the women who wear them so that it becomes possible to slide in and out of identities simply by changing clothes.[44] In analogy with this, Maria is shown to think of her First Communion dress as something that she has to fit rather than the other way round:

> She lies in bed and tries to tell what size she is. When she closes her eyes her tongue is huge and her hands are big, but the bits in between are any size at all. When she opens her eyes she is the size of the dress. Or she might be.[45]

Just before they break down, both Maria and Rose also lose their ability to recognise themselves. Maria cannot identify her own reflection and does not know what she looks like any more, and Rose finds herself unable to fill in the information on the passport form.[46] There is no stability at all, and the characters descend into nothingness.

At the very end of the novel Maria and Rose finally meet and can see themselves in each other. For some reviewers this is a cheap let-down, a simple solution that diminishes the complexity of the work.[47] For others it is a redemptive moment when '[t]win meets twin, England meets Ireland, and there is much rejoicing and comparing of notes', though this comment also carries sarcastic overtones.[48] If the reunion of the twins is placed in a postnationalist context, it could be seen as further underscoring the importance of the present as opposed to the myths of the past. Rose and Maria find at least a temporary stability in the fact that they are 'like' each other. Nevertheless, Enright is anxious to point out that even the likenesses between twins contain elements of coincidence and cannot only be genetically explained. Among the things Rose and Maria discover about each other are the facts that they both had a best friend at school called Emily and that they both have two veins instead of one on the inside of their left elbow, but Enright places these similarities on the same level, though one is purely coincidental and the other a matter of genes.[49] The sources of identity are thus placed in the contemporaneous, in the similarities between siblings instead of in linkage with the past, but at the same time they are shown to be unstable and accidental rather than essential. There are no answers to questions of identity or belonging, only the establishment of a temporary relationship based on likeness, corresponding, perhaps to a postnationalist view of temporary alliances and shared interests. According to Ray Ryan, at least, this preoccupation with the 'now' and its concomitant rejection of history is characteristic of postnationalism as the expression of a 'self-generation unconnected to any collective entity called Ireland'.[50] But this rejection of the past has a price, since there is nothing to take the place of the rejected images. Through her description of Rose in particular, Enright indicates that the negative characteristics of a postnationalist society are alienation and loss. Though obviously critical of nationalist idealisation, Enright does not advocate a happy, utopian mongrelism as a solution, but acknowledges that dismantling old certainties may be disabling, too.

It is possible, perhaps even probable, that Enright's novel could not have been read as a postnationalist text in another literary culture where questions of nationality are less dominant than they are and have been in Irish literature and criticism. As a text that represents life in a modern, urban society no longer in the grip of nationalism it fits a postnationalist paradigm, as does its confrontation with prominent nationalist myths. As a text that probes the importance of genetic and ethnic heritage it is more divided, however. In another cultural context the postnational themes might have been overshadowed or not even detected, because it is certainly possible to interpret *What Are You Like?* also as, for instance, a feminist work describing the insecurity of women who have rejected old female roles but not yet found any certainties to replace them with, or as a moving story about the impossibility of forging true and lasting bonds with other people. Another approach would have been to focus on Enright's poetic use of language and view the novel as a purely aesthetic product. It is striking that, apart from noting the significance of the twin story, the reviewers have all concentrated on different aspects of the book, which of course means that postnationalism is as good a framework as any other, but also demonstrates that the fractured narrative makes a range of interpretations possible. The emphasis on personal responses and emotions could be seen as an attempt to ground the political content in individual experiences instead of constructing overarching narratives or myths. The main criticism directed against the novel, however, is that the characters fail to engage, which ultimately means that their search for identity becomes less interesting and weakens the political power of the text. The absence of linear causality in the tale may be the only appropriate way to mediate a postnationalist experience, but it also means that the postnational society is defined mainly in negative terms: fragmentary, not whole, confusing, not stable, transitory, not solid. In the end, then, Anne Enright's novel becomes as much a critical exposition of modern, urban existence as an attack on the straitjacket of a nationalist past.

Notes

1 Richard Kearney, *On Stories* (London: Routledge, 2002), p. 81.
2 Joe Cleary, *Literature, Partition and the Nation-State: Culture and Conflict in Ireland, Israel and Palestine* (Cambridge: Cambridge University Press, 2002), p. 51.
3 Kearney, *On Stories*, pp. 81–2.
4 Ray Ryan, *Ireland and Scotland: Literature and Culture, State and Nation, 1966–2000* (Oxford: Clarendon Press, 2002), p. 144.
5 Anne Enright, *What Are You Like?* (London: Jonathan Cape, 2000), p. 37.
6 Ryan, p. 143.
7 Quoted in Ryan, p. 144.
8 Frank Davey, *Postnational Arguments: The Politics of the Anglophone-Canadian Novel since 1967* (Toronto: University of Toronto Press, 1993), pp. 259–60.
9 Richard Kearney, *Postnationalist Ireland: Politics, Culture, Philosophy* (London: Routledge, 1997), p. 2.
10 Edward W. Said, *Culture and Imperialism* (London: Vintage, 1994), p. xxviii.

11   Cleary, p. 77.
12   Kearney, *Postnationalist Ireland*, pp. 2–5.
13   Ibid., p. 1.
14   Cairns Craig, *The Modern Scottish Novel: Narrative and the National Imagination* (Edinburgh: Edinburgh University Press, 1999), p. 9.
15   Penelope Fitzgerald, 'Bringers of Ill Luck and Bad Weather', *London Review of Books*, 2 March 2000, p. 8.
16   It would be possible, however, to claim that Enright actually attaches to traditional Irish storytelling since there are endless varieties of the Irish myths and it is impossible to determine which version should take precedence. But within the confines of each version there is usually coherence, a linear progression from beginning to end and a satisfactory explanation of events. See, for instance, Georges Zimmermann, *The Irish Storyteller* (Dublin: Four Courts, 2001).
17   Kearney, *Postnationalist Ireland*, p. 113.
18   Colm Tóibín, Introduction, in Colm Tóibín (ed.), *The Penguin Book of Irish Fiction*, (Harmondsworth: Viking, 1999), p. xxxiii.
19   Kearney, *Postnationalist Ireland*, p. 61.
20   Ibid., p. 124.
21   Enright, p. 13.
22   Ibid., p. 14.
23   Ibid., p. 14.
24   Ibid., p. 148.
25   Ibid., p. 41.
26   Ibid., p. 129.
27   Ibid., p. 136.
28   Ibid., pp. 140–1.
29   Ibid., p. 159.
30   Neil Corcoran, *After Yeats and Joyce: Reading Modern Irish Literature* (Oxford: Oxford University Press, 1997), p. 57.
31   Ibid., p. 58.
32   Enright, pp. 44–5.
33   Ibid., p. 51.
34   Ibid., p. 108.
35   Ibid., p. 140.
36   Ibid., p. 84, p. 29.
37   Gabriele Annan, 'Twin Peaks', *New York Review of Books*, 21 September 2000, p. 90.
38   Ruth Scurr, 'Novel of the Week', *New Statesman*, 10 April 2000, p. 61.
39   Fitzgerald, p. 8.
40   Annan, p. 90.
41   Christine St Peter, *Changing Ireland: Strategies in Contemporary Women's Fiction* (Houndmills: Macmillan, 2000), p. 45.
42   Enright, p. 63.
43   Ryan, p. 166.
44   Enright, p. 201.

45 Ibid., p. 28.
46 Ibid., pp. 145–6.
47 Robert Karron, 'What Are You Like?', *Boston Review*, http://bostonreview.
mit.edu/BR25.5/karron.html (accessed on 5 February 2003).
48 Robert MacFarlane, 'Separated at Birth', *Times Literary Supplement*,
3 March 2000, p. 21.
49 Enright, pp. 255–6.
50 Ryan, p. 147.

13

'Sacred spaces': writing home in recent Irish memoirs and autobiographies (John McGahern's *Memoir*, Hugo Hamilton's *The Speckled People*, Seamus Deane's *Reading in the Dark* and John Walsh's *The Falling Angels*)

Stephen Regan

One of the familiar conventions of autobiography is its revelation of an individual life through a compelling first-person narrative voice. To work upon its readers most effectively, autobiography needs to present the life in question as both unique and typical; it must offer an appealing account of an existence that is special enough and significant enough to warrant attention, but it must also sustain that attention through an insistence on common human dilemmas and a shared sense of endeavour. At the same time as presenting a single life as unfolding and uncertain, shaped by that which can only be dimly discerned, the work of autobiography can, with hindsight, be immensely assured and authoritative about the way things turned out. The reader's gratification is intimately connected with the process by which the individual life, in all its stumbling unpredictability and waywardness, is given shape and structure. There is a special pleasure, too, in being persuaded that the autobiographical narrative is a truthful record of events, while knowing all along that what we are reading is an elaborate, stylised fiction.

Memoir similarly suggests a recollection of actual events and experiences, with an implicit trust in the faithfulness of memory being shared by author and reader. The term implies historical knowledge, an informed account of one's own life and times, but the distinctions between autobiography and memoir are not easy to establish and maintain. In a very general sense, autobiography tends to offer a comprehensive account of a single life in a mode that is personal, if not confessional, while memoir often presents a series of recollections that form only part of the life in question, in a mode that appears more discursive and objective. Memoir, however, often brings with it the personal, emotional intensity of autobiography, and it is just as likely to employ the devices and techniques of fiction.

For many Irish writers, autobiography inevitably takes on the kind of public, historical aura associated with memoir, for the simple reason that the individual life is so frequently and so inseparably entwined with the troubled life of the nation. The awakening of consciousness is also therefore an awakening to the political urgencies of a particular place and time. For late nineteenth-century and early twentieth-century memoirists in Ireland, the unfinished business of one's own life is coterminous with an uncertain political future, so that notions of identity, for both self and nation, tend to take on a curiously suspended form. Autobiographical fiction finds its consummate form in *A Portrait of the Artist as a Young Man*, and Stephen Dedalus, flying by the nets of language, nationality and religion, becomes the exemplary type of the artist struggling to create anew the conscience of his race. For a later generation of writers, the memory of growing up in Ireland carries with it the powerful imprint of revolution, civil war and partition, and the violent repercussions of that convulsive history extend across the later twentieth century and into the autobiographical writings of the present time. Those writers born in the 1930s and 1940s are, not surprisingly, acutely susceptible to seeing their own coming to maturity as unavoidably implicated in the difficult and traumatic passage of the nascent Irish Free State and its eventual transformation into the Irish Republic in 1949.

Most autobiographies and most memoirs rely very heavily on a vividly realised account of place and time. These are the structural co-ordinates through which the self is most obviously recreated and refashioned. In recent Irish autobiography, however, the intense relationship between the psychology of the self and the politics of nationhood has been rendered through an especially powerful and experimental preoccupation with place and time. One of the unusual and distinctive features of recent autobiographical writing has been its tendency to highlight its own spatial and temporal complexities as a way of denoting the problematic nature of identity. A strong commitment to the co-ordinates of place and time might well be expected in nationalist memoirs and autobiographical writings by Irish authors, but place and time are figured with a new intensity and self-consciousness in recent Irish migrant or second-generation autobiographies, which have increasingly become a special category or sub-genre in the study of modern Irish literature.

John McGahern's starkly titled *Memoir* (2005) opens with a vivid
account of the lanes and fields of Co. Leitrim, where he walked as a
boy in the 1930s and 1940s, and where he returned to live in the 1970s.
Despite its poor soil, that landscape possesses a primal power for
McGahern: 'My relationship with these lanes and fields extended
back to the very beginning of my life'.[1] It is also as near as he gets to
imagining heaven, as he recalls his mother naming the flowers for him
as they walk to school. There is a touching candour in McGahern's
insistence on his own abundant happiness on these occasions, almost
as if he challenges his memory to prove otherwise: 'I must have been
extraordinarily happy walking that lane to school' (p. 4). With that one
simple sentence we get an immediate sense of the complexity of any
autobiographical narrative that seeks to capture both the intensity of
childhood feelings and the more circumspect nature of adult recollection. It is not surprising, therefore, that initially McGahern appears to
invoke the romantic idealism of Wordsworth, for whom the child is
father of the man:

> There are many such lanes all around where I live, and in certain rare
> moments over the years while walking in these lanes I have come into
> an extraordinary sense of security, a deep peace, in which I feel that I
> can live for ever. I suspect it is no more than the actual lane and the lost
> lane becoming one for a moment in an intensity of feeling, but without
> the usual attendants of pain and loss. These moments disappear as
> suddenly and as inexplicably as they come, and long before they can be
> recognized and placed. (p. 4)

If the passage acknowledges Wordsworthian spots of time, it also
acquires a more modern, existentialist outlook, reminiscent of Edward
Thomas, for whom the lane was a fitting place for meditating on
beginnings and endings. The lane, which might otherwise function as
a paltry image of Irish pastoralism, takes on a dynamic, cognitive role
as memory and imagination begin to interact. It serves as a vital point
of entry into and exit out of the buried life of the feelings. Walking
down the country lanes provides an intense momentary release, an action
beyond words that is reminiscent of the dancing in Brian Friel's
Dancing at Lughnasa (1990). The movement and rhythm of walking
constitute a structuring element in the memoir, leading us towards the
magnificent final pages in which McGahern imagines a tender reunion
with his mother, gently reconciling her unquestioning belief with his
own unshakeable disbelief:

> If we could walk together through those summer lanes, with their banks
> of wild flowers that 'cast a spell', we probably would not be able to speak,

though I would want to tell her all the local news . . . I would want no shadow to fall on her joy and deep trust in God. She would face no false reproaches. As we retraced our steps, I would pick for her the wild orchid and the windflower. (p. 272)

If the Irish countryside and a caring mother offer peace and security, what they contend with in McGahern's life is political conflict and a violent father. Outside the reassuring lanes with their wild flowers are the police barracks (Garda Siochana), where the father is stationed as a young sergeant in the new Free State. The life that McGahern recounts so movingly is one in which the Civil War has left a bitter legacy of hatred that erupts irrationally and finds its destructive expression in the violence and cruelty of the father. The barracks are a brutal, stifling and enclosing place, the memories of which are associated with childhood humiliation and abject misery. Against the spirit of freedom that informed The Easter Proclamation of the Irish Republic in 1916, the State that emerges is 'a theocracy in all but name' (p. 210). By 1950, the Church has come to exercise power over much of civil life, including education and entertainment, and McGahern's sense of enclosure and confinement is once again defined in terms of buildings: 'the hospitals, the orphanages, the juvenile prison systems, the parish halls' (p. 210).

Even for a later generation of writers, the Civil War casts a long shadow. Hugo Hamilton, in *The Speckled People* (2003), recalls his father explaining the events that took place in west Cork in the 1920s:

He tells us about the time when the British soldiers came to their house in Leap, threatening to burn it down because they thought the rebels were shooting from the upstairs window . . . And then the very same thing happened again after the British had gone and the Irish started fighting among themselves, because that's what they had learned from the British. Then one day they had to leave the house a second time when Irish Free State soldiers said they would burn it down, because they were sure they saw IRA snipers in the upstairs window.[2]

Hamilton adopts the kind of *faux naïf* voice and perspective that makes for comedy, but as with Frank McCourt's *Angela's Ashes* (1998) this wide-eyed credulity is apt to become monotonous and the comic effects can soon wear thin. Where *The Speckled People* excels is in its exploration of 'new' Irish identities: 'My father says we have nothing to worry about because we are the new Irish. Partly from Ireland and partly from somewhere else, half-Irish and half-German. We're the speckled people' (p. 7). What is striking in terms of technique is the representation of this uncertain identity through radical spatial and temporal shifts which are nevertheless in keeping with a child's view of the world: 'When I was small I woke up in Germany . . . Then I got up and looked out the window and saw Ireland. And after breakfast we all went out the door to Ireland and walked down to Mass' (p. 1). At the end of the book, after their father's death, the children stand with their German mother on the road, unsure of where home might be.

The Speckled People presents itself as a memoir rather than an autobiography, and this is how it was generally treated in reviews. Even so, several reviewers paid tribute to its inventiveness and its storytelling vivacity. There was greater uncertainty about whether Seamus Deane's *Reading in the Dark* (1996) was memoir or fiction. Blake Morrison, in a sensitive and discerning review in the *Independent on Sunday*, paid tribute to 'Seamus Deane's marvellous memoir, or novel, about growing up in Derry in the 1950s'.[3] Morrison sees the book modulating between the *Bildungsroman*, a novel of early life and development, and 'a kind of whodunnit', though he nevertheless insists that its strength and control of storytelling make questions about fiction and non-fiction seem irrelevant. For Edna Longley, writing in *Fortnight*, *Reading in the Dark* was autobiographical fiction, 'less a novel than an essay in sensibility of a type more common at the turn of the century', a work full of the epiphanies and self-communings of Joyce's Stephen Dedalus.[4]

Reading in the Dark evades any easy categorisation in terms of its narrative style. Its structure seems simple and obvious, with chapters and parts conforming to the written conventions of narrative, but its use of episodic tales and its colloquial, anecdotal technique owe much to the oral tradition of storytelling. The book consists of three parts, each containing two chapters, with each chapter subdivided into numerous short episodes. These episodes are precisely dated, from February 1945 to July 1971, creating the impression of a diary or journal, though in many ways they resemble snapshots that become increasingly fluid and cinematic. The faded photograph on the dust jacket shows Seamus Deane and his brother, arms folded, celebrating their first holy communion. As if simultaneously inviting and denying the suggestion of autobiography, the book cover also reveals a cracked photographic plate.

The unnamed narrator of *Reading in the Dark*, about five years old in 1945, is the third of seven Catholic children growing up in the city of Derry. Despite its seemingly chronological trajectory, the book repeatedly and obsessively turns back on itself, both starting and ending at the foot of the stairs in a house overlooking the cathedral. There is no single linear narrative, but instead a proliferation of narrative possibilities that have to do with the absence of any secure knowledge. The mental and emotional torment that fuses these different narrative strands arises when a boy so loves his parents that he wants to know everything about them, and in seeking to acquire that knowledge he uncovers a secret that bitterly divides him from them and ends up destroying the love he cherished. The most prominent and poignant verb in the book is the verb *to know*, and while in some ways a universal, archetypal infinitive, it cannot in this instance be abstracted from the cultural and political pressures under which the boy's psychology is so tragically thwarted.

As Edna Longley's review makes clear, *Reading in the Dark* shares with *The Field Day Anthology of Irish Writing* an interest in memoir and autobiography as significant narratives of Ireland. In his introduction to a section of the *Anthology* titled 'Autobiography and Memoirs 1890–1988', Deane declares his interest in 'what gives the self definition'. Autobiography, he suggests, is never simply about the self, but also about 'the hostile or liberating energy' which 'made the self come into consciousness and thereby gave to existence a pattern or the beginnings of a pattern of explanation'.[5] *Reading in the Dark* has its origins in precisely this kind of speculation about selfhood and identity. In a colonial or neo-colonial context, Deane continues, the oppressive agencies with which the self contends are 'multiple and blatant', and so the writing of an autobiography or memoir produces an unusually intense enquiry into the nature of identity, personal or national. The growth of consciousness in such writing is not likely to be registered as a smooth and uninterrupted process but one of profound unease and disturbance. This, Deane asserts, is 'one of the obsessive marks of cultures that have been compelled to inquire into the legitimacy of their own existence by the presence of another culture that is forever foreign and forever intimate'.[6]

In the context of political repression, the autobiographer or writer of memoirs is likely to ask if identity can be more securely established or otherwise simply abandoned and forgotten. What is articulated in the process of self-examination is a familiar relationship between 'Edenic' and 'utopian' responses, one pushing back to a condition of primal innocence, and the other looking forward to some ideal resolution. What most often prevails, however, is 'a radical privation . . . the sense of a missing feature or energy'. *Reading in the Dark* is a meditation on that missing agency, an anguished search for some alternative to what Deane terms 'the obduracy of existing conditions'.[7] The boy's act of reading in the dark is one of both existential necessity and political expediency, a matter of 're-imagining all I had read, the various ways the plot might unravel, the novel opening into endless possibilities in the dark'.[8]

A further explanation of the generic indeterminacy of *Reading in the Dark* is evident in Deane's searching and appreciative review of Terry Eagleton's *Heathcliff and the Great Hunger* (1995). Here, Deane reflects on the cultural forms appropriate to a society in which the conflict between modernity and tradition has been unusually fraught. In literary terms, there is the imaginative world of the realist novel, with its temporal, everyday rhythms, but there is also 'that other world, variously described as the legendary, the mythical, the timeless'. One of the distinctive features of Irish literary culture, according to Deane, is its simultaneous perception of these different dimensions or cultural chronologies. Irish fiction is endowed with a facility for incorporating 'canonical realist forms . . . and other forms subversive of or merely different from them'.[9] *Reading in the Dark* possesses this facility for sliding subtly and uncannily between different imaginative discourses or dimensions. If it embraces the everyday rhythms of realist fiction, it is also powerfully imbued with the rhythms of Gothic supernaturalism. Ostensibly a novel about growing up in a particular place at a particular time, it is also an excursion into the realm of the fantastic, a harrowing story of hauntings, possessions and exorcisms.

The opening episode of *Reading in the Dark* establishes a strange and uneasy conjunction between exactness and ineffability, between that which can be physically measured or registered by the senses and that which lies beyond recovery or comprehension:

> On the stairs, there was a clear, plain silence.
>   It was a short staircase, fourteen steps in all, covered in lino from which the original pattern had been polished away to the point where it had the look of a faint memory. Eleven steps took you to the turn of the stairs where the cathedral and the sky always hung in the window frame. Three more steps took you on to the landing, about six feet long. (p. 5)

The look of the lino and the loss of its original pattern exert a powerful metonymic and characteristically realist effect at the outset of a narrative obsessively concerned with the processes of memory. At the same time, the unsettling description of silence as being clearly and plainly there 'on the stairs' prepares us for the appearance of a shadow that the boy and his mother can feel but not see. The strict denotation of realist narrative subsides into the ghostly imprecision of the Gothic: 'The house was all cobweb tremors' (p. 6). Accompanying the immediacy of the child's enthralment is the adult narrator's retrospective assessment of the mother–child relationship: 'I loved her then', a plain and sorrowful declaration of the breakdown that follows. Similarly, the dialogue presents the shadow as 'something there between us', obdurately and tragically anticipating their separation (p. 5).

The collusion of realist narrative and elements that subtly undermine it produces a highly distinctive and striking prose style. A clean, spare diction and simple, uncluttered syntax reminiscent of journal narratives suddenly opens into a richly embellished and heavily adjectival prose. The opening of the episode, dated 'November 1947', is characteristic:

> It was a fierce winter, that year. The snow covered the air-raid shelters. At night, from the stair window, the field was a white paradise of loneliness, and a starlit wind made the glass shake like loose, black water and the ice snore on the sill, while we slept, and the shadow watched. (p. 9)

Here, a passage that specifies the season, the year and the post-war environment modulates into a world of strange and supernatural occurrences.

Reading in the Dark takes its epigraph from a popular song, 'She Moved Through the Fair': 'The people were saying no two were e'er wed / But one had a sorrow that never was said'.[10] The disjunction between what is said in public and what is not said in private is just one point of contact between the book and the song. The quotation acquires significance as the marriage between the narrator's parents begins to founder on his mother's agonising and obstinate silence. The reluctance or inability to speak about disturbing events is a common affliction in the book, and the narrator himself frequently confides, with shame and frustration, that 'I said nothing'. In a more general way, the epigraph points to the persistence of popular cultural forms, including folklore, songs and legends.

The early episode titled 'Disappearances' establishes the significance of myth, superstition and illusion in the narrator's developing consciousness: 'people with green eyes were close to the fairies, we were told; they were just here for a little while, looking for a human child they could take away'. Catholic doctrine asserts a different, though no less compelling, mythological notion of destination and disappearance, prefiguring hell as 'a great whirlpool of flames' where 'you disappeared forever' (p. 7). In the same episode, we encounter Bamboozelem, a magician with Duffy's Circus, who performs a celebrated disappearing act. The child at the circus hesitates between the power of magic and the rational explanation that Bamboozelem has slipped through a trapdoor: 'Everyone was laughing and clapping but I felt uneasy. How could they all be so sure?' (p. 8).

So often, in the narrator's perceptions, mythical or magical incidents have their counterparts in actuality, though the diverse episodes in the book are so neatly imbricated that no easy distinction between the imagined and the real can be drawn. It is typical of Deane's skilful intercutting of scenes that the 'Disappearances' episode should be followed immediately with the story of 'the big shoot-out at the distillery between the IRA and the police, when Uncle Eddie disappeared'. The story of Uncle Eddie's disappearance is one among many, but its exact dating – April, 1922 – firmly links it to the founding of the Irish Free State and the subsequent events of Irish political history. The repercussions of Eddie's involvement in the Republican movement produce the secrecy and silence that dominate the family life of a later generation: 'Certainly he had never returned, although my father would not speak of it at all' (p. 9).

A powerful instance of realist chronology intersecting with the mythic can be found in the episode titled 'Field of the Disappeared, *August 1950*'. The narrator and his brother, Liam, are taken by their father to see a 'stretch of green' close to the sea. The father explains that the souls of all those from the area who had disappeared, including lost fishermen, would gather on certain feast days like St Brigid's Day or Christmas Day, 'to cry like birds and look down on the fields where they had been born' (p. 53). The narrator suspects that there is 'something more to be told', but his father says nothing. Then the boy intuitively makes the connection with his father's lost brother: 'Is this, I wondered, where Eddie's soul comes to cry for his lost fields?' (p. 54).

'Field of the Disappeared' is a startling instance of Deane's simultaneous apprehension of different cultural chronologies. What it suggests, however, is that the hybrid realism of *Reading in the Dark* is founded not just on intersecting temporal dimensions but on intersecting spatial dimensions as well. One of the most impressive aspects of the book is its sense of place, its meticulous way of mapping cultural and political anxieties on to the city of Derry and its rural environs, at the same time dissolving the boundaries between the real and the legendary. All of the principal places in the book, including the stairs on which it opens and closes, appear to cast a shadow. The Field of the Disappeared, the ruined distillery, the lost farmhouse and the old fort of Grianan are all exactly realised and all imaginatively elevated as legend.

'We begin to think where we live', as Raymond Williams was fond of remarking, and that observation has a special acuity if the place happens to be Derry.[11] The contradictory impulses which Derry provokes in the mind of the young boy growing up there are hauntingly and beautifully evoked by Deane in an episode titled 'Fire'. 'It was a city of bonfires', the narrator tells us, and he goes on to recall how 'Fire was what I loved to hear of and to see. It transformed the grey air and streets, excited and exciting' (p. 33). Of course, the bonfires also inflame the deep sectarian divisions within Derry ('The Protestants had more than we had'), keeping alive a bitter history of triumph and defeat: the 'liberation' of Derry from besieging Catholics in 1689 or the Battle of the Boyne in 1690. Fire also plays a significant role in the events of 1922 and the burning down of Watt's distillery. The occupation of the distillery by IRA gunmen was 'a last-minute protest at the founding of the new state' (p. 35). What remains is 'a burnt space in the heart of the neighbourhood' (p. 36). Place, then, is not a neutral entity or simply a convenient setting for the narrative in *Reading in the Dark*. It is where the long, protracted struggle for meaning and definition goes on.

Deane shows the complex interaction between spatial relations and social relations in a brilliantly evocative and highly animated way. The passage that follows conveys the sights, smells and sounds of the city, but also that complicated experience in which intimate belonging and sullen disenchantment seem inseparable:

> The dismembered streets lay strewn all around the ruined distillery where Uncle Eddie had fought, aching with a long, dolorous absence. With the distillery had gone the smell of vaporised whiskey and heated red brick, the sullen glow that must have loomed over the crouching houses like an amber sunset. Now, instead, we had the high Gothic cathedral and the parochial house, standing above the area in a permanent greystone winter overlooking the abandoned site that seemed to me a faithless and desolate patch, rinsed of its colour, pale and bald in the midst of the tumble of small houses, unpaved streets and the giant moraine of debris that had slid from the foot of the city walls down a sloping embankment to where our territory began. In the early winter evenings, people angled past like shadows under the weak street lights, voices would say goodnight and be gone. (p. 34)

Deane's recreation of the city is both majestic and desolate. The scattered streets and the 'tumble' of houses suggest a casual, unplanned filling of space, and yet the lines of territorial possession are clearly demarcated. Even as a child, the narrator is in no doubt about 'where our territory began'. The contradictory response that Derry elicits is evident, too, in the relentless personification with which it is invested. Its 'heart' is a burnt space, its streets are 'dismembered', and yet its will to live is irrepressible: 'The town lay entranced, embraced by the great sleeping light of the river and the green beyond of the border. It woke now and then, like someone startled and shouting from a dream, in clamour at its abandonment' (p. 36). This romantic evocation, reminiscent of Wordsworth's London in his sonnet 'Composed Upon Westminster Bridge', is brutally undercut with the recollection of a St Patrick's Day riot, when 'the police had baton-charged a march and pursued us into our territory'. The episode ends with another fire – a burning police car – and a sudden spatial distortion: 'The whole street seemed to be bent sideways, tilted by the blazing hoardings in to the old Gaelic football ground' (p. 36).

The Derry of *Reading in the Dark* is possessed of those equal tugs of attachment and disavowal that Deane describes so well in *The Field Day Anthology*: 'To the extent that the world, especially the world of childhood and youth, is restored in writing to its full presence, there is a corresponding sense of its inadequacy. It is always something to escape from'. The search for an alternative, Deane suggests, is 'one of the symptoms of a culture that believes itself always to be provincial, always to be in need of a metropolitan world elsewhere'.[12] Like Gar in Brian Friel's *Philadelphia, Here I Come!*, the narrator of *Reading in the Dark* dreams of American cities: 'Chicago was a place I longed to see' (p. 37). As the boy reaches adolescence and prepares for university, the crisis Deane describes seems imminent. The provincial city must be left, and yet there is no other place that can be as fully realised.

Along with the ruined distillery, there are two other places of deep significance in the geography of the child's imagination. He dreams of a lost farmhouse and longs to go there, but his dream is disrupted by the repercussions of a family feud and by the revelation that Uncle Eddie was interrogated there before he 'disappeared'. The other place is the ancient fort of Grianan (the Fort of Light), where the sleeping warriors of the legendary Fianna are thought to rest. According to the prophecies of St Columcille, the sleeping Fianna will awake to a trumpet call and fight the last battle somewhere between Derry and Strabane, 'after which the one remaining English ship would sail out of Lough Foyle and away from Ireland forever' (p. 57). The old stone ring of Grianan is one of those symbolic places that Deane describes as 'romantic' ruins, signifying 'not only loss but also the native endurance that will prevail even over and through the destruction of the buildings it once created'.[13] Once again, however, these places of dream and legend and imagination are found to be implicated in the harsh political actualities of the present. The narrator discovers that Grianan is where his Uncle Eddie was shot by fellow Republicans on suspicion of being an informer.

So much of *Reading in the Dark* exemplifies what Fredric Jameson calls 'cognitive mapping', an exploration of socio-spatial relations and their political causes and consequences.[14] The landscape where the narrator grows up is 'border country', physically marked by bridges and streams, but also indelibly scored in the mind. A stream, crossed by a hump-backed bridge, marks 'part of the red line that wriggled around the city on the map and hemmed it in to the waters of Lough Foyle'. At one end of the bridge 'the Free State began – a grassy road that ran straight for thirty yards' (p. 49). The physical and mental contours of the narrator's territory are compactly described in a single sentence: 'So there it was, our territory, with the old fort of Grianan on one hill overlooking Lough Foyle, the feud farmhouse on another hill, gazing on Lough Swilly, the thick neck of the Inishowen peninsula between, Derry gauzed in smoke at the end of Lough Foyle, the border writhing behind it' (p. 59).

Across the border, Donegal exerts its own distinctive cultural rhythms, while in Derry the pace of modernity is quickening. By the end of 1958 a firm called 'Birmingham Sound Reproducers' has opened a factory for making record-players. Whereas previously it was the women who occupied the jobs in the local shirt factory, it is now the men who take the available work. As the narrator observes, 'It changed the whole pattern of movement in the neighbourhood' (p. 219). On a crucial day when the narrator's father is about to reveal what he knows of Uncle Eddie's death, he takes the boy and his brother to one of his favourite childhood haunts. Across the river from Culmore Point the British Oxygen plant is being built, and his father explains that the whole embankment is going to 'disappear' in a short time. The ironies here are multiple. It is not just that the Birmingham record-player company and British Oxygen are perceived to be modernising agents that have come from 'outside' and are therefore indicative of a continuing cultural and economic incursion into the area, it is also that one hints at the replaying of a familiar historical record, while the other manufactures oxygen in a place of continuing suffocation.

Given the narrator's sensitivity to the politics of place, it is hardly surprising that his own family's tragic break-up and dispersal should be construed in terms of spatial relations. Dwelling on the broken links of the family and his father's agonised suppression of speech, the narrator reflects: 'I felt we lived in an empty space with a long cry from him ramifying through it. At other times, it appeared to be as cunning and articulate as a labyrinth, closely designed, with someone sobbing at the heart of it' (p. 43). At the end of the book, the narrator leaves Derry for a university education in Belfast, sensing acutely that there is already an unbridgeable gap between himself and his family: 'I had created a distance between my parents and myself that had become my only way of loving them' (p. 225). The boy realises, too, that there is wisdom in Crazy Joe's conundrum: 'There's a place where a man died but lived on as a ghost, and where another man lived as a ghost but died as a man, and where another man would have died as a man but ran away to live as a ghost. Where would that place be?' (p. 221). The melting of solid forms into shadows finally afflicts the boy and his mother. 'She was nearly gone from me now', he remarks towards the end of the book, 'Now the haunting meant something new to me – now I had become the shadow' (p. 217). If the image of the shadow suggests an encroaching darkness and an unremitting sense of guilt and complicity, it also recalls the uncanny resemblances between the missing Uncle Eddie and other family members, as if they are all in some way implicated in his fate.

It is entirely in keeping with the complicity of private and public grief in *Reading in the Dark* that the narrator's mother should suffer a stroke and lose the power of speech at the onset of the Troubles in October 1968. The closing episode, simply titled 'After', shows a community reeling under gunfire, explosions and the smashing of batons on riot shields. On the day the narrator's father dies, a curfew is called and armoured personnel carriers move through the streets. The narrator stays awake until dawn and is roused by the noise of horse-hooves. He watches 'a young gypsy boy jog sedately through the scurf of debris astride a grey-mottled horse'. Although the curfew is still going on, the boy rides through the streets, holding on to the horse's mane. The narrator recalls how 'The clip-clop of hooves echoed in the still streets after he had disappeared' (p. 233). That striking image of the boy on horseback functions on a number of levels. It carries with it the stirring energy of Jack B. Yeats's equestrian paintings, challenging and resisting authority and conformity, but like the painter's fabulous horsemen and their horses it seems to be conjured up out of the imaginative remnants of an older Ireland. Like so much in *Reading in the Dark*, there is a powerful sense of presence in the very acknowledgement of absence and disappearance.

In its moving depiction of a community caught between modernity and tradition, *Reading in the Dark* sedulously avoids both sentimentality and dogmatism. It is all too well aware of that naively utopian plenitude of selfhood and nationhood that seems to beckon in such desperate circumstances. The book does not allow a simple-minded politics of identity to offer itself as cause and explanation, but nor does it cynically or despairingly relinquish the processes of self-definition and interpretation. If reading in the dark is a way of making sense of history, of infusing interpretation with imagination, so too is the writing of fiction. The boy who reads in the dark is effectively inventing fictions of his own and quietly learning the subtle distinction between telling it as it is and telling it as it might be.

A self-reflexive concern with reading and writing, and with the nature of artistic vocation, provides the strongest point of contact with Joyce's *Portrait of the Artist as a Young Man*. Like Stephen Dedalus, the narrator of *Reading in the Dark* comes to consciousness amidst a competing and bewildering array of aesthetic, religious and political imperatives, and there are moments when he has to announce, 'I will not serve'. An education with the Christian Brothers provides Deane's narrator with some magnificent opportunities for ribald comedy and satirical deflation. Like Joyce's novel, *Reading in the Dark* makes its difficult way between the politics of affiliation and attachment and the politics of disavowal and denial. In the process, language, nationality and religion are exposed to those destabilising ironies so character-istic of Joyce. In the Cold War episode titled 'Political Education, *November 1956*', a priest in British Army Uniform tells a group of school-boys that in comparison with the great threat of Communism, 'Our internal disputes are no more than family quarrels'. The boys wonder if it's the Germans, the Russians or the IRA who are causing all the problems. 'Global vision', the narrator muses, 'I needed that' (p. 197).

Where Seamus Deane's autobiographical novel explores the con-sciousness of a Catholic, Republican community in a border town in Northern Ireland, John Walsh's memoir *The Falling Angels* is much more obviously concerned with the fate of migrant or diasporic Irish com-munities, and in particular the uncertain identities of the émigré Irish middle class. In stark contrast to Deane's emphasis on working-class Derry, Walsh (the son of an Irish doctor) gives us what at first appears to be a picture of comfortable affluence in Battersea, South London. But if Walsh finds space for comedy in his anatomy of Irish migrant identity, he is also alert to the painfulness of division and separation. Like *Reading in the Dark*, *The Falling Angels* is about family disinteg-ration and it, too, records the loss of the narrator's mother and father and the bleakness of trying to reinvent and redefine oneself in the emptiness that is left behind. Walsh's memoir is subtitled 'An Irish Romance', but that love of romantic Ireland is severely undercut by the narrator's persistent sense of displacement. In many ways, Walsh's writing exhibits those distinguishing characteristics identified by Deane in his account of Irish memoir and autobiography in the Field Day anthology. If at one level, there is an urge towards consolidation of a secure identity, there is at another level a counter-urge towards com-plete abandonment of any such notion. *The Falling Angels* is suspended between those backward-looking Edenic impulses and those forward-looking utopian impulses that Deane registers so acutely, but it brings with it a special sense of spatial and temporal complexity that derives from its status as a second-generation memoir essentially conceived outside of Ireland.

The Falling Angels gives us an opportunity for examining diasporic Irish identity, especially that of second-generation Irish children growing up in England. Aidan Arrowsmith's analysis of displaced Irishness is helpful here, though as Liam Harte points out, it needs to be modified with reference to the peculiarly indeterminate or suspended identity that second-generation children acquire.[15] Arrowsmith's model is based on a tripartite pattern of development. The uncertainty of identity associated with second-generation affiliation to a lost homeland leads initially to a rejection of parental heritage, involving a desire to conform to English cultural norms. This is followed by a reassessment of cultural origins and by nostalgia for some authentic ideal of Irishness. This nostalgia than mutates into a more mature and enquiring third position, in which the displaced subject begins to question whether there can ever be an authentic state of being and comes to accept the provisionality and hybridity of identity.

What is unusual about *The Falling Angels*, according to Liam Harte, is that it seems to bypass this linear, progressive model of identity and instead shows us different notions of identity co-existing in a much more problematic and unresolved way.[16] Walsh, who studied English Literature at Oxford and then Irish Literature at University College Dublin, and who now writes for the *Independent* newspaper, has a powerfully engaging rhetorical style in which he is able to expose and ridicule the obvious stereotypes of romantic attachment to Ireland while simultaneously suggesting just how strong and seductive those ideals of Irishness actually are. At the same time as revealing that second-generation Irishness entails a whole range of possible identities that might be performed or improvised, the memoir also continues to yearn for some fixed point of security in the old ancestral homeland.

It is towards the west of Ireland, the place of myth and folklore and Irish language, that the memoir is drawn. The title recalls another literary work of indeterminate genre, John Millington Synge's book *The Aran Islands*, in which the Irish playwright in the guise of anthropologist encounters the denizens of those far-flung islands. In his account of his visits to Inishmore, the largest of the islands, Synge recalls how he met an old blind fisherman called Mairtin Conneely, who told him the story of how Satan and his angels were thrown out of heaven, and how one of the archangels pleaded with God to spare some of Satan's followers. The old man explains to Synge: 'those that were falling are in the air still, and have power to wreck ships and to work evil in the world'.[17] Walsh finds a compelling parallel with those exiled Irish, like himself, who seem cursed to spend their lives in a state of suspense, caught between Ireland and England. He seizes on the image of falling angels to explain the predicament of those who are 'eternally in transit between one place and another, deprived of a sanctuary, denied a final refuge, never finding a real home' (p. 30).

What complicates Walsh's already confused sense of identity is the powerful attraction of 1960s popular culture in London in his teen years, with the Beatles and the Rolling Stones now competing with the traditional Irish music enjoyed by his parents and their Irish friends. For much of the memoir, the narrator oscillates between the need for assimilation in middle-class English culture and the powerful attraction of Irish otherness, seeking an identity that will somehow embrace both nationalities. After the death of his mother, Anne, the narrator takes a long journey through Ireland, a rite of passage in which he hopes to find a secure sense of origin and belonging, but to no avail. At the funeral of his mother's sister, his Aunt Dolly, he talks to a nun about his search for home:

> I fell into conversation with Sister Brid, from the Presentation Convent in Athenry. We talked about Dolly's in-between status – how neither she nor Anne could quite stay, or grow, or become 'really themselves' in England; but neither could they go back to what they'd known and rejected in Ireland. I told the nun about my own wonderings about where my home was.
>
> 'It's very simple,' she said. 'Wherever your parents may be buried, your true home is with the next generation. So with you it's London, where your children are growing up. But the human heart allows itself to have *sacred spaces*, where you feel most alive, even if they're not your home.'
>
> That sounded about right. But I still hadn't found the home I sought, somewhere between London and Galway, sharing the essences of Englishness and Irishness, somewhere beyond both. (pp. 279–80)

Although Sister Brid's distinction between one's 'true home' and the 'sacred spaces' of the human heart provides a flexible model of attachment and identification, it still invokes the binary categories of England and Ireland, of 'here' and 'there'. It insists too strongly on generational divides as the final arbiters of what constitutes home.

The narrator's search for somewhere beyond both London and Galway takes him further west and back out to the Aran Islands, following the footsteps of John Millington Synge. He discovers in his reading about the islands that there was an English military presence there in the seventeenth and eighteenth centuries and that the people of the islands are not the pure-bred Irish that Synge and Yeats believed them to be. The Aran Islands as a place once thought to be the repository of authentic Irishnness turns out to be a more heterogeneous, hybridised place than Ireland's writers imagined. It provides a space in which English and Irish identities might be joined and transcended. In a moment of reconciliation strongly reminiscent of Wordsworth turning to his sister at the end of 'Tintern Abbey', the narrator addresses his sister, Madelyn, both suggesting a recovered sense of unity and allowing the memoir to end with a question:

> I looked to the right, where the Cliffs of Moher bulked in the sunlight, showing a more friendly, piebald aspect than ever before. I looked left and saw the edge of Connemara, the great lunar landscape of Galway rock, from where the airplane would soon land to take us back to civilisation. The Cliffs and the stone desert, my favourite sights in Ireland, seemed suddenly drawn together, forming a mystic triangle, somewhere beyond England and Ireland. Here, where Synge's fishermen believed that angels were always falling through the air and wreaking havoc in the world, here was the place where they might fall to earth at last.
>
> 'Madelyn,' I said. 'How'd you like to build a house here?' (pp. 281–2)

Looking to the right and then looking to the left are gestures of caution, but the west of Ireland landscape, for all that it retains suggestions of being beyond 'civilisation', even 'lunar' in its remoteness, is friendly and inviting. The question remains, however, whether this is the real home that the narrator has repeatedly sought. We are asked, perhaps, to consider the difference between a house and a home, and to reflect upon the possibility that a house is only a temporary structure. Liam Harte's reflections on the nature of the house are instructive here: 'this implied preference for fixity over flux is counterbalanced by the sense that this will be no ordinary or earthly house, but rather one which embodies an idea of "home" as site specific yet free floating, earthed yet deterritorialised, concretely bounded yet transcendently open'.[18]

One of the most remarkable features of Irish autobiographical writing since the 1990s has been its readiness to depart from the usual and familiar conventions through which the self is represented in literature. Often this has involved a flagrant mixing of generic codes, or a self-conscious literariness and allusiveness, so that the fictional component of memoir or autobiography is made more than usually explicit. This unsettling of traditional autobiographical modes has tended to bring with it a strong sense of identity held in abeyance, painfully thwarted, strangely suspended. More striking still has been the extraordinary preoccupation in Irish autobiography and memoir with the spatial and temporal structures through which the self is habitually known and understood. There is no easy rite of passage from childhood to adulthood, even in those works that call upon comedy to relieve the troubling question of what it is to be Irish. John McGahern's country lanes in some ways hold secure the memory of a child happy in the presence of his mother, and they guarantee, as well, an enduring image of Ireland. His *Memoir* seems to move, finally, towards reconciliation and fulfilment by returning us to those lanes in Co. Leitrim. From the outset, though, those leafy lanes are 'a maze . . . a green tunnel pierced by vivid pin-points of light' (p. 2), and what they seem to signify in the end is only a momentary security, a momentary magic. What Irish memoir brings home to us with more than usual intensity is the urgent need to converse with the dead and the impossibility of ever doing so: 'If we could walk together through those summer lanes, with their banks of wild flowers that "cast a spell", we probably would not be able to speak' (p. 272).

Notes

1 John McGahern, *Memoir* (London: Faber, 2005), p. 3. All further references will be given as page numbers in the text.
2 Hugo Hamilton, *The Speckled People* (London: Fourth Estate, 2003), pp. 35–6. All further references will be given as page numbers in the text.
3 Blake Morrison, *Independent on Sunday*, 1 September 1996.
4 Edna Longley, *Fortnight*, November 1996.
5 Seamus Deane (ed.), *The Field Day Anthology of Irish Writing*, 3 vols (Cork: Field Day, 1991), vol. 3, pp. 383, 380.
6 Ibid., p. 5.
7 Ibid., pp. 383, 380.
8 Seamus Deane, *Reading in the Dark* (London: Jonathan Cape, 1996), p. 20. All further references will be given as page numbers in the text.
9 Seamus Deane, Review of Terry Eagleton, *Heathcliff and the Great Hunger*, *London Review of Books*, 19 October 1995.
10 The words are by Padraic Colum. See Stephen Regan (ed.), *Irish Writing: An Anthology of Irish Writing in English 1798–1939* (Oxford: Oxford University Press, 2004), p. 395.
11 Raymond Williams, *Resources of Hope* (London: Verso, 1989), p. 32.
12 Deane, *The Field Day Anthology of Irish Writing*, vol. 3, p. 383.
13 Ibid., p. 381.
14 Fredric Jameson, *Modernism and Imperialism* (Cork: Field Day, 1988), p. 18.
15 See Aidan Arrowsmith, 'Plastic Paddy: Negotiating Identity in Second-generation "Irish-English" Writing', *Irish Studies Review*, 8/1 (2000), pp. 35–43 and Liam Harte, ' "Somewhere beyond England and Ireland": Narratives of "Home" in Second-generation Irish Autobiography', *Irish Studies Review*, 11/3 (2003), pp. 293–305.
16 Harte, p. 297.
17 John Walsh, *The Falling Angels* (London: Harper, 1999), p. 29. All further references will be given as page numbers in the text.
18 Harte, pp. 303–4.

14

Secret gardens: unearthing the truth in Patrick O'Keeffe's *The Hill Road*

Vivian Valvano Lynch

The publication of Patrick O'Keeffe's 2005 collection of four novellas, *The Hill Road*, marked the arrival of a significant new voice in Irish fiction. Born in Ireland in 1963, O'Keeffe grew up on a dairy farm in Limerick near the Tipperary border. At the age of twenty-three he emigrated to the United States, but only became legally resident there in 1989, after winning his green card in a lottery. His stories clearly reflect his own diasporic status, since his characters are frequently haunted by the culture they cannot quite leave behind. While the recurring motifs of buried secrets in an occluded past, painful revelations or half-revelations and thwarted desires hardly rank as new in Irish literary tradition, O'Keeffe's distinctiveness lies in his chronicling of the economic, cultural and spiritual condition of rural Ireland in the decades preceding the 1990s boom.

Only one of the novellas, 'That's Our Name', was published prior to the publication of *The Hill Road*.[1] That all four eventually comprised one volume is fitting. Valuable as individual pieces of fiction, they gain substantial power and currency by adjoining one another. What unifies them are their settings in and around the fictional town of Kilroan, Tipperary,[2] and their unique treatments of time. O'Keeffe's narratives constantly intercut between time present – various decades in the latter half of the twentieth century – and times past. Secrets of the most heartrending, terrible and sometimes gruesome kinds are repeatedly unearthed in these novellas, yet significantly many disclosures turn out on closer inspection to be partial and incomplete. As a result, his narrators, like his readers, are left at once feeling knowledgeable, yet in some strange way bereft.

By providing a detailed, analytical reading of two of the novellas, 'The Hill Road' and 'The Postman's Cottage', this chapter will seek to demonstrate O'Keeffe's concerns and status as an emergent artist. In the title novella, truths gradually emerge about a famous local character, Albert Cagney, who had served as a soldier during the Great War. While it is tempting to read this damaged casualty as emblematic of *many* generations of the lost and hurt, his presence in O'Keeffe's fiction is a sign of what has been only a very recent public recognition in Ireland of the contribution Irish soldiers made during World War I.[3] Through the attention it pays to Cagney's fate, O'Keeffe's novella, like Sebastian Barry's novel, *A Long, Long Way*, participates in an important, more inclusive interpretation of Irish history.

The veteran's story is conveyed by O'Keeffe in non-linear fashion, pieced together by a first-person narrator–investigator, Jack Carmody. The fact that the boy's movement towards maturity is strategically advanced through his relationship with two female characters, his mother and his aunt, is of considerable significance, reflecting as it does Ireland's changing gender politics since the mid-1980s. Jack is himself meticulous in his designation of dates, first recalling family life in Kilroan in the late 1960s, before the arrival even of black-and-white television, when evenings revolved around simple meals, the recitation of the Rosary, listening to the wireless and endless tales about Albert Cagney's return. Jack recalls the local, communal rituals, Sunday Mass and the gatherings at Powers' public house by the men of the neighborhood, and then – most importantly – the transformative effect of a summer spent with his maiden aunt on Conway's hill.

It is during that seminal visit that he learns of his aunt's intimacy with and loss of Albert. Boosted by drink, Mary counsels Jack – as his dying mother later will – to make the *right* choice, which is to leave home in order to achieve success. Mary's and his mother's views, of course, typify those held in rural Ireland in the 1940s, 1950s and 1960s, and lead directly to Jack's becoming the first family exile. Albert Cagney, by contrast, made a *wrong* choice, persuaded by John Redmond's[4] claims that fighting for the British Empire would be the best way of enabling Ireland to achieve her independence. In what will prove to be a recurring feature in *The Hill Road*, the initial impetus for departure comes from the women in the family, a phenomenon which suggests how much O'Keeffe has drawn from the work of John McGahern.[5]

It is through his aunt's whiskey-fuelled, yet apparently faultless, memory that the reader learns of what might now be termed Albert's post-traumatic stress disorder,[6] a condition brought on by his wartime experiences. Harried by nightmares, Albert could no longer function as he did before the war. After discovering that he has made a young girl pregnant, Mary rejects him, unable to accept his breaking of traditional religious and social codes. It is only on his last night at Conway's hill, however, that Jack learns the extent of the tragedy – that Albert had committed suicide. In order to ensure that he received a proper

Catholic burial, local men concocted a story about him being killed by the Black and Tans. A drunken neighbour subsequently reveals this to Mary, unaware that she already knew the truth. She makes Jack promise never to divulge a word of this at home.[7]

O'Keeffe then shifts the narrative forward once more, to 1983 and Jack's mother's deathbed. She startles him with an account of how another local man had pined for her, had tried to woo her away from Jack's father, and had lived to lament his failure. Within days, Jack's mother is dead, and we are left wondering whether her final memories were true or merely the fantasies of a drifting mind. Because of a jarring ellipsis, he, and we, will never know. Particularly vivid at the novella's close are the series of epiphanic moments that Jack experiences. A neo-sophisticate Dubliner now, Jack has come to look down on the old ways at his mother's wake:

> She was gone. Her blood was. And all this pageantry. To have to endure it. Just so that others can have a bit of a get-together. Celebrate the life of the dead you or they don't know a thing about. Their poor mother. Not long after their father. Oh, to be alone! To be alone and far from all of them! Back in my flat in Dublin and dancing on a Saturday night after work, pissed and holding a girl against a wall to the pounding music, and my mickey filled with warm blood. My posters of Bob Dylan and The Smiths above my single bed.[8]

Minutes later Jack attempts a farewell to his parents' world and muses that after death:

> There was only the clay; that's all we all are. I raised my hand and waved good-bye to the cows. I then said good-bye to the fields and the trees. This was Nora Carmody's world. She and Mike Carmody made it. Adam and Eve Carmody. The Easter Rising. The Civil War. The six counties. The Irish Republic. The Troubles. The small farmer. Put up the ditches and made the gaps and plowed the fields, milked the cows and had their children, listened to the priests and DeValera and those who came after him, praying like they were the chosen ones. (pp. 97–8)

However, closing the novella, Jack discovers that it is not so easy to extricate himself from his ancestral world:

> I saw myself wandering down a street in London and a street in New York, staring at things and the people going by. I wasn't thinking about Dan selling Conway's hill, or that my aunt's cottage had fallen to ruin, as she had predicted and, like Albert and Mr. Cagney's cottage, that it would become a mound of stones and weeds. I thought about my sisters, in an airplane over the Irish Sea, my brothers walking, alone, through a field behind our house, and I saw clearly the petals on the rhododendrons flickering like flames in the bright sunshine of a spring Sunday morning,

feeling safe then, with my mother's warm body beside me, as we made our way home, and I heard my aunt singing: How lucky I was that day I walked through the evergreen trees, to have heard her voice; the single pink rosebush growing through the flagstones and clinging to the gable end of the whitewashed cottage; the land my father was born and raised on. (pp. 98–9)

The passage is a beautiful exile's lament, one reminiscent of the ending of Friel's *Dancing at Lughnasa*, in which the narrator's memories are fittingly accompanied by the fading of lights, inception of soft music, and gentle swaying of the characters onstage: '*As* Michael *begins to speak the stage is lit in a very soft, golden light so that the tableau we see is almost, but not quite, in a haze*'.[9] Michael's words are a prescient fore-runner to Jack's:

> In that memory atmosphere is more real than incident and everything is simultaneously actual and illusory. In that memory, too, the air is nostalgic with the music of the thirties. It drifts in from somewhere far away – a mirage of sound – a dream music that is both heard and imagined; that seems to be both itself and its own echo; a sound so alluring and so mesmeric that the afternoon is bewitched, maybe haunted, by it . . . When I remember it, I think of it as dancing. Dancing with eyes half closed because to open them would break the spell. (p. 71)

Jack Carmody's past, at home, and the more distant past, inherited from his family and his community, are what make him what he is. He finds that time's secrets, whether revealed or not, can neither be escaped nor occluded nor trivialised. What Anna McMullan has written of Friel's Michael could be equally applied to Jack: 'Authority is simultaneously exercised and disavowed, as the narrator himself struggles between analytical detachment and emotional response'.[10]

Perhaps the strongest piece in O'Keeffe's collection is 'The Postman's Cottage', a masterful conjoining of absorbing plot, brilliant characterisation and efficacious narrative strategy. Told by a third-person narrator, the novella focuses on the story of Kate Welsh Dillon, and begins with a finely wrought paragraph evoking a past time:

> Every third or fourth Friday, up till thirty or forty years ago, which is long before milking machines were even heard of, and places not even too far in from the road still didn't have electricity, there used to be autumn Fairs in the village of Pallas. After morning milking, the farmers who were selling would gather their heifers and bullocks and hunt them down the fields, along the byroads and the main road to the square in Pallas. For miles around you could hear the cattle lowing along the roads, although louder than them were the shouts of the farmers themselves swinging at and hitting the often restless beasts with their ash sticks. (p. 153)

The opening is pastoral, peaceful, warm, seductive even in its evocation. In time-present, the 1980s, the widowed Kate is travelling from Dublin, where she has been visiting her only son, back home to the house her husband, Tom Dillon had inherited, the Postman's Cottage. Serendipitously, on the train Kate meets Timmy, nephew of the late Eoin O'Rourke. It transpires that long ago Eoin had sold five bullocks for a grand price at a Pallas Fair and then disappeared; a suicide note was found with his belongings, but the sale money was gone. An investigation had been conducted, which concluded that he may have simply become drunken and fallen somewhere into a trench. Gallows humour is deployed in depicting the incompetence of the local police officer:

> He halted all searches at the end of the week and he announced in the barracks he now definitely believed young O'Rourke did run mad, screaming, splashing, and laughing, with the money in hand, into the bog, where the fierce waters of the Main Trench brought him to the Shannon and his body was dragged out like a coffin ship itself into the miserable and unforgiving Atlantic Ocean. (pp. 162–3)

On Kate's train journey, meanwhile, matters darken. The reader learns just how detached Christy, her son, had been in Dublin, and that he is about to set off for an engineering job in Qatar. Like Davie Conlon in *The Hill Road*'s second novella ('Her Black Mantilla'), Christy's travels will take him to an alternative space infused with 'eastern' mystique, but which equally represents a new form of transnational mobility that differs markedly from previous patterns of emigration.[11] Kate opens up to the young stranger, Timmy, gradually discovering his kinship to the lost Eoin. The O'Rourkes, Timmy's family, had told him that Uncle Eoin had left for America and never contacted them again. Kate does not disabuse him, but she does tell him that she and Eoin 'walked out once or twice' (p. 179).[12] The reader becomes privy, however, to deeper disclosures, that Kate and Eoin had loved each other, but that her family opposed the match. Suddenly introspective, Timmy announces, as they arrive in Kilroan, that 'Home never is what you thought it was in the first place' (p. 186), a maxim that applies to all of *The Hill Road* tales.[13]

Characteristically, O'Keeffe releases morsels of information, but withholds total, forthright disclosure. In yet another flashback, it is revealed how, when her son was a baby, Kate had found money under a floorboard. Obviously lying, her husband suggested that his own father must have hidden it long ago. On the night of Eoin's disappearance, all those years ago, Kate had waited, as arranged, for her sometime beau, Tom. When he arrived, she sees that his clothes and boots are drenched and muddy, and his bicycle broken:

He then began to cry. He tottered before her, pulled her to him, and kissed her fervently on the face and mouth, his two mucky hands clutching her head and soiling her scarf. She finally got his hand off her head and persuaded him to sit on the graveyard wall. . . . She rubbed his hands in hers, in an attempt to warm him, but he squeezed her hands tightly and cried loudly, I love you Katie. You're mine, Katie, and no one else's, now and forever, you'll never need no-one else. (pp. 196–7)

Kate envisions a terrifying picture of Eoin's murder and its concealment: 'A young man, a good-natured boy, who must have cried and cried not to die like that in the dark, without his mother, calling against that beaten, cruel, and bloody land, and not a soul there to help him. Christ Jesus. Christ Jesus' (p. 197).[14] Once more, O'Keeffe exposes a hidden crime, and, by means of great observational and analytical skill, carries us deeply into the consciousness of the tale's central character, Kate. In the words of Ada Calhoun, 'O'Keeffe conveys the pain that comes from standing over the corpse of a loved one, as well as the greater suffering that comes when there's no body over which to stand'.[15]

What characterises the novellas in *The Hill Road* is their emphasis on the masking of history, and on moments of submerged violence. *The Hill Road* exemplifies Eve Patten's contentions about contemporary Irish fiction:

> For the most part, it remained formally conservative: beyond a prevalent social realism, its chief stylistic hallmark was a neo-Gothic idiom which signaled a haunted or traumatized Irish society and deep-seated disturbances in the national psyche.[16]

Gerry Smyth's comment that 'Pastoralism failed to acknowledge both the complexity and the banality of Irish rural life' is certainly one which contemporary writers like O'Keeffe disprove.[17] In O'Keeffe's novellas, rural Ireland's apparent day-to-day banality belies intense actual complexity. Time's passage heals, at best, very little, and memory refuses to remain submerged. Perhaps like his characters and fellow exiles, O'Keeffe recognises how tied he remains to his place of origin, remembering that 'I cannot deny my past to which my self is wed / The woven figure cannot undo its thread'.[18]

Notes

1   'That's Our Name', in slightly different form, was published as 'Looby's Hill' in *DoubleTake* (winter 2001).
2   A real Kilroan parish exists in Cork, and the real Kilroan Bay is off the Scottish coast.

3 Indeed, the Island of Ireland Peace Park at Messines in Flanders only joined the gallery of other European Great War monuments in November 1998. In a characteristically pointed yet eloquent speech, President Mary McAleese paid tribute to the soldiers while reminding her listeners of how the battles of World War I were concurrent with the struggle for independence in Ireland. Standing alongside the current British monarch, Queen Elizabeth II, at the park's unveiling, President McAleese said: 'Today's ceremony at the Peace Park was not just another journey down a well-travelled path. For much of the past eighty years, the very idea of such a ceremony would probably have been unthinkable. Those whom we commemorate here were doubly tragic. They fell victim to a war against oppression in Europe. Their memory too fell victim to a war for independence at home in Ireland. . . . The Peace Park does not invite us to forget the past but to remember it differently. We are asked to look with sorrow and respect on the memory of our countrymen who died with such courage far from the common homeland they loved deeply. . . . These too are Ireland's children as those who fought for her independence are her children, and those who fought against each other in our country's civil war – and of course the dead of recent decades': Mary McAleese, 'Speeches: Messines Peace Tower, Belgium', Irish President's Website, 11 November 1998, www.president.ie (accessed 2 August 2007). (Note: The acknowledgments to Sebastian Barry's *A Long Long Way* cites ten titles on Ireland and the Great War, eight of them published since 1995.)

4 John Redmond (1856–1918) was the Nationalist Party Leader at the outbreak of World War I.

5 There are strong resemblances between Aunt Mary and Mrs Carmody and McGahern's decisive feminine characters in *Amongst Women*. In that novel, Rose, Moran's second wife, at first seems to have a secondary role, but ultimately emerges as a person of integral importance and influence. For a discussion of her character, see Robert F. Garratt, 'John McGahern's *Amongst Women*: Representation, Memory, and Trauma', *Irish University Review* 35/1 (spring/summer 2005): pp. 121–35.

6 For an account of this condition, see the Royal College of Psychiatrists' Public Education website: www.rcpsych.ac.uk/mentalhealthinformation/ mentalhealthproblems/posttraumaticstressdisorder/posttraumaticstressdis order.aspx (accessed 13 December 2006).

7 Buried secrets abound in Irish literature and, for that matter, Irish history. In his parleying with secret pasts, O'Keeffe is undoubtedly indebted to Seamus Deane's *Reading in the Dark* (1996; New York: Knopf, 1997), discussed earlier in this volume by Stephen Regan. See also below, endnote 14.

8 Patrick O'Keeffe, *The Hill Road* (2005; New York: Penguin, 2006), p. 96. Subsequent references will be cited parenthetically in the text.

9 Brian Friel, *Dancing at Lughnasa* (London: Faber, 1998), p. 70. Subsequent references will be cited parenthetically in the text.

10 Anna McMullan, '"In touch with some otherness": Gender, Authority and the Body in *Dancing at Lughnasa*', *Irish University Review*, 29/1 (spring/summer 1999), p. 99.

11 In his depiction of the eastbound Christy, soon to be representative of a new Irish diaspora, O'Keeffe deftly alludes to Joyce's stifled, eastern-yearning boy narrator in 'Araby'.

12 In Kate one senses the shadow of Gretta Conroy remembering Michael Furey in Joyce's 'The Dead'.

13 I am compelled to remember here the words of the American poet Robert Frost in 'The Death of the Hired Man', ll. 122–3: 'Home is the place where, when you have to go there, / They have to take you in'. Many of O'Keeffe's characters would be forced to disagree.

14 It is illuminating to compare O'Keeffe's novella at this point with Deane's *Reading in the Dark*. When Deane's narrator's mother realises that her father, an IRA leader, had her husband's brother Eddie killed as a traitor back in 1922, she cries, 'Eddie, dear God Eddie. This will kill us all' (p. 123). *Reading*'s hermeneutics lie far deeper: Eddie was innocent; the mother's old boyfriend, McIlhenny, was the actual traitor who set Eddie up for execution. McIlhenny's treachery was eventually discovered, and his life was obviously not worth a farthing. But the mother, although jilted by McIlhenny in favour of her own sister, tipped him off, and he escaped to Chicago. Ironically, akin to Timmy O'Rourke's belief that his Uncle Eoin is alive in America, fabrications of sightings of Eddie in Chicago and in Melbourne passed around Derry through the years, but the reader is certain of his death. The tangled web of betrayals, deceits, and secrets makes for a tortuous relationship between Deane's inquisitive narrator and his agonised mother. O'Keeffe has flipped the situation somewhat: a formidable woman again holds secrets that haunt her and discovers new ones, but Kate's son is gone at the time of her discovery, and he was never too interested in his mother in the first place. For further discussion of *Reading*'s concealments and revelations, see Vivian Valvano Lynch, 'Seamus Deane's *Reading in the Dark* yields "a door into the light"', *Working Papers in Irish Studies*, 3 (2000), pp. 16–22.

15 Ada Calhoun, 'Fiction Chronicle', *New York Times*, 14 August 2005.

16 Eve Patten, 'Contemporary Irish Fiction', in John Wilson Foster (ed.), *The Cambridge Companion to the Irish Novel* (Cambridge: Cambridge University Press, 2006), p. 259.

17 Gerry Smyth, *The Novel and the Nation: Studies in the New Irish Fiction* (London: Pluto Press, 1997), p. 60.

18 Louis MacNeice, 'Valediction', *Collected Poems*, ed. E.R. Dodds (1966; London: Faber, 1979), p. 53.

15

'What's it like being Irish?' The return of the repressed in Roddy Doyle's *Paula Spencer*

Jennifer M. Jeffers

'The Irish are the niggers of Europe, lads.' (Roddy Doyle, *The Commitments*)[1]

In a notorious incident in January 2002, a young Chinese man, Zhao Liulao, was beaten to death in a late-night fight in a Dublin suburb, after being taunted by racist youths. This death occurred against a background of reports of increased attacks on immigrants in the north inner-city area of Dublin, in an area designated in media accounts as 'Little Africa'. (Luke Gibbons, *Beyond the Pale*).[2]

In a recent, brief essay, 'Green Yodel No. 1', Roddy Doyle stresses that Irish identity is in an exciting period of transformation because of the influx of immigrants from such places as Nigeria, Latvia and China. Instead of a reactive response to preserve Irish homogeneity, Doyle welcomes the chance for the Irish 'to invent new stories, new art, new voices, new music. . . . New love stories, family sagas, new jealousies, rivalries, new beginning and new endings. We live in exciting times, if we want them.'[3] Doyle himself has begun to celebrate these new beginnings in what he calls 'episodic short stories' which feature racially heterogeneous immigrants.[4] For example, in 'I Understand' we are exposed to the life of an undocumented male African immigrant who works two unskilled labour jobs and is threatened by local thugs to join their drug-running outfit. Eventually he finds friendship with co-workers and potentially romantic love with a local Irish girl.[5] In 'Green Yodel No. 1' Doyle provides the first page or so of 'I Understand', and then claims: 'What's the narrator's name? I don't know, but I have a short-list of good ones. What happens in the story? I really don't know. . . . Will it end happily? Yes, it will. It's in my hands, and I'll make this one end happily'.[6] With this story and others in the recently released *The Deportees* (2007), Doyle has established himself as an advocate of diversity who creates narratives in order to combat racism in Ireland.

Although Doyle's 2006 novel *Paula Spencer* overtly revolves around the 48-year-old recovering alcoholic Paula Spencer, Doyle packs as many details concerning the new multicultural and multiracial Ireland as he possibly and plausibly can. Doyle first created Paula Spencer in his 1996 novel *The Woman Who Walked Into Doors*. In the ten years between the Paula Spencer narratives not only has Paula's life changed, but all of Dublin has undergone a transformation. As Doyle's indigenous-working-class-white-Irish-Catholic-Dubliner spokesperson, Paula bears witness throughout the novel to the societal, cultural and economic changes in Dublin. In fact, Paula specifically references the intense period of immigration following Ireland's economic prosperity of the 1990s. The Irish Census of April 2006 shows that in the four years since the previous survey, the Irish population grew by 322,645.[7] This statistic becomes more meaningful when we consider that non-Irish work permits went from fewer than 6,000 in 1999 to about 50,000 in 2003.[8]

In the conclusion to my critique of Irish novels published between 1989 and 1999, I noted that the rapid economic growth of the 1990s and the wave of consumerist global culture that would follow in its wake would present a new set of issues for Ireland:

> While the so-called Celtic Tiger roars on, another more subtle change is taking place in the Republic and will be an issue of contention in the coming decades. With the wealth of successful economic globalization comes the attraction to Ireland by refugees and asylum-seekers, as well as a migrant work force. An increase in diversity, a multiracial, multiethnic, and multicultural population looms in Ireland's future. The conservative reaction in England to a multiracial and multiethnic society has been extreme. Race riots and politicians' proclamations that England is becoming a 'mongrel race' are just two examples of the unpleasant side effects of a global economy.[9]

In *Racism and Social Change in the Republic of Ireland* Bryan Fanning confirms some of my predictions when he reports that the British 'new racism' is now emerging as an extreme conservative reaction in Ireland, where it similarly attracts a segment of the white, economically deprived population. According to Fanning, the conservative reactionary questions the refugee's right to stay in Ireland, 'why did you come here? When are you going back, when will you leave Ireland?'[10] This position leads Fanning to comment: 'in common with British "new racism", the fears of the dominant community of being swamped, usurped or exploited by black and ethnic minority minorities have been portrayed as reasonable'.[11]

In my above account I was anticipating the future that Ireland would face with multiculturalism; however, I failed to note that Ireland already had logged several centuries of Irish-Ireland racism toward Jews and Travellers, in particular; racism that had nothing to do with colonisation or Britain. For example, the founder of Sinn Féin and well-known anti-Semite Arthur Griffin, who also participated in the Limerick Pogrom of 1904–06, was the author of numerous anti-Semitic essays, including this editorial printed in the *United Irishman* in 1904:

> No thoughtful Irishman or woman can view without apprehension the continuous influx of Jews into Ireland . . . strange people, alien to us in thought, alien to us in sympathy, from Russia, Poland, Germany and Austria – people who come to live amongst us, but who never become of us . . . Our sympathy – insular as it may be – goes wholly to our country-man the artisan whom the Jew deprives of the means of livelihood, to our countryman the trader whom he ruins in business by unscrupulous methods, to our countryman the farmer whom he draws into his usurer's toils and drives to the workhouse across the water.[12]

These early documents defeat claims that the Irish cannot possibly be racist or xenophobic because they have very little or no experience of racially or culturally different people. Yet, even in the 1990s the idea of the Irish as racialist 'innocent' persisted:

> On the one hand, Irish insularity was seen as responsible for discrimina-tion because it generates fear of foreigners, and of cultural and physical differences. On the other hand, Irish insularity and homogeneity means that Irish people lack knowledge about other societies and cultures, and have no experience of living with difference. So from this perspective, Irish people do not intend to discriminate, they simply do not know any better, yet.[13]

This depiction of 'Irish insularity', published in the 1998 *The Irish Are Friendly but . . . : A Report on Racism and International Students and Racism in Ireland*, overlooks, due to its focus, other areas of Irish racism, most obviously the discrimination against Travellers in terms of cultural and racial Otherness that predates the famine.[14]

In the twenty-first century, according to Doyle, the question 'What's it like being Irish?' no longer comes from 'a Guinness commercial or a *Bord Failte* promotion', but is essentially 'unanswerable'.[15] As he is already comfortable with the role of intercessor for the subjugated with *The Woman Who Walked Into Doors*, it is not surprising that Doyle attempts to rewrite the stories of 'racist youth' and discredit those who promote Irish homogeneity. Doyle exposes the fiction that the patriarchal-white-Catholic-Irish-male is the definition of authentic Irishness. No one would have thought of Paula Spencer as 'typically Irish' in the late 1990s, but Doyle brought domestic violence and chronic alcoholism to national attention with *The Woman Who Walked Into Doors*. In the novel Doyle challenges masculine-dominant Irish narratives, and the entire legal and cultural system which by 'turning a blind eye' in effect sanctions domestic violence and masculine heterosexual dominance. In the first novel, Paula corresponds at almost every level with the identifying characteristics of the battered wife syndrome; Charlo Spencer, her husband, too, follows closely the 'textbook' case of the abuser or batterer:

> a history of temper tantrums, insecurity, need to keep the environment stable, easily threatened by minor upsets, jealousy, possessiveness, and the ability to be charming, manipulative and seductive to get what he wants, and hostile, nasty and mean when he doesn't succeed. If alcohol abuse problems are included, the pattern becomes classic.[16]

Charlo's abuse of Paula extends across the full spectrum of punishment and domestic violence. According to Pat O'Connor in *Emerging Voices: Women in Contemporary Irish Society*, late 1990s Irish heterosexual society still harbours the idea that women should serve the emotional, material and sexual needs of men. Her study indicates that in Irish society, in comparison to other EU countries, women still perform 'the bulk of household labour, including the care of children – despite the fact that they are increasingly participating in paid employment, largely on a full-time basis'.[17] This cultural and societal setting provides sufficient evidence to suggest that women are still not equal to men, and that masculinity in the Irish context preserves its dominance. Power is not individualistic but tied to an elaborate system of privileges. O'Connor theorises that images of masculinity ultimately legitimise physical dominance and violence:

> The idea that the ability and willingness to use force is a 'normal' element in the definition of masculinity and hence an element in the social and cultural construction of heterosexuality offers a potentially fertile source of legitimisation for male violence whether in physical violence towards a spouse or indeed towards any woman, and also in pornography, rape, and sexual abuse. Evanson (1982) has suggested that the causes of marital violence were 'the deeper assumptions of husbands that they have a right to dominate and the powerlessness of wives which make them legitimate outlets for aggression which cannot be vented on others'. Typically, however, such issues and those relating to men's greater cultural value, and the legitimacy of their dominance, are ignored.[18]

There is also 'implicit colluding' on the part of the government officials with those who commit domestic violence; only one in five women, in a recent study on domestic violence, actually report violence to the Gardai. The women in the study stated that the men who committed the violence

were rarely arrested.[19] In fact, O'Connor reports that based on the level
of funding available to combat domestic violence, to train social workers
to recognise signs of abuse and help the abused, Ireland clearly perceives this violence as a 'private problem'. The private versus public
distinction is paramount. If domestic violence was rare and an infre-
quent occurrence, then it would be such an anomaly that it would be
taken seriously and the offender punished. But if domestic violence is
widespread and frequent, then it is accepted (by the police, other males
in the family, the neighbourhood) because it is so *common* and because
the culture and legal system sanction it. Therefore, the battered woman
syndrome exists because, at some level, society and culture support this
kind of manifestation of power.

In *The Woman Who Walked Into Doors* Doyle presents the reader
with the inside version of this 'private problem' indicating, at least implicitly, that this problem is *not* private. Instead, this 'private problem'
ravages the family and from there unfurls exponentially outward into
society. In an interview Doyle states that the novel comes out of his
experience of screenwriting for a BBC television series, *Family* (1994),
in which the last episode is from the wife's point of view. Pleased with
the episode, Doyle believed that there was an entire novel to be written
from this woman's perspective. As it turns out, Doyle was writing the
book when the episode was broadcast:

> When I started the novel, the episode was broadcast in Ireland, and then
> there were all sorts of denunciations. There's virtually nothing in the novel
> that is in the television series, which is very gritty, very hard hitting. And
> the denunciations came from all sorts of politicians, from priests, my old
> teachers union, virtually everybody queued up to condemn it in some way.[20]

When Doyle is asked, 'What was their problem with it?', he replies that
he became the subject of religious sermons and a target for condemnation by those claiming he was, 'undermining the sanctity of marriage.
Which of course was exactly what I was doing'.[21] Ironically, in *The
Woman Who Walked Into Doors* both Paula and her sister Carmel turn
to marriage as a way to flee their abusive father.

In the first novel about the Spencers, the motivating force of Paula's
narrative is her need to grasp the relevance and impact of Mrs
Fleming's murder. The reader has had a few instances of Charlo's treatment of Paula, but not a full account. Near the end of the novel Paula
acknowledges the reader's perverse desire to know *exactly* what Charlo
did to her, 'Ask me. Ask me. Ask me'.[22] With a 'Here goes', Paula provides the reader with a ghastly list of injuries she suffered at the hands
of Charlo:

Broken nose. Loose teeth. Cracked ribs. Broken finger. Black eyes. I don't know how many. A ruptured eardrum. Burns. Cigarettes on my arms and legs. He dragged me around the house by my clothes and by my hair. He kicked me up and he kicked me down the stairs. Bruised me, scalded me, threatened me. For seventeen years. Hit me, thumped me, raped me. He hurt me and hurt me and hurt me. He killed parts of me. He killed most of me. He killed all of me. Bruised, burnt and broken. He never gave up. Months went by and nothing happened, but it was always there – the promise of it. (pp. 175–6)

Charlo is a characteristic wife-batterer who mixes physical abuse with emotional and psychological terror for the victim. Yet, whereas most batterers feel that they have a defence for their behaviour ('I lost control') or a justification ('she provoked me'), Paula presents Charlo as never apologetic, and always in control. Many times after Charlo has hit or beaten Paula, he baits her and asks her how she got that black eye:

– Where'd you get that?
– What?
– The eye.
It was a test. I was thumping inside. He was playing with me.
There was only one right answer.
– I walked into the door.
– Is that right?
– Yeah.
– Looks sore.
– It's not too bad.
– Good.

He was messing with me, playing. Like a cat with an injured bird. With his black armband, the fucker. Keeping me on my toes, keeping me in my place. Pretending he didn't remember. Pretending he'd never seen black and red around and in that eye before. Pretending he cared. (p. 181)

In other parts of her narrative, Paula blames herself, which is typical of a woman in abusive situation, and yet she now sees the absurdity of her own culpability: 'He hit me, he hit his children, he hit other people, he killed a woman – I kept blaming myself. For provoking him' (p. 170). One aspect that is certain, Charlo's behaviour is sanctioned by the authorities and by Irish culture. When visiting a doctor about her injuries, Paula is asked if she had been drinking: 'Have you had a drink Mrs Spencer?' And friends and family members ask her what she said to him to provoke him: 'Did you say something to him Paula?' and ultimately: 'Why did you marry him then, Paula?' (p. 171). Judged culpable by society, Paula wins our sympathy as Doyle shows clearly that she is not only a victim of Charlo, but of Irish patriarchal society. At the end of the novel, instead of a major catharsis, Paula reconciles what she is able to at this point in her life; perhaps this is more faithful to a 'realistic' narrative of a woman who has been mentally, physically and psychologically abused for nearly twenty years.

With *Paula Spencer* Doyle moves from speaking for all women who must endure men like the insidious Charlo and the Irish cultural and legal system that sanctions domestic violence, to portraying one who advocates tolerance and acceptance of racial diversity in the new Ireland. While Doyle does not disappoint the reader in regard to Paula's amiability and our empathy towards her ongoing struggles to overcome her past, *Paula Spencer* lacks the urgency of Paula's psychological crisis following Charlo's death at the hands of the Garda in the first novel. The new novel opens with Paula returning home from work and the acknowledgement that she has been sober 'four months and five days'.[23] As she walks home she thinks to herself, 'This place has changed' (p. 2). This thought stands independently on the page and it will be in course of the next several pages that we understand what it means: new money and new people replacing the old. Paula muses to herself, 'it's changing, the whole place. One of the old shops is a café now, opened a few weeks ago. An Italian place, real Italians in it. Not chipper Italians. Selling bread and coffee and oil and other expensive stuff Paula would love to load up on' (p. 12). These references begin the novel's constant charting of new Dublin. The new Dublin is characterised by immaculate and expensive shops in place of the grungy and provincially Irish shops, along with the foreigners who work in the new and old shops, and the foreigners with whom Paula works. In many respects, just as Joyce charted the day in the life of turn-of-the-century Leopold Bloom, Doyle maps a year in the life of twenty-first-century Paula Spencer.

In fact, one might quarrel with Doyle concerning the intent of his novel. Does he want to tell the story of a victimised recovering alcoholic, whose every reflection concerning her children invariably deals with her guilt and sorrow because she neglected them when she was drinking, or does he wish to use her as a vehicle to record and to interact with multiracial Dublin – a mouthpiece for 'New stories, family sagas, new jealousies, rivalries, new beginnings and new endings'?[24] For the first half of the text, especially, Doyle wants to be an advocate for the immigrants in Dublin. It seems that every few pages the novel records Paula's amazement as she strides through her old neighbourhood or takes the DART to work. In some ways, it as though she has just awakened and discovered that Dublin now has 50,000 immigrants. In the novel there are two particularly insightful instances of the newly awakened Paula that show her interacting with multicultural Dublin. In each example Paula empathises with the immigrants. In the second example she has to identify and compare her life to theirs, which leads Paula to suddenly see herself as no longer *Irish*.

With the first example we encounter the new Dublin with Paula at the shops. In the midst of a passage where Paula is thinking about her children and her sisters, the reader is treated to the new grocery shopping experience that Dublin now affords. Still patronising the old shops and noting that this is the unfashionable, old Dublin, Paula remarks that 'The women on the check-out are nearly all foreign. That's the only real change' (p. 24). Mixed in with thoughts about her sisters and kids, the narrative strays into 'contemporary African politics':

> There's an African woman on the check-out. Nigerian, or one of the others. What other African countries do they come from? Paula doesn't know. There are wars everywhere; you could never keep up. It's the first time she's seen a black woman working here. Good luck to her. She's lovely. Her hair up in a scarf. Her long cheekbones. Lovely straight back. (pp. 25–6)

This is not Joyce's hegemonic white Ireland, and Doyle wants to make sure that you understand that multiracial people are everywhere – in the most common of daily places – on the DART or in the Spar. In this way, Paula's musing upon the African woman is natural enough: taking note on the woman at the market, the meat shop or pharmacy is an everyday occurrence. When Paula's thoughts turn to Charlo, the text further accentuates the positive in the immigrant: 'What would Charlo think? she wonders. What would he have said about it? Charlo was her husband. He died before all these people started arriving. Before the Celtic Tiger thing' (p. 26). On the one hand, Doyle is tracing out the contours of identity in contemporary Ireland with Paula attempting to think through a would-be reaction by Charlo to the immigrants in new Ireland. On the other hand, there is something a little uneven about this mental dialogue. Doyle wishes to give the reader a tour of multiracial Ireland and encourage us to be sympathetic to it, yet at the same time he has to position our female protagonist in a practical situation or all is lost in terms of realism. Therefore in two pages of discourse, Doyle has Paula discuss the prevalence of multicultural workers, Charlo from the last novel, his death, 'the Celtic Tiger thing', and to establish Paula's tone of acceptance, admiration even for these 'foreigners':

She's beautiful. Charlo would have called Paula a lezzer for thinking that, for saying it. It's funny, she doesn't know if he was a racist or not. She hasn't a clue. She'd know these days quickly enough. They're all over the place, the foreigners, the black people. Is that racist? They're all over the place. She doesn't know. She means no harm. It's just a phrase. And she doesn't mind it. She likes to look at all the foreigners. Some of them scare her a bit. The Romanians, the women. They're a bit frightening – wild, like they've come straight out of a war. But most of them are grand. (p. 26)

Readers of *The Woman Who Walked Into Doors* know that Charlo would be in the group with the 'racist youths', maybe leader of the gang, who beats to death foreigners in places like 'Little Africa'. Therefore, evoking Charlo, especially with his 'lezzer' label for Paula, further unites the disenfranchised Paula and the immigrants. From a patriarchal heterosexual perspective, is there anything more threatening to the masculinity of a man like Charlo than being completely sexually excluded and unwanted by women? Doyle's strategy to unite the victimised and those of minority status subtly evokes empathy from the reader.

Although Paula is compassionate toward most of the non-Irish in the novel, she is keenly aware of the fact she is working alongside and at the same level as the immigrants. These 'foreigners' are doing the work that the Irish no longer have to do: cleaning houses and offices, washing dishes, and all forms of manual labour. The 'real' Irish, like Paula's sister Carmel, are buying apartments in Bulgaria in anticipation of its joining the EU: 'When Bulgaria joins the EU the value of those apartments will go through the fuckin' roof' (p. 29). On the bus, en route to the pertinently named 'Marley Park' where Paula and several other women will clean up the grounds after a concert, Paula reflects on her past and the wasted years. Intensely aware that she is the only white woman on the bus, Paula reflects:

She's a failure. She shouldn't be in this van. She should be outside, looking at it going by. On her way home from work. Already home – on her way out again. Irishwomen don't do this work. Only Paula. . . . Ten years ago there wouldn't have been one black woman on this bus – less than ten years. It would have been Paula and women like Paula. Same age, from the same area, same kids. Where are those women now? Carmel used to do cleaning and now she's buying flats in Bulgaria. (p. 56)

Paula answers our question 'What does it mean to be Irish?' by stating that she is not Irish: she is a subordinate just like the Africans, Romanians and Latvians in Ireland. The immigrants and Paula are tethered to bottom of the economic class system in Ireland. Abused for twenty years of her married life and a faithful alcoholic for another ten, Paula missed the 'Celtic Tiger' wave; most other 'Irishwomen' caught the wave, but Paula didn't because she was drowning in vodka at the time. Similar to many of the immigrants who came to Dublin to escape persecution, poverty and war, Paula, too, was a victim, first of Charlo, and then, second, of alcoholism and poverty.

In this way, to be Irish is redefined to include only those who prospered during the boom years of the 1990s. In 'Speed Limits: Ireland, Globalisation and the War against Time', Michael Cronin defines the problem in terms of driving metaphors: those who prospered and entered fast-moving consumerist society and those who failed, like Paula, to do well in the 1990s and who are now in the 'slow lane'. The slow lane is not only failure to prosper, but failure to participate in postmodern global culture; it is a failure to live in your own time:

> Stasis is stigma. Those who are grounded by poverty, disability or prejudice are keenly aware of an isolation that is both social and geographical. They are Irish locals who can watch the Irish globals riverdancing from Paris to Paraguay but who find themselves trapped in the slow lane of neglect and indifference.[25]

However, it is uncanny in that the 'more things change, the more they stay the same'. If we recall that Doyle's 1987 novel *The Commitments* featured impoverished characters from Northern Dublin who sought refuge in aligning themselves with black Americans, then twenty years after *The Commitments* the alliance of lower-class Dubliners with racial minorities could be seen to come full-circle in *Paula Spencer*. The metaphor that Paula uses, that she should be on the outside looking into the bus of multiracial cleaners because she is white Irish, should, in fact, be turned inside-out. Paula is the one outside looking in at post-Celtic-Tiger Ireland: the Italian shop with 'real' Italians who sell costly coffee and olive oil, her successful daughter Nicola's expensive presents, her sister Denise's very-middle-class affair with a dad at her son's school and Carmel's property investments.

In what I am calling the return of the repressed, Doyle's preoccupation with the marginalised in Dublin occurs at both the psychological and the socio-historical levels. First, Doyle is unable to resist repeating the stories of the disenfranchised – from *The Commitments* to *Paula Spencer* to *The Deportees*, which again features Jimmy Rabbitte from *The Commitments*. On one level, Doyle cannot stop 'racist youth' no matter how many stories he makes end 'happily'. This repetition compulsion, of course, parallels Freud's theorising in *Beyond the Pleasure Principle* when he ponders why his grandson stages the *fort/da* game:

'The child cannot possibly have felt his mother's departure as something agreeable or even indifferent. How then does his repetition of this
distressing experience as a game fit in with the pleasure principle?'[26]
The answer Freud formulates is that the child lacked control over his
mother's departures and returns so he enacts a simulation of 'gone' and
'there' in an attempt to master the situation:

> At the outset he was in a *passive* situation – he was overpowered by the
> experience; but, by repeating it, unpleasurable though it was, as a game,
> he took on an *active* part. These efforts might be put down to an instinct
> for mastery that was acting independently of whether the memory was
> in itself pleasurable or not. . . . We are therefore left in doubt as to whether
> the impulse to work over in the mind some overpowering experience so
> as to make oneself master of it can find expression as a primary event,
> and independently of the pleasure principle. For, in the case we have been
> discussing, the child may, after all, only have been able to repeat his unpleas-
> ant experience in play because the repetition carried along with it a yield
> of pleasure of another sort but none the less a direct one.[27]

According to Freud, what starts out as a game of mastery becomes a
game of punishment: 'Go to the fwont!' exclaims the angry boy when
he wishes to make something gone (*fort*).[28]

In order to take back control over the plight of the working class
and poor of Northern Dublin in his fiction, Doyle enacts scenes of
personal and social trauma and repulsion which are repeated from text
to text. While many might consider *The Commitments* only a comic
novel, there are objectionable experiences in it that Doyle repeats in
Paula Spencer. For example, early in *The Commitments* Jimmy's now-
famous pep talk to his band aligns the Barrytown working class and
poor with the racially Other and disenfranchised:

> – The Irish are the niggers of Europe, lads.
>
> They nearly gasped: it was so true.
>
> – An' Dubliners are the niggers of Ireland. The culchies have fuckin' every-
> thin'. An' the northside Dubliners are the niggers o' Dublin. – Say it loud,
> I'm black an' I'm proud.[29]

Late in *Paula Spencer*, Doyle stages a return of the repressed:

> If she stops working, she never worked. She's never been happy with it,
> but it's all there ever was. And all there is. If she doesn't do it, other
> people will. She knows, she sees them. It's why they're here. Go back to
> your own fuckin' country. That's not her; that's not Paula. There's
> plenty of work. (p. 248)

So, what happens when the Irish are no longer the 'niggers of Europe'
because of economic prosperity and the country's ability to reinvent

itself for the twenty-first century? They become the oppressors. Paula's moment of uncertainty shows that, lurking in the back of her mind, she does not want to be in the same group as the new 'niggers of Europe', the immigrant workers in Ireland.

With the novel *Paula Spencer* we are at a crossroads of Irish identity. In Doyle's universe, Paula and her immigrant cohorts are the truly Irish, 'the niggers of Europe', as a long-suffering, economically depressed people. Yet, in terms of the rest of Ireland and the idea of global Ireland, Paula and the immigrants are decidedly not Irish. Doyle is pushing against the wealthy, insular Ireland by repeatedly creating stories about the marginalised and the victimised. In new Ireland, those generally held to be the most un-Irish people in Dublin are always the characters Doyle defends as belonging to Dublin.

As Paula struggles to stay sober, work and keep the fragile relationships with her children intact, we are constantly reminded of her years after Charlo's death, during the prosperous years of the mid- to late 1990s. These reflections provide the Other of 'Irish' identity and lifestyle; not the lifestyle of wealthy Europe flocking to Dublin – such as Becks and Posh Spice's wedding in 1999 – but the lifestyle of ordinary Dubliners with problems who have not quite copped on to globalisation. One would think that the pain of being abused for twenty years and addicted to alcohol for nearly thirty years, and the devastating effects on her children that are endlessly recounted in *Paula Spencer*, would be enough hardship for Paula. But there is another level of suffering in the novel – that is, Paula's twenty-first-century realisation that she has been deserted by her country. As I have shown, Doyle's return of the repressed repeatedly records life from the perspective of the poor and marginalised in Dublin in order to challenge the complacent, homogeneous view of Irish identity. *Paula Spencer* confirms that, historically speaking, the repressed will always *return*, despite the Arthur Griffiths of Ireland, as assimilation of multicultural immigrants in Ireland in the twenty-first century is imminent. Or, at the very least, in Doyle's fictional world of multiracial, working-class Dublin in the era of new Ireland, the stories of the oppressed he will 'make end happily' in an effort to overcome, once and for all, the return of the repressed.

Notes

1 Roddy Doyle, *The Commitments* (New York: Penguin, 1995), p. 13.
2 Luke Gibbons, 'Beyond the Pale: Race, Ethnicity, and Irish Culture', in Andrew Higgins Wyndham (ed.), *Re-Imagining Ireland* (Charlottesville: University of Virginia Press, 2006), p. 51.

3 Roddy Doyle, 'Green Yodel No. 1', in Higgins (ed.), *Re-Imagining Ireland*, pp. 69–71.
4 Ibid., p. 70.
5 Roddy Doyle, 'I Understand', *McSweeney's*, 15 (2004), pp. 39–65.
6 Doyle, 'Green Yodel No. 1', p. 71.
7 The *New York Times*, 19 August 2007, p. 3.
8 www.migrationinformation.org: 'Ireland: A Crash Course in Immigration Policy', p. 1.
9 Jennifer M. Jeffers, *The Irish Novel at the End of the Twentieth Century: Gender, Bodies, and Power* (New York: Palgrave, 2002), p. 178.
10 B. Fanning, S. Loyal and C. Staunton, *Asylum Seekers and the Right to Work in Ireland* (Dublin: Irish Refugee Council, 2000), p. 21. Quoted in Bryan Fanning, *Racism and Social Change in the Republic of Ireland* (Manchester: Manchester University Press, 2002), p. 24.
11 Fanning, p. 24.
12 Arthur Griffith, *United Irishman* (13 January 1904). Fanning, 42.
13 From *The Irish Are Friendly but . . . : A Report on Racism and International Students and Racism in Ireland* (Dublin: Irish Council for International Students, 1998), p. 6.
14 Fanning, p. 48.
15 Doyle, 'Green Yodel', p. 70.
16 Lenore E. Walker, *The Battered Woman Syndrome* (New York: Springer Publishing Co., 1984), p. 203.
17 See Pat O'Connor, *Emerging Voices: Women in Contemporary Irish Society* (Dublin: Institute of Public Administration, 1998), pp. 69–70.
18 See O'Connor, pp. 70–1. See also E. Evanson, *Hidden Violence: A Study of Battered Women in Northern Ireland* (Belfast: Farset Press, 1982).
19 O'Connor, pp. 70–1.
20 See the Roddy Doyle *Salon* interview with Charles Taylor at www.salon.com/books/feature/1999/10/28/doyle/Index2, p. 3 (accessed on 28 August 2007).
21 Doyle, *Salon* interview, p. 3.
22 Roddy Doyle, *The Woman Who Walked Into Doors* (New York: Viking 1996), pp. 175–6. All subsequent references are to this edition and will appear in the text.
23 Roddy Doyle, *Paula Spencer* (New York: Viking, 2006), p. 1. All subsequent references are to this edition and will appear in the text.
24 Doyle, 'Green Yodel', p. 69.
25 Michael Cronin, 'Speed Limits: Ireland, Globalisation and the War against Time', in Peadar Kirby, Luke Gibbons and Michael Cronin (eds), *Reinventing Ireland: Culture, Society and the Global Economy* (London: Pluto, 2002), p. 62.
26 Sigmund Freud, *Beyond the Pleasure Principle*, ed. and trans. James Strachey (New York: W.W. Norton, 1990), p. 15. In this famous example, Freud's grandson throws a spool out of his cot and announces *fort* or 'gone'. As the child reels the spool in, he states *da* or 'there'. Thus,

according to Freud, the child is staging his mother's departure and return in order to gain mastery over the situation. The child goes from passivity, the inability to control the departure, to mastery, the ability to control the departure, with the game. Freud notes that *fort* is only bearable because of the promise of *da*.

27   Ibid., pp. 15–16.
28   Ibid., p. 15.
29   Doyle, *The Commitments*, p. 13.

16

Remembering to forget: Northern Irish fiction after the Troubles

Neal Alexander

To speak of post-Troubles fiction, or even fiction 'after' the Troubles, is perhaps as problematic as it is unavoidable. Nearly a decade since the Good Friday Agreement of 1998, the political accord for which it paved the way remains fraught and uncertain. And if it can be said with at least some certainty that the war is finally over, then it is equally certain that Northern Ireland's troubles are not. The latest edition of *Lost Lives* includes entries for 195 Troubles-related deaths in the period after the IRA ceasefire announced on 31 August 1994.[1] Moreover, the very real social and political gains that have followed on from the republican and loyalist ceasefires, the Agreement, and IRA decommissioning have to be set against the now regular disputes over Orange marches, continuing paramilitary activity – punishment beatings, feuds, black-marketeering, gangsterism – and the repeated suspensions of Northern Ireland's devolved Assembly. Responding to the latter events, the novelist Glenn Patterson observes that in the present political climate '[c]risis management has become indistinguishable from actual government'.[2] Patterson's misgivings, bordering on disillusionment, have been echoed by a number of critics and commentators upon the faltering 'peace process', who suggest that whilst the outward signs of conflict have diminished considerably its underlying causes remain largely unaddressed. For Richard Bourke these causes are to be traced to a fundamental problem of legitimacy affecting all modern democracies, whereby the principle of majority decision is conflated with that of popular sovereignty. As Bourke shows, it was on the basis of this confusion that after partition 'a form of democratic government was established as an instrument for maintaining Northern Ireland as an undemocratic state'.[3] And by retaining the principle of majority decision concerning allegiance (or not) to the Union with Great Britain, the Agreement is 'reverting to the problematic principle which provoked the original crisis in Northern Ireland'.[4] Similarly, Colin Graham has recently argued that the language and practice of the peace process is structured in such a way as to preclude engagement with the issues of identity and cultural difference that have always been at the basis of the conflict. Indeed, he goes on to warn of the dangers of 'constructing a political process which forgets rather than remembers, which detaches itself for survival, which regards identity, in its widest sense, as a danger rather than as the very substance of the matter', because without an acknowledgment of this sort Northern Irish society will remain mired in 'patterns of repression and recurrence'.[5]

These are dangers to which post-ceasefire and post-Agreement novels are often keenly attuned. Deirdre Madden's *One by One in the Darkness* (1996) is set shortly before the IRA ceasefire in the summer of 1994, although it is also haunted by the violence of the 1970s and specifically the murder of the Quinn sisters' father, Charlie, by loyalist paramilitaries. Towards the end of the novel, Cate Quinn muses on what she feels is the imminent possibility of peace and the accompanying necessity for some sort of memorial to the dead:

> She imagined a room, a perfectly square room. Three of its walls, unbroken by windows, would be covered by neat rows of names, over three thousand of them; and the fourth wall would be nothing but a window. The whole structure would be built where the horizon was low, the sky huge. It would be a place which afforded dignity to memory, where you could bring your anger, as well as your grief.[6]

Cate's imagined memorial combines the functions of remembrance and catharsis, providing a space for the working out of anger, pain and conflict rather than their repression or deferral. It is, however, a telling instance of the often-noted equivocality of post-ceasefire fiction[7] that Sally Quinn's response to her sister's imaginative optimism is to ask what makes her think the Troubles are going to end. 'I'll believe it's going to end,' Sally says, 'when it ends.'[8] Caution against false hope modulates into a rather more caustic form of cynicism in another post-ceasefire novel, Robert McLiam Wilson's *Eureka Street* (1996), where Jake Jackson's sullen meditations serve to undercut naïve post-ceasefire euphoria with the cold facts of low-intensity violence: 'A fortnight in and only five people had been shot murkily dead and thirty-eight people beaten half to death with baseball bats.'[9] Indeed, many of the characters in the novel view the IRA ceasefire chiefly in terms of its economic potential and set about opportunistically cashing in on Belfast's peace dividend. In this at least, Wilson's novel is prescient regarding subsequent developments, although *Eureka Street* also goes much further than *One by One in the Darkness* in looking forward exuberantly to the post-Troubles future. On the final page of the novel Wilson writes: 'It's a big world and there's room for all kinds of endings and any number of commencements.'[10] Indeed, on the basis of this apparent article of faith it may be possible to hazard a broad distinction between the respective orientations of post-ceasefire and post-Agreement fictional trends. For if post-ceasefire novels such as *One by One in the Darkness* and *Eureka Street* can be characterised as *proleptic*, anticipating Northern Ireland's possible futures with varying degrees of optimism and enthusiasm, then many post-Agreement novels are better described as *retrospective* because of their tendency towards recreating a particular moment in the past in an effort to illuminate the North's contemporary predicament.

While it should be regarded as neither hard nor fast, this distinction can be illustrated by contrasting Wilson's expectancy of multiple new beginnings with the more sombre note struck in the final line of Glenn Patterson's *The International* (1999): 'We're powerful people for remembering here, I hope that's one thing we don't forget.'[11] Patterson's novel is set in Belfast's International Hotel one Saturday in January 1967, and is narrated retrospectively by Danny Hamilton, an International barman working that day. By locating the events of the novel so specifically in space and time Patterson deliberately invokes a particular historical moment – the inaugural meeting of the Northern Ireland Civil Rights Association, which took place the following day in the hotel – only to leave it as an absence in the text. In doing so he allows the larger political and historical ramifications of his context to inform, but not obscure, the central concerns of the narrative, which are bound up with the ostensibly humdrum experiences of working, drinking and falling in love in Belfast in the late 1960s. Consequently, *The International* is much concerned with the themes of memory and forgetting, and Danny's recollections of pre-Troubles Belfast self-consciously register the distortions and uncertainties that are inherent in the act of remembering:

> I wish I could describe for you Belfast as it was then, before it was brought shaking, quaking and laying about it with batons and stones on to the world's small screens, but I'm afraid I was not in the habit of noticing it much myself. What reason was there to, after all?[12]

But if Patterson, in spite of the difficulties involved, is concerned to excavate and recover the forgotten or neglected history of the city before its was effectively consumed by its Troubles, then the novel also undertakes a deliberate act of remembrance through its focus upon the absent presence of Peter Ward, another International barman who was murdered by the UVF in June 1966. Indeed, it is Peter Ward's memory, rather than that of some spurious age of innocence in the city, that most importantly informs the novel's tone and procedures, its deft interweaving of fact and fiction. As the novel unfolds it becomes clear that Danny is Peter Ward's replacement, and his view of events from behind the bar is constantly but unobtrusively inflected by his predecessor's palpable absence. In the concluding pages of the novel, Danny's thoughts return to Peter Ward via the announcement on 13 October 1994 of a loyalist ceasefire. The statement of the Combined Loyalist Military Command is read to the press by Gusty Spence, one of three UVF men given life sentences for the murder of Peter Ward. Through the figures of Peter Ward and Gusty Spence – victim and killer respectively – Patterson spans the twenty-five years and more of the Troubles, connecting the events that were initially to foster violence with those that would ostensibly bring it to an end. However, the narrative thus constructed is not one of seamless continuity but of fracture and disjunction, and it is to the lapses and absences in the text of Northern Ireland's history that Patterson seeks to draw attention:

> Peter Ward was a good barman. He was earning eight pounds eight shillings at the time of his death, twenty-five shillings above the union rate.
>
> I can't tell you much else about him, except that those who knew him thought the world of him. He is, I realise, an absence in this story. I wish it were not so, but guns do that, create holes which no amount of words can fill.[13]

The injunction to remember with which *The International* concludes is then also an injunction not to forget, and in this sense Patterson's novel strives to fulfil what Paul Ricoeur calls 'the duty to remember', a duty 'to keep alive the memory of suffering over against the general tendency of history to celebrate the victors. . . . To memorise the victims of history – the sufferers, the humiliated, the forgotten – should be a task for all of us at the end of this century.'[14] Interestingly, though, Ricoeur speculates that there may also be a duty to forget, connecting this positive function of forgetting with the concept of amnesty and concluding that 'there can be an institution of *amnesty*, which does not mean *amnesia*'.[15] These speculations upon the non-symmetrical but abiding relationship between memory and forgetting are developed further by Slavoj Žižek in the course of his response to the 9/11 attacks in New York. The 'true choice apropos of historical traumas is not the one between remembering or forgetting them', argues Žižek, as those events we are unable or unwilling to remember haunt us all the more forcefully: 'We should therefore accept the paradox that, in order really to forget an event, we must first summon up the strength to remember it properly.'[16] In the aftermath of historical trauma, then, 'forgetting' is only an option if precisely those events and circumstances from the past that the society in question would rather repress or ignore are made available for conscious reflection. This dilemma speaks directly to Northern Ireland's contemporary situation and, as I have already suggested, the issues of memory, remembrance, and forgetting upon which it turns are central to many novels of the post-Agreement period. In this regard, it is worth noting that three recent novels by established writers are each set at a significant historical remove from the North's current interregnum. Bernard McLaverty's *The Anatomy School* (2001) is a semi-autobiographical novel of Northern Catholic adolescence and sexual awakening against the backdrop of late 1960s Belfast; Eoin McNamee's *The Blue Tango* (2001) reconstructs the circumstances surrounding the murder of Patricia Curran at Whiteabbey on 13 November 1952; and David Park's *The Big Snow* (2002) unfolds its loosely interwoven stories during the unprecedented snowfalls of 1963. All three novels recreate moments out of time from the decades prior to the Troubles but also each refer obliquely to a contemporary situation in which the 'past-ness' of the past is yet to be established. For example, MacLaverty's *The Anatomy School* employs the recurrent image of a man rowing a boat on the river of history, gesturing towards the disaster to come but also allegorising the position of the contemporary Northern novelist in retrospective mode: 'We are all like a man rowing a boat. We have our backs to the way we're going. We can't look ahead, can't see the future. All we can see is the past behind us.'[17] Park's *The Big Snow* and McNamee's *The Blue Tango* both draw self-consciously upon the conventions of crime fiction, tracing corruption and murder to the heart of the Unionist establishment, and so might each be read as veiled expressions of contemporary distrust concerning Northern Ireland's governance and political processes. But whereas Park's characters find their muffled, snow-transformed surroundings both sinister and enchanting, 'a temporary release from the predictable',[18] McNamee's fictional world is unrelentingly noir, its grim investigative rigour and gothic air of elaborate contrivance combining to give a sense of 'the voices of the past coming through, a subtle, evasive whispering.'[19]

This unsettling awareness of the past's insistence upon the present is also powerfully apparent in two further novels which deserve more detailed discussion, Eoin McNamee's *The Ultras* (2004) and Glenn Patterson's *That Which Was* (2004). Stylistically, Patterson and McNamee could hardly be more different writers. Patterson writes in unshowy, naturalistic and deceptively simple prose that is nonetheless finely attuned to the subtleties of social relationships and historical connections, whereas McNamee's metafictional narratives acquire 'textual density'[20] through an ironic tendency towards stylistic excess that not only destabilises its own claims to authority but also gestures to what lies beyond or between the words on the page. Despite these prominent differences, however, *That Which Was* and *The Ultras* are texts that each deal centrally with troubled memories – memories of the Troubles that give rise to troubles *with* memory at both an individual and a collective level. Set in the early twenty-first century, both novels focus upon the processes of reconstruction and recall in order to emphasise the uncertainties and confusions attendant upon any imperative to 'remember properly', often highlighting the seemingly irresistible impulse to mythologise what has happened. Both texts also draw self-consciously upon the conventions of the thriller, the dominant form in Troubles fiction, and their detective protagonists can be thought of as inverted mirror images of each other. In *That Which Was* Ken Avery, a Presbyterian minister, investigates the case of Larry, who believes he is responsible for the murder of three people in a city centre bar in 1976 and claims that his memories of the event have been surgically wiped by elements in the security forces. Avery's role as amateur sleuth is complicated by his other duties as minister, husband and father, and the events of the novel take place against a backdrop of violent loyalist feuds, the ongoing Bloody Sunday tribunal and prisoner releases that are themselves catalysts for uncomfortable returns of repressed memory and guilt. As one character observes: 'There are a lot of damaged people walking about this city.'[21] *The Ultras* centres upon the figure of Captain Robert Nairac, the Special Forces operative who disappeared near the border in 1977 and whose body has never been recovered. This corporeal void is the narrative ellipsis around which the novel is constructed and which fixates Blair Agnew, a disgraced ex-RUC officer navigating a 'world of whispered conspiracies, webs of deceit'[22] in an effort to come to terms with his own part in events he is struggling to understand. Agnew's 'unhealthy obsession with the past'[23] leads him to believe that the seemingly peripheral figure of Nairac, who appears to move at the edge of consciousness itself, has in fact been central both to the British 'dirty war' against the PIRA in the mid-1970s, and to the clandestine rivalries and antagonisms between the different intelligence agencies themselves.

As Mark Urban notes, the growing professionalism of the PIRA in the early to mid-1970s provoked a shift of British military strategy towards intelligence-gathering activities and low-intensity operations, and gave rise to several 'undercover' units whose operations were 'hidden beneath an extraordinary web of cover names and secrecy'.[24] This is the febrile world of subterfuge and infiltration that McNamee's

fictionalisation of real events seeks to explore, and *The Ultras* takes the
Four Square laundry and Gemini massage parlour operations as examples of a new, austerely modern logic of warfare: 'War as subtext.'[25]
But if, on the one hand, the novel elaborates a fairly familiar, though
complex, narrative of collusion, whereby Nairac works alongside loyalist paramilitaries and is implicated in the Miami Showband murders
of 1975, it is also concerned, on the other, to show Nairac operating
'in the spaces between organizations',[26] thereby leading the reader into
an ultimately ungraspable labyrinth of conspiracies and collusions, fac-
tions and double-deceits, that cumulatively intimates 'the knowledge of
clandestine governance, the dark polity'[27] lurking behind the façade of
democratic deliberation. In this regard, *The Ultras* can be read as an
example of what Fredric Jameson calls a 'conspiratorial text',[28] because
its self-conscious investment in 'conspiracy culture' can be understood
as 'an attempt to make sense, albeit in a distorted fashion, of the deeper
conflicts which reside not in the psyche but in society.'[29] Importantly,
however, it is not just military and government agencies that are shown
to be untrustworthy in *The Ultras*, but also language itself, for the
novel's metafictional commentary and borrowings from literary noir[30]
produce an uncomfortable sense that the linguistic resources currently
available are ultimately inadequate to the events and situations they
are called upon to describe: 'Agnew knew that words alone were no
good. You had to go outside the words. The meanings were unspoken,
had not been formed into words.'[31] In a recurrent device, the meanings
of specific words are glossed precisely and compulsively, as if in an
attempt to ward off the white noise of disinformation and propaganda
that threatens to engulf the novel, and both Agnew and his anorexic
daughter Lorna are aware that they are each 'in pursuit of something
coded, allusive'.[32] To this end, Agnew compulsively accumulates documents, files, statements and interviews concerning Nairac's activities,
a 'lonely blizzard of paper'[33] that becomes his one reason for existing.
However, as Eamonn Hughes has perceptively observed: 'Agnew is not
so much looking for the solution to the mystery surrounding Nairac
and his activities, as amassing an archive which is less concerned
with fact than with tracking the generation of narrative possibilities.'[34]
Thus, whilst Agnew's obsessive researches illustrate Pierre Nora's
observation that '[m]odern memory is, above all, archival',[35] his labour
of remembering is directed not at uncovering a final and authoritative
version of what happened but towards an understanding of how
conflicting recollections of the same events come to be produced, and
how history and myth become entangled in the narrative constructions
of memory.

Memories are not objects or artefacts that can be filed away or conveniently accessed at will, nor are they literal records of experiences. Rather, as the psychologist Martin Conway points out, memories 'are *interpretations* of experiences and they preserve what is relevant to the individual at the time of particular experiences and, later, when they are remembered'.[36] Moreover, the disjunction that often pertains between these two distinct time frames – the past of remembered experience and the present moment of recollection – means that memories can be wrong. This problem is engaged by Patterson's *That Which Was*, which concerns the partial recovery by Larry, some thirty-four years later, of memories that have apparently been deliberately suppressed from his consciousness by persons unknown, and the difficulties faced by Ken Avery in determining their truth or falsity. In this regard, the novel's faintly farcical central conceit gestures allegorically to the dangers of political amnesia in post-Agreement Northern Ireland – 'memories come back to haunt you, even when someone has tried to erase them',[37] warns Larry. But Patterson's characters are also a good deal more sceptical than McNamee's of the value or legitimacy of paranoia in the contemporary period, even as they recognise the enduring currency of conspiracy theories for popular understandings of the Troubles: 'Someone had once quipped to Avery that Northern Ireland divided into two camps, those who believed conspiracy theories and those who thought they were being put around to make us all paranoid.'[38] The humorous deflation involved here accords with Avery's matter-of-fact conviction regarding moral certainties – his favourite biblical quotation is from Romans 14.5: 'Let every man be fully persuaded in his own mind'[39] – but the obvious difficulties Larry has in following this plain injunction lead Avery to take his fears seriously and so begin to suspect some kind of monstrous cover-up involving everyone from the RUC to MI5. In a sense, then, *That Which Was* is a secular parable on belief. Avery's willingness to speak out on Larry's behalf places considerable strain upon his marriage and his position amongst his congregation, but is driven by his desire to dispel the shadows in which 'they' operate. So when Larry is ultimately unmasked as a deluded fantasist Avery's confidence in his powers of judgement is understandably shaken, but the necessity and justness of his actions are also affirmed:

Avery told the police how he discovered the truth of his car being stolen. . . . He had been played for a fool frankly.
I thought that was part of your job description, one of the policemen said. To give people the benefit of the doubt. No?[40]

In this way, Patterson intimates some of the delicate negotiations of belief and doubt that frame any attempt to relate the present to the past in Northern Ireland, and Larry's seeming deceit does not invalidate Avery's conviction that '[t]here were difficult truths about the past to be faced'.[41] Indeed, just when it appears to have been established that mental illness rather than official conspiracy lies at the heart of the mystery Avery has been investigating, the novel concludes with an ambiguous textual absence or omission – '*Nothing*'[42] – that confounds any neat sense of resolution and threatens to put the wheels of suspicion and speculation into motion once more.

What is perhaps most significant about *That Which Was*, however, is the central importance that the novel accords to the memory of the dead, the victims of the Troubles, and to the memories of the dead that the living try to remember them by. In a memorable passage Avery dreams that, in an effort to balance the release of paramilitary prisoners, 'the Troubles' dead were being allowed home for the weekend' on temporary release from their respective afterlives: 'The dead were materializing as though from contact with the bus station air. They looked like they had been on a particularly hectic holiday, weary, but full of stories.'[43] This dream vision of the dead repopulating the city is both comforting and disturbing, suggesting the necessity for a collective work of mourning in a society still gripped by post-Troubles melancholia. What it also intimates is the sense of a collective responsibility to narrate, listen and respond to the stories of the dead. Indeed, Patterson's fictional impulse towards remembrance echoes Richard Kearney's affirmation that a key function of narrative memory is empathy: 'Stories bring the horror home to us. They singularise suffering against the anonymity of evil.'[44] Even Larry's false memory of the Ellis's Bar killings and his erroneous assumption of guilt are apparently triggered by a pathological form of empathy for the dead man and women that is exacerbated by his actual intimacy with them in the moments before their deaths. By singularising suffering, *That Which Was* also inevitably shows remembering and forgetting to be unusually painful and difficult experiences. When Avery visits the brother of one of Larry's supposed victims he inadvertently blunders upon the distressing effects of memory's erosion over time: 'Doesn't matter how they died or how you try to keep their memory alive. They sort of get boiled down. They lose their – well, like I say – their substance.'[45] This secondary form of loss on the part of relatives and loved ones may be inevitable, but it is against the similarly disastrous erosion or erasure of memory in the public sphere that Patterson's fictional imagination is engaged. In this respect, however, Patterson's work can be seen as merely part of a larger trend within post-Agreement Northern fiction, what I have here called its 'retrospective' tendency, wherein there is an explicit or implicit preoccupation with the ways in which the unresolved events of the past threaten to disrupt or jeopardise those of the present. As Sigmund Freud recognised, the opposite of remembering is not forgetting but 'repeating', the pathological re-enactment of a repressed trauma that cannot be remembered and so acknowledged.[46] Re-membering – putting together the pieces of a fractured psychological or historical puzzle – is the first step to working through, and eventually forgetting, the long-term effects of trauma, whether at an individual or a collective level. If nothing else, the prominence of the issues of memory, remembrance and forgetting in recent Northern Irish fictions suggests a recognition of the difficulty and importance of such an undertaking in all its cultural, social and political implications.

Notes

1   David McKittrick, Seamus Kelters, Brian Feeney, Chris Thornton and David McVea, *Lost Lives: The Stories of the Men, Women And Children Who Died As A Result Of The Northern Ireland troubles* (Edinburgh: Mainstream Publishing, 2007).

2   Glenn Patterson, *Lapsed Protestant* (Dublin: New Island, 2006), p. 88.

3   Richard Bourke, *Peace in Ireland: The War of Ideas* (London: Pimlico, 2003), p. 193.

4   Ibid., p. 3.

5   Colin Graham, ' "Let's Get Killed": Culture and Peace in Northern Ireland', Wanda Balzano, Anne Mulhall and Moynagh Sullivan (eds), *Irish Postmodernisms and Popular Culture* (Houndmills: Palgrave, 2007), p. 180.

6   Deirdre Madden, *One by One in the Darkness* (London; Boston: Faber and Faber, 1996), p. 149.

7   Edna Longley, for example, notes the alternation of apocalyptic and utopian themes in much post-ceasefire writing, describing it in terms of 'a kind of double indemnity' whereby writers 'insure themselves against false prophecy'. Edna Longley, *Poetry and Posterity* (Newcastle-upon-Tyne: Bloodaxe, 2000), pp. 299–300.

8   Madden, *One by One in the Darkness*, pp. 149–50.

9   Robert McLiam Wilson, *Eureka Street* (London: Secker & Warburg, 1996), p. 343.

10 Ibid., p. 396.

11 Glenn Patterson, *The International* (London: Anchor, 1999), p. 318.

12 Ibid., p. 61.

13 Ibid., p. 318.

14 Paul Ricoeur, 'Memory and Forgetting', in Richard Kearney and Mark Dooley (eds), *Questioning Ethics: Contemporary Debates in Philosophy* (London; New York: Routledge, 1999), pp. 10–11.

15 Ibid., p. 11.
16 Slavoj Žižek, *Welcome to the Desert of the Real!: Five Essays on September 11 and Related Dates* (London; New York: Verso, 2002), p. 22.
17 Bernard MacLaverty, *The Anatomy School* (London: Jonathan Cape, 2001), p. 134.
18 David Park, *The Big Snow* (London: Bloomsbury, 2002), p. 191.
19 Eoin McNamee, *The Blue Tango* (London and Boston: Faber and Faber, 2001), p. 201.
20 Eoin McNamee, *The Ultras* (London and Boston: Faber and Faber, 2004), pp. 5, 28.
21 Glenn Patterson, *That Which Was* (London: Hamish Hamilton, 2004), p. 67.
22 McNamee, *The Ultras*, p. 10.
23 Ibid., p. 17.
24 Mark Urban, *Big Boys' Rules: The Secret Struggle against the IRA* (London and Boston: Faber and Faber, 1992), p. 35.
25 McNamee, *The Ultras*, p. 149.
26 Ibid., p. 223.
27 Ibid., p. 216.
28 Fredric Jameson, *The Geopolitical Aesthetic: Cinema and Space in the World System* (Bloomington: Indiana University Press, 1992), p. 3.
29 Peter Knight, *Conspiracy Culture: From Kennedy to the X Files* (London and New York: Routledge, 2000), p. 18.
30 As Lee Horsley notes, 'noir plots turn on falsehoods, contradictions and misinterpretations, and the extent to which all discourse is flawed and duplicitous is a dominant theme'. Lee Horsley, *The Noir Thriller* (Houndmills: Palgrave, 2001), p. 9.
31 McNamee, *The Ultras*, p. 73.
32 Ibid., p. 20.
33 Ibid., p. 74.
34 Eamonn Hughes, 'Limbo', *The Irish Review*, 33 (2005), p. 140.
35 Pierre Nora, 'Between Memory and History: *Les Lieux de Mémoire*', *Representations*, 26 (1989): p. 13.
36 Martin A. Conway, 'Past and Present: Recovered Memories and False Memories', in Martin A. Conway (ed.), *Recovered Memories and False Memories* (Oxford: Oxford University Press, 1997), p. 150.
37 Patterson, *That Which Was*, p. 49.
38 Ibid., p. 112.
39 Ibid., p. 5.
40 Ibid., p. 265.
41 Ibid., p. 239.
42 Ibid., p. 275.
43 Ibid., p. 107.
44 Richard Kearney, *On Stories* (London and New York: Routledge, 2002), p. 62.

45 Patterson, *That Which Was*, p. 137.
46 Sigmund Freud, 'Remembering, Repeating and Working Through', *The Penguin Freud Reader*, ed. Adam Phillips (Harmondsworth: Penguin, 2006), p. 394.

Part V
After words

17

'What do I say when they wheel out their dead?' The representation of violence in Northern Irish art

Shane Alcobia-Murphy

In one emblematic shot from Midge MacKenzie's *The Sky: A Silent Witness* (1995), a documentary made in collaboration with Amnesty International about human rights abuses, the camera frames the sky's reflection on the surface of water while an unidentified woman recounts the horrifying story of her rape on 3 September 1991, in the midst of the Bosnian conflict. The reflection, as Wendy Hesford identifies, 'reverses, distorts, and contains the sky on the surface of the water'; thus, it 'establishes boundaries where there are none, and therefore draws attention to both the crisis of reference and the crisis of witnessing'.[1] The potent image, enclosing part of the formless, uncontainable sky and rendering the witness visually absent, suggests that the woman's trauma is unattainable, unknowable and, consequently, unrepresentable. Paradoxically, even when an image of violence *is* perfectly legible, its formulation can have the effect of '[dispensing] us from receiving the image in all its scandal'; as Roland Barthes argues, the photograph, when 'reduced to the state of pure language' may not 'disorganize us'.[2] Atrocity can be rendered banal, an unedifying spectacle represented atrociously due to the all-pervasive, and hence 'ultra-familiar', imagery of agony and ruin that is, as Susan Sontag states, 'an unavoidable feature of our camera-mediated knowledge of war'.[3]

In this chapter I want to examine how the activity of creating art in a time of violence brings about an anxiety regarding the artist's role, and how it calls into question the ability to re-present atrocity. More specifically, I want to closely examine how artistic silence and narrative breakdown in texts by Northern Irish writers and visual artists often result from an unwillingness to respond to atrocity due to the need to remain 'expertly civil tongued',[4] from a perception that art lacks efficacy in (what is perceived to be) a cyclical, pre-ordained conflict, and from a sense of being at a disabling temporal, cultural or spatial distance from events. These artists encounter the limitations placed on the artist by his or her medium: the anxiety of the writer or artist brought on by a failure of the linguistic or visual medium to re-present the materiality of violent events; the difficulties in mediating between competing, often mutually exclusive, discourses of the State and the Terrorist, and the necessarily self-reflexive strategies adopted by the artist to foreground the cliché, the stereotype and the empty sign. A tension emerges between what Seamus Heaney calls the text's desire 'to answer back with its clear tongue when the world gets muddied and bloodied'[5] and the need for it 'to understand its place and placing, even if it is a poem of total harmony, total beauty, and apparently total innocence'.[6] 'What do I say when they wheel out their dead?' asks the speaker in Heaney's poem 'Stump': 'I'm cauterized, a black stump of home'.[7] In 'Midnight', a poem by the same author, 'The tongue's / Leashed in my throat'.[8] As we shall see, the formal strategies adopted by writers such as Eoin McNamee, Michael Longley, Seamus Heaney and Medbh McGuckian, and by visual artists such as Willie Doherty, Rita Donagh and Paul Seawright, all implicate the reader/viewer in the construction of narratives about 'The Troubles'. Yet this is neither an abdication of artistic responsibility on their part nor an unwillingness to bear witness due to qualms of voyeuristic prurience. What each work deliberately highlights is the disjunction between event and artefact, the dangers of an aestheticisation of conflict and the pressing need to counteract the narcotic banality and simplicity of media stereotypes, sleepwalking as they do '[t]he line between panic and formulae'.[9]

On 6 December 2002 the Ridiculusmus Theatre Group staged the aptly named production *Say Nothing* at London's Pit Theatre. The two-man play defies paraphrase. It is a hilariously cyclical seventy-minute *tour de force*, a satire on the so-called Peace Process, the lack of progress of which it encapsulates both thematically and stylistically. Kevin, a peace studies graduate, has moved to Derry to work in conflict resolution, running conferences entitled 'Hands Across the Barricades' and encouraging cultural diversity amongst the populace. Dishearteningly, what he meets head-on is prejudice, leading to what can be interpreted as his gradual mental collapse. The play emphasises the lack of communication during the Peace Talks in two key ways: visually, by having the two characters remain within a suitcase full of grass (an emblem of how two fractious communities cling to a differing, yet similarly outmoded sense of place, unwilling to move on); and thematically, by including cyclical motifs in the conversations. None of the depicted characters actually listens to his interlocutor; hence the conversations go round and round, saying nothing. The play's title is another example of repetition as it is an intertextual allusion, revisiting Seamus Heaney's 'Whatever You Say Say Nothing',[10] a poem which establishes a tension between speech and silence:

> The famous
> Northern reticence, the tight gag of place
> And times: yes, yes. Of the 'wee six' I sing
> Where to be saved you only must save face
> And whatever you say, you say nothing

Heaney's poem, like *Say Nothing*, emphasises empty rhetoric, hypocrisy and self-protective reticence. It also focuses on the pressures brought to bear upon the linguistic medium in a time of crisis. The poetic speaker rails against

> . . . the jottings and analyses
> Of politicians and newspapermen
> Who've scribbled down the long campaign from gas
> And protest to gelignite and Sten,
>
> Who proved upon their pulses 'escalate',
> 'Backlash' and 'crack down', 'provisional wing',
> 'Polarization' and 'long-standing hate'.

Complex analysis is the first casualty; quotation marks isolate the already redundant clichés of journalistic shorthand. Must the artist engage in a very public response to the Troubles, and in what form? Must it (or even can it) avoid the conventional terms? Responding to such questions in 'Viking Dublin: Trial Pieces', Heaney depicts the figure of the artist as Hamlet, 'pinioned by ghosts and affections'.[11] As Francis Barker has argued in *The Culture of Violence*, Hamlet's problem lies in 'the difficulty of telling in both the interleaved senses of colloquial speech: that it is difficult to know, and difficult to narrate'.[12] In the Northern Irish context, the speaker is left 'dithering, blabbering' because of his awareness of inherited atavism, the unwillingness towards partisanship and a frustrated sense that the conflict is, as he later states in 'The Marching Season', 'scripted from the start'.[13] In 'Mycenae Lookout', the speaker feels his 'tongue / Like the dropped gangplank of a cattle truck'; he is the liminal figure, 'in-between-times', struck dumb due to competing claims on his loyalty.[14] To avoid such a disabling feeling of inarticulacy, then, writers and artists must, by necessity, adopt strategies other than direct statement.

In his visual artworks Willie Doherty responds to both the performative and narrative dimensions of Northern Irish punishment killings by creating texts which, while silent, are complexly self-reflexive and engage the viewer's own understanding of the Northern Irish conflict.

Doherty's photographic diptych entitled *Small Acts of Deception 1* (1997) at first seems enigmatic, eschewing contextualising detail save for the enigmatic title. It deliberately refrains from presenting the images within an overt interpretative framework: there is no accompanying explanatory text, no biographical details of its subject, no precise geographical co-ordinates. Nevertheless, within the context of his previous work the viewer is led to assume a connection with Northern Ireland.[15]

On the left-hand side of the exhibition space the viewer sees a photograph of a car parked in front of a house; the picture is taken at night, with the flash obscuring the number-plate. Adjacent is a photograph of a body lying on the ground; only one of the bound hands and part of a leg are framed within the photograph. The latter is an already mediated image: it is a photograph of what appears to be a video-still. A comparison with footage from BBC 1's *Panorama* documentary on the IRA (11 July 2003) suggests that the body is that of Francis Hegarty, a suspected IRA informer who was shot by the Republicans on 25 May 1986. The title helps to confirm this,[16] yet the viewer who is unaware of the dead man's identity is left to surmise exactly what acts of deception have been committed, to whom, to what end, and with what effect. In light of the work's subject, is the designation 'small' ironic? How can we judge the scale of the implied deception? Commenting on the titles allocated to each of his works, Doherty contended that '[t]hey propose a narrative, and I'm interested in how the viewer completes that narrative and locates these images within it'.[17] As Paul O'Brien rightly contends, therefore, Doherty's oeuvre consistently raises 'the question of how we fill in meanings to images, in the context of the set of accepted ideological responses'.[18] The viewer may well be fully informed about how the 'performative discourse of the body' operates for punishment killings, how it is part of what Feldman calls 'a theatrical substantiation and ritualization of paramilitary power on the street';[19] or he may encounter the work in ignorance or even prejudice, ideologically pre-disposed against making distinctions between the different kinds of killings in Northern Ireland. Indeed, as Elmer Kennedy-Andrews argues regarding the reception of 'terrorist' acts:

> For the humanistic, bourgeois narrative to maintain its hegemonic control, political violence can be understood only as outside the law, disruptive, discontinuous, unavailable for narration. By representing violence as irrational outrage, anarchy unleashed, the history of domination is made to appear as alegitimate process of civilisation.[20]

Crucially, however, the artwork's form not only engages the viewer's attention by withholding a coherent narrative and by featuring images taken from oblique angles, but it also implicates him within the hermeneutic process. The shiny surface of cibachrome prints reflect back the viewer's image, situating him within the picture's frame: '[t]heir high-gloss reflective surfaces have a mirror-like quality, which insists on the presence of the viewer before them, repelling the viewer's desire to "enter" their imaginary spaces. Paradoxically, they would only be clear where a viewer does not exist'.[21] The viewer's gaze is returned as he formulates a narrative and thus may be forced into considering how he came to his conclusions.

While repetition and silence in a Northern Irish text often suggests a pessimistic outlook regarding the perceived cyclical nature of the conflict and the inability of the artist to meaningfully intervene, with Doherty's single-projection video installation entitled *Sometimes I Imagine It's My Turn* (1998) these motifs are deliberately employed so as to question how narratives concerning violent killings are constructed. Panning across waste ground, the camera comes upon a figure lying face down on the ground. Then, as the exhibition catalogue outlines:

> This establishing shot is quickly followed by a sequence of tracking shots that take us closer and closer to the figure, whose identity is never disclosed. The continuity of this sequence is interrupted by close-up shots of the undergrowth and by short inserts of hand-held footage of the same scene. The growing sense of unease is further heightened by the intrusion of rapid inserts of inserts of television footage, suggesting a link between the subject of the video and actual news coverage.[22]

No commentary is provided; no narrative clues are offered as to the figure's identity or to what has happened to him. The video lasts for three minutes, after which time it is repeated since the projection is on a loop. During each replayed sequence, the viewer looks anew at every detail, trying to answer each unresolved question. What is the link between the different kinds of footage? Why does the camera linger on the body and why is it shot from different heights and angles? What terms do we find ourselves using for the figure ('victim', 'terrorist', 'volunteer', 'member of the public') and why? To a certain extent, the film's silence is matched by our own.

To understand Doherty's intent, one can usefully establish a comparison with Alan Clarke's film *Elephant* (1989), which also employs the key motifs of silence and repetition. The viewer bears witness to a series of sectarian killings in the disused factories and deserted waste grounds of Belfast. Shot by means of a roving steadicam, the film follow killers and victims alike on their journeys through the city without the aid of a situating commentary; it is up to us to articulate the lacunae in the narratives as the camera provides lingering close-ups of each victim's body and killer's hand pulling the trigger. The film lasts for thirty-seven minutes, during which there are eighteen murder sequences each shot following 'a specific structural pattern' described by Michael Walsh as follows:

> Most sequences begin with a long take that serves as an establishing shot and tracks either the killer or the victim onto the killing ground . . . These Steadicam takes are all at least thirty seconds long, with some lasting as long as two and a half minutes, and the locations always either deserted or actually derelict; we see only killers, victims and occasional victim's friends, who for obvious reasons flee. By contrast, each segment pivots on a flurry of shots lasting less than a second – a medium close up of the killer, a close-up of the weapon, often a shot of the victim falling, sometimes more shots of the weapon being emptied into the prostrate body. Each segment then concludes with further long takes which follow the killer's departure and return to a merciless inspection of he unmoving body; these shots of corpses last between twenty and twenty-five seconds. Some segments slightly vary the basic regime, but the essential impression is one of thoroughgoing regularity.[23]

The killings' unrelenting nature and the lack of narrative contextualisation could represent, as Walsh reminds us, 'a pitiless demonstration of what the conflict in the six counties really amounts to, suggesting that for all the history, politics and ideology of Ireland, the stark reality is that anonymous men drive or walk up to other men's front doors or places of work and shoot them down'.[24] Indeed, in his monograph on Northern Irish film Brian McIlroy reads the film in this way, arguing that Clarke's ' "Steadicam aesthetic" provides an affinity with "the murderers" and presents the viewer with a view of the Troubles as "monstrous" '.[25] That which is 'monstrous' is beyond comprehension: it is alien, barbaric and cannot be expressed in language. As such, McIlroy's conclusion typifies the reaction to a Northern Irish atrocity and highlights the inability of language to either faithfully re-present the killing or encapsulate the resulting grief. In a paper entitled 'The Spectacle of Terrorism in Northern Irish Culture', Richard Kirkland argues that 'it has been the traditional role of language in the immediate aftermath of a terrorist atrocity to present itself as unable to capture the overwhelming materiality of the event itself. What, so the argument runs, can words offer in the face of such violence? Understood as such, every terrorist outrage becomes unspeakable'.[26] However, Kirkland's article brilliantly focuses our attention on a different kind of silence, touched on above by Kennedy-Andrews: the occlusion of the terrorist narrative by the British media and by State institutions. By avoiding a situating commentary, Kirkland argues, Clarke forces the viewer to work out a narrative for himself. This emphasis on silence and the highly stylised approach to representing the violence are explained by Andrea Grunert as follows:

> Clarke's stylistic approach underlines the supposition that durational factors generate thoughts which could be integrated in the emotional response in which affective and cognitive factors tend to reinforce each other. The emotional responses created by his films are linked to the symbolic production of meaning and the way they problematize and evaluate violence. Without explaining the motivations of the characters or the reasons of the conflict in Northern Ireland, the films and the spectatorial engagement they encourage help us, the viewers, to face and to understand the nature and mechanisms of individual and collective violence.[27]

As viewers, we are not encouraged to simply take one point of view. Countering McIlroy's interpretation of the 'Steadicam aesthetic', Kirkland rightly contends that Clarke's use of the Steadicam 'gestures towards the implication of the subject that is the classical role of "point of view" while hinting that this interpellation is ultimately conditional, that we can, and will, range beyond our own perspectives as necessary'.[28]

Texts about the Troubles often eschew definitive statements; instead, they foreground multiple, often conflicting perspectives, and demonstrate how individual responses are conditioned by socio-political discursive formations. Since forty years of media coverage has resulted in journalistic shorthand and a proliferation of clichés about the violence, it is little wonder that this has become the critical focus of much artwork.[29] For example, Rita Donagh, a Staffordshire-born artist, responded to ways in which the *Sunday Times* reported and photographed the Talbot Street bombing on 19 May 1974. One work from this series, *Aftermath*, includes a newspaper photograph of people milling about a corpse which has been covered up and shielded from the public gaze. Below this she has drawn an extension of this scene, enlarging (and thus foregrounding) the image of the hidden body. What conceals the person's identity in her drawing are newspaper pages (a motif also included in *Newspaper Vendor, Evening Newspapers* and *Talbot Street, 1974*), the text of which is comprised of meaningless phrases used to indicate the shape of the story waiting to be written. In the catalogue for Donagh's retrospective, Sarat Maharaj convincingly argues that the Talbot Street series shows '[h]ow issues are "covered by" the media, the notion of "news coverage", is set off against the idea that personal facts, painful moments of loss, grieving and shattering of individual lives, tend to get covered up in the interests of a larger story which has to be told'.[30] If a picture tells a thousand stories, which one is 'true'? Can reportage, whether photographic or linguistic, ever represent the event? Can it explain the rationale behind an atrocity, and its consequences for all those involved? It is important to note, however, that Donagh's work self-reflexively calls attention to the failure of representation in her own work. The artwork draws the viewer in, inviting an engagement with the scene's anonymity, to fill in the missing narrative. If, as David Morrison suggests, '[v]iolence . . . draws its meaning only from the totality of the situation within which it occurs and from the meanings that people give to the act within the known structures of its occurrence',[31] then the viewer will necessarily fail in his attempt to fully understand the violence being represented.

Northern Irish fiction has been culpable for proliferating a narrow vision of the Northern Irish conflict and has fostered what Lewis R. Gordon terms 'epistemic closure',[32] the erection of stereotypes resulting in a presumption of total knowledge about 'terrorists' and the 'Troubles' in general. The popularity and sheer pervasiveness of the thriller genre has resulted in the creation of the 'Troubles trash' novel, 'a cult phenomenon in which hardened terrorists race across flat-roofed buildings and blow up sidewalks, misguided idealists die for Erin and lovers are caught in the crossfire'.[33] Thrillers such as Brian Moore's *Lies of Silence* (1990), Chris Pettitt's *The Psalm Killer* (1996), Paul Anthony's *The Fragile Peace* (1996) and Murray Davies' *The Drumbeat of Jimmy Sands* (1999) all peddle simplistic clichés and present conflict as inherently cyclical and sectarian. However, several more sophisticated novels have been produced which disrupt the join between world and text, which focus both on the telling of the tale and on the fictionalising process of history.[34] Such novels are historiographic metafictions, texts which underline 'the realization that "the past is not an 'it' in the sense of an objectified entity that may either be neutrally represented in and for itself or projectively reprocessed in terms of our narrowly 'presentist interests' " '.[35] Such texts do not, of course, deny that certain events happened; rather, they problematise their subsequent representation.

One such novel is Eoin McNamee's *Resurrection Man*,[36] a fictional account of the killings perpetuated by the so-called Shankill Butchers. The novel, when it appeared, was 'much maligned as, variously, a novel that perpetuates the dismissal of Belfast as a hellish stasis left behind by world history, an insult to unionism or loyalism, or an exploitative and voyeuristic example of the "Troubles trash" that has so dehistoricized the conflict in the North'.[37] Indeed, when the novel was made into a film,[38] the critics were cool in their reception. While admiring its 'satanically-vicious violence', Kevin Barry disliked 'the film's stylishness'. Both Michael Dwyer and Gary Mitchell concurred, the former arguing that it 'bordered on the voyeuristic', the latter being abhorred by its 'abundance of bloody, mindless violence and stylish still-frame holds on frenzied idiots'.[39] The critics missed the point entirely: the stylised filming of violence, the slick editing, freeze frames, slow motion and jump-cuts all make the audience aware of an aestheticised violence. Rather than a glorification of violence, the director presents a filmic critique of it. In this regard, the misguided reception of the film matches the misreadings of McNamee's novel. Glenn Patterson, a fellow Northern Irish novelist and contemporary of McNamee, has been scathing in his criticism of the way in which McNamee approaches the topic of the Shankill Butchers:

> I don't like *Resurrection Man*. In fact it is one of the few books I've ever reviewed and I was really angry about it. What I didn't like about the book was stylistic. . . . [B]ecause of the way the book is written, and there's some very fine writing in it, when the characters speak it is quite obvious that the descriptions of the murders are all in a language that I don't believe is available to those characters as he has them speak. Therefore, what I get is Eoin McNamee writing very florid descriptions of murders. There's something of the horror and strange beauty of violence. Violence is not strangely beautiful.[40]

Equally scathing, the critic Richard Haslam states in a recent article that: 'every aesthetic is encoded with a potential ethic: the obligation to do justice, not violence, to one's subject. In *Resurrection Man*, however, the *unglamorous* ethic is missing. Sublime abstractions displace concrete atrocities; the pose obscures the corpse'.[41] But we are *meant* to linger on this corpse; our attention is time and again focused on the pose. When Patterson says that the characters are speaking in a language he does not believe in, that is pointing to the real thematic focus of the novel: the scepticism regarding the novelistic medium to represent violence and to respond to the Troubles. McNamee's text is a metafiction, a novel about the crisis of novelistic representation and avoids the unwanted designation of 'Troubles trash' through its self-reflexivity and intertextual use of differing genres.

The author employs five key strategies to foreground his own intense unease with the linguistic medium. Firstly, McNamee uses a plot element – the severing of a victim's tongue – to state overtly his main thematic concern, namely that language as it currently exists cannot adequately represent the violence perpetrated by the Shankill Butchers: 'The root of the tongue had been severed. New languages would have to be invented'.[42] Secondly, McNamee directly refers to the sensational reportage and mediocre thrillers produced during the worst years of the Troubles:

> The violence had started to produce its own official literature. Mainly hardbacks, with the emphasis on the visual. Photographs of bombs at the moment of detonation, riot scenes, men in balaclavas displaying heavy machine-guns, burnt out vehicles, moments of numbness and shock. There was the inevitable photograph of the civilian victim.[43]

By laying bare the conventions for the reader, McNamee is able to establish the genres that he seeks to avoid in his own text. Thirdly, he insistently establishes a connection between language and violence in a series of macabre similes. For example, looking at photographs of cadavers, one of the characters remarks upon the wounds, 'the marks regular, like the script of some phantom tongue used to record inventions that might be found on the lips of those about to die'.[44] Similarly, when one of the main protagonists, Ryan, looks upon the corpse of Darkie Larch, he notes how 'his torso was incised with small cuts meticulously executed and his head was bent to his chest as though there were something written there he could read, words in a severe tongue'.[45] Each time the author attempts to establish a connection between language and violence, the reader not only notices his recourse to simile ('like'; 'as though'), but also that the narrator can never read what the incisions say. Linked to this is the fourth strategy, namely the way he depicts each character in search of a language: just as the author fails to find a way of representing violence, his own characters suffer a linguistic crisis. Heather's attraction to Victor is partly based on her desire for this new language: 'He looked like he might think in another language. She wondered if he might be an Arab. She had read somewhere that Arabs like plump women and she imagined him discussing the plumpness of women in a strange and cruelly shaped alphabet'.[46] Ryan wants 'to hear an invented language of sex, its expressions of forgetfulness and terror'.[47] Coppinger sits in his parked car, 'chanting names until it seemed that the recitation was an end in itself, a means of fathoming the forces at work. As if the knowledge they were looking for was concealed in the names themselves'.[48] Finally, the narrator plays with different genres throughout the novel and is never able to settle into any of them. Two critics in particular, Gerry Smyth and Nuala Johnson, convincingly argue that the incongruous multiplicity of the novel's languages – discourses of the psychological treatise, crime thriller and *film noir* – points towards 'the suspicion that language cannot adequately circumscribe motive and communicate meaning for politically charged and savagely executed violence in the city of Belfast'.[49] Indeed, the reader bears witness to the author's unwillingness (and inability) to frame his take within a single genre. Although the characters themselves articulate a sense of dislocation – 'the state of civil unrest had made them feel obsolete, abandoned on the perimeter of a sprawling technology of ruin'[50] – it is important to note that their alienation stems from a dissatisfaction with their linguistic resources. While Elmer Kennedy-Andrews correctly argues that the novel's events become textualised (newspaper reportage, anecdotal accounts), and that narration displaces the real into the mediated (that which is re-presented),[51] nevertheless the underlying emphasis of *Resurrection Man* is on the distorting nature of this representation and its ultimate failure to either encompass the primal scene of violence or explain its socio-political cause. The novel's key motif is, in fact, silence. One key scene epitomises this failure of representation. When Victor is in prison and seeks revenge on a fellow inmate, he goes to his cell and forces him to write a confession by holding his wrist:

> When he had finished Victor had difficulty in reading it. The letters did not seem to bear any relationship to others he had seen. At first glance they did not appear to belong to any known language, but were something called up out of months of solitary confinement. It was a language of seclusion: plaintive, elegiac, lost.[52]

Here we have a character who cannot read the words he himself has dictated. It is fitting that Victor's final act in this scene is to smother the inmate by placing a pillow over his face (the latter had already admitted that 'I can't mind the words no more').

Of course, Northern Irish writers' acute sensitivity to the problematics of re-presenting atrocity is not confined to their engagement with the Northern Irish conflict. Indeed, their constant vigilance towards, and avoidance of, the hackneyed phrase and the clichéd response have served them well when approaching other violent events such as the extermination of the Jews under the Nazi regime. One poet in particular, Michael Longley, has been especially vocal in his desire to avoid treating the Holocaust as 'a mere subject':

> The German philosopher Adorno suggested that there could be no more poetry after Auschwitz. Perhaps he meant that after the holocaust poetry could not remain the same. In which case I agree with him. But I also believe that if poetry is incapable of approaching so huge and horrible a subject, then there is no future for poetry. A bad poem about the Holocaust will be a crime against the light. So this is dangerous territory. Although there is little we can do imaginatively with the pictures of the piles of bodies, the torture chambers, the gas ovens, we are duty bound to try and work out how we arrived there.[53]

Longley never shirks from what he regards as the poet's responsibilities, and avows his belief in the efficacy of the poetic text: the poet, he says, must make 'the most complex response that can be made with words to the total experience of living' and, in so doing, he 'illuminates and orders it with words'.[54] 'Orders' does not simply connote a sense of containing chaotic violence within a regular metrical scheme; rather, it means to regulate, to direct, and to bring into order or submission to lawful authority, namely that of the poet. Indeed, this is what Seamus Heaney famously calls 'the jurisdiction of achieved form'. Changing the name of an early draft entitled 'Photographs' to 'The Exhibit',[55] Longley not only refers to a cultural artefact on display ('the pile of spectacles in the Auschwitz museum'), but also invokes the legal meaning, implying that the text is produced as evidence both of 'the torments inflicted on the Jews by the Nazis',[56] and of poetry's governing power.

> I see them absentmindedly pat their naked bodies
> Where waistcoat and apron pockets would have been.
> The grandparents turn back and take an eternity
> Rummaging in the tangled pile for their spectacles[57]

The changes made to the early drafts demonstrate a meticulous and justly scrupulous intelligence regarding his choice and arrangement of words. While he changes a demonstrative preposition ('this') to a definite article in 'the tangled pile' to allow for a sense of distance, he crucially alters the opening line of the earlier drafts to intimate his presence (he now includes the phrase 'I see'), conveying his own act of bearing witness and his imaginative intervention at one and the same time. For the reader, this opening gambit embodies the ambiguity inherent within all testimony: as Derrida reminds us, while '[b]y law, a testimony must not be a work of art or fiction', nevertheless since it cannot constitute proof, then 'there is no testimony that does not structurally imply in itself the possibility of fiction . . . that is to say, the possibility of literature . . .'.[58] The poet's opening statement is all the more poignant as the victims themselves are deprived by the Nazis of the power of vision: while they literally cannot see without their spectacles, they also cannot foresee their own death. The Auschwitz exhibition may connote the absence which resulted from the extermination (all that is left is a pile of spectacles), yet Longley's vision reverses the victims' dehumanisation, firstly, by remembering them as people within a familial context ('grandparents') and, secondly, by reconstructing the unbearably affecting moment prior to death when they 'pat their naked bodies / Where waistcoat and apron pockets would have been'. By changing 'turn around' to 'turn back', the poet intimates a temporal dimension, allowing them to forestall the inevitable. Indeed, by literalising, thereby revivifying, the outworn phrase 'spend an eternity', he presents us with an image of the grandparents held in stasis, almost as if they were revenants returning to reclaim what is theirs. Perhaps the most admirably courageous (and ultimately astute) editorial decision taken by Longley was to change the poem's format, deleting what was originally the second section:

> Hundreds in broad daylight are waiting to be shot.
> I pick out one only. Her aging breasts look sore.

While the couplet once again presents a human dimension, the clever ambiguity of 'to be shot' (photographed; executed) is deemed inappropriate, and the poet avoids placing himself in the position of the Nazis ('pick out' is too reminiscent of the selection process whereby the Nazis chose those who were to be eliminated in the crematoria). The concluding image, though tender and humanising, is perhaps also uncomfortably voyeuristic.

In the first section of an earlier poem, 'Ghetto', the speaker describes the impossible predicament of those who were singled out for selection to go to the Jewish ghettoes (the preliminary stage before the death-camps):

> Because you will suffer soon and die, your choices
> Are neither right nor wrong: a spoon will feed you,
> A flannel keep you clean, a toothbrush bring you back
> To your bathroom's view of chimney-pots and gardens.
> With so little time for inventory or leavetaking,
> You are packing now for the rest of your life
> Photographs, medicines, a change of underwear, a book,
> A candlestick, a loaf, sardines, needle and thread.
> These are your heirlooms, perishables, wordly goods.
> What you bring is the same as what you leave behind,
> Your last belonging a list of your belongings.[59]

Opening with a logical conjunction ('Because'), the speaker questions the rationality of a decision to be made within an ethical vacuum. The choice of which articles to take to the ghetto is made, initially, on both practical and sentimental grounds: each is necessary for cleanliness and health, yet also acts as a totemic item of comfort and familiarity. While the associative connections foster a compensatory sense of non-estrangement, the text's insistent emphasis on temporality ('soon'; 'so little time'; 'rest of your life') undercuts the illusory fiction and hints at the victim's imminent demise, and hence at the absence of any real choice. Indeed, the ironic juxtaposition of 'heirlooms, perishables' connotes not only the destruction of all things material, but also the destruction of an entire generation. 'Worldly goods' becomes 'wordly goods' within the 'concentrationary realism'[60] espoused in this poem: through bureaucratic exactitude (list-making), only the words survive for the victim. Such a conclusion may also hint at the author's positive assertion of language's ability to persist, and his desire to confront (and overcome) silence.

Discussing an earlier poem, 'Terezín',[61] Longley states:

> Sometimes the brevity is to do with tact in dealing with momentous subject matter, and the only way to contain it without being offensive is to touch it and no more. A poem for instance that I wrote, 'Terezín', which is about a photograph in Montreal which I'll never forget seeing – it was a photograph of a room in Terezín filled with hundreds of violins that had been confiscated from Jews and were I suppose about to be handed out to young Aryan future Mozarts. It seemed to me that the only way to deal with that was two lines which approached the condition of silence.[62]

In the poem, Longley refers indirectly to the suffering within the concentration camps:

> No room has ever been as silent as the room
> Where hundreds of violins are hung in unison.

The victims are present here only by their absence. Originally entitled 'Silence',[63] the text presents the reader with an image that on first reading could signify the death of art. Much of its power derives from the title which provides an implied context: the ghetto (and transit camp) established by the Nazis north of Prague. To create the spare, haunting image, complemented by an eerie acoustic echo signifying emptiness ('No room . . . room . . . unison'), Longley again employs his better judgement and shortens the original quatrain by two thematically redundant lines. The overall effect is restorative: bearing witness to and opposing a regime that resulted in the death of so many musicians, the text embodies the surviving efficacy of art. Never has a silence been so resonant.

When writing about atrocious events, Seamus Heaney often achieves artistic distance and a sense of objectivity by adopting the strategy of quoting from literary exemplars. When citing approvingly from the work of others, or when alluding to their artistic praxis, the poet not only seeks their *auctoritas*, but also measures his own work against theirs. By constructing an artistic pantheon – a 'self-referential intimacy' – he creates 'a bolstering imaginative system of self-instruction, self-declaration, self-evaluation, and self-rebuke'.[64] However, there is as much 'self-rebuke' as there is 'self-instruction', and Heaney's recourse to a discourse of exemplarity is not always a resolving one, nor one of unqualified self-approval. At times in his poems, therefore, there is a tension between the need to speak out directly, and an attitude of self-censorship result-ing in silence. For example, when writing about the conflict in the Balkans in 'Known World'[65] he finds himself forced to contemplate 'That old sense of a tragedy going on / Uncomprehended', and his first impulse is to invoke an artistic allusion, referring to conflict in aesthetic terms: 'A pity I didn't know then (for Caj's sake) / Hygo Simberg's allegory of Finland'. He translates Simberg's image of the wounded angel into more familiar terms: 'A first communion angel with big white wings . . .'. Yet even when he has transformed the unknown into the known, he self-reflexively meditates on his right to interpret Simberg's allegory: 'who's to know / How to read sorrow rightly, or at all?' At the time he felt 'involved at the moment and closer than usual and yet half-culpably secure'.[66] Having raised the issue of his self-doubt, however, he invokes a further allusion:

> The open door, the jambs, the worn saddle
> And actual granite of the doorstep slab.
> Now enters another angel, fit as ever,
> Past each house with a doorstep daubed 'Serb house'.

Explaining why the houses were 'daubed "Serb house"', Karl Miller, in conversation with Heaney, states: 'This was a message which was painted on thresholds in order to dissuade those who would otherwise enter the house and kill everyone inside'.[67] Referring to the Passover (*Exodus*, 2:12), Heaney makes an implicit link between that genocide and the contemporary circumstances in the Balkans. Overt judgement and condemnation are avoided – the speaker no longer uses the first person singular; intertextuality facilitates indirection while still allow-ing the poet to refer to the war.

Recourse to quotation as a poetic strategy when referring to unspeakable atrocity is perhaps taken to a curious extreme in the work of the final writer examined in this chapter: Medbh McGuckian.[68] Caught between the ethical compulsion to respond and the knowledge that she is not an authoritative witness, McGuckian embeds un-attributed quotations from eye-witness testimonies, using and engaging with the insights of those who have actually experienced the conditions of war. For example, 'Corduroy Road'[69] refers to an unspecified 'historical ground' situated 'not far from Richmond': 'ripe and suffering / is covered with dirt and pitch, / the sentimentalized blossoms, / outlast the stench'. Here she cites from David W. Blight's 'No Desperate Hero: Manhood and Freedom in a Union Soldier's Experience', a study of two hundred American Civil War letters written by Charles Harvey Brewster. Blight's analysis argues that those who fought in the Civil War

experienced conflicting emotions, running 'from naïveté to mature realism, from romantic idealism to sheer terror, from self-pity to enduring
devotion'.[70] The specific line taken from Blight cites his observation that
combatants often mask ugliness and horror when writing about war,
not only as a self-protective measure, but also as a means of shielding
loved ones from atrocity: '[s]entimentalized blossoms so often outlast
and even replace the stench of the dead and the vileness of war'.[71] Within
McGuckian's text, the quotation extends Blight's argument to suggest
that historiography and commemoration can equally render the reality
of war as safe and distant for those in the present: the Corduroy Road
becomes 'that now historical ground'. Yet the poem refuses to participate
in the whitewash and insistently dwells on the psychological effects of
war:[72]

the compass that had been built into me (p. 64)	It was a compass built into me,
militarization of thought (p. 368)	the militarization of my thought,
the crackling shots were to him like voices (p. 65)	their shots were to me like voices . . .

In the context of the American Civil War 'militarization of thought'
refers to what Blight discerns as 'a male tradition deeply ingrained in
American society, and one that common and less literary-inclined men
like Brewster had helped to cultivate. Brewster's own manly compass
sent him irresistibly off to war'.[73] Individual volition is negated due to
the war effort, and Brewster's imagination is left, like Henry Fleming
in Stephen Crane's *The Red Badge of Courage*, tormented by the
sounds of battle; the 'shots' may be 'like voices', but they drown out
his own voice.

McGuckian's poems often deal with situations in which one can
only 'say nothing'. Borrowing from Eugenia Semyonovna Ginzburg's
Journey into the Whirlwind,[74] the opening section of 'Asking for the
Alphabet Back'[75] depicts a prisoner's encroaching speechlessness:[76]

she suddenly forgot all her small stock of Russian words, even, for instance, the word for water (p. 363)	She could not even remember the word
a single drop in a grey wave (p. 353)	for water. A single drop
So he lied to me (p. 17)	in a grey wave lied to her,
The news burned, stung, clawed (p. 25)	singing the news that clawed and stung.
these un-men (p. 60)	The un-men were not only men

it brimmed over (p. 118)	but her men. They brimmed over
symmetrical watchtowers (p. 397)	the symmetrical watchtowers, the wall spoke
Toward evening the wall spoke (p. 82)	as though it were the unbroken Host.

Within an Irish context, one could read the poem as expressing the effects of linguistic colonisation on the speaker, with English replacing Gaelic as the mother tongue, discomfiting not only her sense of place but also her sense of being (the text goes on to talk of 'the bullet through her heart / as English followed the roads, its tidings' / malady amputating the wildscape'). In the section cited above, the quotations present an analogy between British colonisation in mid-nineteenth-century Ireland and Stalinist Russia in the mid-1930s. Ginzburg's autobiography relates a narrative of betrayal by the communist government in which she believed, a tale of sham trials, purges and imprisonment. She tells of how her friend Maria Zacher began to lose 'her small stock of Russian words' while imprisoned at the Magadan camp, and of how news of the widespread mock-trials 'burned, stung, clawed at one's heart'. Freedom, individuality and voice were confiscated by the totalitarian regime: all became 'un-men'. Although the implied analogy is historically inaccurate, the quotations themselves are unacknowledged and thus meant to be untraceable. The views expressed may be extreme, but the use of a fellow writer's text functions as an enabling means by which she can empathise with those who suffer oppression. The lack of statement of intent is of course in line with both the text's (and intertext's) thematics of secrecy and focus on silence.

In conclusion, one can argue that the writer and visual artist may find themselves compelled to 'say nothing' in three crucial circumstances: firstly, when their role as artists is under question, when they contemplate their objectivity and effectiveness; secondly, either when the linguistic and photographic media becomes debased through the prevalence of clichés, or when they find themselves using discourses which are considered to be beyond the pale (republican nationalism; the discourse of the terrorist); thirdly, when there is a severe crisis of representation (through the intrinsic failure of language to represent the actuality of violence, through psychological self-censorship, or through the artist's feeling that he or she lacks authority). However, contemporary artists from Northern Ireland, and those like Alan Clarke and Rita Donagh who are responding to the conflict in this area, tend not to end up as some angst-ridden Hamlet, 'dithering and blathering'. While their artwork tends toward the self-reflexive, using intertextuality and other formal strategies which foreground an artwork's principles of construction, they are not self-enclosed. When speaking of atrocities, they do not speak atrociously.

Notes

1 Wendy S. Hesford, 'Documenting Violations: Rhetorical Witnessing and the Spectacle of Distant Suffering', *Biography*, 27/1 (winter 2004), pp. 104–45, p. 109.
2 Roland Barthes, *The Eiffel Tower and Other Mythologies*, trans. Richard Howard (New York: Hill and Wang, 1979), pp. 71–2.
3 Susan Sontag, *Regarding the Pain of Others* (London: Hamish Hamilton, 2003), p. 21.
4 Seamus Heaney, *North* (London: Faber, 1975), p. 57.
5 Seamus Heaney, '*Us* as in *Versus*: Poetry and the World', *When Hope and History Rhyme: The NUI, Galway, Millennium Lecture Series* (Dublin: Four Courts Press, 2002), p. 50.
6 Seamus Heaney, *Talking with Poets*, ed. Harry Thomas (New York: Handsell Books, 2002), p. 47.
7 Seamus Heaney, *Wintering Out* (London: Faber, 1972), p. 41.
8 Ibid., p. 46.
9 Seamus Heaney, *The Haw Lantern* (London: Faber, 1987), p. 46.
10 Heaney, *North*, pp. 57–60.
11 Heaney, *North*, p. 23.
12 Francis Barker, *The Culture of Violence: Tragedy and History* (Manchester: Manchester University Press, 1993), pp. 36–7.
13 Seamus Heaney, *Electric Light* (London: Faber, 2001): p. 54.
14 Seamus Heaney, *The Spirit Level* (London: Faber, 1996), p. 29.
15 The work formed part of Doherty's retrospective at the Irish Museum of Modern Art, 31 October 2002–2 March 2003. See Carolyn Christov-Bakargiev and Caoimhín Mac Giolla Léith (eds) *Willie Doherty: False Memory* (London: Merrell, 2002), p. 144.
16 It has been alleged that the informer was lured back to Ireland on false promises by Martin McGuinness and that he was subsequently shot. One other person allegedly involved in all of this was Freddie Scappaticci, who may or may not have been a British agent as well. So many deceptions . . .
17 Willie Doherty, 'Like Home', interview by Joan Rothfuss, in Zarina Bhimji et al. (eds), *No Place (Like Home)* (Minneapolis, MN: Walker Art Center, 1997), p. 47.
18 Paul O'Brien, 'Willie Doherty: Language, Imagery and the Real', *Circa* 104 (2003), p. 53.
19 Allen Feldman, 'Retaliate and Punish: Political Violence as Form and Memory in Northern Ireland', *Éire-Ireland* (summer 1998), pp. 195–235: p. 207.

20 Elmer Kennedy-Andrews, *Fiction and the Northern Ireland Troubles since 1969: (De-)constructing the North* (Dublin: Four Courts Press, 2003), p. 12.

21 Brian Hand, 'Swerved in Naught', *Circa*, 76 (1996), p. 22.

22 Christov-Bakargiev and Mac Giolla Léith, *Willie Doherty*, p. 158.

23 Michael Walsh, 'Thinking the Unthinkable: Coming to Terms with Northern Ireland in the 1980s and the 1990s', in Justine Ashby and Andrew Higson (eds), *British Cinema, Past and Present* (London: Routledge, 2003), pp. 288–98: pp. 294–5.

24 Ibid., p. 296.

25 Brian McIlroy, *Shooting to Kill: Filmmaking and the 'Troubles' in Northern Ireland* (Richmond: Steveston Press, 2001), p. 128.

26 Richard Kirkland, 'The Spectacle of Terrorism in Northern Irish Culture'. *Critical Survey*, 15:1 (2003), pp. 77–90: p. 77.

27 Andrea Grunert, 'Emotion and Cognition: About Some Key-Figures in Films by Alan Clarke': www.artbrain.org/journal2/grunert.html (accessed on 12 June 2005).

28 Kirkland, 'The Spectacle of Terrorism', pp. 86–7.

29 See Shane Murphy, 'Don't Mention the War: The Trouble(s) in Northern Irish Poetry', in Michel Hensen and Annette Pankratz (eds), *The Aesthetics and Pragmatics of Violence* (Passau: Verlag Karl Stutz, 2001), pp. 89–102.

30 Sarat Maharaj, 'Rita Donagh: Towards a Map of Her Artwork', *197419841994: Paintings and Drawings* (Manchester: Cornerhouse, 1995), p. 15.

31 David E. Morrison, 'The Idea of Violence', in Andrew Millwood Hargrave (ed.), *Violence in Factual Television: Annual Review* (London: John Libbey, 1993), p. 125.

32 Lewis R. Gordon, 'A Questioning Body of Laughter and Tears', *Parallax* 8/2 (2002), pp. 10–29: p. 16.

33 Eve Patten, 'Fiction in Conflict: Northern Ireland's Prodigal Novelists', in Ian A Bell (ed.), *Peripheral Visions: Images of Nationhood in Contemporary British Fiction* (Cardiff: University of Wales Press, 1995), pp. 128–48, p. 128.

34 See Shane Alcobia-Murphy, *Sympathetic Ink: Intertextual Relations in Northern Irish Poetry* (Liverpool: Liverpool University Press, 2006), pp. 65–87, and Aaron Kelly, *The Thriller and Northern Ireland Since 1696: Utterly Resigned Terror* (Edinburgh: Ashgate, 2005).

35 Linda Hutcheon, *The Politics of Postmodernism* (London: Routledge, 2005), p. 57.

36 Eoin McNamee, *Resurrection Man* (London: Picador, 2005).

37 Aaron Kelly, ' "A Stasis of Hatred, Fear and Mistrust": The Politics of form in representations of Northern Ireland Produced by the "Troubles" Thriller', in P.J. Mathews (ed.), *New Voices in Irish Criticism* (Dublin: Four Courts, 2000), pp. 109–15, p. 109.

38 McNamee wrote the screenplay for the film, which was directed by Mark Evans (1998).

39 See Kevin Barry, *Irish Times*, 13 February 1998, Michael Dwyer, *Irish Times*, 20 February 1998, and Gary Mitchell, *Irish Times*, 27 February 1998.

40 Glenn Patterson, 'Nothing Has to Die', interview by Richard Mills, *NorthernNarratives*, ed. Bill Lazenbatt, *Writing Ulster*, 6 (1999), pp. 113–29: p. 119.

41 Richard Haslam, ' "The Pose Arranged and Lingered Over": Visualizing the "Troubles" ', in Liam Harte and Michael Parker (eds), *Contemporary Irish Fiction: Themes, Tropes, Theories* (Basingstoke: Macmillan, 2000), pp. 192–212, p. 208.

42 McNamee, p. 16.

43 Ibid., p. 92.

44 Ibid., p. 197.

45 Ibid., p. 213.

46 Ibid., p. 42.

47 Ibid., p. 24.

48 Ibid., pp. 34–5.

49 Nuala C. Johnson, 'The Cartographies of Violence: Belfast's *Resurrection Man*', *Environment and Planning D: Society and Space*, 17 (1999), pp. 723–36: p. 724. See also Gerry Smyth, *The Novel and the Nation: Studies in the New Irish Fiction* (London: Pluto Press, 1997), p. 123.

50 Ibid., p. 83.

51 See Elmer Kennedy-Andrews, 'Antic Dispositions in Some Recent Irish Fiction', in Fran Brearton and Eamonn Hughes (eds), *Last Before America: Irish and American Writing* (Belfast: Blackstaff Press, 2001), pp. 134–6.

52 Ibid., p. 103.

53 Longley, 'A Few Thoughts about the Ghetto', Michael Longley Papers, MSS 744, Special Collection, R.W. Woodruff Library, Emory University, Box 38, Folder 15.

54 Longley, 'Definition of Poetry', Michael Longley Papers, MSS 744, Special Collection, R.W. Woodruff Library, Emory University, Box 35, Folder 11.

55 Longley, Drafts of 'The Exhibit', Michael Longley Papers, MSS 744, Special Collection, R.W. Woodruff Library, Emory University, Box 26, Folder 25.

56 Longley, Draft of *Cenotaph of Snow*, Michael Longley Papers, MSS 744, Special Collection, R.W. Woodruff Library, Emory University, Box 35, Folder 7.

57 Michael Longley, *Weather in* Japan (London: Cape, 2000), p. 18.

58 Jacques Derrida, *Demeure: Fiction and Testimony*, trans. E. Rottenberg (Stanford, CA: Stanford University Press, 2000), p. 43.

59 Michael Longley, *Selected Poems* (London: Cape Poetry, 1998), pp. 97–9.

60 See Sidra DeKoven Ezrahi, *By Words Alone: The Holocaust in Literature* (Chicago: The University of Chicago Press, p. 1982), pp. 50–4. 'Worldly

goods' became 'wordly goods' when the poem was included in Longley's *Selected Poems*.

61 Longley, *Selected Poems*, p. 96.
62 Peter McDonald, 'Au Revoir, Oeuvre', interview with Michael Longley, Special Collections, The R.W. Woodruff Library, Box 43, Folder 5.
63 Longley, 'Silence', box 23, folder 30, Special Collections.
64 Neil Corcoran, 'Seamus Heaney and the Art of the Exemplary', *The Yearbook of English Studies*, 17 (1987), pp. 117–27: p. 119.
65 Heaney, *Electric Light*, pp. 19–23.
66 Seamus Heaney, *Seamus Heaney in Conversation with Karl Miller* (London: BTL, 2000), p. 28.
67 Ibid., p. 27.
68 For a fuller discussion of McGuckian's use of intertextuality, see Shane Alcobia-Murphy, *Sympathetic Ink: Intertextual Relations in Northern Irish Poetry* (Liverpool: Liverpool University Press, 2006).
69 Medbh McGuckian, *Had I a Thousand Lives* (Meath: Gallery Press, 2003), pp. 80–1.
70 David W. Blight, 'No Desperate Hero: Manhood and Freedom in a Union Soldier's Experience', in Elizabeth Clinton (ed.), *Divided Houses: Gender and Civil War* (Oxford: Oxford University Press, 1992), pp. 55–75: p. 56.
71 Ibid., p. 68.
72 McGuckian's text is on the right; quotations from Blight (with page numbers to 'No Desperate Hero' in parentheses) are on the left.
73 Blight, 'No Desperate Hero', p. 64.
74 Eugenia Semyonovna Ginzburg, *Journey into the Whirlwind*, trans. Paul Stevenson and Max Hayward, 2nd edn (San Diego: Harcourt, 1995).
75 McGuckian, *Had I a Thousand Lives*, p. 31.
76 McGuckian's text is on the right; quotations from Ginzburg are on the left, with page numbers from *Journey into the Whirlwind* given in parentheses.

Bibliography

Alcobia-Murphy, Shane. *Governing the Tongue in Northern Ireland: The Place of Art / The Art of Place*. Newcastle: Cambridge Scholars Press, 2005.
—— *Sympathetic Ink: Intertextual Relations in Northern Irish Poetry*. Liverpool: Liverpool University Press, 2006.

Allen, Michael, ed. *Seamus Heaney*. London: Macmillan, 1997.

Annan, Gabriele. 'Twin Peaks', *New York Review of Books*, 21 September 2000, 90.

Appadurai, Arjun. *Modernity at Large: Cultural Dimensions of Globalization*. Minneapolis: University of Minnesota Press, 1996.

Arrowsmith, Aidan. 'Plastic Paddy: Negotiating Identity in Second-generation "Irish-English" Writing', *Irish Studies Review* 8/1 (2000): 35–43.
—— 'New Field Day Dawning', *Irish Studies Review* 15/1 (February 2007): 83–8.

Aston, Elaine. *An Introduction to Feminism and Theatre*. London and New York: Routledge, 1995.

Bachelard, Gaston. *The Poetics of Space*, trans. M. Jolas. Boston: Beacon Press, 1994.

Barker, Francis. *The Culture of Violence: Tragedy and History*. Manchester: Manchester University Press, 1993.

Barry, Sebastian. 'Preface' to *Plays 1*. London: Methuen, 1997.
—— *Hinterland*. London: Faber, 2002.

Barthes, Roland. *The Eiffel Tower and Other Mythologies*, trans. Richard Howard. New York: Hill and Wang, 1979.

Batten, Guinn. 'Boland, McGuckian, Ní Chuilleanáin and the Body of the Nation', in *The Cambridge Companion to Contemporary Irish Poetry*, ed. Matthew Campbell. Cambridge: Cambridge University Press, 2003.

Battersby, Eileen. 'Haughey was an Opportunistic Pragmatist', *The Irish Times*, 24 June 2006, 16.

Bauman, Zygmunt. *Globalization: The Human Consequences*. Cambridge: Polity, 1998.

Bew, Paul and Gordon Gillespie, eds. *Northern Ireland: A Chronology of the Troubles*. Dublin: Gill & Macmillan, 1999.

Bhabha, Homi. *The Location of Culture*. London: Routledge, 1994.

Blight, David W. 'No Desperate Hero: Manhood and Freedom in a Union Soldier's Experience', in *Divided Houses: Gender and Civil War*, ed. Elizabeth Clinton. Oxford: Oxford University Press, 1992: 55–75.

Boland, Eavan. *Object Lessons: The Life of the Woman and the Poet in Our Time*. London: Vintage, 1996.

—— *The Lost Land*. Manchester: Carcanet, 1998.

Bolger, Dermot, ed. *The Bright Wave / An Tonn Gheal: Poetry in Irish Now*. Dublin: Raven Arts Press, 1986.

—— *Druids, Dudes and Beauty Queens: The Changing Face of Irish Theatre*. Dublin: New Island, 2001.

—— and Kazem Shahryary. *Départ et Arrivée*. Paris: L'Harmattan, 2004.

Bolton, Jonathan. ' "Customary rhythms": Seamus Heaney and the Rite of Poetry', *Papers on Language and Literature* 37/2 (spring 2001): 205–22.

Böss, Michael and Eamon Maher, eds. *Engaging Modernity: Readings of Irish Politics, Culture and Literature at the Turn of the Century*. Dublin: Veritas, 2003.

Bourke, Angela, Siobhán Kilfeather, Maria Luddy, Margaret MacCurtain, Gerardine Meaney, Máirin Ní Dhonnchadha, Mary O'Dowd and Clair Wills, eds. *The Field Day Anthology of Irish Writing, Vols 4 and 5: Irish Women's Writings and Traditions*. Cork: Cork University Press, 2002.

Bourke, Bernadette. 'Carr's "cut-throats and gargiyles": Grotesque and Carnivalesque Elements in *By the Bog of Cats . . .*', in *The Theatre of Marina Carr: 'before rules was made'*, ed. Cathy Leeney and Anna McMullan. Dublin: Carysfort Press, 2003: 128–44.

Bourke, Richard. *Peace in Ireland: The War of Ideas*. London: Pimlico, 2003.

Bowcott, Owen. 'A Boom Too Far', *The Guardian*, 21 May 2007, 17.

Boyle, Kevin and Tom Hadden. *Ireland: A Positive Proposal*. London: Penguin, 1985.

Bradley, Anthony and Maryann Gialanella Valiulis, eds. Introduction to *Gender and Sexuality in Modern Ireland*. Amherst: University of Massachusetts Press, 1997: 1–7.

Brady, Ciaran, ed. *Interpreting Irish History: The Debate on Historical Revisionism, 1938–1994*. Dublin: Irish Academic Press, 1994.

Brearton, Fran. *The Great War in Irish Poetry*. Oxford: Oxford University Press, 2000.

Breen, John. *Charlie*. Unpublished script, 2003.

Breen, Michael and Eoin Devereux. 'Setting up Margins: Public Attitudes and Media Construction of Poverty and Exclusion in Ireland', *Nordic Irish Studies* 2/1 (2003): 75–94.

Brooks, Peter. *The Melodramatic Imagination: Balzac, Henry James, Melodrama and the Mode of Excess*. New Haven, CT: Yale University Press, 1976.

Brown, John, ed. *Magnetic North: The Emerging Poets*. Derry: Verbal Arts Centre, 2005.

Brown, Terence. *Ireland. A Social and Cultural History: 1922–2002*. London: Harper, 2004.

Butler, Judith. 'Performative Acts and Gender Constitution', in *Literary Theory: An Anthology*, ed. Julie Rivkin and Michael Ryan, second edition. London: Blackwell, 2004: 900–11.

Cairns, David and Shaun Richards, *Writing Ireland: Colonialism, Nationalism and Culture*. Manchester: Manchester University Press, 1988.

Calhoun, Ada. 'Fiction Chronicle', *New York Times*, 14 August 2005 (www.nytimes.com, accessed 13 December 2006).

Carey, John. 'Resurrection Man', *The Times*, 25 March 2006.

Carlson, Marvin. *Performance: A Critical Introduction*. London and New York: Routledge, 1996.

Carr, Marina. *By the Bog of Cats.* . . . Oldcastle: Gallery Press, 1999.

—— *Ariel*. Oldcastle: Gallery Press, 2002.

Carson, Ciaran. *The Irish for No*. Oldcastle: Gallery Press, 1987.

—— *Last Night's Fun*. London: Cape, 1996.

—— *The Star Factory*. London: Granta, 1997.

—— *Fishing for Amber*. London: Granta, 1999.

—— *Shamrock Tea*. London: Granta, 2001.

Carsten, Janet and Stephen Hugh-Jones, eds. *About the House: Levi-Strauss and Beyond*. Cambridge: Cambridge University Press, 1995.

Caruth, Cathy. *Trauma: Explorations in Memory*. Baltimore, MD: Johns Hopkins University Press, 1995.

Cerquoni, Enrica. ' "One Bog, Many Bogs": Theatrical Space, Visual Image, and Meaning in Some Productions of Marina Carr's *By the Bog of Cats . . .*', in *The Theatre of Marina Carr: 'before rules was made'*, ed. Cathy Leeney and Anna McMullan. Dublin: Carysfort Press, 2003: 72–99.

Christov-Bakargiev, Carolyn and Caoimhín Mac Giolla Léith, eds. *Willie Doherty: False Memory*. London: Merrell, 2002.

Cleary, Joe. 'Modernization and Aesthetic Ideology in Contemporary Irish Culture', in *Writing in the Irish Republic: Literature, Culture and Politics 1949–1999*, ed. Ray Ryan. Basingstoke: Macmillan, 2000: 105–29.

—— *Literature, Partition and the Nation-State: Culture and Conflict in Ireland, Israel and Palestine*. Cambridge: Cambridge University Press, 2002.

—— 'Misplaced Ideas? Colonialism, Location and Dislocation in Irish Studies', in *Theorising Ireland*, ed. Claire Connolly. London: Palgrave, 2002: 91–104.

—— *Outrageous Fortune: Capital and Culture in Modern Ireland*. Dublin: Field Day, 2006.

—— 'The World Literary System: Atlas and Epitaph', *Field Day Review*, 2 (2006): 197–219.

Clifton, Harry. 'A Visitor from the Future', in *The Faber Book of Best New Irish Short Stories 2006–7*, ed. David Marcus. London: Faber, 2007.

Collins, Lucy. ' "Why Didn't They Ask the Others": Resisting Disclosure in the Poetry of Eiléan Ní Chuilleanáin', *Engaging Modernity*, ed. Michael Boss and Eamon Maher. Dublin: Veritas, 2003.

Connolly, Claire. 'Postcolonial Ireland: Introducing the Question', *European Journal of English Studies*, 3/3 (December 1999): 255–61.

—— ed. *Theorising Ireland*. London: Palgrave, 2002.

Conrad, Kathryn A. *Locked in the Family Cell: Gender, Sexuality and Political Agency in Irish National Discourse*. Madison: University of Wisconsin Press, 2004.

Conway, Martin A. 'Past and Present: Recovered Memories and False Memories', in *Recovered Memories and False Memories*, ed. Martin A. Conway. Oxford: Oxford University Press, 1997.

Corcoran, Neil. 'Seamus Heaney and the Art of the Exemplary', *The Yearbook of English Studies*, 17 (1987): 117–27.

—— *After Yeats and Joyce: Reading Modern Irish Literature*. Oxford: Oxford University Press, 1997.

Craig, Cairns. *The Modern Scottish Novel: Narrative and the National Imagination*. Edinburgh: Edinburgh University Press, 1999.

Cronin, Michael. 'Speed Limits: Ireland, Globalisation and the War against Time', in *Reinventing Ireland: Culture, Society and the Global Economy*, ed. Peadar Kirby, Luke Gibbons and Michael Cronin. London: Pluto, 2002: 54–66.

—— 'The Unbidden Ireland: Materialism, Knowledge and Interculturality', *The Irish Review*, 31 (2004): 3–10.

—— and Barbara O'Connor. 'From Gombeen to Gubeen: Tourism, Identity and Class in Ireland, 1949–99', in *Writing in the Irish Republic: Literature, Culture and Politics 1949–1999*, ed. Ray Ryan. Basingstoke: Macmillan, 2000: 165–84.

Daly, Nicholas. 'From Elvis to the Fugitive: Globalisation and Recent Irish Cinema', *European Journal of English Studies*, 'Postcolonial Ireland?' 3/3 (December 1999): 262–74.

Davey, Frank. *Postnational Arguments: The Politics of the Anglophone-Canadian Novel since 1967*. Toronto: University of Toronto Press, 1993.

Davis, Alex, John Goodby, Andrew Hadfield and Eve Patten, eds. *Irish Studies: The Essential Glossary*. London: Arnold, 2003.

Davy, Kate. 'Fe/male Impersonation: The Discourse of Camp', in *Critical Theory and Performance*, ed. Janelle G. Reinelt and Joseph R. Roach. Ann Arbor: University of Michigan Press, 1992: 231–46.

Deane, Seamus. *Celtic Revivals: Essays in Modern Irish Literature 1880–1980*. London: Faber, 1985.

—— ed. *Nationalism, Colonialism and Literature*. Minneapolis: University of Minnesota Press, 1990.

—— 'Autobiography and Memoirs 1890–1988', in *The Field Day Anthology of Irish Writing*, ed. Seamus Deane. Derry: Field Day, 1991, vol. 3: 380–3.

—— review of Terry Eagleton, *Heathcliff and the Great Hunger*, *London Review of Books*, 19 October 1995, 28.

—— *Reading in the Dark*. London: Vintage, 1997.

Delanty, Gerard. 'Irish Political Community in Transition', *The Irish Review*, 33 (2005): 13–22.

De Paor, Louis. 'Contemporary Poetry in Irish: 1940–200', in *The Cambridge History of Irish Literature*, ed. Margartet Kelleher and Philip O'Leary. Cambridge: Cambridge University Press, 2006.

Dickinson, Emily. Poem 712, *Final Harvest: Emily Dickinson's Poems*. Boston, Toronto: Little, Brown and Company, 1961: 177–8.

Doherty, Willie. 'Like Home'. Interview by Joan Rothfuss, in *No Place (Like Home)*, ed. Zarina Bhimji et al. Minneapolis: Walker Art Center, 1997.

Dolan, Jill. 'Gender Impersonation Onstage: Destroying or Maintaining the Mirror of Gender Roles?' *Women and Performance: A Journal of Feminist Theory*, 2 (1985): 5–11.

Donoghue, Emma. *Ladies and Gentlemen*. Dublin: New Island Books, 1998.

Doyle, Maria, 'Dead Center: Tragedy and the Reanimated Body in Marina Carr's *The Mai* and *Portia Coughlan*', *Modern Drama*, 49/1 (spring 2006): 41–59.

Doyle, Roddy. *The Commitments*. London: Penguin, 1995.

—— *The Woman Who Walked Into Doors*. New York: Viking, 1996.

—— *Paula Spencer*. New York: Viking, 2006.

—— 'Green Yodel No.1', in *Re-Imagining Ireland*, ed. Andrew Higgins Wyndham, Charlottesville, VA: University of Virginia Press, 2006: 69–71.

Duncan, Dawn. *Postcolonial Theory in Irish Drama from 1800–2000*. Lewiston, Queenston, Lampeter: Edwin Mellen, 2004.

Durcan, Paul. *Greetings to Our Friends in Brazil*. London: Harvill, 1999.

Durden, Mark. ' "The Poetics of Absence": Photography in the "Aftermath" of War', in *Hidden*. London: The Imperial War Museum, 2003: n.p.

Eagleton, Terry. *Heathcliff and the Great Hunger: Studies in Irish Culture*. London: Verso, 1995.

Eldred, Laura G. 'Francie Pig vs. the Fat Green Blob from Outer Space: Horror Films and *The Butcher Boy*', *New Hibernia Review*, 10/3 (2006).

Eliot, T.S. *The Complete Poems and Plays of T.S. Eliot*. London: Faber, 1969.

Elliott, Marianne, ed. *The Long Road to Peace*. Liverpool: Liverpool University Press, 2002.

English, Richard. *The Armed Struggle: A History of the IRA*. London: Macmillan, 2003.

Enright, Anne. *What Are You Like?* London: Jonathan Cape, 2000.

Evanson, E. *Hidden Violence: A Study of Battered Women in Northern Ireland*. Belfast: Farset Press, 1982.

Ezrahi, Sidra DeKoven. *By Words Alone: The Holocaust in Literature*. Chicago: The University of Chicago Press, 1982.

Fallon, Peter and Derek Mahon, eds. *The Penguin Book of Contemporary Irish Poetry*, London: Penguin, 1990.

Fanning, Bryan. *Racism and Social Change in the Republic of Ireland*. Manchester: Manchester University Press, 2002.

Feldman, Allen. 'Retaliate and Punish: Political Violence as Form and Memory in Northern Ireland', *Éire-Ireland* (summer 1998): 195–235.

Finlay, Andrew. 'Irish Studies, Cultural Pluralism and the Peace Process', *Irish Studies Review*, 15/2 (August 2007): 333–46.

Fitzgerald, Penelope. 'Bringers of Ill Luck and Bad Weather', *London Review of Books*, 2 March 2000, 8.

Fitzpatrick, Lisa. 'Metanarratives: Anne Devlin, Christina Reid, Marina Carr, and the Irish Dramatic Repertory', *Irish University Review*, 35/2 (autumn/ winter 2005): 320–33.

Flynn, Leontia. *These Days*. London: Cape, 2004.

Foster, John Wilson. 'The Critical Condition of Ulster', in *Critical Approaches to Anglo-Irish Literature*, ed. Michael Allen and Angela Wilcox. Gerrards Cross: Colin Smythe, 1989: 86–102.

Foster, R.F. *The Irish Story: Telling Tales and Making It Up in Ireland*. Harmondsworth: Penguin, 2002.

—— *Luck and the Irish: A Brief History of Change 1970–2000*. London: Allen Lane, 2007.

Freud, Sigmund. *Beyond the Pleasure Principle*, trans. and ed. James Strachey. New York: W.W. Norton, 1990.

—— 'Remembering, Repeating and Working Through', *The Penguin Freud Reader*, ed. Adam Phillips. Harmondsworth: Penguin, 2006.

Fricker, Karen. Review of *Charlie*, *The Guardian*, 25 April 2003, 10.

Friel, Brian. *The Communication Cord*. Oldcastle: Gallery Press, 1989.

—— *Dancing at Lughnasa*. London: Faber, 1990.

—— *The Home Place*. Oldcastle: Gallery Press, 2005.

Furay, Julia and Redmond O'Hanlon, eds. *Critical Moments: Fintan O'Toole on Modern Irish Theatre*. Dublin: Carysfort Press, 2003.

Gardiner, Juliet and Neil Wenborn, eds. *The History Today Companion to British History*. London: Collins and Brown, 1995.

Garner, Stanton B. *Bodied Spaces: Phenomenology and Performance in Contemporary Drama*. Ithaca, NY and London: Cornell University Press, 1994.

Garner, Steve. 'Guests of the Nation', *Irish Review*, 33 (2005): 78–84.

Garratt, Robert F. 'John McGahern's *Amongst Women*: Representation, Memory and Trauma', *Irish University Review*, 35/1 (spring/summer 2005): 121–35.

Gauthier, Tim. 'Identity, Self-Loathing and the Neocolonial Condition in Patrick McCabe's *The Butcher Boy*', *Critique* 44/2 (winter 2003): 196–211.

Gibbons, Luke. *Transformations in Irish Culture*. Cork: Cork University Press / Field Day, 1996.

—— 'Narratives of the Nation: Fact, Fiction and Irish Cinema', in *Theorising Ireland*, ed. Claire Connolly. London: Palgrave, 2002: 69–75.

—— 'The Global Cure? History, Therapy and the Celtic Tiger', in *Reinventing Ireland: Culture, Society and the Global Economy*, ed. Peadar Kirby, Luke Gibbons and Michael Cronin. London: Pluto, 2002: 89–106.

—— 'Beyond the Pale: Race, Ethnicity, and Irish Culture', in *Re-Imagining Ireland*, ed. Andrew Higgins Wyndham. Charlottesville: University of Virginia Press, 2006.

Gillis, Alan. *Somebody, Somewhere*. Oldcastle: Gallery Press, 2004.

Gilsenan-Nordin, Irene. '"Betwixt and Between": The Body as Liminal Threshold in the Poetry of Eiléan Ní Chuilleanáin', in *Metaphors of the Body and Desire in Contemporary Irish Poetry*, ed. Irene Gilsenan-Nordin. Dublin: Irish Academic Press, 2006: 224–42.

Ging, Debbie. 'Screening the Green: Cinema under the Celtic Tiger', in *Reinventing Ireland: Culture, Society and the Global Economy*, ed. Peadar Kirby, Luke Gibbons and Michael Cronin. London: Pluto, 2002: 177–95.

Ginzburg, Eugenia Semyonovna. *Journey into the Whirlwind*, trans. Paul Stevenson and Max Hayward, second edition. San Diego: Harcourt, 1995.

Gordon, Lewis R. 'A Questioning Body of Laughter and Tears', *Parallax* 8/2 (2002): 10–29.

Gormley, John. 'The Celtic Tiger', *Resurgence*, 200 (May/June 2000): www.resurgence.org/resurgence/issues/gormley200.htm.

Graham, Colin. ' "Liminal Spaces": Post-Colonial Theories and Irish Culture', *The Irish Review*, 16 (1994): 29–43.

—— *Deconstructing Ireland: Identity, Theory, Culture*. Edinburgh: Edinburgh University Press, 1999.

—— ' "Let's Get Killed": Culture and Peace in Northern Ireland', in *Irish Postmodernisms and Popular Culture*, ed. Wanda Balzano, Anne Mulhall and Moynagh Sullivan. Basingstoke: Palgrave, 2007.

—— and Richard Kirkland, eds. *Ireland and Cultural Theory: The Mechanics of Authenticity*. Houndmills: Macmillan, 1998.

Gray, Breda. 'Transnational Negotiations of Migrancy', *Irish Studies Review*, 14/2 (May 2006): 208.

Grene, Nicholas. 'Black Pastoral: 1990s Images of Ireland', *Litteraria Pragensia*, 20: 10 (2000): 67–75.

Grennan, Eamonn. ' "Only What Happens": Mulling Over McGahern', *Irish University Review*, 35/1 (spring/summer 2005): 13–27.

Griffith, Arthur. *United Irishman*, 13 January 1904.

Groarke, Vona. *Shale*. Oldcastle: Gallery Press, 1994.

—— *Other People's Houses*. Oldcastle: Gallery Press, 1999.

—— *Flight*. Oldcastle: Gallery Press, 2002.

—— *Juniper Street*. Oldcastle: Gallery Press, 2006.

Grunert, Andrea. 'Emotion and Cognition: About Some Key-Figures in Films by Alan Clarke', n.d.: www.artbrain.org/journal2/grunert.html.

Guinness, Selima, ed. *The New Irish Poets*. Newcastle-upon-Tyne: Bloodaxe, 2004.

Hamilton, Hugo. *The Speckled People*. London: Fourth Estate, 2003.

—— *The Sailor in the Wardrobe*. London: Fourth Estate, 2006.

Hand, Brian. 'Swerved in Naught', *Circa*, 76 (1996): 22.

Hardy, Thomas. *The Complete Poems*. London: Palgrave, 2001.

Harris, Geraldine. *Staging Femininities: Performance and Performativity*. Manchester: Manchester University Press, 1999.

Harte, Liam. ' "Somewhere beyond England and Ireland": Narratives of "Home" in Second-generation Irish Autobiography', *Irish Studies Review*, 11/3 (2003): 293–305.

—— *Modern Irish Autobiography: Self, Nation and Society*, London: Palgrave Macmillan, 2007.

—— and Michael Parker, eds. *Contemporary Irish Fiction: Themes, Tropes, Theories*. Basingstoke: Macmillan, 2000.

Hartnett, Michael. *Inchicore Haiku*. Dublin: Raven Arts Press, 1985.

Haslam, Richard. ' "The Pose Arranged and Lingered Over": Visualizing the "Troubles" ' in *Contemporary Irish Fiction: Themes, Tropes, Theories*, ed. Liam Harte and Michael Parker. Basingstoke: Macmillan, 2000: 192–212.

Haverty, Anne. *The Free and Easy*. London: Chatto & Windus, 2006.

Healy, Dermot. *The Bend for Home*. London: Harvill, 1996.

Heaney, Seamus. *Death of a Naturalist*. London: Faber, 1966.

—— *Wintering Out*. London: Faber, 1972.

—— *North*. London: Faber, 1975.

—— *Stations*. Belfast: Ulsterman Publications, 1975.

—— *Preoccupations: Selected Prose 1968–1978*. London: Faber, 1980.

—— *Station Island*. London: Faber, 1984.

—— *The Haw Lantern*. London: Faber, 1987.

—— *The Government of the Tongue*. London: Faber, 1988.

—— *Seeing Things*. London: Faber, 1991.

—— *The Spirit Level*. London: Faber, 1995.

—— *Crediting Poetry*. Oldcastle: Gallery Press, 1995.

—— *The Redress of Poetry: Oxford Lectures*. London: Faber, 1995.

—— *Beowulf. A New Translation*. London: Faber, 1999.

—— *Electric Light*. London: Faber, 2001.

—— *Finders Keepers: Selected Prose*. London: Faber, 2002.

—— *Us* as in *Versus*: Poetry and the World. *When Hope and History Rhyme: The NUI, Galway, Millennium Lecture Series*. Dublin: Four Courts Press, 2002.

—— *Talking with Poets*, ed. Harry Thomas. New York: Handsell Books, 2002.

—— 'One Poet in Search of a Title', *The Times*, 25 March 2006.

—— *District and Circle*. London: Faber, 2006.

Heidegger, Martin. 'Building Dwelling Thinking', in *Basic Writings*, ed. David Farrell Krell. London: Routledge, 1993.

Hennessey, Thomas. *The Northern Ireland Peace Process*. Basingstoke: Palgrave, 2001.

Hesford, Wendy S. 'Documenting Violations: Rhetorical Witnessing and the Spectacle of Distant Suffering', *Biography*, 27/1 (winter 2004): 104–45.

Shane Hickey and John Spain. 'Politics and the Arts pay homage to "Voice of a Generation" ', *Irish Independent* (31 March 2006): 10.

Higgins, Roisin. ' "A Drift of Chosen Females": *The Field Day Anthology of Irish Writing*, Vols 4 and 5', *Irish University Review*, 33/2 (autumn/winter 2003): 400–6.

Hill, Tobias. 'Arms Around The World', *Observer*, 2 April 2006.

Horsley, Lee. *The Noir Thriller*. Basingstoke: Palgrave, 2001.

Horton, Patricia. ' "Absent from Home: Family, Community and National Identity in Patrick McCabe's *The Butcher Boy*', *Irish Journal of Feminist Studies*, 3/1 (December 1998): 75–93.

Hughes, Declan. 'Who The Hell Do We Think We Still Are? Reflections on Irish Theatre and Identity,' in *Theatre Stuff: Critical Essays on Contemporary Irish Theatre*, ed. Eamon Jordan. Dublin: Carysfort, 2000: 8–15.

Hughes, Eamonn. 'To Define Your Dissent: The Plays and Polemics of the Field Day Theatre Company', *Theatre Research International*, 15/1 (spring 1990): 67–77.

—— ' "All That Surrounds Our Life": Time, Sex, and Death in *That They May Face the Rising Sun*', *Irish University Review*, 35/1 (spring/summer 2005): 147–63.

—— 'Limbo', *The Irish Review*, 33 (2005): 138–41.

Hutcheon, Linda. *The Politics of Postmodernism*. London: Routledge, 1989.

Hynes, Garry. 'Accepting the Fiction of being National', *Irish Times* (3 May 1993): 12.

—— interviewed by Cathy Leeney, *Theatre Talk: Voices of Irish Theatre Practitioners*. Dublin: Carysfort, 2001: 195–219.

Inglish, Tom. 'Of Irish Prudery: Sexuality and Social Control in Modern Ireland', *Éire-Ireland*, 40/3&4 (fall/winter 2005): 9–37.

Inwood, Michael. *Heidegger: A Very Short Introduction*. Oxford: Oxford University Press, 2000.

Irish Council for International Students. *The Irish Are Friendly but . . . : A Report on Racism and International Students and Racism in Ireland*. Dublin, 1998.

Jaar, Alfredo. *Lament of the Images*, ed. Debra Bricker Balken. Massachusetts: MIT, 1999.

Jackson, Alvin. *Ireland 1798–1998*. Oxford: Blackwell, 1999.

James, Stephen. 'Seamus Heaney's Sway', *Twentieth Century Literature*, 2/3 (fall 2005): 263–84.

Jameson, Fredric. *Modernism and Imperialism*. Cork: Field Day, 1988.

—— *The Geopolitical Aesthetic: Cinema and Space in the World System*. Bloomington: Indiana University Press, 1992.

Jarniewicz, Jerzy. *The Bottomless Centre. The Uses of History in the Poetry of Seamus Heaney*. Łódź: Łódź University Press, 2002.

—— 'After Babel. Translation and Mistranslation in Contemporary British Poetry', *European Journal of English Studies: The New Poetics*, 6:1 (2002): 87–104.

Jeffers, Jennifer M. *The Irish Novel at the End of the Twentieth Century: Gender, Bodies, and Power*. New York: Palgrave, 2002.

Johnson, Nuala C. 'The Cartographies of Violence: Belfast's *Resurrection Man*', *Environment and Planning D: Society and Space*, 17 (1999): 723–36.

Johnston, Dillon. ' "Our bodies' eyes and writing hands": Secrecy and Sensuality in Eiléan Ní Chuilleanáin's Baroque Art', in *Gender and Sexuality in Modern Ireland*, ed. Anthony Bradley and Maryann Gialanella Valiulis. Amherst: University of Massachusetts Press, 1997: 187–211.

Jordan, Eamon, ed. *Theatre Stuff: Critical Essays on Contemporary Irish Theatre* Dublin: Carysfort, 2000.

Joyce, James. Letter to Arthur Power, quoted in Richard Ellmann, *James Joyce*, Oxford: Oxford University Press, 1983.

—— *A Portrait of the Artist as a Young Man*, ed. Seamus Deane. London: Penguin, 1992.

Karron, Robert. "What Are You Like?", *Boston Review*: http://bostonreview. mit.edu/BR25.5/karron.html (accessed on 5 February 2003).

Kearney, Richard, ed. *Across the Frontiers: Ireland in the 1990s*. Dublin: Merlin, 1988.

—— *Postnationalist Ireland: Politics, Culture, Philosophy*. London: Routledge, 1997.

—— *On Stories*. London: Routledge, 2002.

Keena, Colm. 'When Fact Replaced Rumour', *Irish Times*, 14 July 2006, 8.

—— 'Living Beyond his Means', *Irish Times*, 14 July 2006, 9.

Kelly, Aaron. '"A Stasis of Hatred, Fear and Mistrust": The Politics of Form in Representations of Northern Ireland Produced by the "Troubles" Thriller', in *New Voices in Irish Criticism*, Ed. P.J. Mathews. Dublin: Four Courts, 2000: 109–15.

—— 'Reproblematizing the Irish Text', in *Critical Ireland: New Essays in Literature and Culture*, ed. Aaron Kelly and Alan A. Gillis. Dublin: Four Courts, 2001: 124–32.

—— *The Thriller and Northern Ireland Since 1969: Utterly Resigned Terror*. Edinburgh: Ashgate, 2005.

Kennedy, Liam. 'Modern Ireland: Post-colonial Society or Post-colonial Pretensions?' *The Irish Review*, 13 (1992–93): 107–21.

—— *Colonialism, Religion and Nationalism in Ireland*. Belfast: Institute of Irish Studies, 1996.

Kennedy-Andrews, Elmer. 'Antic Dispositions in Some Recent Irish Fiction', in *Last Before America: Irish and American Writing*, ed. Fran Brearton and Eamonn Hughes, Belfast: Blackstaff Press, 2001.

—— *Fiction and the Northern Ireland Troubles since 1969: (De-)constructing the North*. Dublin: Four Courts Press, 2003.

Kennelly, Brendan. *The Book of Judas*, Newcastle-upon-Tyne: Bloodaxe Books, 1991.

Kiberd, Declan. *Inventing Ireland*. London: Jonathan Cape, 1995.

—— 'Dancing at Lughnasa', *The Irish Review*, 27 (summer 2001): 18–39.

—— *The Irish Writer and the World*. Cambridge: Cambridge University Press, 2005.

Kilfeather, Siobhán. 'Irish Feminism', in *The Cambridge Companion to Modern Irish Culture*, ed. Joe Cleary and Claire Connolly. Cambridge: Cambridge University Press, 2005: 96–116.

Kilroy, Tom. 'A Generation of Playwrights', in *Theatre Stuff: Critical Essays on Contemporary Irish Theatre*. Dublin: Carysfort, 2000: 1–7.

King, Jason. 'Interculturalism and Irish Theatre: The Portrayal of Immigrants on the Irish Stage', *The Irish Review*, 33 (2005): 23–39.

Kinsella, Michael A. 'There-You-are-and-Where-are-You', *PN Review* (July–August 2001): 53–4.

Kirby, Peadar. 'Contested Pedigrees of the Celtic Tiger', in *Reinventing Ireland: Culture, Society and the Global Economy*, ed. Peadar Kirby, Luke Gibbons and Michael Cronin. London: Pluto, 2002: 21–37.

——, Luke Gibbons and Michael Cronin, eds. *Reinventing Ireland: Culture, Society and the Global Economy*. London: Pluto, 2002.

Kirkland, Richard. *Literature and Culture in Northern Ireland Since 1965: Moments of Danger*. London: Longman, 1996.

—— 'The Spectacle of Terrorism in Northern Irish Culture', *Critical Survey*, 15/1 (2003): 77–90.

Knight, Peter. *Conspiracy Culture: From Kennedy to the X Files*. London: Routledge, 2000.

Knight, Stephen. 'District and Circle: The bog man cometh (again)', *Independent*, 9 April 2006.

Kostick, Conor and Katherine Moore, eds. *Irish Writers Against War*. Dublin: O'Brien Press, 2003.

Kurdi, Mária. 'Interview with Marina Carr', *Modern Filologiai Kozlemenyek*, 5/2 (2003): 94–100.

—— ' "Really All Danger": An Interview with Sebastian Barry', *New Hibernia Review*, 8/1 (2004): 41–53.

Kuti, Elizabeth. *Treehouses*. London: Methuen, 2000.

Laird, Nick. *To A Fault*. London: Faber, 2005.

—— *Utterly Monkey*. London: Harper, 2005.

Law, Jules David. 'Joyce's "Delicate Siamese" Equation: The Dialectic of Home in *Ulysses*', *PMLA*, 102/2 (March 1987): 197–205.

Leeney, Cathy. 'Marina Carr', in *The UCD Aesthetic: Celebrating 150 Years of UCD Writers*, ed. Anthony Roche. Dublin: New Island Press, 2005: 265–73.

Leersen, Joep. '1798: The Recurrence of Violence and Two Conceptualisations of History', *Irish Review*, 22 (1998): 37–45.

Leith, Sam. 'Return of the Naturalist', *Daily Telegraph*, 2 April 2006.

Lentin, Ronit. 'Black Bodies and Headless Hookers: Alternative Global Narratives for 21st Century Ireland', *The Irish Review*, 33 (2005): 1–12.

Levitas, Ben. *The Theatre of Nation: Irish Drama and Cultural Nationalism 1890–1916*. Oxford: Oxford University Press, 2002.

Linehan, Hugh. 'Myth, Mammon and Mediocrity: The Trouble with Recent Irish Cinema', *Cineaste*, 24:2–3, Contemporary Irish Cinema Supplement (1999): 46–9.

Longley, Edna. *The Living Stream: Literature and Revisionism in Ireland*. Newcastle–upon–Tyne: Bloodaxe, 1994.

—— 'Autobiography as History', *Fortnight*, November 1996, 34.

—— *Poetry and Posterity*. Newcastle-upon-Tyne: Bloodaxe, 2000.

Longley, Michael. *Selected Poems*. London: Cape Poetry, 1998.

Logue, Paddy, ed. *Being Irish: Personal Reflections on Irish Identity today*. Dublin: Oak Tree, 2000.

Lynch, Vivian Valvano. 'Seamus Deane's *Reading in the Dark* Yields "a door into the light" ', *Working Papers in Irish Studies*, 3 (2000): 16–22.

McAleese, Mary. 'Speeches: Messines Peace Tower, Belgium', *Irish President's Website*, 11 November 1998: www.president.ie (accessed 2 August 2007).

McCabe, Patrick. *Winterwood*. London: Bloomsbury, 2006.

McCrum, Robert. 'From Cattle to Battle', *Observer*, 2 April 2006.

McDonald, Henry. 'Blair's last-ditch deal saved Irish talks', 15 October 2006: http://politics.guardian.co.uk/northernirelandassembly/story/0,,1922980,00.html.

—— 'Ahern Comes out Fighting at Anti-corruption Tribunal', *The Guardian*, 14 September 2007, 26.

McDonald, Marianne. 'Classics as Celtic Firebrand: Greek Tragedy, Irish Playwrights, and Colonialism', in *Theatre Stuff: Critical Essays on Contemporary Irish Theatre*, ed. Eamon Jordan. Dublin: Carysfort, 2000: 16–26.

—— ed. with J. Michael Walton. *Amid Our Troubles: Irish Versions of Greek Tragedy*. London: Methuen, 2002.

McDonald, Peter. 'The Clutch of Earth', *Literary Review*, April 2006.

MacFarlane, Robert. 'Separated at Birth', *Times Literary Supplement*, 3 March 2000, 21.

McGahern, John. *Amongst Women*. London: Faber, 1990.

—— *That They May Face the Rising Sun*. London: Faber, 2002.

—— *Memoir*. London: Faber, 2005.

—— 'What is My Language', *Irish University Review*, 35/1 (spring/summer 2005): 5–6.

McGuckian, Medbh. *Had I a Thousand Lives*. Oldcastle: Gallery Press, 2003.

McIlroy, Brian. *Shooting to Kill: Filmmaking and the 'Troubles' in Northern Ireland*. Richmond: Steveston Press, 2001.

McKenzie, John L. *Dictionary of the Bible*. London: Chapman, 1968.

McKittrick, David, Seamus Kelters, Brian Feeney, Chris Thornton and David McVea. *Lost Lives: The Stories of the Men, Women And Children Who Died as a Result of the Northern Ireland Troubles*. Edinburgh: Mainstream Publishing, 2007.

—— and John McVea. *Making Sense of the Troubles*. London: Penguin, 2001.

MacLaverty, Bernard. *The Anatomy School*. London: Jonathan Cape, 2001.

McMillan, Joyce. 'Ireland's Winning Hand', *Irish Theatre Magazine*, 3/15 (2003): 16–18.

McMullan, Anna. 'Reclaiming Performance: The Contemporary Irish Independent Theatre Sector', in *The State of Play: Irish Theatre in the 'Nineties*, ed. Eberhard Bort. Trier: Wissenschaftlicher Verlag Trier, 1996: 29–38.

—— '"In touch with some otherness": Gender, Authority and the Body in *Dancing at Lughnasa*', *Irish University Review*, 29/1 (spring/summer 1999): 90–100.

—— 'Gender, Authorship and Performance in *Selected Plays by Contemporary Irish Women Playwrights*: Mary Elizabeth Burke-Kennedy, Marie Jones, Marina Carr, Emma Donoghue', in *Theatre Stuff: Critical Essays on Contemporary Irish Theatre*, ed. Eamon Jordan. Dublin: Carysfort, 2000: 34–46.

—— 'Unhomely Stages: Women Taking (a) Place in Irish Theatre', in *Druids, Dudes and Beauty Queens: The Changing Face of Irish Theatre*, ed. Dermot Bolger. Dublin: New Island, 2001: 72–90.

—— 'Unhomely Bodies and Dislocated Identities in the Drama of Frank McGuinness and Marina Carr', in *Indeterminate Bodies*, ed. Naomi Segal, Lib Taylor and Roger Cook. London: Palgrave, 2003: 181–91.

McNamee, Eoin. *Resurrection Man*. London: Picador, 1994.

—— *The Blue Tango*. London: Faber, 2001.

—— *The Ultras*. London: Faber and Faber, 2004.

MacNeice, Louis. *Collected Poems*, ed. E.R. Dodds [1966]. London: Faber, 1979.

McSweeney, Kerry. 'Literary Allusion and the Poetry of Seamus Heaney', *Style* 33/1 (spring 1999): 130–43.

Madden, Deirdre. *One by One in the Darkness*. London: Faber, 1996.

Maharaj, Sarat. 'Rita Donagh: Towards a Map of Her Artwork'. *197419841994: Paintings and Drawings*. Manchester: Cornerhouse, 1995.

Mahon, Derek. Foreword to Harry Clifton's *The Desert Route*. Oldcastle: Gallery Press, 1992.

Maley, Willy. 'Nationalism and Revisionism: Ambiviolences and Dissensus', in *Ireland in Proximity: History, Gender, Space*, ed. Scott Brewster, Virginia Crossman, Fiona Becket and David Alderson. London: Routledge, 1999: 12–27.

Marlowe, Lara. 'Lost in translation', *The Irish Times*, 17 November 2004, 14.

Meaney, Helen. Review of Elizabeth Kuti, *The Sugar Wife*, *Irish Theatre Magazine*, 5/23 (2005): 89–93.

Meehan, Paula. *Mysteries of the Home*. Newcastle-upon-Tyne: Bloodaxe, 1996.

—— *Dharmakaya*. Manchester: Carcanet, 2000.

Merriman, Victor. 'Cartographic Connections: Problems of Representation in Calypso Theatre Company's The Business of Blood', *The Irish Review*, 22 (summer 1998): 28–36.

—— 'Songs of Possible Worlds: Nation, Representation and Citizenship in the Work of Calypso Productions', in *Theatre Stuff: Critical Essays on Contemporary Irish Theatre*, ed. Eamon Jordan. Dublin: Carysfort, 2000: 280–91.

—— 'Settling for More : Excess and Success in Contemporary Irish Drama', in *Druids, Dudes and Beauty Queens: The Changing Face of Irish Theatre*, ed. Dermot Bolger. Dublin: New Island, 2001: 55–71.

Miller, Karl. *Seamus Heaney in Conversation with Karl Miller*. London: BTL, 2000.

Moloney, Ed and Andy Pollak. *Paisley*. Dublin: Poolbeg, 1986.

Moore, Caroline. 'The Parochial Pleasures of Famous Seamus', *Telegraph*, 9 April 2006.

Morash, Christopher. *A History of Irish Theatre 1601–2002*, Cambridge: Cambridge University Press, 2002.

Morrison, Blake. *Independent on Sunday*, 1 September 1996.

Morrison, David E. 'The Idea of Violence', in *Violence in Factual Television: Annual Review*, ed. Andrea Millwood Hargrave. London: John Libbey, 1993.

Morrissey, Sinéad. *There Was Fire in Vancouver*, Manchester: Carcanet, 1996.

—— Interview with Annamay McKernan, *Tatler Woman*, 24 June 2002: www.carcanet.co.uk/cgi-bin/reframe.cgi?app=cipher&index=author.

Motion, Andrew. 'Digging Deep', *The Guardian*, 1 April 2006.

Moxley, Gina. *Danti Dan*, in *The Dazzling Dark*, ed. Frank McGuinness. London: Faber, 1996: 1–74.

Mulhern, Francis. 'A Nation, Yet Again: *The Field Day Anthology*', *Radical Philosophy*, 65 (autumn 1993): 23–9.

Murphy, Michael. *Elsewhere*. Nottingham: Shoestring Press, 2003.

Murphy, Paul. 'Inside the Immigrant Mind Nostalgic versus Nomadic Subjectivities in late Twentieth-Century Drama', in *Performing Ireland*, special issue of *Australian Drama Studies*, 43 (October 2003): 128–47.

Murphy, Shane. 'Don't Mention the War: The Trouble(s) in Northern Irish Poetry', in *The Aesthetics and Pragmatics of Violence*, ed. Michel Hensen and Annette Pankratz. Passau: Verlag Karl Stutz, 2001: 89–102.

Murray, Christopher. *Twentieth-century Irish Drama: Mirror up to Nation*. Manchester: Manchester University Press, 1997.

Naparstek, Ben. 'Notes from the Underground', *The Times*, 25 March 2006.

Newhall, Beth. '97 Years and a Day', *Irish Theatre Magazine*, 4/18 (2004): 12–13.

Ní Chuilleanáin, Eiléan. *The Rose Geranium*. Oldcastle: Gallery Press, 1981.

—— *The Second Voyage*. Oldcastle: Gallery Press, 1986.

—— *The Magdalene Sermon*. Oldcastle: Gallery Press, 1989.

—— *The Brazen Serpent*. Oldcastle: Gallery Press, 1994.

—— *The Girl Who Married a Reindeer*. Oldcastle: Gallery Press, 2001.

Ni Dhomhnaill, Nuala. Translations in *The Southern Review*, 'A Special Issue: Contemporary Irish Poetry and Criticism', 31/3 (summer 1995): 444–9.

Nora, Pierre. 'Between Memory and History: *Les Lieux de Mémoire*', *Representations* 26 (1989): 7–25.

O'Brien, Conor Cruise. 'Don't write him off just yet', *Irish Independent*, 25 January 1992, 12.

O'Brien, Eugene. *Seamus Heaney: Creating Irelands of the Mind*. Dublin: The Liffey Press, 2002.

—— *Seamus Heaney and the Place of Writing*. Gainesville: University Press of Florida, 2002.

O'Brien, Harvey. Review of Vincent Woods, *A Cry From Heaven*, in *Irish Theatre Magazine*, 5/24 (2005): 51–3.

O'Brien, Justin. *The Modern Prince: Charles J. Haughey and the Quest for Power*. Dublin: Merlin Publishing, 2002.

O'Brien, Paul. 'Willie Doherty: Language, Imagery and the Real'. *Circa*, 104 (2003): 51–4.

O'Brien, Sean. 'District and Circle by Seamus Heaney: Songs of a Sane Romantic', *Independent*, 7 April 2006.

O'Connor, Pat. *Emerging Voices: Women in Contemporary Irish Society.* Dublin: Institute of Public Administration, 1998.

O'Donnell, Rory, ed. *Europe: The Irish Experience.* Dublin: Institute of European Affairs, 2000: 209–11.

O'Donoghue, Bernard. *Seamus Heaney and the Language of Poetry.* Hemel Hempstead: Simon & Schuster, 1994.

—— 'Poetry in Ireland', in *The Cambridge Companion to Modern Irish Culture*, ed. Joe Cleary and Claire Connolly, Cambridge: Cambridge University Press, 2005: 173–89.

O'Driscoll, Dennis. '"Steady Under Strain and Strong Through Tension"', *Parnassus: Poetry in Review*, 26/2 (2002): 149–67.

O'Faolain, Nuala. *Almost There: The Onward Journey of a Dublin Woman.* London: Michael Joseph, 2003.

—— *Sunday Tribune*, 2 April 2006, 18.

O'Keeffe, Patrick. *The Hill Road.* New York: Penguin, 2005.

O'Kelly, Donal. *Asylum!Asylum!*, in *New Plays from the Abbey Theatre*, ed. Christopher Fitz-Simon and Sanford Sternlicht. New York: Syracuse University Press, 1996.

—— 'Strangers in a Strange Land', *Irish Theatre Magazine*, 1/1 (autumn 1998): 10–13.

Oliver, Kelly, ed. *The Portable Kristeva.* New York: Columbia University Press, 1997.

Oser, Lee. Review of *Electric Light*, *World Literature Today*, 76/1 (winter 2002): 110–11.

O'Sullivan, Michael. ' "Bare Life" and the Garden Politics of Roethke and Heaney', *Mosaic: A Journal for the Interdisciplinary Study of Literature*, 23/4 (December 2005): 17–34.

O'Toole, Fintan. *Black Hole, Green Card: The Disappearance of Ireland.* Dublin: New Island, 1994.

—— *The Ex-Isle of Erin: Images of a Global Ireland.* Dublin: New Island, 1996.

—— 'Introduction: A True History of Lies', in Sebastian Barry, *Plays 1.* London: Methuen, 1997.

—— 'Introducing Irelantis', in Seán Hillen, *Irelantis.* Dublin: Irelantis, 1999.

—— 'Irish Theatre: The State of the Art', in *Theatre Stuff: Critical Essays on Contemporary Irish Theatre*, ed. Eamon Jordan. Dublin: Carysfort, 2000: pp. 47–58.

—— 'Writing the boom', *Irish Times*, 25 January 2001.

—— 'Picking the Lock of Family Secrets', *Irish Times Weekend Review*, 1 April 2006, 3.

—— 'Truth and Tribalism', *The Guardian*, 21 July 2007, 36.

Park, David. *The Big Snow.* London: Bloomsbury, 2002.

Parker, Michael. *Seamus Heaney: The Making of the Poet.* London: Macmillan, 1993.

Patten, Eve. 'Fiction in Conflict: Northern Ireland's Prodigal Novelists', in *Peripheral Visions: Images of Nationhood in Contemporary British Fiction*, ed. Ian A. Bell. Cardiff: University of Wales Press, 1995: 128–48.

—— 'Contemporary Irish Fiction', in *The Cambridge Companion to the Irish Novel*, ed. John Wilson Foster. Cambridge: Cambridge University Press, 2005: 259–75.

Patterson, Glenn. 'Nothing Has to Die', interview by Richard Mills, in *Northern Narratives*, ed. Bill Lazenbatt, *Writing Ulster* 6 (1999): 113–29.

—— *The International*. London: Anchor, 1999.

—— *That Which Was*. London: Hamish Hamilton, 2004.

—— *Lapsed Protestant*. Dublin: New Island, 2006.

Paulin, Tom. *The Invasion Handbook*. London: Faber and Faber, 2002.

Peillon, Michel. 'Agency, Flows and Post-Colonial Structure in Ireland', *The Irish Review*, 30 (2003): 71–81.

Pirie, David. *Shelley*. Milton Keynes: Open University, 1988.

Power, Carla. 'What Happened to Irish Art?', *Newsweek*, 20 August 2001.

Pratt, William. Review of *Finders Keepers: Selected Prose 1971–2001*, *World Literature Today* 76/1 (April–June 2003): 106–7.

Quinn, Antoinette. 'A Prayer for my Daughter: Patriarchy in *Amongst Women*', *Canadian Journal of Irish Studies*, 17/1 (1991): 79–90.

Quinn, Justin. Introduction to *Metre* 3 (autumn 1997): 5–6.

—— 'The Irish Efflorescence', *Poetry Review*, 4/91 (winter 2001/02): 46–50.

Reddy, Maureen T. 'Reading and Writing Race in Ireland: Roddy Doyle and *Metro Eireann*', *Irish University Review*, 35/2 (autumn/winter 2005): 374–88.

Regan, Stephen. *Irish Writing: An Anthology of Irish Writing in English 1798–1939*. Oxford: Oxford University Press, 2004.

Ricoeur, Paul. 'Memory and Forgetting', in *Questioning Ethics: Contemporary Debates in Philosophy*, ed. Richard Kearney and Mark Dooley. London: Routledge, 1999.

Robbins, Ruth. *Subjectivity*. London: Palgrave Macmillan, 2005.

Roche, Billy. *The Wexford Trilogy*. London: Nick Hern, 2000.

Rose, Kieran. *Diverse Communities: The Evolution of Lesbian and Gay Politics in Ireland*, Undercurrents Pamphlet Series. Cork: Cork University Press, 1994.

Russo, Mary. *The Female Grotesque: Risk, Excess and Modernity*. London: Routledge, 1994.

Ryan, Ray, ed. *Writing in the Irish Republic: Literature, Culture and Politics 1949–1999*. Basingstoke: Macmillan, 2000.

—— *Ireland and Scotland: Literature and Culture, State and Nation, 1966–2000*. Oxford: Clarendon Press, 2002.

Said, Edward. *Orientalism*. London: Penguin, 1991 [1978].

—— *Culture and Imperialism*. London: Vintage, 1994.

Sampson, Denis. 'An Irishman's Diary', *Irish Times*, 8 April 2006, 17.

Scurr, Ruth. 'Novel of the Week', *New Statesman*, 10 April 2000, 61.

Seawright, Paul. *Hidden*. London: Imperial War Museum, 2003.

Senelick, Laurence. *The Changing Room: Sex, Drag and Theatre*, London: Routledge, 2000.

Shumaker, Jeanette. 'Uncanny Doubles: The Fiction of Anne Enright', *New Hibernia Review*, 9/3 (2005): 107–22.

Sierz, Aleks. *In-Yer-Face Theatre*. London: Faber, 2000.

Sihra, Melissa. 'A Cautionary Tale: Marina Carr's *By the Bog of Cats . . .*' in *Theatre Stuff: Critical Essays on Contemporary Irish Theatre*, ed. Eamon Jordan. Dublin: Carysfort, 2000: 257–68.

—— 'Greek Myth, Irish Reality: Marina Carr's *By the bog of Cats . . .*', in *Rebel Women: Staging Ancient Greek Drama Today*, ed. John Dillon and S.E. Wilmer. London: Methuen, 2005: 115–37.

Singleton, Brian and Anna McMullan. 'Performing Ireland: New Perspectives on Contemporary Irish Theatre', *Australasian Drama Studies*, 43 (October 2003): 3–15.

Smyth, Damian. 'Totalising Imperative', *Fortnight*, 309 (September 1992): 26–7.

—— 'Seamus Heaney in a Circle of His Own', *Belfast Telegraph*, 15 April 2006.

Smyth, Gerry. *The Novel and the Nation: Studies in the New Irish Fiction*. London: Pluto Press, 1997.

—— *Noisy Island: A Short History of Irish Popular Music*. Cork: Cork University Press, 2005.

—— 'Tiger, Theory, Technology: A Meditation on the Development of Modern Irish Cultural Criticism', *Irish Studies Review*, 15/2 (May 2007): 123–36.

Sontag, Susan. *Regarding the Pain of Others*. London: Hamish Hamilton, 2003.

St Peter, Christine. *Changing Ireland: Strategies in Contemporary Women's Fiction*. Houndmills: Macmillan, 2000.

Steiner, George. *After Babel. Aspects of Language and Translation*. Oxford: Oxford University Press, 1998.

Taylor, John. Review of *Electric Light*, *Poetry* 176/5 (February 2002): 296–8.

Taylor, Lib. 'Shape-shifting and Role-splitting: Theatre, Body and Identity', in *Indeterminate Bodies*, ed. Naomi Segal, Lib Taylor and Roger Cook. London: Palgrave, 2003: 164–80.

Tobin, Daniel. *Passage to the Center: Imagination and the Sacred in the Poetry of Seamus Heaney*. Lexington: The University Press of Kentucky, 1999.

Tóibín, Colm. *The Trial of the Generals: Selected Journalism 1980–1990*. Dublin: Raven Arts Press, 1990.

—— 'New Ways of Killing your Father', *London Review of Books*, 18 November 1993.

—— ed. *Soho Square: New Writing from Ireland*. London: Bloomsbury, 1993.

—— Introduction. *The Penguin Book of Irish Fiction*. ed. Colm Tóibín. Harmondsworth: Viking, 1999: ix–xxxiv.

—— '*Hinterland*: The Public Becomes Private', in *Out of History: Essays on the Writings of Sebastian Barry*, ed. Christina Hunt Mahony. Dublin: Carysfort Press, 2006: 199–208.

Trench, Brian. 'Popular Music', in *The Blackwell Companion to Modern Irish Culture*, ed. W.J. McCormack. Oxford: Blackwell, 2001: 481–2.

Trotter, Mary. *Ireland's National Theaters: Political Performance and the Origins of the Irish Dramatic Movement*. Syracuse, NY: Syracuse University Press, 2001.

Urban, Mark. *Big Boys' Rules: The Secret Struggle against the IRA*. London: Faber and Faber, 1992.

Vendler, Helen. *Seamus Heaney*. London: Harper Collins, 1998.

von Finck, Diana. 'A.R. Ammons's Poetics of Chaos', in *Freedom and Form: Essays in Contemporary American Poetry*, eds Esther Giger and Agnieszka Salska. Łódź: Łódź University Press, 1998: 120–35.

Walker, Brian. '"The Lost Tribes of Ireland": Diversity, Identity and Loss Among the Irish Diaspora', *Irish Studies Review*, 15/3 (August 2007): 267–82.

Walker, Lenore E. *The Battered Woman Syndrome*. New York: Springer Publishing, 1984.

Wallace, Clare. 'Tragic Destiny and Abjection in Marina Carr's *The Mai, Portia Coughlan* and *By the Bog of Cats . . .*', *Irish University Review*, 31/2 (autumn/winter 2001): 431–49.

Walsh, John. *The Falling Angels: An Irish Romance*. London: Flamingo, 2000.

Walsh, Michael. 'Thinking the Unthinkable: Coming to Terms with Northern Ireland in the 1980s and the 1990s', in *British Cinema, Past and Present*, ed. Justine Ashby and Andrew Higson. London: Routledge, 2000: 288–98.

Walshe, Éibhear. 'Wild(e) Ireland', in *Ireland in Proximity: History, Gender, Space*, ed. Scott Brewster, Virginia Crossman, Fiona Becket and David Alderson. London: Routledge, 1999: 64–79.

Waters, John. *An Intelligent Person's Guide to Modern Ireland*. London: Duckworth, 1997.

Watson, George. 'All Europeans Now?', Proceedings of the Cultural Traditions Group conference, 'All Europeans Now?'. Belfast: Institute of Irish Studies, 1991: 49–55.

Wheatley, David. '"That blank mouth": Secrecy, Shibboleths and Silence in Northern Irish Poetry', *Journal of Modern Literature*, 25/1 (fall 2001): 1–16.

—— 'Irish Poetry into the Twenty-First Century', in *Cambridge Companion to Contemporary Irish Poetry*, ed. Matthew Campbell. Cambridge: Cambridge University Press, 2003: 250–67.

Williams, Leslie. 'Interview with Eiléan Ní Chuilleanáin', in *Representing Ireland: Gender, Class, Nationality*, ed. Susan Shaw Sailer. Gainesville: University of Florida Press, 1997: 29–44.

Williams, Raymond. *Resources of Hope*. London: Verso, 1989.

Wilmer, Clive. 'Down to Earth', *New Statesman*, 17 April 2006.

Wilmer, Stephen and John Dillon, eds. *Rebel Women: Staging Ancient Greek Drama Today*. London: Methuen, 2005.

Wilson, Robert McLiam. *Eureka Street*. London: Secker & Warburg, 1996.

Zimmermann, Georges. *The Irish Storyteller*. Dublin: Four Courts Press, 2001.

Žižek, Slavoj. *Welcome to the Desert of the Real! Five Essays on September 11 and Related Dates*. London: Verso, 2002.

Index